THE
HYACINTH
GIRL

THE
HYACINTH
GIRL

T. S. Eliot's Hidden Muse

LYNDALL GORDON

virago

VIRAGO

First published in Great Britain in 2022 by Virago Press

1 3 5 7 9 10 8 6 4 2

Copyright © Lyndall Gordon 2022

The moral right of the author has been asserted.

Extracts from Valerie Eliot and Hugh Haffenden (eds), *The Letters of T. S. Eliot: vols. 1–6*
(New Haven & London: Yale University Press), © Set Copyrights Ltd and © The Estate of
Valerie Eliot, are reprinted by permission of Yale University Press.

A CIP catalogue record for this book
is available from the British Library.

Hardback ISBN 978-0-349-01211-7
Trade Paperback ISBN 978-0-349-01210-0

Typeset in Spectrum by M Rules
Printed and bound in Great Britain by
Clays Ltd, Elcograf S.p.A.

Papers used by Virago are from well-managed forests
and other responsible sources.

Virago Press
An imprint of
Little, Brown Book Group
Carmelite House
50 Victoria Embankment
London EC4Y 0DZ

An Hachette UK Company
www.hachette.co.uk

www.virago.co.uk

In memory of three Eliot readers:
Rhoda Press
Walt Litz
Helen Gardner

CONTENTS

LIST OF ILLUSTRATIONS

Section 1

Section 2

PREFACE

As the greatness of T. S. Eliot spread, the public saw English women at his side: Vivienne Haigh-Wood, a flamboyant wife who ended up in an asylum; a church-going confidante, Mary Trevelyan; and, late in his life, Valerie Fletcher, a devoted secretary, who married him. These were his visible ties. Yet out of sight, by design, was an American called Emily Hale, an actor and drama teacher for whom he concealed a lasting love. She was the 'hyacinth girl' in his poem *The Waste Land*, as he told her in a love-letter eight years later.

He sent in all 1,131 letters to her, more than he had written to anyone else, and insisted on the longest embargo, by far, on any of his writings: fifty years from the death of the survivor. These letters reveal a relationship at the core of Eliot's creativity, spanning his life from the age of twenty-four to his late sixties. She was the first of four women to take part in the poet's transformations as expatriate, convert and, finally, a man 'made for love'.

Eliot protected his privacy in a male world of college, work, clubs and coteries. But these four women came closer and saw him in ways men did not. All recorded what they experienced. Most outspoken was Vivienne, an early supporter whose voice he came to fear. She left her autobiographical sketches and diaries to the Bodleian Library. His sturdy companion in prayer, Mary Trevelyan, was explicit in her memoir about falling in love with Eliot and her difficulties with him. And Miss Fletcher fulfilled all he asked of her and continued throughout her life to guard and perpetuate his legacy. These women felt a profound attraction – no ordinary emotion – that made for a permanent bond on their parts. Each of the four who entered Eliot's private life was keenly perceptive and rare in her own way. This book tells their stories.

Foremost in his life, we now see, was Emily Hale, the 'hyacinth girl' haunting the memory of a man whose life is a wasteland. Throughout his poems and plays he created roles for her as the Weeping Girl, the hyacinth girl, a Rose of memory, a Lady of silences, martyr and star of the stage. Emily was to live on as his creation, and heard from the poet where she was in his lines. She was the secret sharer of the hot moments of inception, the marvellous words that came to him, part of the drama he conceived and played out, before writing lines to last beyond his time. To read Eliot's letters to Emily during the thirties and early forties is to enter poems in the making.

His letters to her grant a new lens: here is an Eliot who is intensely ardent. Among his love-letters are masterpieces in a form unexpected from a man so austere. It is as though he drew Emily into the hearth of a secret self, where he fired emotions vital to his art. He wished her to match his honesty, to call out 'an Emily of fire and violence', but violence, certainly, was not her style.

Her side of the correspondence he destroyed, except for eighteen letters. The full number of Emily's letters to Eliot must have been about the same as his own, for he expected regular letters, and if an awaited one did not arrive, he sometimes cabled her. There must have been, in all, a thousand from her, proof that the Lady of silences did utter opinions and questions as well as words of kindness and compassion, and we can hear this because Eliot often relayed what she said in his replies. With the appearance of these letters a curtain rose. She spoke.

Her voice was her prime gift: she taught speech as well as drama and that voice comes to us, ironically, through Eliot's own letters.

She was spirited, playful, sometimes hurt, always resisting idealisation, for she wished to be loved for herself.

Emily Hale's friend Margaret Farrand married a Princeton professor, Willard Thorp. Together, the Thorps were Emily's guides as she mulled over what to do with the trove of papers by the great poet who'd loved her. They persuaded her that Princeton would keep her treasure safe. In December 1956 the papers were placed in fourteen boxes, sealed with steel bands and stashed away for future generations. For Eliot's sake, there was no talk, no announcement. Emily told the Thorps that only about eight people (including the two of them, two librarians and of course Eliot himself) knew of her donation.

Thirteen boxes of Eliot's letters to Emily Hale, held for over sixty years in the archives at Princeton. A fourteenth box contains her papers, including a short memoir (drafted in 1957 and revised in 1965).

Eliot died in January 1965, Emily Hale nearly five years later in October 1969. So it was that in October 2019 the steel bands were cut, and the letters saw the light; they were opened to readers on 2 January 2020.

I first heard of the letters in 1972 when, as a student in New York, I went to discuss Eliot with the chair of the English department at Princeton. A. Walton Litz told me of Emily Hale and the priceless gift sequestered in Firestone Library. Then he brought in Emily's friend Willard Thorp, whose wife Margaret had died the year after Emily. The two women, Emily and Margaret, had exchanged confidences, the scholars said: these women had taken it in turn to write every fortnight, on an understanding that each would destroy the other's letters.* Walt Litz and Willard Thorp hinted more than they said about a mystery in Eliot's life. I felt privileged to be there, a bit open-mouthed.

Such was the dignity of Professor Litz that I was amazed by his lawless fantasy as we strolled towards the library: if he knew he was dying, he said, it would be his last pleasure to steal into the archives, break open the boxes and read the Eliot–Hale letters. It would satisfy his curiosity and more: unspoken words hovered in the air. Then and there I vowed to live to the day when the letters would be released. I have not been disappointed.

---

* Selected items from their correspondence were in fact included in the Princeton cache, but that was not yet known.

1

HOME WOMEN

Eliot was a master of disguise. Emily Hale knew him as the person he felt himself to be: a poet of acute emotion, who maintained an impenetrable reserve. In his public readings, his voice was a monotonous deadpan. But his ardent letters to Hale reveal how much he used his life – its particular scenes, the people he encountered and private feeling – to inject poems with jolts of authenticity. His famous claim to 'impersonality' was designed to protect poetry so personal that it verged on confession.

He told Hale how widely he was misread, and how he relied on their correspondence to put future readers right. It was one reason to bare his hidden self, his spiritual aims as well as his flaws, to a woman he saw as a kindred spirit. He did so with the same honesty as in his poetry. The beating heart of his poems, like an encounter with the hyacinth girl in *The Waste Land*, is his own inner life of 'memory and desire' breaking through their erudition. Once it's seen that Eliot is telling his life through his poems, striving to devise a spiritual autobiography suited to his time, readers can reach him and bypass his apparent difficulty. He said himself that his poetry is quite simple and in this sense it is.

His letters to Hale uncovered more than to anyone else, yet he also revealed elements of himself to other choice women. Not to men, except to his brother, who knew him anyway. Then it would worry him when women, at first confidantes, heard too much, and he was most at ease with women who asked nothing for themselves.

As an expatriate in London, Eliot was nervous of exposure: might they pick up the tom-tom of a savage? He battened down all he did not wish the English to see, concealed beneath a set of protective resemblances as, bowler-hatted and properly kitted out with a rolled umbrella, he passed invisible in the work-day crowd crossing London Bridge on the stroke of nine.

As a young man, Eliot left America for Paris and then again for Oxford and London, ostensibly to become a European but also to use Europe's multitude of tongues as a mouthpiece for an emissary

'*Under the brown fog of a winter dawn, | A crowd flowed over London Bridge . . . | I had not thought death had undone so many.*'

of New England wielding his pen to express habits of spiritual search, uprightness and purity.

Emily Hale, the daughter of a New England minister, embodied that high-minded character. In her, it stood firm, distanced from the Englishness he adopted together with the costumed rituals of a people 'not wholly commendable, / Of no immediate kin', though touched by their 'common genius'. In Eliot's heart and mind, Emily would remain his superior, so he told her: 'I recognise the spirit when I see it.'

They met for the first time in 1905 in Cambridge, Massachusetts. Emily had just turned fourteen and Tom Eliot, three years older, was then a schoolboy from St Louis, Missouri. A quarter of a century later he could recall the exact year in a letter to Emily, and this by itself suggests how momentous that meeting came to be. The sole verifiable fact is the date, but the circumstances surrounding this encounter tell us more.

In September 1905 Eliot turned seventeen and entered Milton Academy, a top boarding school near Boston. Later in the school year, the headmaster wrote to Eliot's mother to assure her that her son was mixing with other boys, which indicates how apart the new boy had been on arrival. Too far from St Louis to go home for Thanksgiving, it's likely that Eliot spent that holiday in November 1905 with his mother's widowed sister Aunt Susie and her two daughters, Barbara and Eleanor Hinkley, at 1 Berkeley Place in Cambridge. The younger, Eleanor, was Tom Eliot's favourite cousin: her humour and taste for drama enlivened him. And there he met Eleanor's friend Emily Hale.

He saw a girl with long hair, so dark it appeared black, and grey-blue eyes. Emily had pretty, round cheeks but what appealed most was her 'nice smile' — that's how he pictures her in a humorous poem written years afterwards in the cockney voice of Morgan, the Faber office cat, who takes to Miss 'ale's smile because she 'as a kind 'eart.

As well as her smile, the girl's special asset was her voice, one in millions, he told her later when less shy. As 'children', Eliot would recall, 'we were both too shy and reserved to have real conversation'. Thankfully, she did not take much notice of him. A poem he wrote later recalls a boy's mirth when a girl's slipper falls off to reveal stockings with white toes.

Emily and Eleanor, born in 1891, had attended the Berkeley Street School, around the corner from Eleanor's home. Both were keen on acting. At thirteen, Emily had already dedicated herself to a career in theatre, as she told her aunt and uncle, the Reverend John Carroll Perkins and Edith Perkins, who cared for her. Edith was sister to Emily's mother, who had been in a Boston asylum since the birth of Emily's younger brother, or not long after. Emily's father wrote to Edith Perkins about his daughter, aged four: 'I have not told you how gentle Emily is with her brother, and how hard she tries to do what is right – she is a comfort to us all'.

That little brother died and Mrs Hale never returned home. Emily, who loved and visited her mother, was alert to mental pain with no end. Tom Eliot met a girl in a sad situation, known to everyone, who put aside self-pity, determined to pursue her calling.

He had troubles of his own, kept under wraps and serious enough to hold back progress. It would have been in character to silence what he felt, but the anxiety of his mother is patent in her correspondence with the headmaster of his school. One source of his situation took place three years before his birth.

In 1885, Charlotte Champe Eliot, aged forty-two, had given birth to a sixth child. The baby's legs had been frail and there was fluid on the brain. The child was named Theodora, gift of God, and her disability had endeared her the more to the Eliot family. Grief went deep when Theodora died at sixteen months. The Eliots were an old New England family settled in St Louis for three generations. It was their habit to silence emotion, as in the Latin tag the Eliots made their motto: *tace et face*, be silent and act. Two years later Mrs Eliot gave birth to her seventh and last child.

On 26 September 1888 Henry Ware Eliot Sr wrote to his elder brother, a pioneering minister in Oregon, that at seven that morning a son 'came forth'. He was to be called Thomas after this uncle and Stearns after his mother's family.

The letter did not say the child was well. Unmentioned was a congenital double hernia: lasting damage in his groin requiring surgical repair in his teens and lengthy operations in late middle age. Charlotte's grief over Theodora added to her worry over Tom, as he was called at home: a protective circle of his mother, his eldest and quasi-parental sister Ada, aged nineteen, and three other nearly grown sisters, Margaret, Charlotte and Marian, drew about the boy. They were reinforced by a warm-hearted Irish nurse, Annie Dunne.

Tom remembered sitting next to Ada on a step, before he could talk, while she communicated by tapping out rhythms. He caught on quickly, and later, writing poems, said that the beat came to him before the words. He admired Ada for brains on a par with his own. Everything he later told Emily about this sister implied his identification with her position in the family: their gifts were disregarded. This recollection comes in letters written long after his childhood and tinged by Eliot's need for Emily's understanding. What emerged when they came together was not so much fact but how, at the height of his powers as poet, he remembers a child's feelings, especially jealousy. As he saw it, his parents were fonder of his elder brother Henry whose weaknesses, Tom thought, were more 'tolerable' than his own. Their mother favoured his second sister, Margaret, a beauty with dark brown eyes. For much of his life he disparaged Margaret and sided with Ada, whose life, he said, was 'coloured by domestic bitterness' so long as this responsible, clever girl remained at home.

Despite the absence of parental encouragement, Ada was a determined. She fought for a college education, worked in the Tombs prison in New York and wrote professionally on social work. To

Emily, Eliot praised Ada's emotional detachment, an impersonality he thought uncommon in females. She was reserved, as they all were trained to be. Because Emily was disconcerted at times by his own reserve, he wanted her to know that it was from Ada he had learnt to use detachment as a shield. In Eliot's confidential letters to Emily, and to a lesser extent his letters to his English friend Mary Trevelyan, he presents himself as a boy warped (as he saw it) by his parents' emotional distance.

Ada soothed him with her matter-of-fact willingness to tolerate what in him could not be changed. Eliot stressed this to Emily for he hoped Ada's acceptance could be a model for the way he wished to be loved.

Given his sisters' nurture, women were important to Eliot from the start. He could welcome trusted women as confidantes and comforters and they found his homey side unexpected and endearing. Emily's kindness even made it possible for Eliot to mention his hernia: he thought it cured by the time he left Milton in the summer of 1906, though this did not turn out to be so.

To Hale and Trevelyan, Eliot pictured himself as a solitary child, despite his large family. 'I never talked, for who was there to talk to?' His brother, Henry Ware Eliot Jr, was eight years his senior – so not a playmate. There were no friends, none at all, and the reason he gave sounds like the excuse of a solitary trying to justify standoffish behaviour: the Eliots lived in a run-down quarter of St Louis, while better-off people moved away, 'isolating me from other children of my own class'. He thought local boys 'crude' and frightening. Yet an incident he recalled for Mary Trevelyan suggests that his solitude was not a matter of locale or class but physical, an aversion to touch emerging when he can't have been much more than four or five.

Another little boy living on Locust Street longed to have a go at Tom's smart new tricycle and offered him a blow on his whistle in exchange for a ride. The incident aroused his first 'disgust' with human nature. 'Odious,' he said when this memory came back. He told Trevelyan that he would as soon share a toothbrush as put his lips to another boy's whistle.

Solitude suited a boy absorbed by books. His sister Charlotte, who went to art school, painted a portrait of him as a reader, neatly dressed and seated with head bent towards a book he holds in one hand. An informal photograph shows him sprawled backwards on his chair, glued to an open page. This boy read Shakespeare at an early age, and all of Edgar Allan Poe in a dentist's waiting room when he had to go twice a week for two years.* He 'stole' $2 to buy a volume of Shelley, and in a corner, unnoticed, he took in *Prometheus Unbound* 'with secretive delight'.

At a party he was mortified when a girl whispered behind his back to another girl: 'Look at his ears.' That night, his mother found him in bed with rope about his head, hoping to flatten his ears while he slept. He dodged another party by walking the streets until it was time to go home. He still remembered that day in St Louis, in conversation with Mary Trevelyan, when he was nearly sixty-five.

He was no less ill at ease with a set of Boston cousins, the three high-achieving children of his father's younger brother, the Reverend Christopher Rhodes Eliot. There were inevitable comparisons with Frederick, born a year after Tom. Fred's ambitious energy appeared to outdo Tom, who was held back by a depressed languor in the face of a gift he had yet to fulfil. This 'conceit', as he called it to Emily, came up against the successes of the Boston Eliots. He detested Fred whose boasting irritated also his younger sisters, Martha May and Abigail.

Martha and Abby Eliot were more than able; they were great-hearted and effective, as time would tell. Their mother, Mary May, a great-niece of Louisa May Alcott, brought up her daughters to be as blithely independent as Jo March in *Little Women*. How neatly Eliot combines 'Eliot' and 'Alcott' in the name of his character Miss Nancy Ellicott, a female too fast for her own good, in his poem

---

* Eliot gave no reason for these visits.

'Cousin Nancy'. This caricature was Eliot's protest against the May strain of feminism and radicalism that Mary May and her go-ahead daughters brought into the Eliot family.

In the summer of 1904, when Tom Eliot was fifteen, he was invited to join these cousins for the opening of their newly acquired heaven on earth, Camp Maple Hill, on the shore of Lake Memphremagog, thirty-two miles long, stretching from northern Vermont into Canada. The girls wore 'bloomers' instead of long skirts and went bare-legged. They liked to fish, swim, row and climb. The younger, Abby, usually led the way up a mountain like 'Nancy Ellicott', who strode across the barren New England hills 'and broke them'. Coming into focus behind that sarcasm is a weary boy with an invisible weakness, lagging behind a bounding little girl.

While Tom Eliot was there, his sister Charlotte gave birth to Theodora (named for their baby sister who had died in 1886). In August he sent a congratulatory letter in verse, which includes his report of a strenuous expedition with his cousins:

> *We after breakfast took a start,*
> *Four of us, in a two horse cart . . .*
> *To climb a mountain, quite a feat,*
> *3000 ft. and in the heat . . .*

He breaks off when voices call him to help make a raft.

Eliot confided to Emily that Uncle Christopher's camp left him with 'a terror of excessive community, when . . . it means complete deprivation of privacy'. Campers would have had to relieve themselves in not very private holes in the ground. For a fastidious adolescent with an acute sense of smell and a hernia, encumbered by a truss, it would have been a trial. In his 'First Debate between the Body and Soul', a notebook poem he never published, his refrain fixes on bodily functions: 'defecations' and 'masturbations'. The young writer mulls over the humiliations the body can inflict.

The following year, Tom Eliot completed high school in St Louis and entered Milton Academy. He already had a place at Harvard (courtesy of distinguished Eliots before him and a fact that would not have gone unnoticed: he was related to the president of Harvard, Charles William Eliot). But something was wrong, suggested by plummeting grades: a C average with a B in history and an E in physics. Mrs Eliot stressed her son's uncertain health to the headmaster. Yet something remained undisclosed. Why his mother was concerned to delay her son's entry to Harvard was almost certainly his apathy – what Eliot eventually named as *aboulie*. This was no passing adolescent problem. It would prove, he said, 'a lifelong affliction'.

'I had to find out by painful and humiliating experience that I was not so good as I took for granted', he confided to Emily, 'a bitter lesson in humility: Eliots are not naturally humble'.

Eliot took steps to energise himself with body-building exercises and boxing lessons, and then dispelled fastidiousness with verbal caricatures of what it takes to be a man, pumping up his bravado. In contrast to the suffering self-portrait offered to Emily Hale, his self-presentation to selected men was boisterous. The rhymes are about the antics of Columbo (Christopher Columbus, on his voyages to the New World). Spoofing heroes of classic American fiction – Natty Bumppo or Ishmael – Columbo bonds with a savage other, King Bolo, but Eliot deploys the tie quite differently, not as affection but a pretext for scenes of abusive or rampant sex. Bolo has a 'Big Black Kween' whose 'bum is big as a soup tureen'. Snappy rhymes and bouncing rhythms trounce 'a bastard jew named Benny', a doctor, for injecting Columbo's 'prick' with 'Muriatic Acid'. To the jolly Gilbert and Sullivan strains of 'In Enterprise of Martial Kind', a cabin boy scrambles up the 'mast-o' but Columbo tugs him down and rapes him in the 'ass-o'.

It comes as a shock to find a poet of Eliot's distinction parading this. He topped off his offerings with the misogyny of old Scotch ditties (about a 'whanger' so mighty that it rips up a woman, she says, 'from my cunt to my navel'). Some critics suggest that since Eliot was imitating doggerel and comic books, his rhymes are merely exercises in a popular genre. One of the apologists plays it down as 'amiable', another as 'laddish'. Not so. The publication of Eliot's letters has shown that he continued to disseminate ever feebler variations (to men only) into his fifties. In 1964, at the age of seventy-six, he still cheered it on.

Though Eliot kept this vein from Emily, she sensed things she could not know, and what he did acknowledge with striking frankness was 'a kind of Olympian hypocrisy' in his public manner: 'unctuous', he admits, 'preachy'. This he blames on his family who, he said, believed that since Eliots were better than other people, they had to behave better. The Lord took more notice of 'us' than of ordinary people. Ruefully, he offers Emily this explanation for how, in his youth, he came to be a wilful character, contained in public by an iron control. He learnt early to conceal disturbance by following the family's code of conduct. Conformity, he said, was a strategy for hiding part of a divided self, which became habitual over time.

A different justification is implied in an exchange with the publisher Geoffrey Faber in August 1927. On that occasion Eliot commended obscenity, in the manner of Swift, as an eye for evil.

Yet whatever he said by way of excuse cannot dispel the violence. A punitive relish delivers hatred. Victims are helpless. It's tempting to ignore this were it not for the fact that as an adult, Eliot would press these jingles on other men. We can't know what recipients like Pound and Conrad Aiken thought because they were positioned to play up, but Hale, though she never saw a line, recognised that Eliot was not really like other men.

He was a student when he began his 'Columbiad' and a possible context could be private discomfort, for the top-up of his education at Milton failed to serve at Harvard. Despite his dutiful attendance at lectures, too many C grades led the college to put him on probation. (In old age Eliot claimed he had loafed – another normative guise.)

None of the women who entered Eliot's life would see these rhymes, and his second wife only after her marriage. Women's ignorance is not irrelevant because the smut is rooted in fear of females. Eliot's 1908 poem 'Circe's Palace', published in the *Harvard Advocate*, was derived from Nathaniel Hawthorne's retelling of Homer in the *Tanglewood Tales*. It takes up the scene where Odysseus comes upon an enchantress who turns men into animals. Eliot's version has a 'sluggish python' lying along Circe's stairway. The petals of her flowers, 'fanged and red', make men impotent.

Along with fear is discomfort with the body, not only its sexual urges, but also the unease it gives his character Prufrock (conceived in 1910) to notice a woman's arm downed with light brown hair. Society women whose voices proclaim culture as they talk of Michelangelo and whose skirts trail along the floor, are unknown creatures under cover, much as Prufrock, moving among the women, is covered up himself: his necktie mounting to his chin.

Costume and appearance were crucial to Eliot's intentness on disguise. Two others besides Virginia Woolf observed how Eliot's untamed eyes were at odds with his subdued clothing and manners. The artist Wyndham Lewis drew a portrait in which the poet's eyes brood behind a masklike face. Another of his friends, the poet Osbert Sitwell, described Eliot's eyes as yellow – menacing, not mild.

'Came Christ the tiger', Eliot was to write well before his much publicised mid-life conversion. His deity is fierce, the punitive deity of his ancestors, New England Puritans appalled by their sins. The poet's self-caricature 'How unpleasant to meet Mr. Eliot!' mocks the 'brow so grim' and the severity in curbing conversational exchange. The primness and gloom, Eliot believed, came from forebears in the seventeenth century.

'I am by temperament but not in doctrine, an old-style hellfire Calvinist', he said.

Eliot claimed to inherit their nose for evil. 'Can't help smelling out witches', he joked on one occasion and on another, he recalled that 'my great etc. gnd.father used to hang witches (I don't mean with his own hand)'. He was referring to Andrew Eliott,* who made the crossing to the New World in 1669, landed in Beverly near Salem, and entered into its witch-hunt frenzy in 1692.

After the trials and hangings, Andrew Eliott, along with eleven other jurors, put his signature to a confession: this people of the Lord had shed innocent blood. They had been unable to withstand the delusions of the powers of darkness. The signatories blamed the devil for possessing their souls. Their guilt was more gripped by the drama of introspection and repentance than by the fate of their victims – mostly women.

Like them, Tom Eliot felt the presence of evil, not only in the world but within himself. He says as much in 'Animula', a poem drawing on himself, he tells Emily Hale in one of many confessions to her. The growing boy finds himself 'misshapen': 'selfish' and 'irresolute', too hesitant to act. This poor soul backs away from human warmth and fears 'the offered good'. Eliot believed in damnation as the punishment for evil. It bothered Eliot that Emily sustained her Unitarian faith in what he came to oppose: a belief in human progress towards rationality and morality without the need for divine intervention. Eliot, born a Unitarian, came to see his family faith as tepid, confined to conduct and blind to overwhelming questions of mortality and the afterlife.

His chief grievance was the Unitarian code of self-suppression for the sake of others. His grandparents, William Greenleaf Eliot and his wife Abigail Adams Eliot, had practised this as Unitarians. Abigail Eliot lost nine of her fourteen children, and each time a child died, she found the strength to go on helping others. During an epidemic in 1849, when one in ten died in St Louis, she cared for orphaned children. When Eliot spoke of the past to Emily Hale and later to Mary Trevelyan, he waved away his grandfather's achievements: establishing the Unitarian Church in St Louis; anti-slavery

---

* As the name was spelt.

sermons which lost him a quarter of his congregation; and his founding of schools and Washington University. All this, the grandson alleged, was nothing more than 'an Eliot Unitarianism: and unfortunately all Eliots believe that they are born to a more intimate understanding of Unitarianism than other people – in fact that to be a perfect Unitarian you have to be an Eliot.' In confidences of this kind to Emily Hale, he was not speaking only of the past; it's a nudge for a Unitarian correspondent not disposed to convert as he did.

When Eliot was eleven, in 1899, his mother had published a booklet of three poems, *Easter Songs*. 'Deep within this soul of mine', she writes, 'A living principle divine / Awaits its day and hour'. Her aim is to unfold the 'conscious life within!' Here is a formula for her son's poems: be nearer to God on an 'upward path'. The bell that will sound in his *Four Quartets* may hark back to this poem by his mother, where bells ring out 'fleeting joys that tempt us' and ring in 'immortal hopes that shall endure'.

Eliot's confidences to Emily Hale draw parallels between his mother and himself. 'I think that my mother, who wrote a good many religious poems, some of which I think very good, would have liked to believe more firmly than she did'. He too was to experience the unease of those who 'affirm before the world and deny between the rocks'. That kinship with his mother leads him to confess to Emily, to her alone, 'I have wondered sometimes whether, if I had stayed in New England, I should have returned to the Unitarianism from which I had strayed; certainly my change would have been a more painful process there, surrounded by family and historical traditions.'

It was his mother, he acknowledged, 'or some shadowy personality behind her who wants me to make retreats and keep vigils . . . One is hustled . . . by a crowd of shadows'. Figures from the Eliots' past will appear in the finale of *Ash Wednesday*, written after his mother's death: ghosts signal the poet from behind the granite rocks of the New England shore. The pain of expatriation and loss culminates in the poet's cry: 'Suffer me not to be separated'.

A schoolboy exercise required him to write verses in imitation of Ben Jonson, and the polished result was published in his St Louis school magazine, *The Smith Academy Record*. He said nothing at home. But his mother did see it, and walking with him one day in Beaumont Street, around the corner from their house, she remarked that 'A Lyric' was better than anything she'd done. He felt the gravity of this, because, he said later, 'I knew what her poetry meant to her.'

About five years later, when Eliot was a student writing poems for the *Harvard Advocate*, she encouraged him to become a poet in her place. 'I should so have loved a college course, but was obliged to teach before I was nineteen', she told her son.

At the age of sixty-seven, she reflects, 'I made a dead failure'. Her publications in church magazines had placed her, she now saw, in permanent obscurity. Her remaining hope was that her son would fulfil her ambition.

The superior men in Charlotte Eliot's poems purify themselves by shedding what is 'low', including the senses. She sets out ordeals that end in faith and this was to be the pattern her son would follow in his own poetry. Spiritual biography claimed him with absolute authority when he was twenty-one and in his last year as an undergraduate at Harvard. His poem recording this is 'Silence', dated June 1910 in his notebook and unpublished in his lifetime. The sound of Boston dies away and 'the garrulous wires' of life are cut. It is as though the speaker wakes outside his setting to some timeless state of being. This is a formative moment for the poet, the first of such 'moments' in poems to come. 'Silence' concludes that nothing could compare with this beatitude: 'There is nothing else beside.'

2

SCENES IN PARIS

The first time Eliot opposed his mother was his wish for a year in Paris after graduation. She was appalled and made this plain before he left. The French were not to be trusted, Charlotte Eliot warned; she could hardly bear to think of him amongst so immoral a nation. Little did she know it was decadence, in fact, that drew Eliot to Paris. He was finding a voice through French poetry, especially the sophisticated ennui of Jules Laforgue.

He arrived in Paris in October 1910, soon after he turned twenty-two. At 151 bis rue St Jacques, near the Panthéon and the Sorbonne, Mme Casaubon took in students, including Americans. She offered Eliot a small wallpapered room, with a bed in an alcove. She also provided dinner, and each evening her lodgers would see her tuck a napkin between chin and chest while she tossed the salad with wrinkled hands. Seated at the table was a medical student from the Pyrenees, Jean Verdenal. When Verdenal aired 'the listless discouragement in which I have been living', Eliot was pleased to find another who spoke the language of Laforgue.

Imitating Laforgue's air of weary derision constrained by formal courtesy, Eliot began his first great poem, 'The Love Song of

J. Alfred Prufrock'. His character is a nervous man, too timorous to utter words of love or speak at all, who hesitates to 'disturb the universe', no less. The absurdity makes him all the more vulnerable to slights especially from ladies, and so Prufrock must shield himself from them. Indeed, 'Prufrock among the Women' was the poem's alternative title.

Many of Eliot's early poems are observations of women by an inspector in disarming disguise: an immaculate man of their own ilk. His apparent passivity, ineptness and pathos give out intimations of a man disconnected from 'them' – women – like an anthropologist adrift in an alien tribe.

Would women, Prufrock wonders, respond to an overwhelming question about the nature of existence? It's a test, he thinks, they are bound to fail, since women only look for love. Surely ladies attending Boston teas will not penetrate Prufrock's philosophic soul. Prufrock sets himself a secret task: to go among them and remain unknowable.

Back in February, during his final semester as an undergraduate, Eliot had begun another long, ambitious poem, 'Portrait of a Lady', which he took with him to Paris. This poem traces a young man's view of a woman from one season to another in the course of a year during which the young man goes abroad. It's a retort to *The Portrait of a Lady*, the novel by Henry James, in which an American girl affronts the passive destiny expected of women – an efflorescence of the go-ahead Jo March phenomenon. But where James celebrates the free-spoken woman, Eliot derides her presuming voice.

His live source, according to Eliot's friend and fellow poet Conrad Aiken, was a slightly older woman, Adeleine Moffat, who lived behind Boston's State House and invited select students to her teas. She was head supervisor of several settlement houses and, like a number of unconventional Brahmin women, 'a Saph'.*

Eliot began with the interior monologue of a young man

---

* A Sapphist. From Sappho, the ancient Greek poet of Lesbos.

resisting a talkative woman but courtesy forbids him to say so. Soon after arriving in Paris, the poet tried out the Lady's plaintive voice, stating her claims, which prompts a fantasy. The youth appears so normal, so reasonable, so constrained by politeness to submit to her scenarios that it heightens the surprise when suddenly he displays his weapon: a lethal pen. The reader reels at his bland words, 'what if she should die some afternoon . . . / Should die . . .', before he wraps himself again in his hesitating manner.

Prufrock too is not quite as put-upon as he appears. His negatives are revealing, as well as absurd: 'I am no prophet' and 'No! I am not Prince Hamlet'. The negations unveil another side, a visionary and loner who has much in common with Hamlet: an introvert, asking questions; an actor who havers, deferring action. The Hamlet section was the first to be written.

It amused Eliot to keep back details about Prufrock: the J of his suppressed first name stood for Joseph, the dreamer in the Bible who stands out as the chosen of the Lord. Eliot concealed too that an alternative name for Prufrock was Proudfoot. Pride. Visions. A potential force lurks inside an ineffectual man past his prime and unappealing to women.

This caricature of a middle-aged failure can't be equated with Eliot whose rising gift as a poet would attract discerning people. In his early twenties Eliot was strikingly handsome, with hair parted in the centre, the two sides flopping over his brow, and an enigmatic smile – a friend called it his *Mona Lisa* smile.

An unexpected encounter shook Eliot during his first months in Paris. It was an overture from a man with a bony face and unfathomable, deep-set eyes, who held himself stiffly.

Matthew Stewart Prichard was an English art historian, aged forty-five, who had worked in antiquities at the Boston Museum of Fine Arts. He had a well-bred manner and a 'good as gold' brother, Eliot said, an officer in the British army. An introduction from Eliot's brother Henry was sufficient reason to trust Prichard as an expert guide to French art but when we meet his poetic representation he is not that – he is a sinister antiquarian, Mr Silvero, in Eliot's 1919 poem 'Gerontion'. We see the man's hands caressing Limoges porcelain.

Eliot revealed Silvero's identity to Emily Hale and, on two separate occasions (March 1931 and March 1933), talked of their contact, stressing his own naivety. But it was not a confidence about homosexuality. He called Prichard 'an ascetic pervert' who had conquered the body but not the soul. It was his soul that Prichard was after, and for a few seconds, Eliot confessed, he gave way. He felt possessed, taken over by someone subtly evil, even devilish. It bore on him as a 'vision of hell'.

Alone later in his room, he felt sure he had gone over an edge, falling fifty thousand years back in evolution and 'down into the uttermost abyss'.

He went on seeing Prichard after the incident and, at Christmas, accompanied him on a fortnight's tour of southern France. He heard Prichard pacing up and down all night in the next room. Eliot told Emily twenty years on that he still remembered those footsteps, and that night (maybe in Limoges) he recovered his self-possession: 'and I didn't mind; it was all over, the struggle, for me; something had won'.

The struggle remains murky, but clearly he rejected some tug from an older man. Since it was a temptation of the soul, not the body, he seems to have been horrified by demonic possession. It was not only that this man with an air of holiness preyed on him; the shock was to find himself susceptible, taken over, however briefly. It was a state he recognised in his kinship with the jurors in Salem, including Andrew Eliott who came to believe the Devil had been active in him. Eliot felt it necessary to reassure Emily that Prichard was his sole experience of this kind. And to confide in Emily alone was an intimate act: it mattered to him to come clean to a woman he could trust.

Back in Paris, his continued obsession with vice drove the

young Eliot to watch scenes of licence. By day he studied with a literary critic, Alain-Fournier, who was writing for the *Paris-Journal* and later wrote the celebrated novel *Le Grand Meaulnes*. Eliot also attended packed lectures by the philosopher Henri Bergson, and other lectures at the Sorbonne and the Collège de France. By night he roamed the prostitute quarter of Montparnasse, guidebook in hand: the fashionably decadent novel *Bubu de Montparnasse*. In March 1911, in his poem 'Rhapsody on a Windy Night', he observes a street-walker's 'crooked eye', and in his third 'Prelude', composed that July, a man imagines sordid scenes warping a prostitute's soul as she wakes alone after her night's work. He shudders at the thought of 'soiled hands' holding her 'yellow soles'.

He would have had his father's voice in his ear: if a cure for syphilis were to be found, his father said, 'there will be more nastiness, and it will be necessary to emasculate our children to keep them clean'. Henry Ware Eliot Sr looked on extramarital sex as tantamount to consorting with the Devil. His wife reinforced sexual prohibition with a more compelling image of ascetic aspiration:

> *Purge from thy heart all sensual desire,*
> *Let low ambitions perish in the fire*
> *Of higher aims. Then, as the transient dies,*
> *The eternal shall unfold before thy eyes . . .*

To purge lust was to unfold 'immortal gifts'. The force of these parental warnings ensured that their son was an inspector, not a practitioner, of vice – a curious, riveted onlooker.

To be a spectator became his habit, but could not satisfy unfulfilled desires. A safer solution was the desire perpetuated through romantic love.

The most formative experience Eliot had during his year in Paris, a prompt for an alternative image of love, was to witness a performance of the Russian dancer Nijinsky. *Le Spectre de la rose* entranced Paris in

1911. It was the star turn of the Ballets Russes, performed every night between 6 and 18 June at the Théâtre du Châtelet. Proof that Eliot saw *Le Spectre de la rose* is a barely noticed poem, 'Suppressed Complex', about a dancer who enters a girl's bedroom. This short poem in his notebook, written in 1914/15 but unpublished in Eliot's lifetime, draws on this ballet: a man dancing in the presence of a sleeping young woman, who then, in Eliot's phrase, 'passed out of the window'.

Sergei Diaghilev had first brought Russians to Paris in 1909, and then in 1911 the dancers, trained in St Petersburg, arrived as a permanent company and with new ballets that were all the rage. Diaghilev had commissioned a twelve-minute filler for his programme, from his choreographer, Mikhail Fokine, who used a piano piece by Carl Maria von Weber, 'Invitation to the Dance', orchestrated by Berlioz. The result was an innovation in choreography placing the male dancer, Vaslav Nijinsky, centre stage.

Though *Le Spectre de la rose* is a *pas de deux*, the young girl is mostly seated in a chair as she sleeps. It's largely a solo for Nijinsky, the Rose, as a vision of love. He appears out of the dark at a long French window with arms curled about his head. Strung only with petals shaded from pink to mauve, some wilted, some curled about his loins – barely covered with a few fronds – he jetés onto the bedroom floor, and his turns around the dreaming girl reach through her sleep. The Rose is expressively physical with his bulging thighs and long leaps, but it's a masculinity unafraid of its femaleness – it does not seek to overpower. It's not the usual seduction scene, not conquest. The eroticism of the Rose is delicate; he tends the girl's innocence as a quality of her own. It's a visitation, leaving the girl with a presence like a lingering perfume.

For the nine minutes the Rose is on stage, the audience is transported from a familiar scene – a young girl in her bedroom after a ball, breathing in the scent of the rose she has worn and falling asleep in her chair – into a visionary awakening. The Rose's curling and unfurling arms behind her sleeping head rouse her senses, and she moves with him, eyes still closed, as in a dream.

Vaslav Nijinsky and Tamara Karsavina in Le Spectre de la rose.

Then, as her dream takes hold, she dances faster, before dropping back in her chair. Bending over her from behind, the Rose touches his face to hers then runs for the window: five steps, and on the sixth he lifts off in flight. As Nijinsky soared through the window the conductor, Pierre Monteux, held up the beat, like catching a breath in wonder. And no one who saw his leap – never to come down – forgot it.

The girl wakes now to her familiar world. She picks up her rose from the floor and, holding it to her face, plants it in memory.

The dancer whose grace brings timeless love into the human world, the lingering scent of a 'Rose of memory' and a scene in a rose-garden were to recur in Eliot's poetry. Nijinsky said he wished to express as the Rose 'love in its divine sense'. In time Eliot too would elevate love to this level.

Eliot composed much of 'The Love Song of J. Alfred Prufrock' that summer in Munich, while staying at the Pension Bürger at No 50 Louisenstrasse, in July–August 1911. His return to Prufrock had been prompted by another ballet in the same programme as *Le Spectre de la rose*: a clown-marionette, Petroushka, is unable to live and love according to his own impulse. This manipulated flop, shunned by a ballerina, suffers rebuff (as does Prufrock, pinned and wriggling on a wall). Nijinsky painted his face white, obliterating expression, but unable to conceal his wounded eyes. He danced this role with his head on one side to music by Stravinsky – music so alert to jangled private emotions in the midst of a crowd that the musicians laughed when they saw the score. Neither the tragic clown nor Prufrock can bring himself to approach a woman.

During this fertile year abroad, Eliot shifted from writing juve-nilia to launching poems that would make his name. Even though Eliot felt physically weak in Munich, a condition he called cerebral anaemia, he took walks with a woman living in his pension, Marie von Moritz, who was proud of being '*echt Deutsch*', though born in Lithuania. She was in her early forties, about the same age as Eliot's eldest sister, Ada. Eliot knew enough German to converse and take in her memories. She spoke of her exhilaration as a child tobogganing in the mountains: 'Marie, Marie, hold on tight,' they'd say. Since then, her existence had fallen flat. She merely filled vacant time: 'I read much of the night and go south in the winter.' Eliot looked back on this twenty years later, when he told Emily Hale how he had relayed this woman's conversation 'almost word for word!' in *The Waste Land*.

Prufrock's need to frame an 'overwhelming question' and the intellectual stimulus of Paris prompted Eliot's resolve to enrol for a doctoral course in philosophy, a subject in which he had gained A's during his final year as an undergraduate. Following his summer jaunt to Munich and Italy, he found himself back at Harvard and again in his cousin Eleanor's company. She owned a phonograph in a studio of her own, where Eliot attended dances. It wasn't long before he met once more her friend Emily Hale, now grown up.

3

A CHANCE OF LOVE

Eliot returned to America with a polished European air, a Malacca cane and a reproduction of the *Yellow Christ* by Gauguin. He also brought back a sheaf of new poems, including his 'Prelude' about a prostitute, and was ready to complete 'Portrait of a Lady' with its dismissive finale. For all his panache, he began to worry. In his two rooms on the third floor of 16 Ash Street, near Harvard Yard, he suffered from insomnia and began writing undistinguished poems about the world falling apart, together with the mental health of its observer.

'Prufrock's Pervigilium', an addition to 'Prufrock', written in about 1912 and set apart in his notebook, narrows in on a madman in the gutter singing as dawn breaks. Here, Prufrock's confession loses its ironic ruefulness and becomes raw apprehension: 'I heard my Madness chatter before day / I saw the world roll up into a ball / Then suddenly dissolve and fall away.' On the advice of Conrad Aiken, the 'Pervigilium' was not included in the final poem.

This and other night-vigil poems were not publishable, especially a self-harm fantasy, 'Do I know how I feel? Do I know what I think?' A tight-lipped lodger greeting his porter dreads 'what a flash of

madness will reveal'. The poem moves on swiftly to a doctor performing a post-mortem, which is followed by a potential diversion
(a pencil addition on the same page) beginning 'Hidden under the
heron's wing': it's a tender thought of a lovely girl whose arms divide
the evening mist. The dream of hidden love brings a gentleness that
dispels violence.

But tenderness cannot take hold. On the loose is 'a syphilitic
spider', a fear of venereal disease. The after-effect of fear and suppressed sexuality was a will-less apathy, his aboulia. The physical
result was an outbreak of shingles two springs running, and this
may be the reason that Eliot was treated in the Stillman Infirmary
from 17 to 25 March 1912. He knew that this painful illness was
brought on by stress.

The searcher in Eliot chose to study Eastern religions. He took an
elementary course in Sanskrit, followed by a course in Pali, in order to
explore Hindu and Buddhist scriptures. He never forgot the Sanskrit
he studied in J. R. Lanman's course in Indic Philosophy, particularly
the words of wisdom Lanman tipped into the copy he gave his pupil
of *The Twenty-eight Upanishads*: '*da datta, damyata, dayadhvam*' ['give', 'control'
and 'sympathise', with meanings out of the reach of the English
equivalents]. These injunctions would reappear in the finale to *The
Waste Land*. Other voices he heard in his classes would also resound ten
years later. St Augustine's *Confessions*, Books I and VII, came into Eliot's
philosophy course in December 1913 and Dante in January 1914. The
fruits of his poetic gift, fruits that would ripen, had their beginnings
in what seemed to him, at the time, a fruitless period.

Though outwardly a successful philosophy student, he was
studying under duress: forcing himself to become an academic,
what everyone around him expected, his mother above all.
Although he produced a stellar fourth 'Prelude' in 1911–12, a poem
foreseeing *The Waste Land*, he felt himself drying up.

To combat inertia, his reading explored extreme positions on the
outposts of existence: the biblical landscape of spiritual desire and

trial. The earliest fragments of what would become *The Waste Land* take place at these outposts: 'I am the Resurrection', 'So through the evening' (the earliest version of the climactic part V) and a failed 'dancer to God' in 'The Death of St Narcissus'. The opening lines of 'Narcissus' (completed early in 1915), would appear verbatim in *The Waste Land*.

The demands and challenges of a genuine spiritual trial gripped Eliot, first through his mother's poems and then his study of Indian scriptures and Dante. To him Dante was the greatest poet of the spirit's journey, reaching 'deeper degrees of degradation and higher degrees of exaltation'. From 1911 he carried around the Temple Classics edition of *The Divine Comedy*, small enough to keep in his pocket, and he learnt passages by heart on long train journeys between St Louis and Boston.

Eliot's pencil lines in the margins pick out two figures who appeared to Dante in the course of a vision. One is Brunetto Latini, a Florentine writer whose homosexuality lands him in Dante's hell.

Dante finds this fate disturbing because Brunetto's sodomy turns out to determine his afterlife, rather than his best-known book, a popular allegorical journey (influential for Dante himself) called the *Tresor*. Pitifully, Brunetto asks Dante if the *Tresor* (treasure both literally and, for an author, emotionally) is still alive. It's not sodomy itself that appears to upset Dante; it's divine Judgement* giving precedence to sin (what is perceived as sin) over art — no matter how great art is. Dante is filled with empathy for his master, who wants his work to last.

The other figure is Beatrice. In his early reading of the *Paradiso*, Eliot marks at several points the appearance of Dante's great love, his guide in heaven. When Dante meets Beatrice, his nature 'is transmuted to the quality of heaven and he knows not whether he is still in the flesh or no'. Dante is waiting for Beatrice to restore his lost sight: his eyes will be as the gates through which she entered, 'with the fire wherewith I ever burn'. The paradisal fire comes first, called forth by Dante's understanding of a woman's goodness, 'for good . . . kindles love'. The angelic voice of Beatrice represents Divine Wisdom.

Memorising these passages, fretting about his life, Eliot was about to encounter his own Beatrice.

Berkeley Place was, and still is, an old-fashioned street of large, plain wooden houses with steeply pitched roofs to shake off snowfalls, within walking distance of Harvard Yard and Eliot's lodgings in Ash Street. He felt especially at home with his cousin Eleanor, a graduate of Radcliffe College now taking an advanced play-writing course, Harvard's '47 Workshop' (forty-seven were enrolled). She acted with this group, wrote plays for it and liked to dramatise scenes from novels by Austen and Dickens.

Eleanor was a member of the Cambridge Social and Dramatic Club, and Eliot was drawn into the circle. Acting, a chance to

---

* In Canto XV of the *Inferno* it is of course Dante himself who has exercised Judgement and placed Brunetto with those who, in life, had practised sodomy.

immerse in a role, with script and costume, offered a counter to his
worry, a release from a tortured and directionless self. It delighted
him to offer silly scenarios to Eleanor, teasing his cousin that her
play-writing would conform to theatrical clichés. These scenarios caricature female types and the dialogue in subtitles to silent
films. Prominent was a Mexican dancer with rolling eyeballs who
performs to a medley from *Carmen*. Another cliché was the plucky
Native American maiden who dies saving the man she loves, and
there was Effie the Waif, pursuing the truth about her parentage:

'Father, won't you tell me about Mother?'

'Not now, dear.'

Eliot often saw Emily Hale at the Hinkley house. Another young
woman serious about theatre, Emily had the gifts to be an actor: a
command of the stage and her lovely voice. In 1912 she performed in
Through the Looking Glass. At twenty, she was tall with a slim, upright
figure. Her manners combined the familiar decorum of old Boston
with warmth and humour. A photograph shows how her wavy
hair shone when the light fell on it. Eliot was welcome for Sunday
evenings around the fire with comfy suppers of what he remembered as 'nice things'. In after years, faced with English puddings, he
would remember Boston fish-cakes as 'ambrosia'. He felt the 'thrill
& excitement' of eating baked beans on toast with 'Miss Hale'.

One evening, the Hinkleys held a small party: it included Emily
Hale, Eliot and Penelope Noyes, who had been at Radcliffe with
Eleanor. Long afterwards, Eliot reminded Emily of what had been
for him a memorable evening. 'I had been bottled up for a long time.
When I fell in love with you,' he wrote, 'we acted some impromptu
charade in which I stepped on your feet. All I knew at the moment,
being very undeveloped and never having had any such experience
before, was that I wanted dreadfully to see you again; and it was
only when the "stunt show" was proposed and I knew that I should
be able to see you once a week [at rehearsals] that I began to realise
what had happened to me.'

The stunt show took place at the Hinkleys' on 17 February 1913.

Emily, who studied singing in Boston, led each half of the programme with songs. She and Eliot did a scene from *Emma*, devised
by Eleanor, who herself took the role of Emma. The three of them
performed in a small space in front of the fireplace in order to be
visible to all in the inter-leading two-room parlor. Eliot played
Emma's father, Mr Woodhouse. Emily remembered he played the
part of this wrapped-up hypochondriac 'delightfully, while I was
a "natural" for the part of Mrs Elton. I was overawed by the quiet,
reserved very brilliant young man whose low voice made all he
said very difficult to follow, apart from the content of his already
individual thinking. I was given to understand by others that I was
the only girl he paid any attention to.'

Eliot retained a tender memory of Emily's dresses and could recall
them years later. She was 'graceful' in a pretty apricot dress with
fur trimming on a day he felt how 'hopelessly remote' she was.
She wore a blue dress with a scarlet sash the first time he ventured
rather hesitantly to call her by her first name. He watched her performance in a comedy of manners, *The Mollusc*, and years afterwards
still held wryly to his identification with a mollusc fixed to its rock
and determined not to move. He would also remember the 'light
flowered dress' Emily had sported in her role as a matron tenacious
of social conventions, a variation on persistent Mrs Elton.

Emily invited Eliot to join her party, along with her friend
Margaret Farrand, for Wagner's *Tristan und Isolde* at the Boston Opera
House on 1 December 1913. This third memorable event (following
the charade and stunt show) was independent of the Hinkley con-
nection and momentous enough to provide the earliest scenes for
The Waste Land.

The sailors' chorus on board ship in Act I, as the pair fall in love,
was to remain with Eliot and introduce his memory of Emily Hale
as 'the hyacinth girl'. Her effect on him is blind and lasting love. In
Act III of the opera, Tristan, bleeding and fatally wounded, needs
'the healing Lady'; after a delay, Isolde appears but too late to save

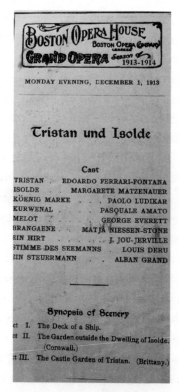

Eliot kept this programme from the night at the opera when he realised he was in love with Emily.

him. She has come to die with him, and her voice calls him back: 'his heart swells and, brave and full, pulses in his breast'. This strain too will stay with the poet. The finale of *The Waste Land* will recall that pulse in the breast as though his own. He would spell out for Emily what followed: 'After that night at the opera I was completely conscious of it [love], and quite shaken to pieces.'*

He invited Emily to a football game and arranged a tea party for the next day, for the purpose of seeing her again. Afterwards, when

---

* Eliot had seen the opera in 1909 and written a poem, 'Opera', unmoved by extravagant emotion. The speaker feels like 'the ghost of youth / At the undertakers' ball'. His newfound affinity for the emotion in 1913 could have been prompted by Verdenal's regard for Wagner as well as by the presence of Emily.

he walked her back to Clement Circle at the end of that Saturday afternoon, he fell into feverish gloom. 'I was so down in the mouth to think those delirious two days were over – it all seemed over – that I nearly spoke to you.'

'I could not / Speak' at the height of the hyacinth girl scene in *The Waste Land* recalls this delirium, a love that goes beyond its object: 'Looking into the heart of light, the silence.'

It was, however, far from clear whether Eliot was bent on courtship. In the end he did speak, but puzzled Emily with a mixed message, as she recalled in a pencil scrawl of 1957, a first draft of a brief memoir about her relationship with the poet to serve as an introduction to his letters: 'he very much embarrassed me by telling me he loved me deeply; no mention of marriage was made'. Here is the telling fact in their story: what he did *not* say. Since he did not speak of marriage, she had to be cautious. He had won a Sheldon travelling scholarship to study for a year at Merton College, Oxford, and made his declaration to Emily when he was leaving. If a man did not commit himself, a woman could not allow, much less return, feeling. Instead, she waited.

Sixteen years later, he took pains to explain.

'I said, that last evening: "I can't ask anything, because I have nothing to offer". That meant simply "I cannot ask you to become engaged to me, I cannot try to induce you to love me, because I am still so far away from being self-supporting". You should know that my only goal and ambition in life was that I might ask you to marry me.'

Though his explanation was persuasively rational, Emily remained unconvinced so he explained further.

'When I first knew you I was immature for my age, timid, discouraged, and intensely egotistical,' he told her. 'At Oxford I was in a very disturbed state; for I knew I should never be a good professor of philosophy, that my heart was not in it, that my mind even was not good enough.'

This rings true. To offer marriage would have been to fix himself in a life he did not want: a jobbing academic supporting a family; not the international poet he wished to be.

Emily had to ask herself if she could read the meaning of Eliot's words. Furled there were needs that veered away from what a person might expect of love: physical closeness, domesticity, security, public acknowledgement.

He had been 'a divided man', he justified his actions in many letters to Emily and in his eventual statement about her to posterity. Between 1911 and 1914 the division in him deepened, as he bound himself to Emily and at the same time contrived a sequence of farewell scenes: first in his Weeping Girl poem. She had to take in the fact that, however much he loved her, he could not commit himself. The situation permitted her no other course than to turn away.

'La Figlia che Piange' foretells a parting. What's curious about this poem is the date: late 1911 or 1912. It means that Eliot composed this scene before, by his own account, he fell in love with Emily, and some two and a half years *before* they parted. It seems prophetic for them that in this poem, love has little chance. An admirer and a girl with her arms full of flowers part artistically, her body posed for maximum effect:

> *Stand on the highest pavement of the stair —*
> *Lean on a garden urn —*
> *Weave, weave the sunlight in your hair —*
> *Clasp your flowers to you with pained surprise —*
> *Fling them on the ground and turn*
> *With a fugitive resentment in your eyes:*
> *But weave, weave the sunlight in your hair.*

Here is a director setting up a scene. His imperatives, one after another, devise a mime; the distressed girl has no lines and she is to enact parting through gesture, eyes and tears alone. The image of the Weeping Girl foreshadows Eliot's poetic idea of Emily as the hyacinth girl of *The Waste Land* – marking again her beauty, hair and arms full of flowers — and the speaker's positioning of the Girl foretells the unlikelihood of their coming together — which is perhaps why Eliot never shared this with Emily in the way he shared other scenes.

The speaker gives no reason for discarding the girl. Certainly, she attracts him, for he considers a love-scene — 'how they should have been together' — but he prefers a scene of parting to fix in memory and art: as statue or poem, she cannot fade. It is what poetry does, Shakespeare tells the beloved of the *Sonnets*: so long as eyes can see, 'So long lives this, and this gives life to thee.'

Eliot's Figlia tantalises us with the kind of novelistic scene at which this poet became master. This is a fragment of a fuller story touching a woman who is loved, then used and rejected — her 'pained surprise'; her trust left 'torn and bruised'. The impact of a man sensitive to the hurt he could inflict is delivered with extraordinary candour.

Unknown to Emily Hale was this: at the time that Eliot did not ask her to marry him or wait for him, he imagined a solitary drama of martyrdom. In June 1914, he wrote 'The Burnt Dancer', a poem about a moth singeing itself in the flame of a candle. A refrain, 'O danse danse mon papillon noir!', urging a dance to the death, sets up a fire narrative as distinct from a love narrative. How early Eliot invents this antinomy: the solo death-dance along with the bedroom dance in the footsteps of the Rose.

And there's yet another complication that Eliot concealed from Emily Hale and all other women. His Bolo and Columbo rhymes, which he was still composing in 1914, and which he put together (taking the time and trouble to copy out the cycle to date) in a separate notebook in 1915, are another counter to the romance of the Rose. What Emily Hale was up against was an adversarial code: a polarisation of the female into innocent Figlia versus the 'whore' of the smutty jingles. The traditional split puts aside living women so as to revel instead in fantasies of sexual assault. How, on deck, Columbo grabbed the bosun's wife round the neck and 'raped her on the bowsprit'.

Tempting though it has been for some to play down the Columbo cycle, it can't be excluded. The violence with an edge of hilarity would enter the poet's public oeuvre, bent on declaring a buried life with total honesty, the sordid and horrible along with the poet's sense of beauty.

Still at Harvard in the spring of 1914, his last semester there, Eliot chose to take a course with a visiting Englishman from Cambridge University, the mathematical philosopher Bertrand Russell. He found Russell's logic 'a ballet of bloodless alphabets'. But Russell took a liking to the silent Eliot, and Eliot admired Russell for his social ease and laughter. In Eliot's poem 'Mr Apollinax', he pictures him as Priapus, god of fertility, in the shrubbery, while his hosts, prim Bostonians with amusingly respectable names, Professor Phlaccus and Mr and Mrs Channing-Cheetah, avert their eyes. The poem favours the disruptive intruder with pointed ears, recognisably Russell's. They would meet again in London, where Russell would play a new role in Eliot's life.

At the beginning of July 1914 Eliot sailed for Europe a second time. His Boston manners and accent led some passengers, many of them students from the West, to take him for an English visitor to America. They found it hard to believe he came from St Louis.

By the end of July, he was ready to send a new poem to Conrad Aiken. The title, 'The Love Song of St Sebastian', suggests a sequel to 'The Love Song of J. Alfred Prufrock', but the scene has shifted from an imagined tea party, populated by unapproachable women, to an untouched figure of a particular woman. Clothed in white, an image of purity, she stands at the top of a stair, watching an act of martyrdom. A would-be saint flogs himself until he is standing in a pool of blood. In pity, the woman takes him up and he dies on her breast.

The second stanza reverses roles: now it's the woman's turn to die. The lover turns out to be a strangler, fingering her ear as he bends her head between his knees. He is in love with the flesh he's

about to destroy. This man articulates a twisted rationale for violence in a manner that prefigures the spiel of present-day terrorists.
In Eliot's version the victim has no story, no character; she exists
solely as a *tabula rasa* for an insane 'saint' seeking power.

Emily Hale lingered in Eliot's mind. He sent Conrad Aiken a postal
order for $4, to order pink or red Killarney roses for the Saturday
night performance of one of her plays that December.

During the Christmas vacation of 1914, Eliot stayed at 1 Gordon
Street in Bloomsbury. It was a boarding house full of transient
Americans. In his first term at Oxford, Eliot had been taken aback
at the right of students at the women's colleges to mix with men. At
the more conservative Harvard, professors keen on women's education had to repeat their lectures at Radcliffe College. It disturbed
Eliot's sense of fitness that women – this would be Vera Brittain's
generation of feminists – came 'right into' a men's college. 'No one
looks at them,' he assured his family.

Yet he could not entirely avert his eyes from women in London.
'One walks about the street with one's desires,' he confided to Aiken
on New Year's Eve. As in Paris, 'nervous sexual attacks' confronted
his wall of shyness and refinement. It worried him to be still a virgin
at the age of twenty-six and he thought how 'very stimulating' it
would be for several women to fall in love with him. Several, he
says, because that would make 'the practical side' less evident. And
he would be 'very sorry for them'.

A continued outlet was ribaldry. Eliot was proud of his rhymes
and elaborated on their bravado to a new friend, the American
poet Ezra Pound, then living in London. Aiken had shown him
'Prufrock' as well as providing Eliot with a personal introduction.
Eliot pretended to Pound to have been fatigued by a non-existent
'debauch'. To impose Bolo on Pound and Aiken was to beckon
them into complicity. Mundane reasons for this performance offer
themselves – protracted juvenility (a common excuse to Emily as he
grew older), unwilling virginity and not least the popular notion of

masculinity current in America at the time – but none seems quite to explain this guise.

Eliot was prepared to publish two of the rhymes, both drafted a few years back in Paris and Munich: 'The Triumph of Bullshit' (November 1910, an address to critical 'Ladies' with a refrain to 'stick it up your ass') and 'Ballade pour la grosse Lulu' (July 1911, with a call to Lulu to put on her rough red drawers 'And come to the Whore House Ball!'). But the artist and writer Wyndham Lewis, to whom these verses were offered for his avant-garde magazine *Blast*, declined to print words 'Ending in -Uck, -Unt and -Ugger'. On 2 February 1915, writing from Merton College, Eliot complained to Pound that Lewis was too 'puritanical'. He nudged Pound to share the hilarity of a new couplet: Bolo's Big Black Kween 'pulled her stockings off / With a frightful cry of "Hauptbahnhof!!"'. In this same letter he enclosed his *Spectre de la rose* poem, 'Suppressed Complex'.

A girl in her bedroom lies prone; the man is at first 'upright' in a corner, then he starts dancing along with the flames of her fire. Nothing is required of the girl but to watch his performance. He stays all night and then, the dancer reports, 'I passed joyously out through the window.'

What is the situation? As with 'La Figlia', the girl is silenced; she protests only with her eyes. The fugitive resentment in La Figlia's eyes when she is discarded and the stubborn eyes of the girl in 'Suppressed Complex' signal discord. Disturbing in both poems is the speaker's awareness of a girl's emotions and his disregard for them.

Eliot drew on yet another ballet that had been a sensation in Paris in the spring of 1911, *Le Martyre de Saint Sébastien*. Beautiful Ida Rubenstein danced barefoot on hot coals, and this found its way into Eliot's Narcissus, who dances barefoot on burning sands. The burnt feet, a follow-on from the burnt moth six months earlier, revives Eliot's fire ordeal. Eliot's early try-outs with fire mock his would-be martyrs as failures.

'St Narcissus' had been accepted by Pound's contact Harriet

Monroe in Chicago for publication in *Poetry*, when Eliot pulled it at the last moment. There is no explanation but Eliot, increasingly under Pound's influence, was turning away from martyrdom towards a hard-edged Modernism. Pound encouraged the satiric element in 'Prufrock'. Not the Prufrock of the hundred visions: Pound had no truck with an unrealised prophet, nor with saints, failed or otherwise, nor with Judaeo-Christian religion. Eliot resolved on a new phase of quick caricatures; and so, the higher aspirations of dance and fire – and, with them, the nearly published 'Saint Narcissus' – were relegated to the back burner.

Encouraged by Pound, Eliot resolved to stay in London and put poetry first.

After he left for Europe, Emily Hale recalled, 'I heard often from him; on certain anniversaries my favorite flower, sweet-peas, always arrived.'* What Emily had meant to him – innocence, unspoiled desire and the silence falling between them – was to flash back in memory like the light of some other possibility: a might-have-been, all the sharper for their separation.

---

* Over the years, he mainly chose roses. The scent of sweet-peas was too overpowering, he once told her.

4

'THE POET'S BRIDE'

Eliot's marriage came as a 'complete surprise' to Emily Hale. He did not warn her or anyone else of this move, neither his parents, nor his sisters, nor Eleanor. All expected him back at Harvard to complete his doctorate.

'I did want to write poetry, and I felt obscurely that I should never write in America; and so I suppose I persuaded myself gradually that I did not love you after all,' he told Emily in a letter of 1930 when he resumed their tie, as though it had been impossible for her to be with him elsewhere. Emily must have questioned this because the following August, he insists: he had to escape the life laid out for him in America.

Disappointingly, the real-life parting from Emily did not prompt the lasting work of art anticipated in the projected farewell scene of 'La Figlia'. Eliot had written nothing since of that calibre. On arrival in England he continued to divert desire into the Columbiad and the masochistic show Narcissus puts on, these knowingly crazed displays a substitute for the romance that he left behind as he sailed for Europe.

All through Hilary term (January to March 1915) Eliot was having

Vivienne Eliot at Garsington Manor. Photographed by Lady Ottoline Morrell, who thought her a spoilt kitten but then was charmed.

a deadly time in an Oxford emptied by war. Immured amongst men in Merton College, his body felt numbed. And then, at a lunch party in March, a vivacious young woman, the daughter of an artist, appeared as one of the guests.

She was dark, petite and put herself forward in a flamboyant manner, unlike the Boston women Eliot had known. The party took place in the grand medieval pile of Magdalen College. Eliot was invited by another American, Scofield Thayer, whose rooms had once been occupied by Lord Alfred Douglas, the lover of Oscar Wilde. Thayer came from a wealthy family on Martha's Vineyard, an island south of Cape Cod in Massachusetts. He had been a year behind Eliot at Milton Academy, attended Harvard and now he too was reading philosophy and writing poems. Thayer had also invited Vivienne Haigh-Wood, a close friend of his cousin Lucy Ely Thayer. The two had met in Vevey in 1908. Vivienne's 1914 diary shows how often she stayed over with Lucy in Bayswater after a late-night jaunt in London. This is where she encountered Scofield. A year-long flirtation was still in play when Eliot entered the scene.

At the time, Vivienne was a governess with a Cambridge family, and freer than most to come and go. She did not look like a governess. Her clothes were dashing, stagey in the manner of the Ballets Russes.

She meant to leave her origins behind. Her grandfather had been a craftsman in Lancashire. He lived in Bury and the name had been Wood. The Haigh came from Vivienne's grandmother, Mary Haigh, from Dublin. Vivienne's father, Charles Haigh-Wood, rose to be a successful Royal Academician, who did portraits and popular drawing-room scenes, including a painting of Vivienne as a little girl in a sash, with curled red lips, looking down at the doll in her arms. His wife was Rose Esther Robinson from London, where the couple had settled in 1891. Two children, a daughter and then a son, were born. The family lived in comfort at 3 Compayne Gardens on the fringe of Hampstead, a respectable address, though not on the arty heights of this north London suburb. Their income was increased by the rentals from seven inherited Dublin properties.

Vivienne was artistic, multi-talented and uncertain which course to follow. At one time or another she tried different arts: dance, writing, music. The range and keenness of her tastes made her unusually alive – almost quivering with life. Ballet was her favourite of the arts and the previous year she had seen Nijinsky's last performances in Le Spectre de la rose and Les Sylphides at the Palace Theatre.

One evening when Eliot came to London during his spring vacation, Vivienne and a friend joined him at one of the dances held on Saturdays in hotels. Vivienne, who had taken ballet lessons, proved a pliant dancer, quick to follow when Eliot started to foxtrot,* the latest from New York. Around them, couples jerk from side to side in the one-step while, coming from St Louis with the rhythm of ragtime in his blood, Eliot dips to the beat and in his arms is a lithe, uninhibited woman with animated eyes.

Small and slight next to this tall American, nearly six foot, Vivienne casts an upward, enquiring glance and lifts a pointed chin. Her grey-green eyes are full of venture as she raps out opinions. Where Eliot reserves observations for his poems, she says what she thinks out loud.

Vivienne. He repeats her 'amusing' name.

She speaks with conviction, even vehemence, and as she speaks she exhales cigarette smoke. It excites him to see a woman smoke, he writes home to Eleanor, struck by Vivienne as 'emancipated', 'sophisticated', a Londoner in the know, an Englishwoman – a species so new to him he cannot as yet exercise judgement.

By now it's the summer term at Oxford, with leaves afloat on the branches and boating parties on the Cherwell. Vivienne is there again, down from London. Scofield Thayer is there too. He's what Gatsby will aspire to be, one of those born to privilege with a voice full of money. He has his eye on Vivienne. And Eliot is there, lean and handsome in white flannels. Neither American is as young as their fellow-students. A year later Eliot will remind Scofield Thayer of this occasion: 'Can it be that a year ago you and I were charming the eyes (and ears) of Char-flappers from one virginal punt'.

That day Vivienne's attention turns from Thayer to his potential rival, silent, more unknowable, more gifted. She knows his poetry and likes what is flagrant and catchy in Eliot's writing. That May, he has produced three caricatures of supposed Boston relatives: the fast Miss Nancy Ellicott and the deadly propriety of a deceased aunt, Miss Helen Slingsby, and another aunt who reads the *Boston Evening Transcript* as a substitute for living. The youth who brings the

---

* Introduced in 1914 by Harry Fox in New York.

paper to his Boston aunt is quite like Prufrock, wearily dutiful, but harbouring the character of a thinker. In June 1915, the month when Eliot turned from America to Europe, 'The Love Song of J. Alfred Prufrock' was published by Harriet Monroe in *Poetry*.

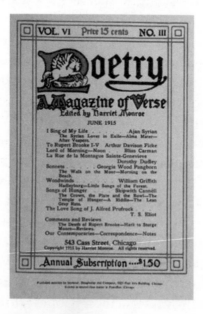

'The Love Song of J. Alfred Prufrock' was published in the same month, June 1915, as Eliot resolved to stay on in England and marry an Englishwoman.

Eliot, about to break with his people, expressed disillusion through those family satires, and Monroe accepted all three for the coming autumn.

That this poet is destined for greatness Vivienne has the wit to discern. She, like Pound, urges Eliot to remain in London, as the centre of the literary world. Despising 'provincialism', Eliot does not want to fall into what he sees as the narrowness of New England. Vivienne's imagination sights a new role while the poet-to-be watches her step from the punt at Magdalen Bridge and into his life.

He is by no means in love in the delirious way it had been with Emily. This is not blood shaking the heart. What he wants is an affair but does not know how. His upbringing, moral and hygienic, forbids casual sex. At twenty-six, he has wished to shed his virginity together with the numbness induced by Oxford, and now opportunity could be thwarted once more by his wall of shyness. Could he change course? His year at Merton will come to an end in the middle of June.

Marriage, then?

Eliot has rarely failed to exercise the option of inaction. His way has been to hold back with Prufrockian indecision. To close now with Vivienne, to act decisively, will take him away from his past with relieving finality.

At twenty-seven, Vivienne is a few months older than Eliot, and totally unlike the single women of his Boston circle, Eleanor Hinkley, Emily Hale and Penelope Noyes, who will all remain single. The assurance of Vivienne's manner implies that she knows what she's about. She is given to disillusion, and while Eliot's disillusion owes a lot to Laforgue, Vivienne has gone and found it for herself.

On 15 June, with Eliot's last day in Oxford at hand, Vivienne is still flirting with Scofield Thayer. Her nudging directness has not so far brought on a proposal. That day she reproaches Thayer for letting her down about a dance at the Savoy the previous Saturday.

'I could have danced like a faun,' she says, alluding to Nijinsky's *Prélude à l'après-midi d'un faune.*

A cultured man like Thayer would have picked up this sophisticated signal, not only Vivienne's allegiance to Modernist choreography but also an erotic innuendo. In this controversial ballet, the face, in profile, is expressionless; the body alone speaks. The sexually explicit finale, the faun stretched face down over the nymph's scarf – Nijinsky, it seemed, masturbating in public view – outraged the first audience in 1912.

A few days later Vivienne was engaged to Eliot, with no inkling that he had dreamed of someone else.

Eliot too had no inkling of Vivienne's past: a dependence on chloral hydrate, prescribed by doctors for nervous episodes since she was fifteen. But even before he left Oxford, he did create a nervous episode, in a prose-poem, 'Hysteria'. The piece sets up a scene in a tea room where a woman loses control of herself. Helpless, the gentleman with her takes in his companion's shaking breasts and open mouth. Her bared teeth and the cavern of her throat, with its rippling muscles, bring on the same sexual fear as in Eliot's student poem where a man, turned into a snake, lies sluggish along Circe's stair.

'Hysteria' is the first fruit of Vivienne's impact on Eliot's work, prompting sharp, agonised scenes of a man and woman who cannot uncouple, two figures apparently at odds. But the unrestrained Vivienne Haigh-Wood and her restrained suitor were not incompatible. On the contrary, they had in common a capacity for emotion, in Eliot contained, in Vivienne uncontained, emotions in search of situations.

Eliot's rationale for his decision to marry Vivienne, as laid out eventually in letters to Emily Hale, was a variation on what became the set story about needing to escape from America 'to some life in which I could write poetry ... I had to persuade myself that I was in love with someone here who could not or would not go to America—I had to pretend to myself that I had cut all ties to home.'

There was also an unspoken intention. Eliot was after a bolt of novel experience, less to do with falling in love and more with ending inhibition, sexual and poetic. His first statement about the marriage, writing seven days later to explain himself to his brother, is that he feels less 'suppressed'. He adds, 'I feel more alive than I ever have before.' Daring herself, daring him, Vivienne stood ready to join herself to the poet in him. She could inject her quick fire into his hope to end hesitation.

As Vivienne saw it, Eliot was the active party, firing her imagination with a role she could offer. Her speech was rapid in contrast with Eliot's slow deliberation; she could seize a telling word amongst the trove of synonyms in the English language. As a poet of the 'tobacco trance', Eliot was of course a master, yet Vivienne was a match in her way: quick in repartee, almost hypnotically rhythmic in her insistent repetitions, and tuned in to the Cockney of the streets. Eliot's commitment to the marriage seemed to appoint her as partner of his poetic venture.

Eliot would later stress his passivity: a man who found himself engaged to a woman with whom he had hardly had the lightest flirtation. He could have been driven by continued rivalry with his Boston cousin Fred Eliot, the success in the family. Can it be merely a coincidence that Tom Eliot chose to marry on 26 June 1915, on the heels of Fred's wedding day, 25 June? Fred's was the full-blown occasion with bridal white and proud mothers. Tom Eliot's, by contrast, was to be downplayed: a registry office. No flummery, no guests. In a letter to his cousin Eleanor, Eliot had spoofed Fred's simpering bride. In fact, Elizabeth Berkeley Lee was a graduate of Radcliffe and well-placed in Boston society, a bride certain to please the family.

When much later Eliot came to justify himself to Emily, he wanted her to believe the short engagement – no more than a few days – with no time to come to his senses, was because Vivienne told him of her previous broken engagement, to a school teacher, Charles Buckle, and claimed that this time she could not stand the strain. Eliot went along out of compunction, he said.

Amongst Vivienne's stories is an early, unpublished one entitled 'Rosa Buckle', about a Victorian woman with her mother's first name, who, at the age of twenty-six, 'very nearly an old maid', gets engaged to an unattractive man called Charles (the name, as it happens, of Vivienne's father as well as her former suitor). He becomes the butt of jokes for Rosa's younger sisters. The telling detail is wild, cruel laughter. The author presents this as a family trait: 'unless they were laughing they were in the dumps. There was nothing between.' This went with a fleeting look of 'utter recklessness'. This kind of recklessness was not a mark of courage or adventure; it was 'self-destruction'.

In 1914 Vivienne's father had settled £500 on her; soon after, she asked him to inform Buckle that the engagement was off. Her mother had agreed with Buckle's mother that the pair should part. So Vivienne was defying a previous disaster when she joined Eliot on 26 June 1915 at the Hampstead Register Office. For both, then, to marry was a rebellion against the lives laid out for them: Eliot as unwilling academic, Vivienne as governess.

It was the very day that Vivienne's nineteen-year-old brother Maurice left for the battlefields in France. For Vivienne to say goodbye to her brother and, the same day, go through with a secret wedding, took some nerve.

She produced the necessary witnesses: her aunt and godmother Lillia Symes, and her friend, Lucy Thayer. Eliot, acting alone, gave an address in Greek Street on the marriage certificate. He must have lodged there, in Soho, for six days after he vacated his rooms in Oxford. The certificate registered 'no occupation'. Once he surrendered his travelling fellowship from Harvard (which would have paid his return fare to America), he had no income.

Vivienne had an annual allowance of £50 from her father (worth about £5,000 today). It's not clear if she retained the £500 her father had settled on her when she became engaged to Mr Buckle. In addition, there were expectations, including a third of the Irish rental income after her father's death and her mother's substantial annual income of £600. Eliot had no income at this point and could expect to earn around £150 a year through full-time teaching, which is what he proposed to do during the school year of 1915–16. With men away at the Front, schoolmasters were in demand, and Eliot's American nationality, which kept him out of the war, was an advantage.

The marriage was announced in *The Times* on 30 June. Eliot also informed Harvard that he'd changed course in favour of poetry, had married in London, and had no intention of living again in the US. The marriage, he claimed in his stiffest manner, had been hastened by 'factors to do with the war'.

Eliot later confided to a friend that he never 'lay' with a woman he liked, loved or was strongly attracted to physically. This confession – if true – cannot but centre on Vivienne, and what was a sad fact for

Eliot was also a sad fact for his bride. In his poem 'Ode', a bridegroom is observed trying to compose himself, smoothing down his hair. The bride lies prone and appears at once pitiful and threatening, a 'Succuba eviscerate'. Not only has the bridegroom harmed this creature but also himself, for instinct has, it seems, betrayed him with a premature ejaculation, some way below the stars.

Eliot's poetic method, he told Aiken, was to use his own experience in an objectified way, as though it were disconnected from himself. He published 'Ode' only once, and not in America, because he did not want his mother to see it.

In no time, Vivienne's rescue role deflated into helplessness: she was 'knocked out completely', Eliot told his brother on 2 July, seven days after becoming her husband. No one knew the cause of 'illness' (presenting as migraine or neuritis or 'glands' or stomach trouble or rheumatism or 'internal displacements'), not the expensive doctors summoned to attend Vivienne, nor Eliot, nor Vivienne herself. Her voice cried 'ill', like a warning gong.

Elements of self-dramatisation and invalidism can't, though, dispel a crucial fact: her vulnerability to assorted doctors who prescribed drugs now known to be dangerous. Since puberty, she had been given chloral, which could damage the liver, and potassium bromide, a sedative whose side-effects fit the otherwise disconnected array of Vivienne's ills: headaches, eye problems, lethargy, confusion, irritation of the stomach and loss of appetite. Another of her prescribed drugs was Hoffmann's Anodyne, a hypnotic consisting of one-part ether to three parts alcohol. Later, the effect of ether rubbed into her skin or soaked into her handkerchief could leave her groping in a daze, and in company the smell of it clung about her. From 1915, the year she married, she had insomnia.

Her 'upsets', the word she used for scenes, were challenging, but they put an end to Eliot's numbness. The crises of his wife's instability together with his own huge leap in the dark — expatriation at any cost — threw him into the kind of action that could animate his poetry.

Vivienne gave back to him pure, distilled, the vision in
'Prufrock's Pervigilium' that the world was falling apart. Where
Emily Hale, or his fantasy of her, had countered the potential disin-
tegration, Vivienne confirmed such fear in the destructive context
of a country at war. Both came to see the war as horribly futile,
along with the pacifist Bertrand Russell, who meant to help Eliot
establish himself in England. Two weeks into the Eliots' marriage,
Russell visited the couple who were staying for the time being with
Vivienne's parents in a Hampstead house with lots of decorative
china and brass. Vivienne told Russell that she had married Eliot to
stimulate him and had found that she could not. Since her husband
was present, reclining listlessly across the table, it was a measure of
Vivienne's disappointment that she spoke so openly. Her need for
reassurance was not lost on Russell, who began to fix his lascivious
eye on this unhappy bride.

Vivienne's impulse to make sexual failure entirely her husband's
fault was cruel: to shame him to a near stranger who was his prime
English connection. She was certainly a disappointed bride, but she
was also simplifying an unfathomable situation at Eliot's expense. It
was only years later that he could bring himself to tell his brother
that Vivienne had treated him as a 'clodhopper'. Some power game
was in play: Vivienne, it seems, competing with Eliot for Russell's
regard, and Eliot, unable to read the signals between his bride and
Russell, humiliated by her disparagement. To defend himself would
have been uncivil to his wife.

It's common to pity this marriage. Yet the couple's letters to others
during their early years contradict this truism if their joined forces
are recognised as theatre. Two days after Vivienne's disclosure to
Russell, Eliot offered a different scenario to Boston's eminent art
collector Isabella Gardner, saying that she would know his marriage was not rash. He trusted this art connoisseur to condone the
all-out ambition that could not be revealed to family because it
was too keen for ordinary people. Unlike commonplace minds, she

could discern what it took to pursue works of art. What Vivienne and Eliot undertook together was more a poetry union than an ordinary marriage; it's something we can't quite label, and was to prove extraordinarily fertile for a long time.

Eliot wrote to his father that Vivienne had been willing to sacrifice herself by marrying a man without money. 'She has everything to give that I want, and she gives it.' He had to drive home that during their first month together he had found her to be 'the one person for me'.

Vivienne too found reason to be pleased. She was proud to be 'the poet's bride' in an announcement by Wyndham Lewis in the July issue of *Blast*. A month later she crows with triumph and teasing self-confidence in her letter to Eliot's defeated rival, Scofield Thayer.

When Eliot came to know his wife's people, he found them 'distinctly outsiders socially'. Since the Eliot family was grander than her own, Vivienne assumed they were well placed to support the new couple. She staked a claim to straitened circumstances owing to the war. Their properties were said to be a liability rather than an asset. Nothing was said about Mr Haigh-Wood's lucrative sideline in illustrations for greeting cards. Eliot's letters to his family convey his sense of sole responsibility for supporting what was now revealed to be a semi-invalid wife. There appears no suggestion that Vivienne was prepared to use her annual income for medical and other expenses. At no point, neither now nor in the future, would she take in the fact that her husband's family did not fit the cliché of rich Americans.

Eliot found a post as a schoolmaster in High Wycombe, a town west of London. The salary was only £120 a year. School would not start until September, so what were Eliot and his wife to live on in the meantime? There was nothing for it but to beg help at home: 'What I want is MONEY!$!£!!' he told Conrad Aiken.

In the wake of the torpedoed liner *Lusitania*, Eliot embarked on a perilous wartime crossing from Liverpool to see his family. On

24 July he sailed on the *St Louis* (a neutral American ship), arriving in New York on 1 August.

His parents were summering as usual at Eastern Point on Cape Ann. His father reminded Tom of the affectionate and dutiful son he had always been. His mother pointed out the low status of a schoolmaster. She foresaw her son as a Pegasus in harness and it disturbed her further that he should continue to take it for granted that whatever he needed must come his way. They were not in the least impressed by his backing from Bertrand Russell and a long screed from Ezra Pound attempting to cheer them with his own transatlantic success.

The family would have relayed the latest achievements of his Boston cousins, Fred, Martha and Abby Eliot. The contrast could not have been starker between their promise and the son of Henry Ware Eliot Sr, who appeared to have messed up his life. After graduating summa cum laude from Harvard, Fred had followed their distinguished grandfather into Harvard Divinity School. In 1915 he was ordained as a Unitarian minister in the First Parish in Cambridge and his path would lead to becoming the foremost Unitarian in America. Martha, meanwhile, was at Johns Hopkins University, which welcomed women into the medical profession (unlike Harvard at that time). Impelled by the many child deaths in the Eliot family, she would set up 'Well Baby' clinics in poor, immigrant, black and rural areas. She was determined to wipe out rickets. The dauntless May character in Martha May Eliot would lead to reform in children's health, eventually through the United Nations as a founder of UNICEF. Her younger sister Abby, a recent graduate of Radcliffe College, was undertaking social work, preparatory to her own pioneering career as founder of free nursery education for the children of working parents who could not otherwise afford it.

A chastened Tom Eliot was persuaded of the need to complete his education and use it to become self-supporting. Professor Ralph Barton Perry, chair of philosophy at Harvard, advised him that it could be difficult to write his dissertation while teaching. So Eliot gave the headmaster notice, aware he was letting the school down.

No sooner did Vivienne hear of a plan to keep her husband in America than alarms about illness tugged him back. His first thought was to accede to Vivienne, and then, when she was better, return to the US to carry out his undertaking. But once she had him in England, Vivienne convinced him to stay. He now had to apologise to his father for his 'blunder'. All the same, he was forced to hold out his hat. It was not a matter of needing help, he said: 'It's a matter of living at all.'

This was not the only issue in play at this fraught time. Vivienne was a creature of contradictions, with quick-change moods as one scene in her repertoire replaced another. Her performances had an extravagance beyond the polite comedies of manners that Emily and Eleanor had played in the Cambridge Dramatic Club. While her husband had been away, Vivienne had sent Thayer (now back home on Martha's Vineyard) a provocative letter, taking the role of a satisfied bride brimming with awakened sensuality, reclining on black silk sheets.

Thayer confessed to Eliot he was 'nettled'.

Eliot's reply was cold. 'You had never given me the impression that your interest in the lady was exclusive – or indeed in the slightest degree a pursuit: and as you did not give her this impression, I presumed that I had wounded your vanity rather than thwarted your passion.'

For a time, Vivienne had held the attention of two uneasy Americans dancing about her. Englishmen took a cooler view: Bertrand Russell, and later Aldous Huxley and Anthony Powell, classed her as vulgar. There was pity for Eliot's mistake. All the same, these high-flyers were charmed, as Eliot was, by Vivienne's darting, forthright views.

Russell reported on the appeal of Vivienne to his former mistress, Lady Ottoline Morrell, aged forty-three, an uninhibited grandee, half-sister of the Duke of Portland. He observed that Vivienne had '*no* physical passion' and actually found maleness 'disgusting'.

Vivienne's scenes with Thayer and Russell appear unfeeling for her husband while he was putting himself through an ordeal for her sake. But it's futile to take sides. Long before Eliot put together *The Waste Land*, Vivienne was a prime player, a 'Lady of Situations' or a doomed Duchess of Malfi or a would-be Cleopatra who will find herself up against a closed-off Hamlet haunted by the past. Each took the lead in a different drama.

Could the invalid be one of the roles in Vivienne's repertoire? Eliot's brother Henry thought so: a demand for attention 'well buttered with sympathy'. Eliot's experience is well known and supported by all who knew the couple at the time: how his wife's deteriorating condition obliged him to reset the course of his life. That position leaves out the question of his own conduct. Privately, he came to agree with his wife that he did harm, adding to her ills.

He later told Emily Hale, 'I did try, again and again, to love as I had promised; but failed utterly; and no one could thrive on what I had left to give.'

Vivienne played up to men who did like her, Thayer and Russell, to boost her fragile self-confidence. What's extraordinary in all this is that nothing could shake her commitment to Eliot's poetry. This vital element in their union was genuine and lasting.

On Eliot's return to England, the pair had a reunion in cheap lodgings at Eastbourne from 4 to 16 September. Russell called it a 'pseudo-honeymoon', with Vivienne swinging from her August high to a low exacerbated by menstrual tension. Vivienne was embarrassed by a bloodstained sheet and took it home to wash. Eliot spent a night in a deck chair on the beach.

He retrieved the job as a schoolmaster in High Wycombe. On weekdays he lodged there and joined Vivienne in London at the weekend. Russell had offered them the use of his flat at Russell Chambers on Bury Place in Bloomsbury. Vivienne was in clover. The alternative of joining her husband did not occur to her. As a lecturer in mathematics and philosophy, Russell lived at Trinity College, Cambridge, but was often in London. It was a questionable situation, with Russell and Vivienne alone in the flat. There was a gentlemanly exchange, with Russell asking Eliot's permission to be in his own home, and Eliot polite in return, He offers civil thanks to this usurper in his marriage.

It's the familiar situation of the American as an innocent abroad falling victim to the corrupt Old World (a variation on Eliot's encounter with the ascetic predator in Paris). Russell told himself and others that his intentions towards Vivienne Eliot were kindly. In November, he said to Lady Ottoline Morrell that he loved Eliot 'as if he were my son' and Lady Ottoline warned Russell not to meddle, both for the Eliots' sake and for his own protection.

Russell did not agree. It pleased him to play the role of benefactor. He was indeed generous in giving the Eliots debentures in an engineering firm, worth £3,000, since, as a pacifist, Russell could not in good conscience profit from a company making munitions. He also paid for Vivienne to take ballet lessons. In return, she typed up Russell's anti-war writing.

There were two bedrooms in the Bury Place flat. The one occupied by Vivienne was behind the kitchen, a former pantry. The single bed was too small for two people, and when Eliot was there he slept in the hall. This arrangement continued until early December, when the Eliots took a flat in St John's Wood for three months.

At this stage Eliot was not thinking of Emily Hale – not yet. At first he exulted in having found the 'force' to change his life. He stood ready to embrace the prospects that would open to him both in the way of writing the kind of Modernist poetry that Pound was calling for, and to take on paid reviews for leading philosophical journals.

Looking back at the start of a new year, on 10 January 1916, he told Aiken that Cambridge (Massachusetts) had been 'a dull nightmare' in contrast to his present 'wonderful life'. He said, 'I have *lived* through material for a score of long poems, in the last six months.'

Sure enough, material that would enter *The Waste Land* was the fruit of a second belated honeymoon that month. This time the venue was Torquay. Russell orchestrated this, taking Vivienne down to Devon for the first few days and paying for rooms at the Torbay Hotel looking out to sea. While Eliot remained in London he commended Russell for 'managing' Vivienne more skilfully than he.

To be giving Vivienne this seaside holiday was, Eliot told him, the 'last straw (so to speak) of generosity'.

Help is how it appeared to this young husband, baffled by his bride. Russell commended Eliot in turn for being 'devoted' to Vivienne, and so he was. But whatever Russell had anticipated, he found himself with an invalid. After five days, once Eliot took over from Russell, things fell apart, with Vivienne on the verge of suicide.

The scene in Torquay in January 1916 was the loveless friction of a couple cooped up together, followed by a taxi ride in the hope of diverting an ill Vivienne one wretched Saturday afternoon.

'My nerves are bad tonight. Yes, bad. Stay with me. / Speak to me. Why do you never speak? Speak.'

So a wife starts the famous non-exchange in *The Waste Land*. A silent husband thinks of an urban alley where 'dead men lost their bones'. She then asks if he's 'alive, or not', and what they will do tomorrow. 'What shall we ever do?' The answer is to follow deadening routine and, to fill the time, 'a closed car at four'.

Pound thought this too photographic, while Vivienne — as co-creator of the scene and whose performance will resonate for ever — would applaud in pencilled capitals climbing sideways up the typescript: 'WONDERFUL, wonderful & wonderful. Yes.'

How rapidly Vivienne and her poet-husband plunge together into the world of *The Waste Land* before it existed on the page. How quickly their non-union created an alternative to a lone allegorical journey beyond the world in 'So through the evening', an earlier fragment of *The Waste Land* manuscript, going back to the first half of 1914. This discarded but all-important source for the climactic part V of the poem Eliot had conceived on his own. Vivienne then provided a foil for the lone journey: a man and a woman stuck together.

As the waste of their day-to-day lives rolled out, Vivienne was driven to humiliate her husband in the manner he feared most: to strip him of cover, or at least threaten to do so. The harm on his part was his unreachable detachment. Missing on both sides was kindness: a wife understanding her husband's unease with intimacy; a husband understanding a wife's need for love.

Russell found, he said, that the Eliots' troubles were what they clung to. It's a skewed and self-serving opinion from a philanderer. Yet there's a grain of truth to it: the pair held together with the rare purpose of living a poem yet in the making.

This bond is more like twinning than marriage. He was the foreigner, she the Englishwoman; they were alien to each other, and yet poetically they were kin. Vivienne was the face of what Eliot felt inside the armour of his politeness. Her free-spoken voice released the poet in him. Vivienne took it on herself to stand up for him to his family and to speak in no uncertain terms.

'Tom knows perfectly well that I share his feeling over the poetry — in fact, of the two of us perhaps I worry most — and rather more often get despondent. I look upon Tom's poetry as real genius — I *do* think he is made to be a great writer — a poet.'

In this way Vivienne saved Eliot, and it was exactly what she set out to do. 'I provide the motive power,' she informed Eliot's brother. 'I *do* shove.' This was no ordinary marriage; it was a rare conjunction, bound up with Eliot's gift.

In March 1916 the Eliots took a high-up flat, number 18, in the newly built five-storey Crawford Mansions on the corner of Crawford Street and Homer Row in Paddington. Vivienne had orange wallpaper for the dining room (a fad for this colour came from the blazing sets for the Ballets Russes), and this room did triple duty as her husband's study and dressing room. Another must-have were black and white stripes for the hall. From the start of 1916 Eliot became 'the American master' at Highgate School, still at a low salary, £160 per annum, and after hours he tried to earn more by reviewing and also by offering evening classes for working people in Yorkshire and Southall.

Vivienne's own gift for writing is abundantly evident in letters to her in-laws in St Louis. They begin with expressions of family warmth and lively domestic detail. But it's plain why the Eliots took against her, for all her many efforts to win their liking: her letters end with nudges for money. In October 1916 the Eliots should know her doctor's opinion that her migraines happen because she's 'starved!' Yes, 'starvation', she repeats, excited by this diagnosis and the poverty-stricken image it begets. The doctor has told her 'not to economise', and they have only £22 in the bank to last until Christmas.

Henry Ware Eliot Sr was already paying the rent. He did this for years, month in, month out. Come 1917 his son, having given up his schoolmaster job without securing something else, asked his father to supply the whole of the next year's rent in advance. Henry Ware Eliot Jr sent gifts of money ranging from $5 to $50. Once, he cabled £20. To have cabled, at an extra cost, he must have thought his brother in dire straits.

Vivienne wrote back, 'I have reason to thank you, for Tom says I am to get my winter clothes out of it.' It's not convincing when she explains the urgency to Henry: she's down to her 'last rag'.

In March 1917 Eliot started as a bank clerk on a salary of £2 10 shillings a week. Vivienne let it be known that, with food prices rising during the war, they would be 'practically starvating' if she did not lock food away from their servant.

Henry Jr was a good man, highly intelligent and bookish, who put up with a rather lonely life in Chicago, earning his keep in an advertising firm. Vivienne sent the same kind of endearing, needy letters to him too. Of all the family, Henry was the one to take most strongly against her, though he continued to be loyal to his brother and anxious for his welfare.

But Vivienne did not act alone. The couple's letters show collusion in money pleas. Vivienne made it clear to Henry that it was a joint solution to Eliot's needs to invite him to join them in London. Her argument went like this: Henry was unsuccessful in America (he could hardly do worse, she tells him), so he might as well take over his brother's reviewing, leaving him free to get going with poems.

A tougher demand came from Eliot, this time in Vivienne's interest: if she were widowed, would Henry undertake to support her?

'<u>Will you do that?</u>' his brother pressed him. 'I depend <u>especially</u> on you.'

The directness is formidable. Vivienne's future security obliterates any consideration that Henry, then thirty-six, might yet marry.

Vivienne wanted her mother-in-law to know that her son's health was at risk, that he was 'always tormented' by extra work, and how 'difficult and harassing' it was 'to procure proper nourishment on the money which Tom is earning'.

The usual approach to this marriage is to list Vivienne's many and varied ills and to conclude, as Eliot's family did, that her demands blocked his freedom to write. An alternative approach has been to take Vivienne's side against Eliot. But Vivienne's many surviving letters, as well as Eliot's comments to intimates, open up a different sense of what mattered to them. This pairing can't fit any familiar model and must be seen on its own terms as a catalyst for a new phase of poetry. From the start Eliot was aware that a failure to compose new poems would disappoint his wife even more than himself. Vivienne, he told his brother, was 'so exceedingly anxious that I should equal ['Prufrock'] and would be bitterly disappointed' if he did not. A month later Vivienne makes her own statement to Henry, 'It is a *constant* canker with me that [poetry] is at a standstill . . . He feels *dried up* – not a bit as if he could write poetry even if he had the leisure and circumstances.' She was more than committed; Vivienne's shove was a force for his poetic future.

Her unafraid voice, emotions at the ready, fed the urban despair Eliot pursued and developed in sharp-edged quatrains over the next few years. Vivienne shared, endorsed and perhaps prompted extreme feelings of what Eliot called 'hatred of life'. The poems set up arbitrary and often routine targets: a Russian ballerina whose bust offers 'pneumatic bliss'; the church lost in a 'miasmal mist'; Jews as vermin undermining society. Prejudice, blatant, shameless, recast in catchy phrases, is designed to infiltrate the minds of read-ers. Hatred comes cased in hilarity like the Bolo targets. Eliot had a justification for his brother, who didn't like these poems: Vivienne, he said, saw, as he did – her endorsement mattered – that his two Sweeney poems were the most 'serious' and 'mature' things he'd ever done. Eliot claimed that hatred of life amounted to a kind of vision, like a biblical warning of a Gomorrah doomed for corrup-tion and licentiousness.

'Sweeney Erect' is set in a brothel. In violent Bolo mode, the lout Sweeney waves a razor at a faceless creature 'slitted below'. The prostitute's fear brings on an epileptic attack, more shaming than sex. 'Sweeney Among the Nightingales' (a code word for prostitutes) is about a plot to kill a man. Here, a Jewish woman, 'Rachel née Rabinowitz', with 'murderous paws', appears to be complicit. The smear of Rachel as murderess is unconvincing, as is the poem's arbi-trary positioning of her as a lowlife comedown from Clytemnestra, who murdered her husband Agamemnon. In Eliot's hands the strict form of the quatrain, with its pat rhymes, is like a straitjacket con-trolling an excess of horror.

Their letters to others prove how indispensable Vivienne was. This was not merely a matter of advice, practical support or being a passive muse. The tie was active. In December 1918, Vivienne spoke of a shared state of mind. She appears to reflect on Eliot's unsuccessful efforts over the previous summer to enter the final stage of the war as an American non-combatant, yet this was the time when quatrains were emerging.* At the same time, too, he was soaking up macabre revenge plays in preparation for evening classes on Jacobean tragedy. He could feel revolted by life to the point of madness, he told Emily Hale years later, in the summer of 1932. Summer 1918 was one such time.

'We were off our heads all the summer,' Vivienne said. 'We'. Not 'I' or 'he'.

Virgil leading Dante through the *Inferno* offers the vigilance of reason. Vivienne dispensed with reason, and her freedom from inhibition stimulated the vehemence of Eliot's flair for the sordid (for him, a counterpoise to beauty). What Vivienne uniquely offered was a daring to match his own, a secret sharer of what was extreme in his aversions. Only, with Vivienne confrontation was naked.

Her virulence consorts oddly with her pretty looks and a tiny body wasted by diets her doctors devised for assorted ailments. Toothache was one of her ills and her in-laws were invited to inspect her drawing of a sizable abscess exposed by an extracted tooth. There's a kind of relish in exhibiting this, forcing the fastidious Eliots to look at the pus.

The marriage was, 'in some respects, the most awful nightmare of anxiety that the mind of man could conceive,' Eliot told his brother, 'but at least it is not dull'. There were 'compensations'.

It took a year for Eliot to find himself still in love with Emily Hale. On 5 September 1916, he asks after her in a letter to Eleanor: 'Tell me how Emily is.' She was staying with her aunt and uncle when the Rev Perkins was called to a Unitarian parish in Seattle. There's a photograph of Emily seated quietly with a book open on the table in a creeper-covered summerhouse. As always, she's associated with gardens. Seattle, on the northwest coast, has a rainy climate like that of England, and Emily's aunt began to cultivate English flowers

---

* 'Whispers of Immortality', 'Mr. Eliot's Sunday Morning Service' and 'Sweeney Among the Nightingales'.

and learn about English gardens. Emily shared in this pursuit and accompanied Mrs Perkins when she lectured on gardens and their design. All the while, Emily remained single, lonely out West. Lonely too when she returned to Boston. The door that had shut between her and Eliot seemed closed for good.

'For a year I was merely dazed and numbed,' he confided to her later. He did not know 'what was the matter; then, quite suddenly, I awoke. Well, I did not know how much, if any, harm I had done to you; but I could know quite well, the harm I had done which was under my eyes; and I came to see that this at all events I must expiate with the rest of my life.'

It did occur to Eliot to end his marriage, he told Emily in August 1931, almost a year after they reunited, but he had been deterred by a practical consideration: if he left his wife, his father would have to fund two homes rather than one, and he could not bring himself to press his father for more.

In order to endure the situation, Eliot curled up like a creature whose name, Possum, he adopted. It's a joke that isn't only a joke. The possum plays dead in the face of threat. This form of withdrawal from their union affected Vivienne. Outwardly a semblance of marriage went on but in the interstices was psychic matter so disturbing that Eliot turns to Poe for an equivalent.

In a set of quatrains under the title 'Elegy', part of *The Waste Land* manuscript, he calls up a bride 'as in a tale by Poe' – like Poe's 'Ligeia', which tells of a man mourning the loss of his 'ethereal' soulmate. His grief is obsessive to the point of 'incipient madness'. He remarries but remains wedded to his beloved's memory, while his new bride, taken into a 'ghastly' bridal chamber, dreads the 'fierce moodiness' of her bridegroom's temper. He 'loathed her with a hatred belonging more to demon than to man'. During the second month of their marriage she falls into a mysterious illness, beset (unknowingly) by the ghost of her predecessor. Unloved and increasingly emaciated, she exists on the edge of mortality but instead of dying, her damaged being grows in excitability and fear. Her chronic illnesses defy the understanding of doctors. She appears dead and shrouded to her bridegroom, with an urge to be rid of her, yet as he gazes, she is taken over by the return of his loved one – an outcome he appears to have willed. Of course the wildness of fantasy does not equate with action but 'Ligeia' lays out a suggestive link between two women with no inkling of each other: Emily as number one and Vivienne as undesired replacement.

As a boy in St Louis, Eliot had read all the way through Poe: a collected edition in his dentist's waiting room. Eliot's essay 'The Three Voices of Poetry' speaks of what he calls the 'first voice' emerging from some dark psychic material, too dark for the specificity of language, which the poet conveys indirectly, as Eliot does through his Poe bride. If we are to reach Vivienne and the effect on her of the death-in-life of her marriage, then 'Elegy' offers a macabre sighting of a relationship no one can fully know. Eliot's mother came to the conclusion that he was afraid of Vivienne; blown up as horror in 'Elegy', a husband fears to look upon the features of 'the injured bride'. Eliot would later acknowledge to Emily that to marry without love had been a greater 'sin' than to marry with 'low' passion.

In 'Elegy' guilt is a prompt to move on to an alternative action: solitary, enclosed, introspective. A future religious scene competes with the gothic drama of the doomed bride. She's displaced from the husband's attention by the fire narrative of the final stanza:

> *God in a rolling ball of fire*
> *Pursues by day my errant feet.*
> *His flames of anger and desire*
> *Pursue me with consuming heat.*

A like turn to faith appears in two discarded lines from a draft of another quatrain poem, 'Whispers of Immortality': 'And when the Female Soul departs / The Sons of Men turn up their eyes.'

The turning point for the Eliot marriage was an emotional withdrawal in favour of Emily. To Eliot it meant loyalty to his first love, but his repeated action in detaching himself from Emily and then from his wife, shows the priority for him was solitude, for want of a better word: a need to divest himself of claims. His rationale for his actions (Vivienne's demands and moods) should not obscure his emerging pattern of behaviour with women, stranger than it appears, that will declare itself more clearly in the course of time. Curiously, it's forecast in the dismissal of 'La Figlia', imagined before any relationship with a woman takes place. With Emily he evaded the question of marriage. With his wife, he sustains a formal commitment but evades the intimacy marriage requires. There is an invisible divide, now and then removed to engage and draw on Vivienne's stimulus, her almost uncanny resemblance to his imaginative venture.

During the month of June 1918 the Eliots occupied a house Vivienne had rented (aided by Russell) on West Street in Marlow, on the Thames. Roses abounded in the back garden where Eliot sat working all day. He was in his element, writing with brilliant originality, as he explored his temperamental affinities with his forebears, Puritan diehards in seventeenth-century New England, in an essay on 'The Hawthorne Aspect' of Henry James. Praising Hawthorne's insights into 'the deeper psychology', he shows how Hawthorne detects a mind-set in Puritan ancestors, which bore on Eliot himself. This peculiar mentality shapes the lives of rare and tormented men who cannot but recognise their superiority: Ethan Brand, Young Goodman Brown, a minister who covers his face with a black veil and another minister, Dimmesdale, concealing his guilt in *The Scarlet Letter*. These men are exceptionally intelligent, introspective and severely moral as diagnosticians of sin, primarily their own.

So it is that when we try to fathom Eliot's capacity for life-long expiation in the way he planned to continue with his wife, Hawthorne can tell us where he came from, in his kinship with men who held themselves apart, alone in the solitude of their hearts.

5

UNDER ENGLISH EYES

To be a newcomer in England was 'a great strain', Eliot admitted to his brother after five years. 'Society is in a way much *harder, not* gentler. People are more aware of you, more critical, and they have no pity for one's mistakes,' he explained. 'They are always intriguing and caballing; one must be very alert. They are sensitive, and easily become enemies.'

He depended on Vivienne to assist him in English ways, and they were at one in the effort to establish his public voice, but he had much to contend with. His Modernist poetry had to assert itself against resistance from the old guard, led by Edmund Gosse and the once-influential J. C. Squire (a long-time editor of the popular *Mercury*). They disliked his disdain for popular taste, his obscure allusions and irreverence.

Traditional gentlemen with old-boy influence were still in place (and for decades yet to come) in the Senior Common Room of All Souls College, Oxford, when they refused, as late as 1926, to admit Eliot as a Fellow. The vote, fourteen yeas and thirty-five nays, went heavily against him. Even the Fellows of his own college, Merton, were slow to notice him.

*

In the early months of 1916 Eliot had been recognisably American to the schoolboys (including John Betjeman) whom he taught in Highgate; by the autumn of that year he had stripped all residue of his American accent. The workers who attended his evening class in Yorkshire reported no sign of it. Only to members of his family, mainly his brother, did Eliot speak now and then as an expatriate, complaining that in England he felt on 'dress parade'.

To Charles William Eliot, ex-President of Harvard, who (on behalf of the family) urged him to return, Eliot promised his writings would be true to the finest temper of old New England.

The blunt retort was: you might as well come home.

But the poet did mean to distil the introspective moral and spiritual character of his native tradition. Eliot positioned himself as James's heir: in living abroad, in writing for the English and Europe, as well as for Americans, James had propagated an American turn of mind in his novels *The American*, *The Europeans*, *Daisy Miller* and *The Sense of the Past*.

Eliot acknowledged the advantages of being, like James, 'everywhere a foreigner'. Coming from a large country 'which no one wants to visit', he felt his kinship with the subtleties of international encounter. Following the death of James, Eliot set out to perpetuate habits of observation close to his own. James 'preyed upon living beings', who became 'the victims of a merciless clairvoyance'. The aim was to detect the 'curious precipitates and explosive gases which are suddenly formed by the contact of mind with mind'. This applies to the poetry that came from his contact with Vivienne as well as his affinity for the moral refinement of old New England.

There the best writers were thought to be the 'best people' and Eliot himself sees 'a halo of dignity' around an elect few in the purlieus of Boston, Concord, Salem and Cambridge: Emerson, Hawthorne, Thoreau, Margaret Fuller (author of *Women in the Nineteenth Century*), the historians Bancroft and Motley, the poet James Russell Lowell, and his own relation, Charles Eliot Norton. Eliot, of course, by virtue of his birth, took it for granted that he was one of the 'best people', as was Emily Hale. (It is impossible to overstate Hale's and Eliot's commitment to the subtler shades of morality. Their letters would sift these almost as though they were characters in a James novel.)

So while Eliot played up to English derision, wit and repartee, he remained privately what he always was; his rectitude, his stiffness and sense of propriety at odds with the licence of his English milieu. Marriage to an Englishwoman was the first step in his adaptation and Vivienne the first of four Englishwomen, all keen readers, who made him welcome. Even as he moved, stage by stage, into his position as English insider and planned to change his nationality from American to British, he became ever more the quintessential Bostonian at a distance from Boston.

His wife's affair with Bertrand Russell was not for a long while apparent to Eliot. From mid-1915 to mid-1917 it may not have gone much beyond flirtation, but in the autumn of 1917, Vivienne told a friend that 'Bertie' wanted to share a country cottage. She predicted: 'That will probably mean being out of the frying pan but *in* the fire!' They slept together on 17 October, while staying at an old place in a forest of pines tucked away in the Surrey hills, six miles from the nearest railway station and four miles from the nearest village. It could be reached only by a cart track, 'a sort of fairy tale farm' to Vivienne.

Five days later, Vivienne nudged her mother-in-law to fund a permanent country cottage. She makes her case at length, solely on grounds of health, in the must-have voice by now familiar to the Eliot family. Tom's mother should know that her son looks white and thin from his struggle to support them and it would ease him if his wife were less constantly ill. Over the last four months she has spent eight weeks away in the country, and has not felt so well since she married. Of course they have to keep on their flat in London, so that Tom can work. A servant there sees to his needs.

This initiative awakened suspicion. Why was Vivienne staying away so much? As always, Eliot stood by his wife, but his letters towards the end of 1917 sound dejected and homesick. Even if he did not know the facts as yet, his family's suspicion did reach him. By the beginning of the following year Russell had a reconciliation with another lover and his affair with Vivienne – limited by her admission to Lady Ottoline Morrell that she was not keen on sex – faded to an end. It was a blow to Eliot to discover that his mentor had betrayed his trust.

'Bertie, because I had admired him so much, is one of my lost illusions,' he later told Lady Ottoline. 'He has done Evil . . .'

The disillusion was so great that it led him to find respite during lunch hours in City churches. By 1919 he was attending mass at St Magnus the Martyr, the high Anglo-Catholic church near his work at Lloyds Bank on Lombard Street. The contemplation of its 'Inexplicable splendour of Ionian white and gold' is one of the non-wasteland moments that break up the urban despair of *The Waste Land*.

In his benevolent aspect, Bertrand Russell had provided an initial entrée to the English intelligentsia when he took the Eliots to Garsington Manor near Oxford. There Lady Ottoline Morrell held court, hosting the most advanced English writers and artists of the day, including members of the Bloomsbury set. A discerning reader, she had taken to Eliot's poetry.

Eliot already had enthusiastic support from Ezra Pound, bent on promoting a Modernist movement led by Americans, chiefly themselves, and Irishmen, Yeats and Joyce, the up-to-date Men of 1914, as they called themselves. Maintaining his character as an American individualist, Pound thought England retrogressive and chose not to adapt. His outsider circle and the insider Garsington court did not mix, apart from the pre-eminent Yeats, who held his own in both worlds.

When Eliot first came to Garsington in April 1916, Lady Ottoline was disappointed by him. Inhibited, reserved, slow of speech in a monotone unlike the switches of tone and pitch swooping gracefully about him, Eliot's sobriety did not entertain, and his hostess even tried French in the hope of rousing him. No luck. She dubbed him 'the undertaker'.

Bejewelled and theatrically costumed, she received her talented guests, amongst them D. H. Lawrence, Katherine Mansfield, Siegfried Sassoon, Lytton Strachey and a recent Oxford graduate, Aldous Huxley, as well as a protegée from Belgium, Maria Nys, who married Huxley.

Lady Ottoline proved a sympathetic friend to Vivienne, who had qualities in common: both women were stylish, charming, cultured and fearlessly flamboyant. She could see that Eliot was unfitted to cope with his wife's 'upsets' and became a confidante to both.

Soon after his initial visit to Garsington, Eliot had encountered another discerning Englishwoman and literary hostess who also took to his poetry. Mary Hutchinson first spotted Eliot sitting alone on a sea wall at Bosham on an inland estuary of Chichester harbour. The Eliots were summering there. Mary's country home, Eleanor House, was near by on the open sea and sands, close to West Wittering.

Not at once but from 1917 on, Mary issued invitations that took the Eliots into another circle. They met the aristocratic Sitwells (the eccentric poet Edith and her two brothers) and the Bloomsbury artists Roger Fry and Duncan Grant.

Mary Hutchinson was not made in the fragile style of Vivienne; her face with its lowering, thick-lipped mouth was sensuously poised above her elegant couture clothes. Matisse drew her in a few curved lines (she had a liaison with his son-in-law, Georges Duthuit); Cecil Beaton photographed her; and Vanessa Bell painted a nude of Mary for her bedhead at River House, her London home in Hammersmith, where a woman offers her pink rondures to the gaze of two swollen crimson poppies.

Born in India, the daughter of a colonial administrator, Mary, along with her brother Jim, was brought up by her grandparents in

The young Eliots lodged at Bosham, near Chichester, in summer 1916.

Florence. After her grandparents died, Mary was sent to boarding school in England and then married a prominent barrister, St John (Jack) Hutchinson.

When the Eliots crossed her path, she was twenty-eight with two small children and linked to the Bloomsbury Group through her cousin, Lytton Strachey, and her lover, Clive Bell, the art historian married to Vanessa Bell and brother-in-law to Virginia Woolf. Mary's open affair with Bell started in 1914 and lasted twelve years. She also had affairs with Vita Sackville-West and with Aldous Huxley, which turned into a *ménage à trois* with his wife. She was actually more taken with Maria. Given Eliot's aversion to sexual licence, his warmth for Mary may seem surprising. But Mary, like Vivienne and Lady Ottoline, was a reader.

She had a sophisticated taste but what drew Eliot more was her 'sensitive' rather than learned readings. He told her how opposed he was to 'a mass of chaotic erudition' (even though this is what his allusive poetry appeared to demand).

'Some people really read too much to be cultivated,' he said. He thought it blocked readers from sensing the personal element well beneath the surface of what he wrote. Mary read his major poems 'Gerontion' and *The Waste Land* on completion.

She rather fancied Eliot and seems to have been open with Vivienne, who waved off her husband as 'impossible at present – very American and obstinate!' In October 1919 she excused Mary from attending his lecture on 'Modern Tendencies in Literature' to the Arts League of Service, saying he was not Fun and not a Flirt and told Mary that from now on she would leave him to handle the perils of Englishness.

Conceivably, for Eliot, the balm of Mary's insight brought him into a measure of tolerance for sexual irregularities, a complaisance he would not otherwise entertain. There were unusually flirtatious sallies, first in May 1919 when he accepted a weekend invitation, saying, 'So you see I can be seduced', and again in June when he went north to lecture in Yorkshire, agreeing to tell her about his 'provincial *amours*' on his return. Non-existent though these were, he signals affection for Mary by entering into her style of banter.

When Eliot later recounted this to Emily Hale, he elaborated on his success in eluding an affair without ill feeling.

He explained himself to Mary Hutchinson as 'a simple natural innocent'. It's the knowing, teasing statement of a newcomer to a cavorting society who has stumbled into a situation almost too dense for his understanding. Eating of the Tree of Knowledge, he was bound to meet a snake (Bertrand Russell, dangling offers from his bough in Bury Place), and such an innocent was bound too to come upon a European woman who could introduce him to a sexual freedom beyond his horizon. James's New Englander in *The Ambassadors*, who encounters the charming but disconcertingly unchaste Mme de Vionnet, finds a way to live all he can in his expanding consciousness without compromising himself morally. It was a telling compliment when Eliot asked Mary to read *The Ambassadors*.

Another compliment was to draw up for Mary alone a list of what mattered to him. This list included Tudor plays, Flaubert (a favourite with Mary), Russian novels and the Russian ballet, a model for devising verse that could communicate immediately with a popular audience, even people with no prior experience of the art. He had feared and distrusted society women, but learnt from Lady Ottoline and Mary Hutchinson that such women could be perceptive readers as well as the kindest of friends.

By the autumn of 1917 Eliot was working for *The Egoist*. It was a monthly successor to *The New Free Woman*, and Pound had leant on Miss Harriet Weaver, the magazine's editor and financial backer, to appoint Eliot as assistant editor. He'd also persuaded her to publish Eliot's *Prufrock* collection in October.

Vivienne had given Mary's slight story 'War' to Eliot. Without further ado, he published it in *The Egoist*. He talked up Mary's story as having no precedent, but the war is the old one between the sexes. It's about a potential affair that doesn't happen, a slice of life in which a male candidate for love turns out to be incidental to the intimacy of two women. But is this really all? There could be a homoerotic subtext to this story, delicately balanced on the border of women's friendship and something keener.

Vivienne's closeness to Mary, rather like her closeness to Lucy Thayer, is recorded in her letters and diary. The two friends picnic, boat and swim together at Eleanor House; confide in each other; and joke about husbands as 'dragons' (Vivienne's 'dragon' disapproves of her taking to bed when she has a period, an attempt to wean her off unnecessary invalidism). Vivienne calls Mary 'little cat' and praises her 'delicious sense of humour'.

'When may I come and spend the night?' she asks, 'I embrace you.' And another time, 'I love you much more than ever.' Many years later, she signed a letter to Mary 'Yr. lover'.

Lady Ottoline, also close to Vivienne (and jealous of Mary), remarked in her journal that it was Vivienne who made her understand how some women fall in love with their own sex. Vivienne's uncomplicated, sleeping-over friendship with Lucy Thayer, the 'love' Eliot's lesbian cousin Abigail Eliot felt on meeting her, Vivienne's readiness to take Abigail around London, Abigail's invitations to Vivienne to travel with her, as well as Vivienne's ease with the bisexual Mary, together with Russell's remark to Lady Ottoline that Vivienne disliked maleness, could all add up. Garsington always welcomed guests who tested the boundaries of gender or who were, as in Bloomsbury, actively homoerotic. Lady Ottoline added Vivienne to her list of women she liked best.

Vivienne's outspoken manner caught the post-war mood, as did Lady Ottoline when in 1919 she cut her hair and dyed it a vivid red. Vivienne admired Mary Hutchinson's chic and, not having her friend's wealth, admitted to finding it hard to enter shops displaying post-war couture. On occasion, though, she told Mary, she did spend 'recklessly', fancying that she could recoup funds by 'cinema acting' with no doubt of success. She writes with frank spontaneity, close to the spoken word, and with a playful vigour, even when she talks (as always) of being ill. Here is Vivienne replying to a reproach from Lady Ottoline, on 4 June 1919:

> My dear − ... you ought not to say 'that was a quick change etc affair'. Believe me it wasn't ... I have been ill in a sort of way, and I had to go into a sort of retirement which is so necessary to me at times that I should die without it. It is a seemingly selfish, closed up, affair, but without something like it at frequent intervals I should cease to exist as a person at all. I am perfectly certain that no one has so little resistance to human contacts as I ... Of course I have been thinking of you. That is the worst of it! I had to.
>
> ... Tom's pyjamas are still at Garsington. Do keep them as a hostage! I can wear them when I come.

Eliot's attraction to England had more to do with its past than the present, as he claimed in an aside to another American trying his luck in London: 'there was a civilisation here'. When it came to selecting from the English past, he was drawn most of all to the sixteenth and early seventeenth centuries for the popularity of verse plays. He too meant to find a popular audience. His first taste of this came from his after-work pupils in Ilkley and Southall, who responded eagerly to his lectures on French poetry, Victorian literature and Jacobean drama. Attendance kept up amazingly and reports of his nervous tic of fiddling with his watch chain were friendly. In America he might have been a conservative but in England, at this stage, he leant towards Labour.

He reminded Mary that he was a *'metic'*, a foreigner, observing and wanting 'to understand you'. His eye was on the English, and the English eye increasingly on *him*.

Virginia Woolf was the most distinguished of the four Englishwomen who welcomed the poet. Her chief impetus to meet Eliot, backed by her husband, Leonard Woolf, was a result of the *Egoist* edition of his first volume of poems, *Prufrock and Other Observations*. Mary's lover Clive Bell took a dozen copies to Garsington, and there Katherine Mansfield read 'Prufrock' aloud to enthusiastic applause. Mansfield, an expatriate herself, understood better than most how insecure Eliot felt, with his side glances and painfully slow speech.

When 'Prufrock' came Leonard Woolf's way, the poem struck him as saying something no one had said before, and as a rarity in that not one line fell below 'the heights'.

Leonard and Virginia Woolf had just then bought a small hand press, planning to print books as a hobby. The machine stood on a table and could print only one page at a time, and the first publication of the Hogarth Press was the couple's own *Two Stories* in 1917. They followed this with Katherine Mansfield's *Prelude*, a wonderfully moving frieze of family scenes from her native New Zealand, seen through the emotional intelligence of a child. In September and October 1918, the Woolfs approached 'Mary's friend', Eliot, about publishing one of his poems.

He was invited to dine at their home, Hogarth House in Richmond, on 15 November, and there he read three or four of his caricatures of humankind: possibly 'Sweeney Among the Nightingales', 'The Hippopotamus' and 'Mr Eliot's Sunday Morning Service'. The Woolfs accepted these and a few other poems for a small collection, the third publication of the Hogarth Press (along with Virginia Woolf's new story, *Kew Gardens*). The Woolfs would do the printing themselves and cover the book with one of Roger Fry's marbled papers. To be taken on by Virginia Woolf was a triumph for Eliot, who informed his family of her standing as her father's daughter. Sir Leslie Stephen had been a leading Victorian man of letters and one-time president of the London Library. It meant acceptance by London's literary elite.

At first, Virginia Woolf was as disconcerted as Lady Ottoline by Eliot's speech: slow, with each word allotted a special finish. She couldn't quite make out what he was saying. The problem, perhaps, was his effort to strip every word of its American intonation, but he came across as pedantic — what his prospective publisher called 'intellectual' (not a compliment). Woolf detected intolerance 'beneath the surface'. Then too she was put out by his allegiance to Wyndham Lewis, Joyce and Pound, whose brand of unconventionality was too blasting for Bloomsbury, which cultivated nuance and a light, comic touch. Why is Mr Eliot 'stuck in that mud', Virginia Woolf asked herself, addressing him formally as 'Mr Eliot', calling him 'Eliot' to her friends, not as yet 'Tom'. Meanwhile, she joked about Eliot's over-done Englishness.

Despite acceptance by the Hogarth Press, at the end of 1918 Eliot was weak and depressed after a bout of flu, yet again unconvinced he could fulfil his gift. His recent poems, tight quatrains, were composed under the eye of Pound, who urged sharp-edged conclusiveness, verging on invective. Vivienne too encouraged this cutting vein. It's not that Eliot couldn't hit his targets with lethal words, but rather he was writing somewhat against the grain. He was an explorer, not an expounder. By nature he was hesitant, and his greatest works make a virtue of it.

Eliot's Anglicisation seemed to tighten over his features as an irremovable mask. 'I have acquired the habit of a society so different that it is difficult to find common terms to define the difference,' he informed Professor Woods at Harvard. Conrad Aiken noticed the change in him when he came to England after the war, an impression of his distancing himself. For Eliot wished to belong wholly to his English milieu. Though courtesy obliged him to meet this old friend now and then, in private he shrugged off Aiken as 'stupid'.

The publication of Eliot's *Poems* did not go smoothly. The Woolfs finished printing in March 1919 and Eliot supplied them with a requested list of contacts who might receive copies. Just then, unused as he was to the gossip that circulated in Bloomsbury, he incautiously concurred with Mary Hutchinson's jealous criticism of Virginia Woolf. Clive Bell promptly passed this disagreeable morsel to Woolf herself, who took it in at the very time she had been setting type for Eliot's book. A long silence followed, and Eliot was unnerved to discover that none of his contacts had received copies.

At this point Vivienne stirred paranoia. She suggested to her husband that the Woolfs were taking revenge by dumping his book.

The truth finally came out: whatever they felt about his slight, the Woolfs had merely lost Eliot's list. He supplied another and worked hard to appease Virginia Woolf. Both were invited to a weekend at Garsington, where the guests watched. Eliot went out of his way to praise Virginia Woolf to all her friends and refused a nudge from Jack Hutchinson to malign her. Virginia then invited the Eliots for lunch (together with Bloomsbury insiders Marjorie Strachey, Lytton's vibrant sister, and Walter Lamb), remarking sardonically in her diary that she now sees Eliot as 'a stick since he no longer likes me'. His wife she nailed as a washed-out little woman. Vivienne, intimidated, would never shine in Virginia Woolf's company, as she did with Mary and Lady Ottoline.

Poems appeared on 12 May. There was an adverse review in the *TLS*, while Virginia Woolf's *Kew Gardens*, published the same day, was an unexpected success with orders pouring in, necessitating a second edition of a thousand copies.

There could have been more to this. The Woolfs, who took to 'Prufrock', were not quite so thrilled by meeting Eliot in person. That fact is not in question. But what if Leonard Woolf (whose story 'Three Jews' shows how sensitive he was to Jewishness), was less than pleased with Eliot's portrait of Rachel née Rabinowitz as a low predator with 'murderous paws' in a poem that Eliot regarded as the best and most serious he'd ever done? When asked late in life, Leonard Woolf replied evenly that Eliot would not have regarded himself as particularly antisemitic. But his 1919 letters to the poet are curt. Cold. There was a silent change of plan: the Hogarth Press had initially intended a print run of four hundred. Leonard Woolf, who did the machining, printed only one hundred and ninety copies. In time, all these were sold and, once production costs were deducted, Eliot eventually received £3 and a few pence.

Time passed and Virginia Woolf's regard for Eliot grew. When he came to dine a year later, she marked 'the driving power' in him: 'my word what concentration of the eye when he argues!' She came to find herself akin to Eliot in her reserves and subterfuges. She too was an explorer of the inner life defined by 'moments of being', as climactic as Eliot's 'unattended moments'. Both, as experimental Modernists, abjured the nineteenth-century narrative of getting on from tea to dinner. And both edge towards the unspoken. For all that, they did not discuss work, not the way Virginia Woolf would sift 'our precious art' with Katherine Mansfield.

Where Virginia Woolf was generous — setting type for Eliot's publications, inviting him for tea and weekends — Eliot tended to faint praise of her writing. He conceded that there was 'astonishing beauty' in her language, carefully deployed by 'unremitting toil of arrangement'. Toil is a routine misogynist putdown: women toil in contrast with the spontaneity of true genius. Once, to her satisfaction, he admired an early story, 'String Quartet'; but on another occasion, in September 1920, when Eliot spent a weekend with the

Woolfs at Monk's House in Sussex and she confronted him with not reading her, his answer was evasive: since he hardly ever read fiction apart from detective novels, he claimed, he had read more than she thought.

She noticed that his young hazel eyes seemed to escape from his heavy sculpted face, pale, with no upper lip.

Though Woolf prided herself on not being 'submerged', the waters did rise once or twice when, she said, Eliot 'completely neglected my claims to be a writer'. She thought, 'had I been meek, I suppose I should have gone under'. The after-effect was to find herself halted in composing her novel *Jacob's Room*. His visit had 'cast a shade', left her 'listless'.

Privately, Eliot remarked to Pound that there were 'no women worth printing'.* He meant primarily Katherine Mansfield, a rival expatriate and ahead of him at the Hogarth Press, but he also disparaged Virginia Woolf. This is explicit in a letter to Emily Hale, who read her keenly: 'I do not in my heart admire her work quite as much as I am sure she likes it (naturally) to be admired.' Friendship and Eliot's willingness to accept her hospitality contented Woolf, who over the years took little notice of his self-absorption – a 'scimitar keenness' curving round to himself – and disregard for her work. Except once, in her diary, fancying Vivienne is after her and Ottoline with a knife, imagining them to be Eliot's mistresses, Virginia Woolf pretended to be put out: 'as I never had a favour from that man it's hard to give my life on the pavement'.

She did not allow anger to get the better of her admiration for Eliot's poetry. The more he published, the clearer his distinction appeared: there was 'well-water in him, cold & pure', she observes in her diary. He noticed how it warmed her to discover his family connection with her father's New England friend Charles Eliot Norton. Leslie Stephen had enjoyed his ties with the New England literati

---

* The context is the appearance of TSE's new journal, the *Criterion*. He made the remark on 7 November 1922.

and, when Virginia was born, had asked James Russell Lowell to be
her godfather. In time, Eliot told Emily Hale that he was 'happiest
with the Woolfs', and years later, when he spent his birthday weekend with the Woolfs in Sussex, Virginia remarks in her diary, 'Tom
in some ways – with his sensitive, shrinking, timid but idiosyncratic
nature – is very like myself.'

6

CONFIDING LINES

Penelope Noyes, who had been part of the Cambridge circle, visited England, bringing her photo album. Among her snapshots was a 'rather lovely' one of Emily. She was kneeling with her hand on a dog's head.

Five years after they had parted, Eliot wrote to Emily suddenly. The letter has not survived, but he mentioned it to Eleanor: 'I hope it was a nice letter. I should, I think, like her to know what a keen interest I take in everything that happens to her.'

At twenty-eight, Hale was still single, her mother still in an asylum, and she had taken her ailing father to the warmer South for the sake of his health. He had died two years later, in 1918. It's likely that his income as a clergyman had supported her while he was alive, for it was from this date that she had to earn a living. At Simmons College, a women's college in Boston, she had led a theatre club intermittently since 1916. She now took a post as matron in the dormitory.

It was the start of a way of life, a cloistered existence in colleges where Miss Hale met few men and threw herself into her work. There was no romance, she would later tell a surprised Eliot. Why was she not sought after, given her looks, manners and connections? The fact that she had to earn her living, unlike other women of her class, and then too the blot of mental illness in her mother, could have made men cautious.

Emily found lasting friends at Simmons. One was Louise Andrews Kent, who had studied library science and become a writer in Brookline. Louise Kent remained 'Lulie', while Emily was 'Tubby' – a joke, because Emily was always thin despite the roundness of her smiling-cherub face with softly curved cheeks.

The friends who mattered were all women, some of them students. They all remembered Miss Hale as fun. In their reports she appears a born teacher, asking bracing questions and ready to know the girls' characters and aspirations. And wherever she worked, she put on plays. At Simmons, she worked with Lucia Briggs in the English department to stage Yeats's *Land of Heart's Desire* and a play by Lady Gregory. She hoped that dormitory duties could in time shift towards a more fulfilling position in speech and drama.

In London, Eliot's severance from the past set up a sharper divide between his outer and inner existence. More than ever, he confided to his brother, he felt a stranger, transplanted in an unreal world, separated by a fearful space from all he had known. In 1919 there was a continued inward allegiance to a woman whose memory stirred a disillusioned poet to speak to her. Not intimately in the letter he sent but openly, confessionally, in poems of that year. Here he spoke not to Emily as an actual woman, but more a ghostly presence. 'Our sighs pursue the vanishd shade', was a line left out of 'Whispers of Immortality', his macabre poem about the afterlife.

One of several drafts recalls, in a final stanza, a girl once known as Pipit, whom Eliot later identified as Emily Hale. In memory she is childlike and unassuming, as Emily could have been when they met in the homey setting of Berkeley Place in 1905. The poet, as playful as she, casts her as a little songbird beside the big names of lasting fame, Donne and Webster, to whose posthumous company this poet aspires. But in his heart of hearts the poet wants Pipit's company, and this stanza testifies to this preference: 'As long as Pipit is alive / One can be mischievous and brave', he writes, and when living is done, 'I would like my bones flung into her grave.'

How insignificant is a little bird and her quiet domestic setting in the public record of a great life? It used to be a challenge to give substance to the tie between Emily Hale and Eliot, when for years there were no meetings and almost no communication; no facts outside the poetry. Some have disbelieved such a bond even existed, reinforced by Eliot himself, late in life.

But now, thanks to his letters, he confirms guesses ventured in the past and gives incontrovertible evidence of Emily's presence in his memory over the years he was married to Vivienne. Forming here at the interface of life and art are Eliot's distillations of womanhood, with Emily Hale representing innocence and Vivienne representing a wan bride. Such a woman senses some part of her husband who is not with her. Vivienne voiced that role – visible, insistent, trying in vain to oust the ghost of memory that haunts her husband as he traverses the crossways of an unreal city.

This is the psychic space where expatriates live. He speaks not only personally but universally to the present-day expatriate who becomes, like him, a stranger everywhere. To be far from home is to see the remembered place and remembered faces ever more clearly because the mix of distance, memory and desire composes the past so as to re-experience it, in somewhat the same way as Joyce in *Ulysses* saw his native Dublin all the more keenly from Trieste. Eliot speaks to searchers for meaning but also, given his regret for his first love and the unreality of existence without her, he speaks to the increasing numbers who migrate with a view to the future and who find their core left behind in the past.

Pipit then reappears, a more distinct figure of innocence from far away and a far-off past – 'Some distance from where I was sitting' – in the obscurely named poem 'A Cooking Egg'. I recall the renowned Eliot scholar Helen Gardner saying that we cannot understand this poem without knowing who Pipit was. For a century her identity remained unknown, until it came to light at last in a letter from Eliot to Emily Hale. On 3 November 1930 he asked Emily to compare Pipit on the one hand and a guiding Lady (a Beatrice figure) on the other (in his recent poem, *Ash Wednesday*) 'and see if they do not convince you that my love for you has steadily grown into something finer and finer. And I shall always write primarily for you.'

In the Cooking Egg poem she's cast as an 'upright' young woman with whom the speaker has been in a separate youthful world, sharing some simple pleasure. There's a screen, as it were, between the two innocents and whatever is to be their grown-up fates.

The emotions of this poem are buried even more deeply than usual below an obscuring surface, with glittering shards of narrative in the Modernist manner. Three big alluring nouns, in capitals – Honour, Capital and Society – side-line an unassuming Pipit. Yet beneath distracting wickedness (the Borgias) and money-power (a contemporary financier, Sir Alfred Mond) and the faddish spiritualism of the medium (Madame Blavatsky), there persists a cherished memory of a girl who, beside celebrities past and present, appears a nobody, a little pip.

Her negligibility persists only in her worldly aspect. The speaker invests her with an otherworldly reverence through his glance at Piccarda, the first blessed soul whom Dante meets in paradise. In the personal hinterland of Eliot's poem, Pipit and Piccarda are women with souls whom the young Eliot had encountered in that distant time and place where he studied Dante and fell in love.

Another clue to buried emotion lies amongst Pipit's paraphernalia, eyed by the speaker who visited her. Can it be the knitting on the table? Is it a photographic book on Oxford colleges – has the speaker, off to Oxford, brought it as a farewell gift? On her mantelpiece are old family photographs and there the clue lies between them:

Daguerreotypes and silhouettes,
　Her grandfather and great-great aunts,
Supported on the mantelpiece
　An Invitation to the Dance.

Invitation to the Dance is the music for *Le Spectre de la rose*. It can't be the score: Pipit is not a musician and you don't keep a score on the mantelpiece. Placed together with photographic mementos, it has to be a scene from the ballet that provided a template for exhilarating love.

Yet another clue to buried feeling is the poem's *date*: it must have been composed in 1919 because it was too late to be included in the collection of poems* which the Woolfs printed in March. It was published separately in *Coterie* on 1 May. In January of that year Henry Ware Eliot Sr had died. The news came unexpectedly, shockingly, by cable before his son could change, as he longed to do, his father's conclusion that his youngest, 'my Tom', had made a mess of his life.

The Pipit poem, then, was composed in a period of acute grief. If read in personal terms, it's an admission that the poet's father had been right about his son's life, and the poem starts where that mess began: relegating Pipit's innocence to the past and adopting in her place corrupt old Europe, where 'Lucretia Borgia shall be my Bride'. To go on with this false marriage is to banish faith in goodness, specifically the comfort of the twenty-third Psalm, 'The Lord is my shepherd, I shall not want'. That balm is lost not only for a lifetime but for the afterlife as well, in what the poem ironically calls 'heaven'. It's to Pipit's credit that she has no place in the fake 'heaven' of celebrities: 'I shall not want Pipit in Heaven,' says the bridegroom, who is locked to the likes of Lucretia Borgia. Lucretia, not to be relied on for fidelity, is aligned with others on the make, Alfred Mond and 'red-eyed scavengers'. The message is to pity the

---

* The second collection includes 'Whispers of Immortality', which had the first mention of Pipit in draft.

speaker his Fall into a licentious and greedy world where innocence remains no more than a distant memory.

A month or two after the Pipit poem appeared, about July 1919, Eliot gave Mary Hutchinson a draft of a new poem. In 'Gerontion', an untrustworthy, decayed world, recycling its destructive history, is cut off from an otherworldly 'sign' or vision. The speaker, a man looking back on an unlived life, would welcome a reviving bolt like the coming of Christ. He imagines divinity as 'Christ the tiger', an unfathomable and terrible fierceness like Blake's 'Tyger Tyger, burning bright'.

Revulsion and distrust of worldly people in the Pipit poem continue in the sinister character of Mr Silvero, aka Matthew Prichard, ex-Boston Art Museum. Gerontion then turns from his appalled denunciation of human nature and history to a low-voiced confession. Suddenly, he blurts out his personal losses: 'I would meet you upon this honestly. / I that was near your heart am removed therefrom . . . I have lost my passion.' Who, then, is 'you', the listener to this lament?

There is someone screened from our sight: nameless, faceless, a memory who provides a measure for a wasted life. Gerontion elaborates on the lost passion, the effect on his body: 'I have lost my sight, smell, hearing, taste and touch: / How should I use them for your closer contact?' His senses are numbed and deadened. Eliot later explained to Emily Hale how he had to deaden himself during these waste years without her. 'I tried to pretend that my love for you was dead, though I could only do so by pretending to myself that my heart was dead.' What appears in the poem as a disembodied figment of the imagination did, after all, have a face and name.

At the centre of Gerontion's confession is a rhetorical question: why should a man keep passion alive, 'since what is kept must be adulterated?' The corrosion of adultery, the poet's painful discovery about his wife and Russell, is coiled inside the ambiguity of 'adulterated'.

Eliot slides confession into his poetry. Gerontion admits how damaged he is. This is the poet talking about himself in full view on the surface of a poem, in a favourite disguise as weary old man, a successor to Prufrock saying 'I grow old . . . I grow old'. He confides the betrayal and its consequence, his deadened state, to a woman he can trust. It's a statement of loss and regret for what might have been.

However much Eliot kept Emily in mind as secret listener, he was married to Vivienne and both tried now and then to revitalise their marriage. Vivienne confided to Mary 'an affair' with her own husband. It began with 'the Peace weekend' (18–20 July 1919),* and went on until 9 August, when Eliot left for a three-week walking holiday with Pound in the Dordogne. Vivienne asks Mary if she too doesn't find that staying in another house is conducive to 'passion'. The Eliots were staying in Eastbourne at the holiday place of new friends, Sydney and Violet Schiff, who made much of Vivienne; they liked her 'natural sincerity'.†

When Abigail Eliot visited London in January 1920 she reported back to the family that her cousin's marriage was not a mismatch. At tea in their pleasant flat, she found Tom affable and hungry for family news. Abigail was the first Eliot whom Vivienne had met after four and a half years of marriage, and she warmed to her friendliness and agreed to take her about London, while Abigail's beautiful manners eased Eliot with the breath of the family. Abigail, who went on to have a loyal same-sex tie, 'loved'

---

* The Treaty of Versailles, ending the state of war between Germany and the Allies, was signed on 28 June 1919. On 19 July 1919 official Peace celebrations with bands and fireworks were held throughout Britain.

† Schiff was a generous patron of the arts, a novelist and a translator of Proust and Hermann Hesse. At their home Eliot met the long admired Arthur Symons (whose book on French poetry had introduced him to Laforgue), Delius, Katherine Mansfield and Lady Rothermere who was to sponsor Eliot's journal, the *Criterion*.

Vivienne ('love' was not a word she said lightly) and approved of
the way Tom and Vivienne shared 'radical' political views, deplor-
ing the futile horror of war and the treatment of Germany, and
expressing their regret that the American President, Woodrow
Wilson, had proved weak at Versailles, where the vindictive post-
war treaty was drawn up. They all agreed that to starve Central
Europe was criminal. Most emphatically, Abigail told her people
back home in Boston that Vivienne was 'a dear' who put much-
needed love into Tom.

The bond between Vivienne and her husband was palpable once
more when John Middleton Murry, editor of the *Athenaeum*, invited
the Eliots for dinner in May 1920. Murry's wife, Katherine Mansfield,
who was fond of Eliot, witnessed what seemed to her a fixation on
Vivienne. She observed Eliot 'leaning towards [his wife], listening,
making the most of her – really minding'.

The pleasure the Eliots could take in each other seems to have
been mutual that summer. Eliot was due to take a fortnight's
cycling holiday in France, this time with Wyndham Lewis. Before

*Abigail Adams Eliot took to Vivienne when she studied at Oxford as an external student. Abigail
then returned to England in 1921 to train in nursery education at the Rachel McMillan Nursery
and Training Centre, visited here by Queen Mary. Abigail (in glasses) is on the right.*

he left, Eliot sent his mother some photographs that Lady Ottoline had taken of Vivienne at Garsington. How attractive she looks, he thinks. Her lacy petticoat dips out under her skirt and one leg is bent back on a balustrade, showing the grace of a dancer.

But then, while her husband was away Vivienne shifted into anxiety mode, feeling more than dependence. She tensed up as though fearing she would lose him. She stayed again with the Schiffs in Eastbourne, who encouraged her confidence. They got up home theatricals and Vivienne shone. In a letter to 'Wonkypenky', her husband, she signs herself 'Yr. most adoring V' or 'Wee', and calls him 'darling', but she tugs at him, saying how she felt ill and went to her room and cried 'and called yr. name'. She tells him to post her his address each day, as he travels from place to place – Brittany, then Tours and Saumur along the Loire – so that she can, as she puts it, 'get at you'. She was aware of being 'a drag on Tom'.

Vivienne's nag is brilliantly recreated in *The Waste Land*. A wife tries in vain to get at her husband, to get through to him. All the while, he feels trapped by her battering voice and the hopeless diversion of the closed car, which goes back to the disastrous holiday in Torquay in January 1916. What should be heard as dialogue is audible only as the wife's monologue; the husband is mute: what comes from him, sotto voce, is a rebarbative inward voice.

The wife craves communication; the husband shuts her out.

'Do you remember / Nothing?' she prods.

'I remember / The hyacinth garden' is his silent, inexorable reply in a line Eliot saw fit to cut.

In the hinterland of composition, what prevails? The wife is blotted out, together with all that is ephemeral in the waste. What holds is the memory of the girl in the first part of *The Waste Land*, also composed in 1921. The poem speaks to her of 'we' coming back from the hyacinth garden, 'Your arms full' of flowers, just like the La Figlia poem with 'her arms full of flowers'. Called 'the hyacinth girl', she is named for a flower a god creates to lament lost love. In this short scene, the remembered girl – Emily Hale – is stilled as an image of purity, elevated above the dross of daily contacts.

The girl is introduced in *The Waste Land* with a song from Act I of *Tristan und Isolde*, when love is about to take off. The sea wind fills the sails of their ship, though it's carrying them into a situation, marriage to someone else, that will part them. When Tristan lies wounded in the final act, it seems that Isolde is not approaching with her potion. The sea is empty, a look-out sings: 'Oed' und leer das Meer' is the line Eliot adds by hand to his typescript of part I early in 1921. Isolde finally arrives, but it is too late. Instead she is transfigured (*Verklärung*, Wagner called it). There follows the famous *Liebestod*, an aria for lovers who find bliss through death or beyond death. Her voice seems to call him briefly back to life: 'his heart swells and, brave and full, pulses in his breast'. The finale of *The Waste Land* will recall that pulse of 'blood shaking my heart'.

Eliot's memory of his hyacinth girl, held intact through all the years, is the most personal of the lyric moments that counter the waste of the present. Speaking once more to Emily Hale from afar, through the confessional intimacy of his poem he recalls for her that night when they were joined as 'we'. In the poet's fancy, 'we' came back late from the garden. For 'we', Emily should read 'I', Eliot said to her nine years after he recreated this scene in the poetry of 1921. He did not expect falling in love to have been as decisive for her as it had been for him, a night that defines his life. ('By this, and this only, we have existed').

He tells her, 'I could not / Speak, . . . / Looking into the heart of light, the silence'. That 'could not speak' was and remains the high point, as it had been for the young Eliot after the night at the

Boston Opera in Emily's party. His emotion, followed by loss of will, becomes the very movement of his poetry: a visionary moment followed by emptiness.

Towards the end of the poem the confidential voice returns to recall the daring of emotional surrender, overcoming his habit of 'prudence', as the poem enters on its thunderous finale. The message of the Thunder, to 'give', *Datta*, is delivered in the Sanskrit the young Eliot was studying when his attachment to Emily Hale came to life.

To see Emily Hale and Vivienne Eliot in the ur-scenes of *The Waste Land* is not to suggest there is no other way to approach the poem. It speaks to all of the unlived life, the degradation of promiscuity and the need for spiritual renewal. It is not necessary to know the author's private life, but it helps to understand how the poem evolved over the eight years of its gestation, going far back to 1913–14, the poet's last years in America. 'Tom's autobiography – a melancholy one' is the way Mary Hutchinson, one of the first to know the poem, described *The Waste Land*. She could discern the substratum beneath the Modernist manner. His mother was given to understand the same: 'Tom wrote to me before it was published that he had put so much of his own life into it.' Most telling of all, Eliot's unveilings to Emily Hale make it clear how much this poet needed an actual pulse shaking the heart to authenticate the experience he opens up to us. Unless these unveilings in his letters were preserved, he told her, 'my life and work will be misunderstood to the end of time'.

7

A PRIVATE WASTELAND

'*The Waste Land* . . . has become a part of me (or I of it) this last year,' Vivienne exulted to Sydney Schiff on 16 October 1922, the day the poem appeared in the first issue of Eliot's own journal, the *Criterion*. The following month it appeared in a New York magazine, the *Dial*, edited by Scofield Thayer. The poem won the prestigious *Dial* prize of $2,000, and from then on Eliot, aged thirty-four, was hailed as a leading poet in Britain, the Empire, Europe and America.

Vivienne had been her husband's partner in their private wasteland. He confirmed it, and whatever else they endured together, their union proved, as both had hoped, fertile for his art. Eliot never told Emily that Vivienne shared his private poetry workshop: she sharpened 'When Lil's husband was coming back out of the Transport Corps' to 'When Lil's husband was demobbed'. Instead of the call 'Good night, Lou' when the Larrik, the nearby pub, shut, Vivienne, with her ear for Cockney, slurred this as 'Goo' night'. When a worn, working-class wife has had an abortion, her fancy-free friend says, 'What you get married for if you don't want children?' That was Vivienne's line, in the voice of the Eliots' servant – 'pure Ellen Kellond', they agreed. (It was also a jab at a sore spot, their own childlessness.) Though to all appearances Vivienne depended on him, Eliot needed her to encourage the poem and provide him with her own rhythmic voice.

There was, though, a more private space – call it silence or memory mixed with desire (in the opening of the poem), a love-place – to which Vivienne had no access: the inward bar against the nervy wife trying to reach her husband, whose mind sheers off to the hyacinth garden.

But it wasn't just a private wasteland that drove his writing. That April ('the cruellest month'), the poet felt oppressed by the 'horror' (he repeats the word) of contemporary politics (a coal-miners' strike lasting from 1 April until 1 July, his 'contempt' for all parties in government and 'hatred' of democracy). It was 'like the feeling of growing madness in one's own brain. It is rather a horror to be sane in the midst of this.' This emotion, he went on, 'goes too far for rage'. His original epigraph to the poem found a parallel in Conrad's *Heart of Darkness*: 'The Horror! the horror!' at what humans can perpetrate.

The Waste Land can be read as a prophetic public poem, a lament for a fallen world after a pointless war. At the same time it is a psychic state, packed with personal reference and embedded confessions. A sequence of ordeals immediately preceded the poem.

The first trial, in June 1921, was the Eliot family's arrival in London: his mother, together with his brother Henry and sister Marian. Eliot had longed for his mother, whom he had not seen since his visit to Eastern Point in August 1915. He had worried that she might die, as his father had, before he saw her again.

The visitors were to occupy the flat where the Eliots were now living at 9 Clarence Gate Gardens while Tom and Vivienne would stay in Lucy Thayer's stuffy quarters on Wigmore Street.

Vivienne became ill as soon as her husband's people arrived. The Eliot family had been apart for six years, but Vivienne's health demanded prime attention – from them all. The only time that Tom Eliot was not loving to his mother was the one day she did not visit Vivienne.

Eliot and his mother Charlotte Eliot when she came to visit him in the summer of 1921. He broke down after she left in August.

Charlotte Eliot met Vivienne's mother without taking to her. The Haigh-Woods had a 'lovely' home, she saw. That word says enough about the Haigh-Woods being reportedly unable to contribute towards their daughter's support. When the Eliot family left on 20 August, Vivienne, seeing them off, had what she called a fit. If she seemed to them like an 'animal', she excused herself afterwards to Henry, they should know that the English are less conformist than New Englanders in showing their true feelings.

After Eliot's mother departed, he broke down, so badly that the bank gave him three months' leave of absence. Vivienne joked that her own breakdown wasn't finished, yet she did try to help and accompanied him to Margate for his recuperation. From 15 October to 12 November he stayed at the Albemarle Hotel, a guesthouse overlooking a park, with a deserted bandstand and the sea beyond.

Sitting each day in the Nayland Rock shelter on Margate sands,

Eliot drafted part III of *The Waste Land*. This opens with yet another portrait of a lady, this time a pampered English socialite who writes dark poems to a measure of critical acclaim. Her name is Fresca.

An actual woman writer behind the fictional Fresca has come to light, through Eliot's testimony to Emily combined with the lady's own arch memories, too secretive in tone to be relied on but hinting at their knowing each other for some years. At the very least, she had him in her sights long before he drafted *The Waste Land*.

Nancy Cunard was a high-society heiress, only child of Sir Bache Cunard, whose immensely wealthy grandfather had founded the Cunard steamship line. Nancy's American mother, 'Emerald' Cunard, flourished as a leader of English society. As a fledgling poet herself during the war, Nancy fell in love with 'Prufrock'. She heard of the poem from Pound, who visited Emerald, Lady Cunard in 1915 with a view to soliciting support for Joyce and other writers in need. As a very young, impressionable poet, she recalled leaving her mother's box at the ballet and chasing in vain along a corridor to find the gifted young American who was taking in a year at Oxford. Eliot attended Cunard parties in high style, wearing make-up: a 'peculiar' green powder he had acquired in Paris, which under artificial light made him look 'corpselike'. It went with his flair for acting and disguise and was, he said, a 'great success'.

Nancy Cunard sported kohl-ringed eyes and a tulle scarf tied across her eyebrows. She was flat and straight with the lean-and-hungry look of a wolf, and she could be a candidate for the *lupus* in his portrait of 'Princess Volupine' in 'Burbank with a Baedeker', which Eliot wrote in 1919, before the Fresca portrait in *The Waste Land*. Cunard's emaciation fits the 'phthisic hand' the Princess extends to lovers. Burbank, an American on tour in a rotting Venice, is due for a momentous Fall (in the biblical sense) when he meets her at a small hotel. 'Princess Volupine arrived, / They were together, and he fell.'

She exudes an allure like Cleopatra in her barge that 'Burned on the water all the day', or like a temptress interrupting a grail quest, for as her ship sails on it seemed 'that all the water brente after her'.

Cunard's two strands of hair curved along her cheekbones set the fashion for the Jazz Age. She wore huge African bangles up and down her thin arms and took experimental writers and artists as lovers, including Ezra Pound.

In the end Pound edited out the Fresca portrait in *The Waste Land*, along with other longer scenes, to create a more fragmented Modernist composite. But in the original schema Fresca, dreaming of 'pleasant rapes', loomed large, 'a sort of can-can salonnière', introducing scenes of sexual degradation and violence in part III. Sex defiles other women in this section, while it serves the empowered Fresca. But her portrait is filled with misogyny, its rhyming couplets spitting venom.

> *Odours, confected by the cunning French,*
> *Disguise the good old hearty female stench . . .*
> *Women grown intellectual grow dull,*
> *And lose the mother wit of natural trull . . .*

Vivienne stayed in Margate for two of the three weeks that Eliot was there. Collaboration is suggested by the fact that two and a half years later she published a redone Fresca portrait as her own.* Still in Margate on 4 November and by then on his own, Eliot wrote to Schiff that the third part of *The Waste Land*, called 'The Fire Sermon', 'must wait for Vivien's opinion as to whether it is printable'.

Vivienne, it seems, saw room for improvement. Her portrait of Fresca omits promiscuity ('a doorstep dunged by every dog in town') and the dismissal of women as predators: 'Unreal emotions and real appetite.'

She herself had been happy to flirt with Scofield Thayer, sleep with Bertrand Russell and beckon Mary Hutchinson's brother. While Eliot was in Margate, Vivienne put out feelers to Thayer, whose marriage had ended. He was in Vienna, having psychoanalysis with

---

* In her piece 'Letters of the Moment: II' in the *Criterion* in April 1924.

Freud. Vivienne told Thayer she might turn up there – she meant alone, because her husband was going to Lausanne. She accompanied Eliot as far as Paris and remained there from later November and throughout December 1921. A letter to Mary Hutchinson shows the panic that hit her on separation.

Tuesday
Hôtel du Pas-de-Calais,
59 rue des Saints-Pères, Paris

Mary!

... The first few days with Tom were very perfect, and it was only after I saw him climb into that dreadful Swiss train, and me left on the platform, at 9.20 in the evening, that I felt someone had taken a broomstick and knocked me on the head ... I have even forgotten Tom. No-one seems at all real to me. At the end of ten days I decided to go to Cologne. I knew a man there ...

Now, my dear, dear Mary ... I adore the thought of you ... About Tom – I don't know I don't know ... Have I behaved even worse than usual? ...

Ever,

V.

The man from Cologne arrives tomorrow – will stay with me. After that I don't know ...

There's no desire in reaching out to different men, only an acute sense of displacement and unreality, like Eliot's, when her husband went away for treatment.

Lady Ottoline had recommended Dr Roger Vittoz in Lausanne to help cure Eliot's breakdown, and Eliot followed her advice so closely that when he arrived he even stayed in the same room she had at the Hôtel Sainte Luce. It was an easy walk down the sloping cobbled street to the doctor's consulting room in his house on the rue de Tilleuls. His wife was a French aristocrat and many of his patients came from that background. Joseph Conrad and the psychologist William James had also been his patients, as had the evolutionary biologist Julian Huxley who wrote encouragingly to Eliot.

Eliot suffered from insomnia, which sounds like a recurrence of the night-time disturbance he had experienced before, when his vigil poems, including 'Prufrock's Pervigilium', had voiced fear of madness. In his book *Treatment of Neurasthenia by Teaching Brain Control*, Dr Vittoz describes 'Aboulie', want of will, in a passage Eliot marked in his copy of an edition published in 1921. The problem made the patient changeable, with thoughts sliding from the present to the past or future. Dr Vittoz restored the sense of control through a simple mental exercise. A patient would visualise a scene or a series of numbers and then eliminate a small part of it. This would train the patient to eliminate what Eliot called worry. At the same time, the doctor laid on calming hands.

Eliot's energy returned and, in an inspired outpouring, he wrote part V of *The Waste Land*, the all-important alternative to the Unreal City: a journey into unknown mountainous territory – the poet could see across the lake to the mountains from his room – craving the water of spiritual refreshment. His poem ends with a possibility of 'Shantih shantih shantih' (the Peace which passeth understanding). There is no full stop; peace could be coming on or fading.

Sadly, to leave Lausanne was to return to a deadened state. While in Switzerland, Eliot had grateful thoughts of Vivienne's help but once he was back with her in London his moodiness made her want to escape. To separate did occur to her, but she had not the courage. 'In the Cage' was the original title of part II of *The Waste Land*, with its failed marriages. A cage is evoked again in the poem's epigraph about the Sybil who keeps the gateway to the Underworld in classical myth. It's the Sybil's fate to atrophy in a cage, and when asked what she wants, all she can say is 'I want to die'.*

Vivienne identified with this caged woman in choosing the name Sybilla for the wife who reads a handbook on the art of fading away in the autobiographical stories she began to write. They were in this private wasteland together, she and Eliot.

It was soon after completing *The Waste Land* that Eliot had an affair for the first and only time. Nancy Cunard again. She named him in a poem called 'The Letter', describing how they met once more at a party, attended by the Prince of Wales, in 1922, and how she had preferred Eliot to dancing with the 'P. of W.':

> *We met, you and I, first, that summer night of 1922,*
> *At a ball — you in 'smoking', I in a panniered dress*
> *Of Poiret: red, gold, with cascading white tulle on the hips.*
> *The P. of W. was there (so polite, lovely face) and we danced together;*
> *. . . Bored by it all was I. After many dances, we went down*
> *Alone, by the grand staircase to the supper room.*
> *It was then, Eliot, you came in, alone too . . .*

The following night, they had a 'tryst' at the fashionably arty Restaurant de la Tour Eiffel on Percy Street. It was a favourite meeting place for Cunard, the artist Augustus John, Wyndham Lewis, his *Blast* circle and other avant-garde artists. In a private room upstairs, sitting on the floor in front of a gas fire, Cunard recalls 'thawing' Eliot with talk of passion and repression, together with a confession how his poetry had 'put its frenzy into me' and 'changed my life'.

---

* TSE quotes from the *Satyricon* of Petronius. This 'Sybil' epigraph replaced the original epigraph from Conrad's *Heart of Darkness*, which Pound cut when Eliot passed again through Paris early in January to fetch Vivienne on their return to London. Eliot protested over losing the Conrad epigraph, saying it had been 'somewhat elucidatory'.

They sat so long that Joe, the Austrian waiter, came to check and found them 'as close as could be'.

'Not every life's-moment is recalled,' Cunard said, 'though all of that night certainly is.' She obeyed Eliot's wish to say nothing for the rest of his life, and revealed 'The Letter' only after he had died.

Eliot deplored that lapse. Years later, when he confessed this to Emily Hale, he told her that it had left a taste of ashes he could never forget. The sense of sin was such that he had felt he must end his life, and it was then that the alternative of celibacy occurred to him.

From 1922, after the publication of *The Waste Land*, until the mid-twenties, Eliot was moving privately towards conversion. This course that was to surprise his contemporaries does follow from certain unpublished poems, the visionary 'Silence' and the failed martyr poems of 1914–15. A clue to this direction lurks also in Eliot's curious remark about 'The Life of a Great Sinner', a plan for an unfinished novel by Dostoevsky, which Eliot published in the first issue of the *Criterion*. He considered it 'the most important thing in no. 1' – that is, more important than his own poem.

This comment comes in a letter to a refugee from the Ukraine, Samuel Solomonovitch Koteliansky,* who, together with Virginia Woolf, translated this work. It's easy to overlook Eliot's words as a mere courtesy to the translators or else a gesture of self-deprecation. But Dostoevsky's incorrigible Sinner pointed to a route he could take beyond *The Waste Land*.

The Sinner proposes to expose, with ruthless honesty, a man's

---

* S. S. Koteliansky, known as 'Kot', had come to England in 1911. He provided a channel for Russian literature at a time of growing interest, when reliable English translations were few and far between. (In 1911, when Eliot had been in Paris, he had read Dostoevsky in French and seen a production of *The Brothers Karamazov*.) Kot became friends with the Woolfs, who wished to publish unknown Russian texts. The Hogarth Press was due to publish the notes for 'The Life of a Great Sinner' at the end of 1922, and Leonard Woolf allowed TSE prior journal rights.

most shameful flaws and doubts, unearthing the character of some-one of exceptional powers, who has known from childhood that he is destined to be extraordinary. Yet this man hesitates. His 'incessant thinking' asks 'What shall I be and how shall I do it all?'

Certain traits in the Sinner reflect traits in Eliot. One is the 'state of *wavering*'; another an 'insatiable desire for the ideal, looking for a fixed point to rest upon'; and yet another mirrors Eliot's fear that his protective disguise, his English appearance, would be blown to expose that savage he had feared he was. Dostoevsky's Sinner is stripped of manners. There's no concealment: he admits to supe-rior contempt for others and a need to 'defile' or subjugate them to his controlling will. He owns also to violent impulses and utters harsh judgements. The Sinner confounds our distinction between superior man and base criminal. What he confesses is abnormal, especially a deathbed confession of a crime. In Dostoevsky, abnor-mality is overt; in Eliot, concealed, but declared with startling honesty in his poetry.

Eliot had confided to Eleanor Hinkley that he was *not* living in a novel by Jane Austen, but in one by Dostoevsky. As Eliot would admit eventually to Emily Hale, he was an egotist. He had a Temper with a capital T.

Dostoevsky sets out how readily his Sinner's unused endowment can turn to violence, 'hatred' and 'filth'. This character trounces others, honing his will and exercising it without compunction – almost without noticing. He becomes detached from common humanity and from his own soil and people.

Unlikely though it may seem to align this temperamental Russian with the well-conducted Eliot, we remember Eliot's supe-riority, contempt and Bolo filth. Dostoevsky does not side-line filth; 'debauchery' is at the centre of the life he lays out. The Sinner must astound himself with 'the hollowness, dirt and absurdity of immorality' on his way to a monastery, where he learns a cura-tive humility.

*

A shadow falls on Eliot in his mid-thirties. It's hard to see who he is behind the aura of fame lighting up with the publication of *The Waste Land*. As pre-publication copies circulated during 1922, and afterwards, as the decades followed, it came to be recognised as the poem of the century. But for the poet himself, that year, 1922, and that poem located largely in London as an Unreal City deprived of the hyacinth garden, marked the end of an era. The 'waste' was stale, he repeated.

Was the soul dead, he asks in 'The Burial of the Dead', part I of the poem. Could it sprout again? He repeats this question to John Middleton Murry. To come alive, to unbury, he needed to move on in his work along the lines of the journey opening up to a pilgrim at the end of *The Waste Land*. His mother understood this to be a grail quest. But if he pursued this quasi-medieval course, what repercussions would this have for Vivienne and the Modernist project they had shared?

If Vivienne proved beyond rescue then both were doomed. Did he have a right to save himself at her expense?

So began a contest for survival. The right to save himself, that moral issue that will haunt him through the next phase of his life, turned on one question and one only: had *The Waste Land* proved him to be the great poet of his age who, by virtue of that, must grant priority to his gift? Because Eliot's conscience was so scrupulous and his sense of responsibility for Vivienne so strong, the issue could not be resolved in any simple manner, but an answer came in June 1922 when he disclosed the poem to the Woolfs. They were enthralled when, over dinner, Eliot did not just read *The Waste Land* but performed it. 'He sang it & chanted it rhythmed it. It has great beauty and force of phrase,' Virginia Woolf reports in her diary. 'What connects it together I'm not so sure ... One was left however with some strong emotion.' This assured showing, a verve unlike the austere public readings, had to do with the Woolfs' hurrah: an audience of two who had the measure of his achievement and their immediate decision to publish the poem as a book. That very night they planned for it to come out in the autumn. It was deferred by journal publication, but this affirmation from the heart of the English intelligentsia mattered hugely. From now on Eliot was not only 'Tom', he was 'great Tom', one of the literary 'Gods'.

Virginia Woolf saw he had grown 'supple as an eel': familiar, friendly, jocular. Her charmed impression hints at chemistry – a clue to her much later confidence to her sister that they could have been lovers. The sinuousness of an eel explains a charm – not apparent in photographs – that Eliot could exercise, when he chose, with various women drawn to him even as he aged.

Hearing the poem that June, Virginia Woolf had an impulse to rescue so great a poet from toiling as a bank clerk. In league with Lady Ottoline Morrell, she initiated an Eliot Fellowship Fund. Pound too had a rescue scheme called Bel Esprit, to which a New York lawyer, John Quinn, promised a big contribution. Eliot himself was wary: they would have to collect £3,000 to yield an income of £300 a year (less than his steady rises at the bank to £500 a year by the mid-twenties) and the interest would be subject to fluctuation. No security then for his wife.

His father had not left money outright to his younger son, unlike the bequests to his five other children. The sum was in trust, for use during his lifetime; after that, the capital would revert to the Eliot family. Henry Sr had not liked Vivienne, who'd gone on cadging funds beyond the rent he'd been compelled to pay. As a responsible parent, there had been no alternative, and it had been easier to deplore his son's wife than 'my Tom'.

In January 1923 Vivienne was all for more expenditure, using pet names for her husband: 'Wing' and 'Wang' (some kind of double act). Addressing 'Dearest darling Wing', she begs him to take Saturday off from the bank to keep her company, and then, to Wang, she is 'pining' to see a second flat they could rent, '– just *mad* to see it'. From 1923, they rented a workplace at 38 Burleigh Mansions

in the Charing Cross Road. That autumn, Vivienne craved a house
with a garden in central London.

The Woolfs proposed Eliot as editor of the *Nation* (now incorpo-
rating what had been Murry's *Athenaeum* with its impressive array
of contributors, Eliot himself, Katherine Mansfield, Virginia Woolf,
Aldous Huxley, Robert Graves, Thomas Hardy and Edith Sitwell).
It was a top literary post, what Eliot had dreamt of when he came
to England, and it carried a higher salary than he had at the bank.
Early in 1923 this presented an agonising temptation because Eliot
had to recognise that it wouldn't do for his wife: despite the salary
and literary prestige, the position did not offer the bank's guaran-
tees of security nor a widow's pension.

Vivienne said she did not want to die in a humble cot. If her husband took the opportunity on offer, she told Mary Hutchinson, she
would bear him 'a considerable grudge'.

In the end, Eliot turned the *Nation* down, and Leonard Woolf took
up the position. Eliot blamed himself for his prolonged hesitation
because he thought this had undermined Vivienne.

She 'was utterly worn out and *ruined* by my indecision', he told
Mary. 'I know that the strain of that was deadly to her.'

That spring Vivienne wasted away to a skeleton – weighing only
eighty pounds – and nearly died seven or eight times. There was
some serious and deep-seated disorder, impossible to label with any
confidence. Doctors did not know at the time and they certainly
were part of the problem with their diets, addictive medications and
misdiagnoses. Too little is known of her childhood problems. She
spoke of tuberculosis of the bone in her left arm, and many operations. This history, if true, suggests physical and mental pain in
early childhood, trauma that became a way of life and left her damaged. Self-starvation followed doctor's orders, as Eliot saw it, but
Vivienne carried this out with a severity and strictness common to
anorexics. There was a physical illness, colitis, yet doctors thought
this a symptom of a condition they could not determine.

During the following year, Vivienne became desperate enough

to contemplate suicide, and warned her husband that she would leave a letter for his loyal supporter Ezra Pound. She wrote to Lady Ottoline about coming back from death, 'still gasping for breath and just *hanging on*'.

One of Vivienne's Sibylla stories, 'Medicine à la Mode', an unpublished one written in 1924, pictures herself after an impersonal treatment by a doctor with strained blue eyes, as though the doctor is too preoccupied to attend properly to her patient: 'Sibylla stood just outside the open door, her short dark hair untidily disposed on her head, standing on end in fact, & her thin hands clasping & rubbing her emaciated body in the places where the treatment had been most severe. She looked a strange little bony object in her shrunken grey flannel dressing gown with all her life in her keen face & her startled grey eyes.'

Eliot had to take leave from the bank to nurse Vivienne. The crisis swallowed all of his annual three-week holiday allowance. Vivienne, fearing that he would leave her, cried out for support to Lady Ottoline and Murry, yet even as she did so, fear led her to distrust Eliot's friends. Seeing him harassed, pale, weary from lack of sleep could win their sympathy. She thought he was merely playing a role of 'poor whipped dog'. It was a dire situation, replaying the marital impasse in *The Waste Land*, to which there seemed no solution.

Eliot's temptation to leave the bank, followed in April 1923 by Vivienne's close encounters with death, was a challenge he could not deny. He blames himself in his letters, feeling he must never again consider a future that did not cover that of his wife. He tells his mother he is 'crumbling' and can hardly go on.

To forestall another breakdown, Charlotte Eliot was forced to go against her husband's will. When the outcries from London came to a confrontation, her son refusing to accept an inheritance that excluded his wife, she drew up a codicil granting Vivienne an income should she become a widow. (A further plan was to take out a life insurance of $20,000, with Vivienne as beneficiary and her husband's brother paying the first premium of $558.) Forced to give priority to Vivienne, Charlotte Eliot was led to play down the insufficiencies of her daughter Charlotte Eliot Smith, who was ailing more quietly. Her architect husband was not successful, there were two daughters to support and no home help, in comparison with Vivienne, who was never without a servant. As it turned out, Charlotte Smith, in a weakened condition, did not survive an operation for peritonitis three years later.

Vivienne's bout of colitis died down in May, only to be replaced by other ills. These kept her state of extremis at fever point. She despaired of a cure, while her husband felt forever trapped. His guilt at damaging his wife by his prolonged hesitation over the *Nation* was compounded by guilt at his affair. It was this abashed man whom Emily Hale met when she came to London with her aunt and uncle.

8

A SIGHTING IN ECCLESTON SQUARE

Some nine years had gone by since they had parted in 1914. During this time Emily Hale went on with singing lessons for seven years and took courses at the Leland Powers School of Dramatic Art in Boston and at the Cornish School of Drama in Seattle. She was fascinated, she said, by the history of the theatre and by the 'make-believe' of the stage.

In 1921 she was invited to join Lucia Briggs, the new president of a women's college, Milwaukee-Downer, in Wisconsin (eventually part of the University of Wisconsin). It was another dormitory post but the lure for Hale was an opportunity to build up spoken English and drama at the college.

It was her policy to put on new plays as well as theatrical classics. In 1922, when she was thirty-one, she took the lead in a Pulitzer Prize-winning play, *Miss Lulu Bett*, in Milwaukee's main theatre. She infused this downtrodden role with dry wit. At Downer, in the same year, she directed *Le Bourgeois Gentilhomme* to celebrate the tercentenary of Molière's birth, taking part herself as the painted and white-wigged marchioness Dorimène, waving an enormous feathered fan to emphasise her panache. She excelled in comic roles requiring articulate delivery of lines. In speech classes she trained young women to move lazy tongues and shape their words through opened, flexible mouths. On stage they were told to stand tall, straightening their backs. Her most important lesson was integrity: to bring qualities from within to visible roles, honesty above all. For her, performance was not a disguise to put something over, but an art of genuine expression.

Hale used some summer vacations to travel and take courses that would enhance her work, and it's likely that 1923 was the summer she took a course at the Speech Institute in London. She and Eliot arranged an after-hours meeting in Eccleston Square in Pimlico, its garden surrounded by elegant buildings. Both were aware that feelings were likely to have dimmed with the passage of time. But for Eliot the opposite happened. Here was a woman who was not only lovely but straight in the New England manner that meant home to him, a moral being who could be trusted. In command of her own life, she was determined to fulfil her vocation as best she could. Eliot knew at once that he still loved her.

Emily Hale recalled this scene decades later in her memoir-introduction to Eliot's letters, after she donated her collection to Princeton. 'I was dismayed when he confessed, after seeing me again, that his affection for me was stronger than ever.' Eliot's second declaration of love led her to put a question to him. It was vital enough for Emily to remember this vexed question and to bring it up again, still in need of an answer. Eliot himself took this seriously enough to lay it out in a letter of 18 September 1931. We can't know what the question was, but do know that the last time this man had invited her to respond to a declaration of love, it had come with no prospect for her. Again, in Eccleston Square, he invites her to hear him without, it appears, a plan. She is dismayed when he will not reply to her question. She turns away, and they do not see each other for some time.

'The night at Eccleston Square was too confusing, too painful, to make reasonable action possible,' she told Eliot in September 1931, when she reminded him of that unanswered question. When she broached this issue, after committing herself to a warmer tie, she was still asking for a clarification.

To reply, he said, would have meant explaining the whole history of his relations with Vivienne. He put it to her that his silence had been scrupulous. It would have been wrong to tug her into his situation, when he had been 'hopelessly separated' from her.

Hale remained entirely disengaged at the meeting in Eccleston Square. Her self-protective reserve was part of her appeal; she was grave, austere, and did not allow herself to respond to a married man unwilling to explain his intentions.

For his part, Eliot was elated. Here, in person, was his hyacinth girl, unaware of her place in his poetry. At thirty-two she still bore out his idealisation of her in memory as the girl who could take a poet into 'the heart of light'. Here was a glimmer of rescue from the 'ashes' of his private life.

After she departed for the new academic year, he sent her two gifts. On 5 September 1923 he dated and signed a copy of his 1920 collection of poems, *Ara Vos Prec*. Was there something he still needed to say to her, through the collection's title? 'Ara vos prec' are the words of Arnaut Daniel, the sinner who, in Dante's *Purgatorio*, owns to lust and accepts his punishment, yet cries out for pity: 'I beseech you . . . take pity on my pain.'

A conventional inscription on the flyleaf, 'For Emily Hale with the author's humble compliments, T. S. Eliot', is followed by another Dantean inscription that resonates with private import:

> *'sieti raccommandato il mio Tesoro*
> *nel qual io vivo ancora, e più non cheggio.'*
> *Poi si rivolse.*

('"Keep my Treasure, where I yet live on, and I ask not more." Then he turned round.') From the hell or purgatory of his present existence, he asks Hale to hold on to what will last of him, his work, and to keep him in her memory, before he turns back to his punishment.

Soon after, on 14 September, he asked his printer, Cobden Sanderson, to send the next year's issues of the *Criterion* to Miss Hale in Milwaukee where she lived in college in Johnston Hall. In 1924 he wrote a poem called 'Eyes that last I saw in tears' through 'division': their parting and, behind it, the tearful scene devised for 'La Figlia che Piange'. These eyes, which now 'outlast' the tears, reappear as a 'golden vision' in a dream. These are eyes he will meet again, as eyes of judgement, possibly deriding his mistake, on the other side of death. The meeting with Emily Hale opens up this once-opaque poem in terms of his life. Here could be the answer to Hale's unanswered question: what he actually intended was for her to take part in his poetic phantasmagoria.

The immediate result of the encounter with Hale was that he began to look towards beatitude as a counter to the 'hell' he experienced with Vivienne: the new poetic path he would take away from *The Waste Land*. In September 1923 he began a little-known essay about what he calls 'duality', as practised by sinners in Dante and Dostoevsky who want to be close to God. These characters live on two planes of reality, the ordinary life being only the veil of another action taking place behind it. They are aware, as Eliot was, of the futility of their visible lives, as they listen for other voices and appear to be conducting 'a conversation with spectres'.

FIGHTS TO THE DEATH

Two words, 'death' and 'paralysis', resound between Vivienne and Eliot, a mirrored wretchedness. At the height of the colitis episode in April 1923, Eliot had told Schiff about the struggle to get Vivienne to a rented cottage in the country: 'we could die with less effort in London'. A 'paralysis from misery' had stopped his poetry once more. In 1924 Vivienne wrote a story called 'The Paralysed Woman', set in a high-up flat they took that summer in Eastbourne. Sybilla, a writer married to a preoccupied husband, observes a paralysed woman in a wheelchair, who sits looking out from the flat opposite. The two women bond as watchers and secret sharers. Sybilla, meanwhile, pores over a book called *Holy Dying*.

Vivienne was 'at death's door' again, Eliot told Mary Hutchinson in March 1925; at times he thought she must 'die from exhaustion'.

'I ought never to have married you,' Vivienne would say during dreadful nights. 'I am useless and better dead.' Her husband would deny this and promise anything, feeling it his fault for being unbalanced. But in the morning it would be just as bad. 'Oh I am such a trouble to you, I ought to die.' Then, again, her tears would flow. In a retrospect on the marriage decades later, in 1960, Eliot mirrors her still, saying she 'nearly was the death of me'. It was a 'nightmare agony', but he continued to believe that this conjoined agony protected him from what otherwise would have been a 'mediocre' life. He confirms that Vivienne kept him alive as a poet.

She did more. She lent more than a hand in bringing out the quarterly issues of the *Criterion* (with help from Eliot's able assistant, Irene Pearl Fassett, whose governess had been none other than Vivienne). Vivienne claimed to Pound that she wrote almost all of one issue in the spring of 1924 – except the good bits, she added modestly. After his day at the bank Eliot had only evening hours to produce a journal. To do this alone was a farce to make one laugh, he said, 'if any Eliot could ever laugh'. It made sense for Vivienne to undertake the business side. She could be professional, as when she writes to one of their contributors, Schiff, about the sketches they both were writing that year and which each hopes to collect as a book. Where Schiff, she points out, was writing each piece from the point of view of a different person involved, hers were to be from the point of view of an intimate outsider, someone who does not participate.

There was an unexpected advantage to Vivienne when Eliot moved from the bank to join Faber & Gwyer in September 1925, bringing with him the *Criterion*. Geoffrey Faber wanted it to be more a 'fireside' journal than a highbrow one for the gentlemen's clubs. Vivienne's domestic sketches, sometimes with Eliot collaborating, fitted the idea. Her edgy, ironic slices of life, with mismatched couples trying to go on, are candid in the manner of Katherine Mansfield. In an unpublished fragment she sums up her wry character, Sybilla, in a way that makes sense of the rebel in Vivienne herself: 'Although she was constantly engaged in acting violent parts, or simulating various & definite characteristics, inwardly she had invariably rebelled from taking the cues offered to her by tedious & only half conscious performers – because it was this that she feared & dreaded . . . & she would take the most fantastic courses to preserve herself from being thrust into such a position.'

Vivienne applies this to her mother-in-law when Charlotte Eliot visited London once more in 1924. Another story, 'Au Revoir', describes a farewell call when the 'old lady of eighty' did not face the fact that she would never see Sybilla and her son again. In Sybilla's pitiless view 'everything must be faced, & what was more, slapped in the face – to show one was not afraid of it & knew it for what it was'.

Eliot did not publish 'Au Revoir' but did praise Vivienne's new literary voice. It's a direct transmission of her spoken voice. Years later, the editor of her stories, Ann Pasternak Slater, would suggest that 'the dispassionately observed subjectivity' precedes that of Sylvia Plath in *The Bell Jar*. Eliot published a number of Vivienne's stories in 1924–5 under various pseudonyms, all with the initials FM. Why, then, is this not a history of two writers who live fruitfully together, coping with occasional illness, as Virginia and Leonard Woolf did? The wish to emulate the success of their marriage is why Eliot went to talk over his problems with Leonard Woolf, whom he recognised to be 'a good man'. Leonard's advice was practical, to do with choice of doctors, warning the Eliots off a brusque leading man, Sir Henry Head. (After a consultation back in 1913, Virginia Woolf had attempted suicide.)

Eliot confided more darkly in John Middleton Murry. A certain Dr Marten, a German, had encouraged Vivienne to look back into her past. 'It paralyses action,' Eliot said, for her to dwell on 'the damage that people have done her (and I am not the least important of them).' His confession to Murry is as eloquently introspective and tormented as a Shakespearian soliloquy, as he looks back on what the relationship with Vivienne has done to them both.

In the last ten years – gradually, but deliberately – I have made myself into a *machine*. I have done it deliberately – in order to endure, in order not to feel – *but it has killed* V . . . I hope to become less of a machine – but yet I am frightened – because I don't know what it will do to me – and to V. – should I come alive again. I have deliberately killed my senses– I have deliberately died in order to go on with the outward form of living – This I did in 1915. What will happen if I live again? 'I am I* but with what feelings, with what results to others – Have I the right to be I – But the dilemma – to kill another person by being dead, or to kill them by being alive? Is it best to make oneself a machine, and kill them by not giving nourishment, or to be alive and kill them by wanting something that one cannot get from that person? Does it happen that two persons' lives are absolutely hostile? Is it true that sometimes one can only live by another's dying?

Bringing in his desire for another to whom he would give 'life', he does not explain what we know about Emily Hale:

... Is there a way in which I can lay down my life and gain it? ... Can I exorcise this desire for what I cannot have, for someone I cannot see, and give to her, life, and save my soul? ...

Murry advised Eliot in no uncertain terms. He must come alive again. 'You have done a great wrong to yourself, and a great wrong has been done to her ... What you choose to do *for* her, you must do with all yourself; what you refuse to do for her, you must refuse with all yourself.'

Eliot felt he had yet to drive his guilt home to Murry, a feeling he had expressed most painfully in his poem about the eyes of judgement. 'I know I have killed <u>her</u>. And this terrible sense of the most subtle form of <u>guilt</u> is itself paralysing and deadening ... I give her nothing to live for, I have blocked every outlet.'

In order to give her a first-class outlet, the following month, May 1925, Eliot submitted her 'amazingly brilliant and humorous and horrible' story, 'The Paralysed Woman', to the *Dial* in New York. Under her real name, the story was sent to the assistant editor, Ellen Thayer, sister of Lucy and cousin to Scofield. The editor, the poet Marianne

---

* Richard III in Act V, scene iii of Shakespeare's play, accepting his deeds.

Moore, rejected 'The Paralysed Woman' early in June and Eliot responded with rage on the grounds that he had supported Moore as a poet: 'I have championed you in the face of derision and indifference, and I had the right to expect better treatment from you.'

Vivienne then topped up the rage by alleging abuse. Her story, as relayed to Pound, was that, at her doctor's consulting rooms, Lucy Thayer '[k]nelt down beside me and asked me if I loved her, & made love. I could not get at anyone to help me & so nearly went mad. Helpless. Not dressed. Alone … Spouse [Eliot] cursed out Ellen and Marrrriannnne & Lucy.' Eliot banned Lucy from coming to their home. But this seems not what Vivienne really wanted, because eighteen months later Lucy was back, staying amicably with the Eliots.

The only residue of this scene was Vivienne's line about Lucy as abusive lover: 'she has done me in'. In 1925–6 Eliot appropriated it for his play *Sweeney Agonistes*, when Sweeney justifies destroying a woman in a Lysol bath: 'Any man has to, needs to, wants to / Once in a lifetime, do a girl in.'

In this union, two self-dramatists, given to fantasy, fought each other while preserving some mutual support. Then Vivienne's trust in her husband's support dropped away sharply in November–December 1925 when she was persuaded to enter nursing homes, first at Elmsleigh, near Southampton. Initially she was calm and sent a rational letter to her husband, thinking about wages for Ellen Kellond (who was leaving to marry), and care for her cat, Lulu. She says sorry for driving him mad. In the margin of the letter she asks him to let her doctor know that their married life had been 'good', to contradict a false impression amongst the staff. Eliot was to write and say 'the truth, that we have had sexual relations'.*

At the next nursing home, the Stanboroughs in Watford, she detected a collusion, initiated by her husband, to keep her from troubling him. She thought that his agents – a doctor called Hubert

---

* Crossed out.

Higgins and a nurse – were obeying his signals (conveyed through chill tones) to undermine her position. At Elmsleigh she had been treated as inferior to what she knew herself to be; her attendants felt licensed, it seemed, to disparage her hoarse voice and her common-ness, as though she were unfit to be the wife of so fine a gentleman. She felt at their mercy.

Vivienne called on the Schiffs to witness her unwilling imprison-ment in Watford. She threatened suicide in letters to Ellen Kellond and to Dr Higgins, who had been assigned the task of reporting to her husband while he was abroad. The suicide threats meant that a night nurse had to stay in Vivienne's room.

While Dr Higgins monitored Vivienne, he was treating Eliot's mental health, assuring him that his symptoms came from his 'imprisonment', hyping it as an 'oubliette', a dungeon with a hole in the ceiling, dark and narrow to increase mental torture as the prisoner died. Vivienne was indeed under the control of a doctor who favoured her husband.

He, also on the edge of breakdown, lay low in La Turbie in the Alpes-Maritimes. Vivienne was not given his address, though he did inform 'Wee' of his intention to spend a last few days with Pound, who had settled in Rapallo, south of Genoa, on the west coast of Italy. Pound made a mistake when he tried to assure Vivienne that Eliot arrived looking fit, as Vivienne took this to mean she had been duped into believing her husband was about to collapse.

When he returned, according to plan, he found Vivienne affec-tionate. His tone made light of her ructions, reporting to Pound they were, as expected, mere 'moonshine'. He acted swiftly to smooth over the situation with friends, fearing they believed Vivienne (as recalled to Mary Trevelyan many years later).

Though the Eliots were reunited, all was not well at 9 Clarence Gate Gardens over Christmas and the New Year of 1926. Vivienne was threatening to sue her husband for putting her away. If she carried this out, it would mean a scandal. Vivienne, who had not physically hurt herself or anyone else, had habeas corpus on her side.

In the dim underworld of the imagination, Eliot's bogey of himself as killer looked to two murderous men in novels. One was Bill Sikes in *Oliver Twist*, who murders his partner Nancy, and the other was Kurtz, the colonial exploiter in *Heart of Darkness*. 'Kill the brutes' is his mad mantra in the Belgian Congo, covered by high-toned talk.

Dickens introduced the guilt-haunted Sikes into his public readings in the last two years of his life, between 1868 and his death in 1870. To perform this murder became for him a kind of addiction. His performance was hugely popular – rock-star popular, unprecedented in history – and, each time, when he came to an end, the audience would be silent. Afterwards, Dickens himself was silent. Spent, he would lie on the sofa in his dressing room. Then he'd do it again, night after night, city after city, across the British Isles and America. He was bent on feeling that violence. His pulse would go up from 72 to 112. He liked to joke about his own 'murderous instincts', as though the fictional violence came from himself.

Like Dickens before him, Eliot tries to induce his audience, each person there, to acknowledge in his secret self a capacity for violence, in the same way that Kurtz faces up to the horror of savagery in himself and all men beneath a veneer of civility. Kurtz has this insight as he confronts mortality. The report, 'Mistah Kurtz – he dead', is the epigraph to 'The Hollow Men' (one of the last touches to this poem, which Eliot completed and published in November 1925).

It was Eliot's second use of an epigraph from *Heart of Darkness*. The first, the original epigraph to *The Waste Land*, had been 'The horror! the horror!' The reader is persuaded to bear witness, like Conrad's fictional counterpart returned to Europe and moving through a sepulchral city, maddened by his encounter with what lurks in men's hearts: 'I daresay,' he mutters, 'I was not very well at that time.' To *see* brings on mental breakdown.

In Eliot's play horror and guilt function in the repetitive manner of nightmare, what the killer Sikes undergoes in *Oliver Twist*. As Sikes flees, the eyes of his ghostly victim follow and fix upon him. Eliot replays a victim's eyes in preceding poems of the early to mid-twenties. The accusing eyes in a face that 'sweats with tears' loom in the dark of night and take the poet to the brink-of-hell scenes in 'The Hollow Men' and then into the guilt in *Sweeney Agonistes*.

The play, Eliot's first, drafted in 1925–6, transforms a loutish Sweeney into a moral being. Here the poet resurrects the 'ape-neck' lout in 'Sweeney Erect' and again in *The Waste Land*, where Sweeney is once more on his jolly way to Mrs Porter's brothel. Sweeney, wielding a razor, is a variety of Columbo: to 'straddle' a female is an act of aggression. Sweeney disproves an idealised notion of the human species, for which the poem blames Emerson, the philosopher and one-time Unitarian minister who had hailed the Unitarian church that Eliot's New England grandfather established on the frontier. But then, Sweeney 'Erect', turns into Sweeney 'Agonistes', a character with the dimensions of Milton's Samson. It's an awakening to a moral order. The hot breath of violence and guilt come close as Sweeney relates a murder. The killer's guilt is a daily inescapable hell. He's pursued by 'the hoo-ha's', a joke that's not really a joke.

What comes over as an experimental Jazz Age drama with syncopated beats is a sermon of sorts with retribution brought home, knocking at the soul's door – the relentless 'KNOCK KNOCK' on and on, nine KNOCKS, are the last words of a sermon, so that although Eliot called the play unfinished, it takes the audience, together with the sinner, to a terrifying climax like the terror the Puritan divines used to batter into congregants in their ominous jeremiads.

While Eliot conceived and wrote these scenes, the Eliots themselves were moving into a state of extremity. Vivienne sensed a 'menace', and tried to explain this to John Middleton Murry:

It is my fear of Tom . . . His presence, still terribly longed for, gives me a feeling of such utter isolation. *I can't tell you.* Each time I see him it is a shock.

And whenever he speaks to me, about himself, & his interests, work, thoughts, desires, I know so frightfully that *I simply do not understand* him, that sometimes when I am tired or overwrought, it gives me the sensation that he is mad. Sometimes that he is mad or else that he is most *frightfully* & subtly *wicked* and *dangerous* . . . That I must either somehow cut free & run, run, run . . . Or else that I shall . . . be stifled to death.

The need to run comes into Vivienne's poem 'perque domos ditis vacuas' ('through the empty halls of Dis', the Underworld, from Virgil):

> *It was after the acrobats*
> *And I left my box*
> *And ran along the corridor*
> *Fast*
> *Because I wanted to get into the air into the air*
> *And in the suffused light of the empty corridor*
> *And in the stale air and soft suffused light of the corridor*
> *In the deathly airlessness of the silent corridor*
> *I met my own eyes*
> *In another face.*

This poem is so like Eliot that it could be a hybrid, except that the panic is Vivienne's. The repetitions, like Eliot's, convey a mind locked in nagging thoughts.

In the spring of 1926 Eliot and Vivienne joined Henry Eliot and his new wife Theresa on their honeymoon tour of the Continent. Vivienne became increasingly anxious, fearing a plot against her. At the railway station in Milan, at seven in the morning, she implored strangers to rescue her from a police pursuit. She was hearing voices, hallucinating, convinced she was on the brink of death.

The honeymooners were on their way to Nice. The two couples parted in Milan and Eliot took his wife north to Freiburg – a secret destination – to consult Dr Marten, who had treated Vivienne before, in London. Her husband took the view that her paranoia was caused by drugs – she was 'soaked in bromides', he said, and drugs have remained a common explanation of Vivienne's downfall – but paranoia doesn't mean there is no grain of truth. The pursuit she fancied sounds like a variation on the terror that beset her in the Stanboroughs six months before: she'd felt trapped by the force of authority (the doctor she'd feared there, and the German doctor she was about to see).

In Freiburg, Dr Marten's treatment proved a disaster. Not only did he put Vivienne on his standard starvation diet, he ventured on psychoanalysis with its narrative of damage. Vivienne now became so distrustful that her husband thought it better to remove himself. He left Vivienne with Pound and his wife Dorothy in Paris while he returned to work in London. But Vivienne remained so terrified that she had to sleep on the floor of the Pounds' room. The Pounds found the situation too far gone. Vivienne tried to kill herself by swallowing 'poison' (her word). It's not known what the substance was or how she obtained it. Quite possibly Vivienne had chloral to hand and overdosed.

Pound helped to place Vivienne in the Sanatorium de la Malmaison about ten kilometres west of Paris, at Rueil. It was famously humane and enlightened. Henri Claude, Vivienne's doctor, was Professor of Psychiatry at the University of Paris and soon to be elected to the Académie de Médecine. He kept her in a special room for suicidal patients, watched day and night. High-level medical opinion took her alarm seriously. Eliot commuted from London but neither he nor his wife's parents were permitted at first to see her.

The horror that took Vivienne over from late May to early June 1926 revives the 'injured bride' who had appeared in Eliot's Poe-like 'Elegy'. Vivienne's mounting feverishness is reminiscent not only of Poe's fictional bride Ligeia but, even more perhaps, of the Ushers in the strangest of Poe's horror tales. 'The Fall of the House of Usher' looks into a fatal link between a man and a woman who, twinned, share a state of terminal extremity. Later, Vivienne was to recall their mental affinity in an uncanny claim: 'As to Tom's mind, I *am* his mind.'

The extremity and terror in this marriage was mutual. If Vivienne had reason to fear Eliot, he feared her in turn, as his mother had observed when she saw them together in 1921.

Murry advised Vivienne to keep calm and quiet.

'I managed to for that day, but you know, I *can't*,' she replied from Malmaison. 'I can't keep calm & quiet John. It's no use,' she went on. 'You know I love Tom in a way that destroys us both. And it is *all* my life. Nothing remains.'

She divined quite accurately what was in her husband's mind. Later, in August 1927, he conveyed an intent to his brother: he was waiting for Vivienne either to make a more lethal attempt on her life – to be seen to have injured herself – or else to commit some public offence that would make her committal feasible.

However patiently devoted he seemed, he admitted 'the kink in my brain' that made life 'an unremitting strain' and was 'at the bottom of a good many things about me that you object to'. Eliot had regarded his aboulia as a lifelong 'emotional derangement'. Vivienne was not the sole cause of trouble; she was a co-sufferer. When their 'kinks' competed, she had one advantage. Losing face did not concern her. Her flagrant loss of control challenged Eliot's sense of fitness.

The experts at Malmaison found no insanity in Vivienne Eliot; the persecution, what she foresaw, they said, was a projection of emotional anguish. Her husband accepted he had some part in this. Long ago he had owned to 'a great many mistakes, which are largely the cause of her present catastrophic state of health'.

Eliot too became a patient at Malmaison for a three-week cure in August 1926, in part to treat his addictions to whisky and smoking. Later, he confided to Emily Hale that he had been 'in a state of dark dry death'. He was housed separately from his wife, but her doctors meant to test how she might react to his presence.

Vivienne remained uncertain. She wrote to Osbert Sitwell,

asking him to advise her whether or not to return to her husband. She told him that she had been in a 'scandal', which would bring disgrace upon him. For Vivienne this action was of a piece with her letters to the Schiffs and Murry, calling for help. These friends, who were also Eliot's friends, were in an impossible position because they felt called upon to adjudicate in a situation wholly beyond them. She also commanded the Sitwells not to reveal to Eliot that she was seeking their advice. Assuming Eliot would want his freedom, they did not reply. Vivienne took their silence to heart and this ended the Eliots' friendship with the mystified Sitwells. For Eliot sided with Vivienne as he unfailingly did when his wife confronted others.

After Eliot's treatment, he and Vivienne (who had responded well to kindness at Malmaison) tried out a reunion under medical supervision at another sanatorium, Divonne-les-Bains, in the mountains near Geneva. They felt dismal, blaming the place, but had to bear the stress of being together. Another English patient, the writer Robert Sencourt, never forgot his sight of Vivienne walking alone along a woodland path, her hair dank, her face blotched and her expression acutely sad.

Vivienne's accomplished stories, some published in 1924 and 1925, some like the 'Paralysed Woman' unpublished, had turned her imagination to effect. She saw this as a long-clogged fount spurting. So why did it dry up? One reason could be simple: the presence of a third person in the marriage.

Until Eliot's letters to Emily Hale were released in 2020 no one could fully know the force of his memory of her. 'I remember the hyacinth garden.' That recollection in *The Waste Land* silenced, cancelled in the manuscript, persisted, shutting off the voice of the unloved wife. At what Eliot called the blackest moment of his life, this memory was renewed not only as a figure from his past but for the future. It came to him that an alternative to marital hell could be heavenly perfection as the measure for all things: the renewal of a frame of mind to be found in the twelfth and thirteenth centuries – at its finest in Dante's *New Life*, the *Vita Nuova*, a spiritual autobiography of Dante's youth, drawing on poems he wrote during the decade before completing it in 1294. It was composed in memory of an elevating love that could remake a man and outlast life itself. In the last chapter Dante hopes to put forward 'what has not before been written of any woman'.

Eliot's new poetry was about to turn from the promiscuous Fresca, the abused women and the agitated wife of *The Waste Land*, and fix instead on a rarer 'Lady' destined to watch over his 'turning' or conversion. He meant to write 'my Hymn to the Virgin', the earliest idea for a 'Salutation' to a 'Lady', like the salutation of Dante and Beatrice in the *Vita Nuova*. On 21 August 1926 Eliot, while still at Malmaison, mentioned his forthcoming 'Hymn' to Marguerite Caetani, née Margaret Chapin, an American he called 'cousin', who was married to an Italian prince. She had founded a literary journal, *Commerce*, to which Eliot contributed. He told her that he had not managed to write this poem as yet. When eventually he did so, it was infused with a private dream of what Emily Hale might be to him.

After six years at Downer, in 1927 Hale was appointed assistant professor at a salary of $1,000 a year. She was also granted half a year's leave of absence. That spring she surprised Eliot with a letter from Florence, the city of Beatrice. It gave him a lift as he walked around Russell Square with a friend. Eliot did not mention her name, identifying her only as a 'girl' from Boston he had not heard from for years.

His confidant that day was the Reverend William Force Stead, a fellow-American, also from St Louis and coping with a disturbed wife. Stead had been ordained in the Church of England and encouraged Eliot's conversion. The priest had drawn Eliot's attention to Lancelot Andrewes in the seventeenth century, whose 'pure', 'medieval' temper did not stir the emotions so much as stress a resolute will to holiness. The poems of Eliot's mother tracing the ordeals of Catholics had prepared the way for her son's attachment to Anglo-Catholicism. As a Unitarian, he had not been baptised in the name of the Trinity, so Stead agreed to baptise him anew in his own village of Finstock in Oxfordshire. This took place on Wednesday 29 June 1927. The doors of Finstock Church were closed to spectators and Stead poured the water of regeneration over his head. Next morning he was confirmed as an Anglican. For him it meant more than commitment. It augured transformation. Later that year he addressed a Beatrice figure, the 'Lady' of his poem 'Salutation', asking her to witness the dismemberment of the person he had been.

By then Emily Hale, turning thirty-six, was back in Milwaukee, teaching, acting and putting on plays. Far from her New England milieu, her single life was lonely. That year a lesbian pupil called Olga became infatuated, but her teacher did not respond (though she kept Olga's letters fantasising about 'Miss Hale' in bed in her silk nightgown with gold sleeves). She could not have conceived the drama in store for her: a famous man thousands of miles away, who was planning to love her in the medieval manner.

10

'ROSE OF MEMORY'

Emily Hale spent the summer of 1930 in England. She attended the Shaw festival at Great Malvern and spoke on American poetry at the Lyceum Club in London. She also addressed the American Women's Club.

In September she stayed with her aunt and uncle at a guesthouse called Calendar's on Sheep Street in the sloping Cotswold town of Burford. This is where Eliot wrote to 'Emily' in a helpful, not personal manner, his use of her first name the only sign that she was an old friend. He was answering her request for advice on Modern poetry in view of her series of lectures to be held over the winter of 1930–1 at the Commander Hotel in Cambridge, Massachusetts. Eliot's letter appears to offer no more than the civility of his myriad letters to people with claims on his attention. But later that month came a moment when Emily was admitted to an intimacy the poet had allowed no one else.

Just before, Emily's oldest friend, Margaret Farrand, met Eliot. The two were born in East Orange, New Jersey. Margaret studied at Smith College, joined the American Red Cross when her country entered the war and then wrote for various papers. She was a

Emily Hale speaking at the American Women's Club, London, 1930.

wealthy, witty, independent woman, almost forty when, in 1930, she married Willard Thorp and settled with him in Princeton. Both were academics: Margaret had been an assistant professor at Smith during the twenties and studied for a doctorate at Yale; Professor Thorp, eight years younger, had taught literature at Princeton since 1926.

Eliot had received the new-married Thorps in a small reception room at Faber & Faber. Margaret recorded her impression: 'Mr Eliot appears tall, grey-suited with black mourning band & tie [in mourning for his mother, who had died the year before]. His face is a little heavy, the eyes underlined and tired. His hair is thin.' He mopped the sweat running down his brow with 'a sopping hand-kerchief' on the hottest day that summer.

Their talk was about having to accept absurdly unwelcome

gifts and his anecdotes presented an image of kindly politeness, downplayed with humour. 'He has a slow, deliberate way of talking, will not leave off an idea until it is quite finished. Several times we interrupted, thinking it was time for us to take the ball; but no, he had still a sentence or a paragraph unsaid.' His carefully measured speech and joking preserved his distance from people; even the folksy Uncle Remus lingo with Pound was a performance that kept intimacy at bay. He was less distant with confident women, Mary Hutchinson, Virginia Woolf and Lady Ottoline Morrell, who offered the domestic affection Eliot missed. But even with friendly Englishwomen, Eliot did not lower his guard in the way he was about to do with Emily.

At the very last moment before her return to Boston (in late September or at the start of October) Eliot invited her to a tea party he and Vivienne held at 68 Clarence Gate Gardens (another of their succession of flats in this Edwardian block around the corner from the Baker Street haunt of Sherlock Holmes – a character Eliot liked to imitate). Emily was staying close by, within walking distance, at Ford's Hotel on Manchester Street. Was this move a belated impulse? It would be in character to leave a meeting too late for action, with Emily poised to sail away across the ocean. Just then, on 25 September, he had published a homesick poem, *Marina*, his favourite of all the poems he had written so far. It's about a crossing to the grey rocks of the Maine shore, the granite islands with the scent of pine and bird calls, where a long-lost woman waits to greet the battered voyager.

The sight of her dazed him. Emily, now thirty-nine, was smartly turned out in a hat and a 'very pretty' dress. He told her later he had to struggle to maintain the polite detachment of his public face. From the moment that Emily came into the room, Eliot felt 'something very strong and deep' between them so that everyone else there seemed 'quite unreal'.

Overwhelmed by emotion, he nearly spilt his tea. It was the same response as the evening they had met in Eccleston Square. In the flesh another idealised woman might have dissipated a poetic memory; Emily validated it. Amongst strangers at this English gathering she appeared to triumph with 'an unusual spiritual maturity'. It made her 'more radiantly beautiful'.

He managed to conceal signs of agitation from an unsuspecting Vivienne, who had a similar response to Emily. Vivienne, he told her afterwards, had liked her 'to the point of infatuation!'

After she sailed, he posted a handwritten letter (more private than his customary typed letters) from his office in Russell Square to her Boston address, 41 Brimmer Street.

'I am heartily sorry every day & every night of my life for my mistake & fault', he wrote, 'and for the ruin it has made: but I am not sorry for loving and adoring you, for it has given me the very best that I have had in my life.' This third declaration assured her of intentions 'as pure & unseeking as any love can be'.

He revealed Emily's part in his struggle for purity of spirit, his move towards faith. 'It has become to me a part of the Love which "overcomes the world" and in the midst of agony a deep peace & resignation springs – "not as the world giveth" – but the peace of God. Of course there were many concurrent paths leading me to the Altar – but I doubt whether I should have arrived but for you. And now there is no need to explain "Ash Wednesday" to you. No one else will ever understand it.'

In *Ash Wednesday*, the poem he had published earlier that year, he wrote:

> *Lady of silences*
> *Calm and distressed*
> *Torn and most whole*
> *Rose of memory . . .*

He invites Emily to read him personally, beckoning her into his secret. It has the effect of a startlingly intimate whisper behind his hand.

Rose of memory
Rose of forgetfulness . . .

Was the forgetfulness hers? His appeal to their past was capped by another: he offers her presence a tender touch. At the tea, he tells her in his letter, he'd detected signs of pain she had gone through since last they met, a sadness that made him want to stroke her forehead. As the Rose had captivated a sleeping girl with his leaps, turns and parting touch to her face, so Eliot exercised an enthralling art. He approached Emily first in poetry; then then by letter.

At the age of forty-two, what Eliot calls his 'first love-letter' asks her to trust an enduring passion. What he felt on seeing her now was not sudden; it had been there always. He assures her further that if she knew 'what pages and pages of tenderness I am <u>not</u> writing now, I think you <u>would</u> trust me'.

A visionary prospect lies behind Eliot's post-conversion address to Emily Hale, beginning with *Ash Wednesday*. In his sights was 'the multifoliate rose' of Dante's *Paradiso*. Dante relates how 'Beatrice drew me . . . into the yellow glow of the eternal rose [*la rosa sempiterna*], that rises layer on layer, and exudes the perfume of praise.' For Eliot, this rose had flashed into sight in 1924–5 as 'The hope only / Of empty men' in 'The Hollow Men'. Such a man may glimpse the rose formation of the blessed on the highest level of paradise, where each of its thousand petals is a soul who sits in the divine light. Dante, led by the shade of Beatrice, is granted this pre-vision, and once she has shown heaven to him, she takes her place amongst the rose-petals.

How far did Emily Hale see into the particular nature of the love on offer, and take in Eliot's need as a poet to fly ever higher? Did she notice that his address to her as 'Lady' in his first letter is identical with an address to 'Lady' in *Ash Wednesday*? 'Salutation' was the first section of that poem to be written. The title, later cut, looks back to Dante's salutation of the still-living Beatrice ('the Lady of the salutation') when, aged eighteen, after adoring her from afar for nine years, he met her on the Ponte Vecchio in Florence one

May morning in 1283. Dante's *La Vita Nuova*, eleven years on, recalls his dazed joy. When Eliot declares to Emily how dazed he feels on beholding her in person, he recovers this emotion.

Dante is secretive about his love. To conceal it, he takes up with a 'screen' lady, though it's no more than a charade. When he encounters Beatrice again, she's disengaged by his apparent defection. On the verge of collapse, he tries to regain her gaze, hoping to be healed. There follows a declaration that Eliot quoted in a lecture on Dantean love in 1926: 'The end and aim of my Love was the salutation of that lady ... wherein alone I found the beatitude which is the goal of desire.'

A greeting from Beatrice acts on Dante like a sign from on high. Eliot's 'Salutation' speaks to a 'Lady' who is to watch over a penitent as he discards his warped self. Before her, he lies dismembered. The bones want this; relieved of the flesh, they 'chirp' as though it had been a burden. Emily Hale would not have known that this scene harks back to the destruction of the body, watched by a girl in the first stanza of 'The Love Song of St Sebastian', written as Eliot had sailed for Europe after their parting. Unknown to her also was an incident in Rome in 1926 when Eliot had fallen on his knees before Michelangelo's *Pietà*, the Virgin gazing down on the martyred body of Jesus.

'Salutation' appeared in December 1927; soon after, the religious scenario was cast into doubt: with Vivienne's return from another long stay in the sanatorium in February 1928, the design alters. First must come the convert's effort to 'turn' in all honesty, because he finds himself too far from where he needs to be. 'Salutation' (minus its title) then became the second part of *Ash Wednesday*, and the next part is a purgatorial sequence, climbing a stair and fighting off the devil within.

Partway up, the climber recalls a woman's sweet brown hair blown over her mouth. The penitential ordeal requires him to see and renounce natural love in favour of a disembodied love, close to worship. The role Eliot assigned Emily is spelt out in *Ash Wednesday* just before his letters to her began: 'Redeem / The unread vision in the higher dream'. The dream-lady bends her head in agreement to the Dantean plea to take pity (*'Sovegna vos'*) on a man putting himself through fire as penance for lust.

In the higher reaches of the climb, the Lady is positioned to be remote, her body 'veiled' and 'sheathed'; she wears Mary's colours, blue and white, and takes on the character of the Virgin. Here is the fulfilment of the 'Hymn to the Virgin', which Eliot had intended to write while undergoing a cure at the sanatorium in August 1926. As an angelic being, this woman can restore water to the parched ground that once had been *The Waste Land*. In her imagined presence, all the poet had craved comes to pass: 'the fountain sprang up'; the 'sign' appears; and words, unheard, unspoken, are potential tokens of the Word.

It's a faceless as well as silent woman who oversees this destiny: who she is, the reader is not told. She has no name. Yet this unidentified 'Who', with a capital letter, is driving the lines: 'Who walked . . . / Talking of trivial things . . . / Who then made strong the fountains and made fresh the springs'. Eliot's puzzling dedication of *Ash Wednesday* 'To my wife' makes sense only if he was positioning Vivienne to be like Dante's screen lady: a distraction from the poet's love for the unseen 'Who'.

Soon after the publication of the complete poem in 1930, A. L. Rowse, a Fellow of All Souls, expressed his disappointment to Eliot that *Ash Wednesday* did not reach a promised land. Eliot agreed. He was disappointed himself, he said. He believed the penitent was stalled in the act of conversion and Eliot told Rowse that he himself had still a long way to go. A poet has to be honest 'about the stage one has got to and really knows'. The promised land remained a remote possibility that would take, he judged, another ten or fifteen years. What if his Beatrice figure was too 'withdrawn' to offer access to his promised land? He needed her closer contact.

*

There was a long pause before Emily responded. Might she back off as she had from two previous declarations?

Three days after Eliot mailed his love-letter, he sent another in his formal voice. On 6 October he tells Emily that he is sending a few useful books on Modernism. His wish is merely that she had a good crossing. It was as though he were offering an alternative, a safety net: to continue as old friends.

Emily took time to consider. To be cast as a 'Lady of silences' meant a role without a script. Her prime gift was a resonant onstage voice; her own purpose was to pursue a theatre career. In Milwaukee she had put on about five productions a year, including Shakespeare each summer in the woods behind the college. In 1929 she had staged the balcony scene in *Romeo and Juliet*, playing Juliet herself, in one of these outdoor productions. After resigning her post at the end of that academic year, she'd resolved to lecture on American and European theatre, and to give dramatic recitals and programmes of American and foreign poetry while living for extended periods in Back Bay as a companion to a benevolent and wealthy Bostonian called Mary Lee Ware.

During the preceding summer, she had travelled abroad with Margaret Farrand, taking in theatre developments in Germany, France and England. Emily was especially taken with Irish drama in reaction against the dominance of the Abbey Theatre. She was alerted to Seán O'Casey, to a new experimental theatre in Limerick, and to the Gate Theatre in Dublin, newly set up in 1928 to put on modern plays. Her most stimulating experience was to speak to the Gate's founder, Micheál Mac Liammóir, in his dressing-room. J. J. Hayes, theatre critic for the *Irish Times* and *New York Times,* urged her to put on Irish plays in the US.

When Emily re-encountered Eliot in the late summer of 1930, she was not short of parts for the following year, and not really in need of a silent role as a poet's muse. And like his mother and brother, she was not all that taken with his poems. Her notes for a lecture characterise his work as 'bitter'. She respected him as an authority on Modernism and pitied his unhappiness.

Eliot did not hear from her for a whole month. Back and forth, London to Boston, Boston to London, each sea passage took about a week. It means that Emily Hale took at least two weeks to consider what to do. At last, on 1 November, her reply came, addressed to his Faber office.

She wished, she said, to make him 'perfectly happy'.

Her restrained generosity was exactly right. Whatever this response meant to her, it accorded with the love Eliot had in mind. In the thirteenth century it was the fashion to cherish love for a lady too superior, too immured behind walls, too distant to be available. Her part was to respond to feeling with delicacy, pity and kindness. It was irrelevant to Dante that he was married to Gemma Donati. Who she was or what she felt didn't come into it. Nor the probability that Beatrice had married a banker called Portinari. The higher love of a pilgrim soul had to do with another order of being moving towards a life to come; it had everything to do with poetry close to prayer, fixed on awe and reverence. Dante singled out Beatrice as bearer of divine love. All that mattered was that she inclined to his salutation as she passed on the Ponte Vecchio.

In Eliot's 1929 essay on Dante, he warns that this love is remote from ours. As a sop to the Modern mind, he offers the word 'sublimation' as the closest equivalent. But that once-modish term is too pat. Nor does it convey the medieval regard for chastity.

The manner of courtly love, cultivated by French troubadours, was elevated by Dante into worship. This love did not exist outside the imagination. It had its outlet in poetry or song; its purpose was art, not action. It was not directed towards marriage; the underlying situation was in fact adulterous. That this love could never be consummated made it more, not less, intense.

Emily Hale's kindness freed Eliot to uncover more fully in an exultant second letter, this time typed (as were almost all subsequent letters). He promised Emily privacy – he would keep no carbons – writing to her on 3 November from his cream-coloured top-floor office, overlooking Woburn Square and Gordon Square beyond.

His letter calls hers 'saintly' and pictures for her his preparedness with scenes of prayer, communion and on Friday, the day before the letter arrived, a confession to his spiritual director, Fr Francis Underhill, who was in charge of Grosvenor Chapel in Mayfair. Fr Underhill had reassured him that it was not wrong 'to cherish' the image of Emily; it was 'a gift of God' to help his spiritual progress and alleviate his tribulations. His happiness, beyond anything he had known, was elevated, 'a kind of supernatural ecstasy'. Looking back, he sees his love for Emily had been 'the one great thing' in his life, and looking ahead, he expects to depend upon her 'utterly' as 'a friend, and as long as you are in the world I shall want to stay here too'.

Endearingly, he tells her he is 'capable of knowing you ... as no one else can – I <u>do</u> appreciate spirituality when I meet it, and by that word I mean something very rare and precious indeed. And I like to believe that I am capable of more intense and deep devotion to one person than are most men.'

Most tellingly, the letter ends with the revelations we already know about specific lines and poems she had inspired. It is here that he asks her to 're-read the hyacinth lines in The Waste Land Part I, and the lines toward the very end beginning "friend, blood shaking my heart [/ The awful daring of a moment's surrender / Which an age of prudence can never retract / By this and this only I* have existed ...]" and compare them with Pipit on the one hand and Ash Wednesday on the other, and see if they do not convince you that my love for you has steadily grown into something finer and finer. And I shall always write primarily for you.'

*

---

* TSE adds '(where <u>we</u> means privately of course <u>I</u>)'. I have inserted 'I' in place of 'we' to convey how he intends EH to read the line.

Without Hale's letters there's no knowing how far she took in the role on offer, but her assent gave rise to a tidal wave of love-letters. It swells with the unanswered question she had asked in Eccleston Square. Eliot was still unwilling to answer, 'because it involves unnecessary and painful detail', and this avoidance worried her.

It's not hard to see why. Once again, Eliot was inviting her to hear and respond without offering any distinct proposal. As a single woman, she had to care for herself. In Milwaukee there had been at first no official recognition for her work in drama. It was regarded as a side-line, at her own pleasure. Without the credentials for a permanent post, she had presided over the dormitories at Downer and had to wait six years before she was appointed to a teaching post. All those years she had stuck it out far from home. Her letters to friends never prevented a loneliness that seems to have been part of her – possibly because in early childhood her mother had been removed. Her tie to her aunt was based on respect and gratitude for invitations to stay for extended periods, and in time she took on a role as her helper, keen to please and alert to needs. Her attitude was brave and grateful rather than heartfelt. There was an orphan feeling in her that craved nurture, safety, position.

Did the question Eliot would not answer have to do with his marital status? Separation from Vivienne was an issue long in the air. Vivienne's most constant doctor, a Catholic called Dr Miller, had advised separation, as did Fr Underhill. Lady Ottoline too had ventured to suggest this, presumably after Vivienne, writing from the Sanatorium de la Malmaison in January 1928, had blurted out that her husband 'hates the sight of me'. She had signed herself 'Your outcasted friend'. Whenever Eliot himself brought up separation, Vivienne would not consider it, preferring to put up with his cold devotion. But to Lady Ottoline she gave this warning: 'If you hear of me being murdered don't be surprised!'

When Emily asked if anything could be done to improve his marriage, Eliot made three points. To Emily, as to others, he pictured Vivienne as a dependent child who could not grow up. This was a simplification that overrode a more intricate bond, including the fact that Vivienne's sophisticated stories are filled with adult ennui and hopelessness. Eliot made the further dubious claim that Vivienne, being a child, did not suffer as an adult would. The character of a child-wife served to warn Emily of his unfree position: he could not relinquish this responsibility.

Secondly, he analysed Vivienne's problems, stressing the fact that she had once been jilted, which had put 'a finishing touch' to an inferiority complex 'from years before'. His wife, he believed, did not find their marriage as intolerable as he did because of her capacity for self-deception. Her mind was 'fundamentally dishonest'. She dodged truth, and to force it upon her would kill her.

The third point was an attempt to reassure Emily: he said that Vivienne might have loved him had he been the sort of man who could love her. The implication was that Emily had been and remained the only woman for him.

At or about the time that Eliot had made his first post-conversion confession to Fr Underhill in February 1928, he had resolved on celibacy. Partly this was a continued – and fiercer – effort to control his body, partly a reaction to his fling with Nancy Cunard, and partly it was to underpin his distance from his wife: an alternative to separation. This resolve had coincided with Vivienne's unwelcome decision to return to him after another stint at Malmaison. Celibacy was no longer a matter of inclination; it became a rule. Eliot was attempting to void the marriage as far as possible, with the backing of the church.

Vivienne called his piety 'monastic', and then a dark idea grew on her: what if celibacy were a cover for a mistress? Her suspects were Lady Ottoline and Virginia Woolf. The Eliots had tea with the Woolfs at their house in Tavistock Square on 6 November. Vivienne quivered with suspicion and challenged whatever their hostess said. What appeared as paranoia was in unison with Eliot's 'high emotional fever' (as he described his state to Emily) – a mood Vivienne had never witnessed.

Virginia Woolf, opening a jar of honey from the garden at Rodmell, retaliated to Vivienne's insinuation about her and Eliot by asking if she too kept bees.

Vivienne retorted, 'No, hornets.'

'But where?'

'Under the bed.'

This image of marital torment told against Vivienne. 'Sane to the point of insanity' was Virginia Woolf's report, for of course this scene circulated in Bloomsbury. Famously, she pictured Vivienne as a bag of ferrets around Tom's neck. He was pitied for loyalty to his wife and respected for playing this down. Virginia Woolf saw a man who looked 'leaden and sinister'. From the letters we now know that he actually longed to be rid of his wife – to have her certified, if only English law would permit it. But no one at that time, including Vivienne, knew of his attachment elsewhere.

Something in Eliot's second letter jarred Emily Hale. He was distressed, he replies, 'that my words should have bruised the wings of my dove'. Was it the question of 'wrong' discussed with Fr Underhill, whose reassurance of Eliot might not have reassured Hale? Love might come to Eliot as a gift of God, but neither he nor Fr Underhill, brushing 'wrong' aside, considered her position. Might it be wrong to receive love from a married man – unless he meant to leave his wife?

The other troubling words could have been Eliot's frankness about his nature. Looking back to youth, he regrets his 'immaturity and egotism'. This character dominates his confessional poem 'Animula' (1929), where the child's small soul twists in adolescence:

> Irresolute and selfish, misshapen, lame,
> Unable to fare forward or retreat,
> Fearing the warm reality, the offered good,
> Denying the importunity of the blood,
> Shadow of its own shadows, spectre in its own gloom . . .

To bare his off-putting traits to Emily was intended as a fair warning of what she was taking on. She offered some flaw in return, which he pats down as not blameworthy. He was still 'ecstatically happy with so marvellous a response'. He denies that he 'overrated' her. Eliot sometimes quotes back her words and phrases, and his letters take up issues she raises. And playing into her voice are Eliot's private revelations: first, that his bond with her is a clue to his poetry and, second, that he dates his move towards faith from seeing her in Eccleston Square. He put it to her, 'you have made me'.

During the first period of Hale's correspondence with Eliot, from autumn 1930 until spring 1932, she was trying to fulfil her undertaking to make Eliot happy. But now and then a testy note sounds in his letters. His muse was proving not quite cooperative.

As a man 'living to live' in a time beyond him, Eliot brought up the question of posterity at the outset. His fourth letter, dated 8 December 1930, asks Emily Hale to share his posthumous reputation. He presents the matter diffidently, introduced by 'if': if his name is to last two generations beyond their lifetime, what are they to do with their letters?

His wish for privacy prompted a passing impulse to leave an instruction to Geoffrey Faber, his possible executor, to burn Emily's letters (so far, only three or four, but he foresaw many more) in a locked tin box. But his preferred plan was to deposit them in Oxford's Bodleian Library, with a proviso that they should not be opened for sixty years after his death.

The astonishing speed with which this concern for posterity came up suggests the poet had it already in mind to collect letters to prove a particular woman had been at the heart of his oeuvre, not a figment of the imagination. Though he would change his mind about this, initially it seems to be a plan to amaze the future by flying in the face of his supposed impersonality along with his poems' superstructure of allusion, as proffered in his notes to *The Waste Land*.

This is not to suggest that Emily was not also dear to him in so far as he had cherished her memory and still did cherish her, but clearly the relationship was stranger — on his side — than it has formerly appeared. He planned to obscure Emily Hale to his own generation yet leave letters as tangible proof — and the more letters, the stronger the proof — that a tie of import to his poetry had existed. Was it his way of keeping himself private (and inspired) in his time, yet truly understood by readers long after his death?

At first Emily made nothing of the Bodleian plan, trusting his forethought and expecting he would act on it in due course. Surprisingly, he sped into action and with an urgency that disregarded the closure of the university over New Year until term began in mid-January. Early in January he contacted the Master of University College, Michael Sadler, who earlier had approached Eliot about manuscripts for the Bodleian. Sadler replied by return to say that the Librarian would be pleased to archive Eliot's private papers. At this point Emily Hale hesitated.

It was not what Eliot expected. His voice sharpened. Though he said that he didn't care what people would think of him after he died, his posthumous reputation seems to have mattered so much that, conceivably, it was one motive for initiating the correspondence. It pleased him to find Emily's early letters showing him 'in a rather favourable light'. He urges her, saying he wanted what he owed to her to burst one day upon the world.

On 12 January 1931, three months into their correspondence, Eliot urges her once more. He wishes, he says, to archive her 'beautiful' letters. These are 'the only documents in <u>my</u> possession which cast any light on my life and work'. The future must know 'how very very great is, will be and always was, my debt to <u>you</u>'.

He took it for granted that Emily would be in agreement. It annoyed him to find he was wrong. Something about this troubled her and it's clear that she did not yield to Eliot's intention. For her, writing to him was a gesture of kindness in answer to his plea. When she agreed to correspond, she was not in love but in sympathy, aware of his rarity and grateful for his feeling. But this business of papers was unforeseen.

He had been open about egotism, but had distanced it as the youthful kind – a flaw of the past. But now she sensed the keen edge of his present self-interest, honed by a far-reaching purpose. For this he needed his real-life Lady to testify on paper and permit her 'lovely' letters, with first-hand portraits of him, to be earmarked for the future. He was baffled that she was not entranced by this prospect.

If she did not wish her letters to be preserved, she should have said so, he wrote.

It's a reproach for her present 'stipulation – which you did not make at the time, because I did ask your permission first, and I can prove that – I should never have bothered to make the arrangement at all!'

If she persisted in withholding her side of the correspondence, he went on, 'there will be little to throw any new light whatever'.

There will be so much in existence to give a very false impression of me, and so few clues to the truth. Can I make clear to you my feeling, I wonder. I admit that it is egotistic and perhaps selfish; but is it not natural, when one has had to live in a mask all one's life, to be able to hope that some day people can know the truth, if they want it. I have again and again seen the impression I have made and have longed to be able to cry 'no you all are wrong about me, it isn't like that at all; the truth is perfectly simple and intelligible, and here it is in a few words'. I shall revert to this. But meanwhile be assured that however painful to myself, the decision shall be in your hands. But I hope meanwhile to persuade you to my view.

A month later, Eliot grew impatient: 'what I do not yet understand is what motive of delicacy, modesty or what, is in your mind now, that you should wish your name erased from my history'. If she wished not to be associated with him, there would be no papers for posterity, 'only a blank'. He assured Emily the disclosure would not happen for nearly a hundred years. So far off in the future there would be no feeling about them as people, apart from 'pity for all concerned'. All. That is, not only their two selves. He includes his wife, in case Emily does not want to go down in history as the woman who came between a couple. He wants her to trust that no one in the future will care who she was or what she did. What matters is how people of the future will read his poetry. And this he tried to cover up:

'As for my selfish motive please believe that I care little about posthumous fame.'

The issue came up yet again during 1932 because Emily continued to be wary. He told her that it did 'canker' to feel that his life and work would be misunderstood always. Her acceptance of this tie and response to mentions of her presence in his work, there on the page in black and white, would serve his plan to reignite interest in his writings in time to come.

This posthumous outcome really does not involve her as a person; it's about his poetry, her impact on it. It is consistent with what 'La Figlia che Piange' reveals of an artist's frame of mind. The girl posed as a statue, an image, is what this artist desires more than coming together. Though he likes to fantasise about coming together (as Eliot himself fantasised on waking), he is not bent on union.

Eliot restated his case for preservation on 6 July 1932, declaring Emily's letters were 'testimonies of the most important matter in my life', which should not 'perish altogether'.

In place of an archive, Emily then suggested handing his letters to Willard Thorp for safe keeping.

Eliot replied that she 'may entrust them to Thorp, or to any person who has your confidence'.

Emily pressed further, asking if he would allow Professor Thorp to go through the letters and make 'extracts' that were sufficiently general and impersonal 'to give out'. Almost certainly, the Thorps themselves were having a say behind the scenes.

Eliot took in the fact that Emily was coming to know Willard 'perhaps almost as well as Margaret'. Though he did not exclude Thorp, he put forward an alternative in Geoffrey Faber, said to be collecting Eliot's papers for the Bodleian. He was an Oxford man, long-time bursar of All Souls, and Eliot preferred a colleague who was loyal to him. He went on to undermine Thorp in a veiled way by questioning an assumption that a husband and wife – the Thorps – are the same in a matter of trust.

The issue of preserving their letters was to surface every so often without resolution. At times, unexpressed, it entered Eliot's mind, as when he chose to teach *The Aspern Papers* by Henry James in 1933. Given Eliot's concern for his own papers, it's not surprising that he would return late in his life to this tale of conflict over the posthumous papers of a famed American, a poet called Jeffrey Aspern. On the one side is the woman he had loved, who retains the author's papers as a private possession; on the other, a devotee of Aspern, who makes it his mission to secure the papers. Intense feelings are trained on these papers and the vexed question: who will keep them?

At this time, Eliot reminded Emily they had agreed to write whatever came to mind, charged with authentic emotion and ignoring the fact that other eyes would eventually see their letters. Even so, future readers hover on the far-off horizon.

His private harshness towards others had an outlet in his letters to Emily Hale and led her to protest. Eliot still insisted she must allow him to say exactly what he felt. We may wonder if this too was intended for posterity: a window on his disgust with humanity that, in public, courtesies walled off.

Eliot always agreed with Emily that their relations were 'peculiar'. His tone is impenetrable but certainly not apologetic. On the contrary, he sounds proud to be 'peculiar' and, with exaggerated politeness, he positions Emily in a space that excludes claims: 'all I ask is that Emily should <u>allow</u> me to give myself up to her: without any claim, but only with the great gratitude of self-surrender'. Chivalry leaves her no recourse but to accept a devotion that offers words alone. There's grace in this, a writer's way; as Yeats put it, 'Words alone are certain good.' Yet Yeats, unlike Eliot, can entertain a contrary impulse, if only Maud Gonne, his muse, could love him:

> *I might have thrown poor words away*
> *And been content to live.*

In the case of Eliot and his muse there are two incontrovertible facts a century on: one is that it was Eliot who originated the idea of preservation, held back by Emily Hale. The issue was put on hold with Eliot still hoping, as he'd said, to persuade her to his point of view. This was her first, but not only, divergence from Eliot's masterplan.

The other fact is that, against all odds, including burnt papers, Hale has continued to exist in her own right, alongside the poet's image, and her later papers and actions show this is as she would have wished.

11

ACTOR AND MUSE

Emily Hale's career in theatre took her far from the passivity of a traditional muse. She would have succeeded on the public stage, even Eliot saw, because she was made for it, especially her voice. But he took a low view of theatre people who were given, he told her, to spite and jealousy. On New Year's Day 1931, Eliot disapproved of her latest role in *The Yellow Jacket*, a play opening up Chinese theatrical traditions to an American audience.

'And so you are now . . . to put yellow on your face and slant your eyes and get up as a Chinese Lady[.] Well, well.'

His casual racism did not deter Hale, who performed in the same role a year later, and this time Eliot, having seen the play in the meantime, deplored her stage make-up more strongly on the grounds that this look would not show her beauty 'to advantage!' If she ever sent a photo, 'not in this role please'.

He responded by reinstating her Lady role. 'I lit a little candle praying for you, before the Virgin this morning. Does all that seem fantastic make believe to you?' and he adds, by hand, a phrase from *Ash Wednesday*: 'I don't know how to address you this week – you seem to have withdrawn to contemplation? But always "my Lady".'

Later that year he urged, 'I should like to see you in the role of
Beatrice!' To do him justice, he wanted her to play more articulate
parts, Antigone, Clytemnestra and – best for her, he thought –
Cleopatra. In February he called her 'madonna Olivia', bringing
back to mind her role in *Twelfth Night* in 1914. He sat up at her recollec-
tions of playing Roxane back in 1915, an intellectual Frenchwoman
of the seventeenth century in the verse play *Cyrano de Bergerac*. This
hero has a physical handicap, an enormous nose, which he believes
disqualifies him as a lover, but as a master of words he writes wonderful love-letters on behalf of a friend who is courting Roxane.
She falls in love with those words, and only too late, when Cyrano
is dying, does she realise that the words come from this man, her
true mate. It's understandable why the letter-writing Eliot now
fantasised playing opposite Emily in the role of Cyrano.

He asked her to send him texts of the plays she was in, so as to
imagine her performance. Gradually she brought him to see how
her work in theatre freed her, as he put it, from 'the restrictions
which Boston birth and breeding imposes upon one'.

One of her roles that appealed to him was in a play based on *A
Sense of the Past*, a late novel by Henry James. The play was a restaging
in 1931 of *Berkeley Square*, which two years earlier had had a long run
on Broadway, directed by Leslie Howard (who later took the lead in
the film version). It's a time-travel story of a young American, Peter
Standish, who inherits an eighteenth-century house in London,
and when he crosses the threshold finds himself in the past of his
ancestors with whom he becomes involved. Eliot promised Emily
to go to Berkeley Square on her opening night, to be with her in
spirit; his invitations to Emily to participate in a ghostly form of
love resonate.

In September 1931 Emily felt closer to Eliot than before, and in
that mood she enclosed a sonnet she had written about mourners
in a painting: it's an Eastern scene and the mourners are Muslims.
Eliot's marginalia were excessively carping, and he did not comment on Hale's empathy with prayers to Allah: 'The head is bent /

As if in prayer. "Allah is good, Allah is — " over and over he sought /
To say . . .'.

Eliot's advice to Emily was to use a work of art not for its own
sake but to open up another topic. Eliot went so far as to call this
poem a failure. If she tried her hand at other poems, she never sent
him one again.

After only three months of correspondence Emily had boldly confronted him with the idea that he was 'abnormal'. Yes, he calmly
agreed, he was, and their relationship would be more abnormal
if he pretended to her or to himself this was not so. Emily would
not have known of his 'lifelong affliction', the damage his aboulia
caused: the fatigue brought on by contact with others and the safe-
guards he put in place. His honesty invites her to accept what was
already plain: there could be no prospect of normality.

Ideally, he would like to write to his 'dearest Lady' every day, and
this he proceeds to do for three days in succession. He wants to live
in their exchange of letters with 'a dizzy sense of awe at gradually
penetrating, or so it seems to me, into the depths of your saintly
soul. Is it wrong to feel that, I wonder.'

In the margin he writes in pencil: 'I mean, is it wrong to crave
such complete spiritual possession and union as I do. Of course the
situation is "abnormal".' But then he adds, as he often does, an irresistible sweetener. He cannot pretend either, he says, that 'I do not
long to be with you always; there are times when my arms literally
ache with the emptiness. I need not say this <u>twice</u>.'

In effect, the tug of desire against its prohibition is stirring, even
seductive — enhanced by distance. Hale's words acted in somewhat
the same way, enhanced by verbal restraint. She was prepared to say
that she admired him.

'Well, my paragon,' he replied, 'your words made me nearly
giddy with excitement.' He had never expected to find someone so
'sympathetic and understanding' in the presence of a reserve much
like his own.

But then, the very next day, 8 January 1931, he admits to an 'odd' desire for a solitude that would exclude her. His fantasy of a stay in a New England village does *not* say he wants to see her (even though his arms had been aching to hold her).

This seesaw only makes sense if what Eliot tells Emily repeatedly is true: he claims that if he saw her, he might be unable to control a palpitating desire. Anticipation starts alarm bells for fear of his body's responses – he might tremble, even 'blub' – an anxiety so acute that he must ban proximity. It's the danger of uncontrollable desire in a man who is not a natural celibate. St Augustine had been such a man and had prayed for chastity and self-control (*da mihi castitatem et continentiam*) at the same time as wishing chastity could be deferred. The confession is startling, and Eliot too is honest in stressing his struggle to tame an intractable body.

He explained this frankly to Emily: meeting her in person would make celibacy harder, and this justified putting his need above hers. Nancy Cunard might have relieved his body, but this had reduced him to ashes. He had already put the problem of bodily love to his Lady in a way that made physicality untenable: 'Terminate torment / Of love unsatisfied / The greater torment / Of love satisfied'.

What about plans for the summer, Hale asked. She might be in England again. On 9 January, the third of the run of daily letters, Eliot blocked this as well. To meet, he said, would be unlikely. He saw few women and never alone.

Hale tried to understand the 'difficulty' of coming together. Apprehension was to be expected with two reserved people. She herself was inexperienced; there had never been a man in her life, and Eliot had never felt unreserved with anybody before. 'Indeed,' he said, 'my life has made me more clam-like than I am by nature – I think that the few women who have offered me quite desirable and pleasant friendships have always found me singularly stiff, formal and roundabout.' It was different with Emily. He was more at ease with her chaste refinement, and to turn to her brought home how

'Weave, weave the sunlight in your hair'.
Eliot first drew on poetic feeling for
Emily when she was twenty.

Eliot fell in love with Emily while he was
a philosophy student from 1911 to 1914

Charlotte Eliot was a teacher who wished to be a poet. She wrote on the trials of the spirit.

A circle of sisters with Henry Ware Eliot Jr, as later the sisters would protect their younger brother, Tom. *Left to right*: Marian, Charlotte, Margaret and Ada, *c.* 1883–4.

Emily at the Berkeley Street School in Cambridge, aged about twelve, two years before Eliot met her. She and her father, the Reverend Edward Hale (*below*), were bereft of her mother and brother.

Editors of the *Harvard Advocate*. Eliot is seated in the front row, third from the left. Conrad Aiken is seated second from the right.

At Eastern Point with his sister Marian.

Emily Hale 'all in pink', holding flowers.
This oil portrait hung in the Perkinses' hall.

Emily Hale in performance.

Emily's lifelong friend Margaret Farrand in her
American Red Cross uniform. France, 1918.

Englishwomen with Bloomsbury associations
made the poet 'one of us'

Lady Ottoline Morrell with Eliot at Garsington.

Seated: Mary Hutchinson with lover, Clive Bell; standing left, Duncan Grant, who did a portrait of her, and E. M. Forster in the walled garden at Charleston.

'She was to me like a member of my own family.' Eliot with his publisher, Virginia Woolf, at Garsington.

'To me [our union] brought the state of mind out of which came *The Waste Land*.' Photo (1920) from Vivienne Eliot's unused American passport.

First book edition of *The Waste Land*, hand set by Virginia Woolf for the Hogarth Press.

Nancy Cunard and Eliot had the briefest of flings. 'They were together, and he fell.'

Mr and Mrs Eliot at home in
Crawford Mansions.

To Emily Hale in Seattle in 1915,
the door that had shut between her
and Eliot seemed closed for good.

alien he was to 'a certain kind of corrupt vulgarity' in his London circle, a casual looseness too sophisticated to appear as gross as he felt it was.

Hale repeatedly made a point of urging Eliot not to 'overrate' her; he was not to 'idealise' her. Tall, good-looking, adept at business, he didn't *look* like a man in a medieval dream. There was a restrained force that attracted women and made it reasonable for Hale to hope she might encourage normal responses in this man who loved her. The semi-divine Lady in a tie that would never wake up was his dream, not hers.

He denied idealisation. He had no alternative if the relationship was to continue, and in the course of the ninety letters he wrote during 1931 switched from addressing her as 'Lady' and 'Saint' to 'Turtle' and 'Dove'. And he sets aside awe for tenderness in his first poems after renewing contact: 'Triumphal March' (published in October 1931) and 'Difficulties of a Statesman' (written by then but not published until early in 1932).

An exquisitely delicate feeling lies secreted in a public hero obsessed with power, a modern equivalent of Coriolanus leading a Roman Triumph. Eliot looks at brute force as a travesty of manhood; he erodes the edifice of militarised society, with its fake authority, weaponry, useless committees and self-important busyness. True manhood is to keep alive an unseen emotion.

The character of Eliot's Statesman presents a contrast to Prufrock, who shies away from women when he goes among them. The Statesman parades for the crowd, yet inwardly he too sheers away. So armoured is the Statesman in his extreme masculinity, and so insistent and contrived is his façade, that he is shut off from himself except for a soft spot like a dove kept in his breast.

'Coriolan',* as Eliot called this sequence, is enigmatically personal, like Eliot's songbird, Pipit. Biographical facts are needed to

---

* TSE told EH on 16 March 1931 that Beethoven's Coriolan Overture had moved him: 'I have wanted to do a Coriolan in verse.'

read the two poems: Emily Hale was given the code for unlocking them (Pipit, Dove, Turtle, also Bird and Birdie) in early letters.

Unknown to readers until the release of the letters is that Emily Hale reminded Eliot of his recently dead mother – a woman who understood him and his spiritual quest. In approaching Emily he sought some replacement of his mother's unconditional sympathy. 'Coriolan' exposes the poet as never before to the public gaze: a patrician and man of destiny, divided between pride as he rides above the crumpet-crunching crowd and hidden feelings – 'O hidden' – for two women, his mother and his 'dove'.

Eliot believed that a poet must write of his life as though it were someone else's, plumbing the depths of character. Through the arrogance of the Roman victor, Coriolanus, glorious, fastidious and indifferent to the contemptible mob, the poet bares himself, together with his dependence on his hidden dove who heartens him.

A refrain of 'hidden' goes back to the time when the young Eliot fell in love with Emily. A tender poem, 'Hidden Under the Heron's Wing', undated and unpublished in Eliot's lifetime, was copied into his student notebook. Now a public figure, he gropes to retrieve from memory words of undeclared love between 1911 and 1914: 'O hidden under the ... Hidden under the ... Where the dove's foot rested and locked for a moment, / A still moment'. Fuelled by disclosure in letters to Emily, the poetic lines find release: 'O hidden under the dove's wing, hidden in the turtle's breast ... / At the still point of the turning world. O hidden.' The still point signals the divine, linking the private dove with the wings of the dove in the Psalms.

Eliot wished to become 'Emily's Tom'. Over the next year she was no longer the Lady of silences; she found words of her own to unblock him and release words, phrases and poetic designs for *Four Quartets*. The letters quickly become a test ground for the masterpiece the poet eventually composed between 1935 and 1942.

As early as 16 March 1931 Emily was the first to hear his inspired response to Beethoven's A minor quartet on the gramophone. 'I like Beethoven so much that I can hardly endure anything else, except some Brahms (the Tristan music is too painful for me to listen to). There is some kind of supernatural gaiety, almost an angelic frivolity, about Beethoven's later music, as of a man who had gone through all human suffering and come out into some strange country – which I would give my life to be able to translate into poetry.'*

No more than three days after Eliot relayed his wish to measure up to Beethoven, he tested out an *Alice in Wonderland* trope, a revival of his paradisal hyacinth garden. Even though Eliot had closed down the prospect of meeting, he admits to Emily his own frustration. It's a spring day with lilacs coming up, and he feels cut off from 'life' like Alice's longing to get into a garden and her frustration when she can't enter.

Stirred by the breakthrough to another realm in Beethoven and by the longing for the garden, yet another idea for the *Quartets*, to subdue human desire with a view to a higher existence, burst out in his 2 April letter. Emily praised one of his letters as 'more normal', to which Eliot explained that at Easter he had undergone a 'rending' self-examination. He must tear the soul from the body. His unruly body was 'still so passionate' that he had to struggle to subdue it. All he could do was hold on, sweating like one undergoing surgery without an anaesthetic. In a further letter a few months later he likens this operation to that of cutting out his physical desire for her. This anticipates a surgical scene in the second quartet, while the agony goes back to Eliot's anticipatory poem about La Figlia in 1911–12 where, on parting, the soul leaves the body 'torn and bruised'.

*

---

* After Beethoven, the poet took in also 'the wonderful string quartets of Tsaikowsky' (*sic*), followed by hearing Beethoven's Razumovsky Quartet at a concert in Boston in November 1932. His response to these appears only in confidence to Emily Hale.

At first, Emily did what she could to resist the disembodied aspect of their relationship. She took in the strangeness of what Eliot wanted from her and the challenge he presented but hesitation about taking him on gave her pause, and towards the end of 1931 and into the early months of 1932, morale dropped. However much she admired him, should she eliminate her own needs in order to serve those of the poet?

Whenever Emily's letters stopped flowing, Eliot became agitated. Was she preoccupied with acting? To judge by the succession of plays in which she performed, it can't have been her career that brought her low. It could have been worry over money. She was not paid for performances in non-commercial theatre, so if she were living on savings her freedom to pursue acting was probably coming to an end and she had to think of supporting herself once more. This, alongside Eliot's insistence that their relationship must continue to be 'abnormal'. Three times during 1931 she broke it to him that she was in 'despair' – an unlikely word from a reserved woman.

Eliot did not discuss the content of her despair. He regarded despair as a sin on the part of a person who presumes to think she deserves better and traced despair to egotism.

To Emily, this came as a 'blast'.

His formidable return was to take her place as the blasted party, a man at the mercy of a threatening female. Her anger was hurtful to him, he warned. 'I am very much disturbed – please, Madam, I should be too <u>frightened</u> ever to <u>want</u> to anger you.' Had he been impertinent? 'Dear me, I must control my elephantine gambollings, if I tread on the beautiful lady's toe.'

At this, she fell silent.

Eliot worried in case she was ill. It was borne in on him that with no formal connection to her, he had no right to make enquiries. Feeling miserably helpless, he begged her to cable and set his mind at rest.

She did. Then a letter followed admitting she had stopped writing. When he said how wholly his well-being depended on her regular letters, compassion came back. She said no more about despair but he had not finished with the subject.

Hope, he said, is a <u>duty</u>. To despair is to be defective in humility. Who are you, he puts it to her, 'that you should have the right to be exasperated with yourself for being merely human?' A sermon allowed him to wall himself off, as though her state of mind had nothing to do with him. A woman with less humility might have walked away at this point. Hale did not. She was attentive. What he said was of use to her, she said.

But he was still relentless (disturbing even) in his teasing control. 'I should like to send you a good kiss,' he said, 'instead of the smack of another kind which I felt like giving you at the time.'

When she ventured to confide her difficulties as a child, he turned talk back to himself. And when she brought up her sense of inadequacy, he happened to be in a rush.

Both Hale and Eliot were in need of income when, in October 1931, Harvard offered Eliot the prestigious Norton lectureship for the academic year 1932–3. It carried what was then a bountiful stipend of $10,000. Given his debts and arrears in taxes, he could not afford to refuse. A bonus was that Vivienne would not accompany him. He had made it clear that he couldn't carry out the work expected if he had to look after her.

One early plan was for Vivienne to return to Malmaison for the seven or eight months Eliot was to be away. The cost could use up the bulk of his American earnings, but if it was Vivienne's preference, Eliot said, 'she shall go'. It turned out *not* to be her preference. An alternative plan was a paid companion, and this solution too Vivienne turned down.

It would not have taken much for her acute intelligence to read her husband's mind: a return to America and a period apart might offer an opportunity to leave her. Her instinctive response was to play up her needy and childlike aspect to keep a hold on her husband and ensure his return by refusing to have anyone else look after her. She did not intend for him to have a way out. Pitifully, she was motivated by fear and, unfairly, her husband alleged it was her sole emotion.

Aurelia Bolliger ('Bolly'), an American friend,* stayed with the Eliots early in 1932 and witnessed Vivienne having a tantrum on the phone to her husband, calling him 'you cautious, over-cautious coward!', banging her fists on the table. She told Aurelia he was 'a sadist' who wanted to make her squirm. Aurelia observed the Eliots' ordinary marital life during that last year together: they shared a bedroom; Eliot at ease in pyjamas; Vivienne saying 'come to bed, Tom'; her apology to him after losing her temper, holding up her face for a kiss. Once, when Vivienne undressed, Aurelia was puzzled by marks on her back that looked to her like measles. Sympathetic to both Eliot and Vivienne, she set down observations, including a visit to Vivienne's mother in a rather over-furnished home with a canopied bed and a photograph of Vivienne as an exceptionally beautiful young woman with large eyes, full lips and rounded body.

For the time being, Eliot's marital position was one reason for the boundary imposed on Emily Hale. But how, then, were he and Emily to conduct themselves when the lectureship brought him to her home town?

'We shall make our plans quite irrespective of each other,' he said.

Treading carefully, Emily asked what she was to expect.

His reply was measured, the tone cautious to cold. First, he must see his sisters and other family members, and then he would phone or perhaps see her just once. He writes uncertainly about a face-to-face encounter; if this took place, he would be shaken and dazed.

The way to cope, he decided, would be to take his formal stance. He warned Emily that she would find him different from her ardent correspondent. He would appear the stiff, forbidding man no one

---

* She was a teacher and missionary in Japan, attached to the English poet Ralph Hodgson, who married in her in Japan in 1933 after obtaining a divorce.

could approach. For seven or eight months they would not lay eyes on each other, and then, before he left Boston for London, he would pay her a farewell call.

An obvious reason for the proposed arrangement was to avoid scandal as a married man. He foresaw, for instance, that Eleanor Hinkley and Penelope Noyes would invite both him and Emily together for dinners in a town filled with their connections. And there was also a more delicate issue: concern for celibacy.

Throughout the months in Boston, he would depend on Emily, he told her, to keep the letters coming. It's like a strange tale by Nathaniel Hawthorne about a man who leaves his wife; she never sets eyes on him again, though all the while he's living nearby and intent on all she does. The spectatorial fixation, especially with an intimate, is not untrue to the stalker in an artist, and to secretive quirks of character familiar to Hawthorne. Along with Eliot's reasonable excuses to Emily, there is a weird satisfaction as he contemplates eluding Emily while living near her and all the while receiving letters hot from her hand, overnight, instead of waiting up to ten days as they cross the Atlantic.

Before Eliot's offer from Harvard became official, another had arrived for Miss Hale from Scripps College, the only women's college in the West. To move far away amongst strangers did not appeal and the post would put an end to the gains and plaudits she had won for acting. Her immediate impulse was to turn the job down. But Eliot urged her to accept it. He might visit her, much as he detested California. It was a possibility he offered in a reluctant tone and hedged with qualifiers: the claims that were bound to press upon him once in Boston.

'I don't know how much, or in what circumstances, I can endure to see you; but I shall tell you frankly when I do know.'

He was 'severe', she protested, and at this he flinched. As before, he fell back on poetic feeling: 'my beautiful Lady, my Dove'. But as though he realised this would be inadequate, he writes on New Year's Eve, 1931, about his poetry: rarely, now and then, he would apprehend a 'pattern' in existence. Still more rarely, his future flashed before him 'in a way which neither makes possible, or even desirable, that we should alter our course'.

There was nothing for it. Early in 1932, Hale accepted the Scripps post. She had to commit herself for at least two years.

Eliot was jubilant. He warmed to Emily for making herself unavailable and commended her pluck. 'You are just what I would have you be! . . . I am very proud of you.' He hoped that she hadn't sacrificed herself for his sake and tried to present Scripps as romantically exotic. No luck. She remained depressed.

If she was having a 'little' breakdown, he was glad to hear that she was staying with Penelope Noyes, who would take the best care of an invalid. To console her, he went so far as to talk up Unitarianism. The idea was for her faith, and especially her uncle, the Rev John Carroll Perkins, to comfort Emily.

Her actions in the early months of 1932 signalled resistance. She wrote infrequently in February and threatened to withdraw her letters from his plan to preserve them in the Bodleian.

He wanted her to know that he was haunted by worries about her, and that 'a man visited by the muse is haunted ever after'. He pleaded how 'corrosive' it was to his mind not to be able to express himself in his usual confidences. Early in March he sent a pleading poetic cry composed in the Underground: 'O when will the creaking heart cease?' The insistent self-pity is almost comically out of kilter with the normality she despaired of inducing.

Even as Hale withdrew, Eliot firmed up the prospect of a visit to see her.

He might fly, she suggested in her practical way.

'Fly!' he exclaimed, 'no thank you madam.' He was too old for such 'monkeyshines'.

Pining more, he realised how 'violently' dependent he had become. He would see her, he decided finally.

She kept cool. 'No plan can be made yet.'

On 15 March, Eliot acknowledged her admission that she no

longer felt stirred by him. He took to brooding over her photographs, 'memorising' them and feeling 'intoxicated' himself.

Drawn back into the conversation, she disparaged the way she looked, a 'washed out, soft-looking creature' in a 'poor state of control', to which he retorts 'ridiculous'. He saw 'a very firm and formed character . . . nothing prettypretty about it at all, but the real thing.'

On 12 April 1932 he sent her a bravura statement, a continuation of his December revelation about his purpose. This letter, with its mix of desire, intoxication, regret and reaching towards a timeless design, resonates with echoes of *The Waste Land* and premonitions of *Four Quartets*.

He begins with the same feeling that opens *The Waste Land*. April is an unkind month. He finds the first intimations of spring, its sweet smells and the last smokes and damp leaves of autumn, the most troubling times of the year, reviving memories 'one must subdue'. At other times, one is working like a mole or a seaman in a submarine. One can't help coming to the surface with a realisation how intense life can be, or how it was, or how it might have been. This thought will find its poignant way into the opening of his first *Quartet*: 'What might have been and what has been'.

That day Eliot looked towards 'fulfilling a part . . . in some purpose or design so large that it can only rarely be grasped, and of transcending oneself in a satisfaction that gives reconciliation'.

In the *Quartets*, and more particularly in *East Coker*, he was to develop this idea of a transcendent design in which he partakes. And his sense of 'reconciliation' will receive its finest summation in an essay, 'Poetry and Drama': 'It is ultimately the function of art, in imposing a credible order upon ordinary reality, and thereby eliciting some perception of an order *in* reality, to bring us to a condition of serenity, stillness, and reconciliation.'

Every moment matters, he says, and one is always following a curve either up or down.

These two ways constitute an aim that can't be measured on the scale of happiness. Beside 'the Peace that passeth understanding', happiness or unhappiness does not matter. Happiness is for those (unlike himself) who have no destiny. At this moment in the spring of 1932 Eliot is flooded with what he has yet to achieve. Years of work open up before him.

Imagine Emily Hale receiving this letter a week or so later. She reads the words of the godlike creator who has chosen her for his mate, calling out her reciprocal power to generate this unfolding.

There is nothing explicit about secrecy in the Eliot–Hale letters, but Emily wanted Margaret Thorp to know Eliot better. During their sabbatical in London in 1931–2 Eliot was hospitable to the Thorps, aware of them as Emily's friends, and he would mention 'Emily Hale' or just 'Emily' quite openly.

The Thorps' impressions of Eliot and also of his wife were almost certainly relayed to Emily in confidential letters they agreed to destroy. Eliot's first invitation was to a monthly *Criterion* Club dinner on 14 October. They noted that Eliot 'was a little tight so that he mixed words & talked bawdy & was shouted down'.

Ten days later the Thorps had tea at the Eliots' home, and again Margaret set down her impressions: 'His mind moves slowly but with deadly accuracy . . . I felt the whole time as if we were – all four of us – doing a sword dance. If one misstep had been made, we might have brought all the blades down at once.'

During the visit Vivienne, with straight bobbed hair and glasses, was nervous, prowling about and asking abrupt, disconcerting questions. She remarked on 'faces changing so that one sees a well-known person disappearing before one'. The Thorps wondered if this bore on the changing façades of her husband. But she could have had the Harvard job in mind or, conceivably, Vivienne's remark was another instance of foresight, since her husband did have it in mind to disappear from her sight. What appeared hallucinatory could have been another instance of super-clarity, like the far-sighted terror back in 1925–6 that her existence was at risk.

A third invitation for the Thorps was to a party at the Eliots' flat in January 1932. Eliot commended Vivienne for organising this, effective once more when she chose to back the poet. Another guest was Alida Monro, wife and helper of Harold Monro, who ran the Poetry Bookshop. She came from Eastern Europe; her name before her marriage had been Klementaski. She had given a reading of Eliot's poems in the bookshop and Vivienne had her read again. Eliot himself read an unpublished fragment, possibly 'Difficulties of a Statesman', soon to appear.

Secretly he shared with Emily his relish of Margaret as 'one person present who had been at a certain performance of *Tristan* and was quite ignorant of its significance'. The two couples met for dinner and cards (the game of *ombre*) at regular intervals – once at the Thorps' lodgings at 20 Lincoln's Inn Old Buildings. Eliot appreciated Margaret as educated and sensitive, and her bland, chubby-faced husband proved more acute than on first appearance. Eliot reported to Emily that he was growing to like Willard Thorp as a person of delicacy, refinement and goodness. Vivienne, warming too to Margaret, felt moved to accompany Eliot to Harvard. 'Thanks to you, I am going to America,' she told Margaret.

When the Thorps came to dine Eliot wondered to himself how much they knew about him and Emily, and he pressed her to disclose what she had told them and others about him. Had she confided in Eleanor? He was relieved to hear that she had not. He confided in no one, he said.

Often, he told her, he would lie awake at night thinking 'of what we are to each other'. He thought about her physically: not only about what she wore, her dresses and earrings, but also her hair, wanting her to draw it back to show her ears and the shape of her neck.

Once, when Emily felt doubtful of their future, she asked him if it had happened, after all, 'too late'.

The answer came quick and sure: '"Too late?" you say. – my dear, you are only at the beginning.'

After living in the past, haunted for years by their night at the opera and other events she too remembered, he was living in the present and future, avid for the next letter from his 'western star'. He imagined how, if she were ill, he might nurse her. He would dab her with eau de cologne. A photo of herself as a child, sent to him, was to be kissed and put to bed in the box and looked at as often as possible. There's a spontaneous rush of ardour: 'It is beyond words to express how I cling to you, adore you ...' Despite himself, he had never felt so natural and ready to enjoy friends. An immediate benefit of her letters was to find himself 'suddenly and completely freed from the sexual strain of celibacy'.

He was unafraid to tell her that age had not cooled his passions. There were times, he said, 'when I desire you so much that neither religion, nor work, nor distraction, and certainly not dissipation could relieve it – it is like a pain that no sedative will deaden, or an operation without anaesthetic – nothing to do but be still and wait'.

To come alive in this way made him long for more – more letters. He wanted them to belong to each other, all the time deflecting her need to meet in the ordinary way.

Could he win her to his way of loving? How far could she lend herself?

Time is the big player in this relationship, time in combination with Eliot's erratic character, seesawing (as he admits to Emily) between exaltation and agony. On his part, he did not hesitate to hold her fast with an absolute conviction that she was right for him; on her part, there were frequent hesitations: times when she backed off from the prompt replies he demanded. Was this demand too much at this point when she was not in love and had to cope with strange evasions?

A simple answer lies in her loneliness. But there's another answer, linked with the poet's baring of his aims. He speaks to Emily of finding 'something <u>very</u> rarely identical in us', beyond sympathy and understanding, which at this stage seems to him like a 'miracle'. What if the power of Eliot's colloquial and confessional eloquence, the combined power of his poetic lines and love-letters, actually did call up in Emily Hale something akin to that medieval ideal of pity welling into generous attentiveness? As a director of plays skilled at drawing out the best from her players, it would not be out of character for her to extend this skill to shaping 'Tom', as he declared she did. If so, there was something in it for her in continuing their exchange.

In this first phase of their union it's striking how quickly Hale questions, probes and resists Eliot's Dantean narrative, while words of love hearten her to keep his narrative going. Eliot's control of the situation triumphed, with Hale acceding to a further phase of separation through their simultaneous moves to different places for the 1932–3 academic year. This would preserve distance, perpetuating an epistolary relationship.

Within these bounds she found words of her own to complement those of a great poet and to unblock his habitual barriers. Her words piling up in his locked tin box had to be there beside him, he told her, words he re-read until he knew them by heart. It satisfied him to touch the paper where her hand had moved. Her name at the end of a letter brought to mind her mouth and he kissed it again and again. Her absent presence promised a fount of 'new verse', as the 'new years' walked their way through time towards the 'unread vision' this love must bring.

12

A QUESTION OF DIVORCE

Vivienne felt the 'cruel pain of losing Tom' when he set out for Harvard in September 1932. She knew his wish to separate and could hardly have been unaware that, three months before he departed, he commissioned Foyles bookshop to make an inventory of his library: some 650 books at 68 Clarence Gate Gardens; his first practical arrangement for moving out. Vivienne clung to the fact that he was due to return after eight months, but this did not quiet her fears that he would remain in America.

Her anxiety shows all too plainly in Leonard Woolf's photograph of Eliot's farewell visit to the Woolfs at Monk's House in Rodmell on 2 September 1932. In the rainy garden Virginia Woolf looks aloof in sturdy lace-ups and casual cardigan, one hand on her hip, the other stretching a pocket; she and Eliot stand together, while Vivienne, like a doll in white with matching white shoes, is apart, her small face woeful under the brim of her hat. Virginia Woolf's diary mocks her as a mad Ophelia, who now and then 'lapsed' into sense.

At the time of the visit, the Eliots were spending four days at the Lansdowne Hotel in Eastbourne, a return to where they'd been on honeymoon in July 1915, like the echo-hell of *Sweeney Agonistes*

A forlorn Vivienne, aware that her husband wished to leave her, accompanied him on a visit to the Woolfs at Monk's House in 1932. Leonard Woolf took this telling photograph.

where characters (as conceived in draft) are doomed to repeat a set of actions. Eliot had dreaded this holiday, he told Emily, yet it was a duty conscience demanded.

Two nights before Eliot sailed, Vivienne invited friends to a farewell. The guests included Lady Ottoline Morrell; a young bibliophile, John Hayward; and a young writer, Hope Mirrlees, author of *Paris*, a fragmented, Modernist precursor of *The Waste Land*, also published by the Hogarth Press. Lady Ottoline wrote in her journal how little she could bear Vivienne's agitated company; Hope Mirrlees later did an imitation (caught on camera) of Vivienne's jumpiness, looking as though she saw 'a goblin ghost'. She exhausted visitors; they felt 'sucked dry'. All pitied 'poor Tom'. Mirrlees remarked on Vivienne's 'ashy-white, tormented, angry, drug-addict's face. She

had a streak of poetical sensibility. She was a mixture of Ophelia
& a spirit in hell . . . She cried wildly "Now I will give you a toast –
TOM!" I can still see Tom sitting there with an enigmatic smile
looking like a cross between a tomcat & the Mona Lisa.'

The last day, 17 September, as they set off in a taxi to catch the
boat train at Waterloo, Eliot discovered that a bag was missing, the
vital bag with his papers including lecture notes. Alida Monro,
who accompanied them, dashed off in another taxi to retrieve the
bag from the flat. She discovered that Vivienne had locked it in the
bathroom. The window was too small to admit an adult, so Monro
had to find a boy small enough to squeeze through. And quickly.
She made it to the train with only minutes to spare.

Alida Monro, by now a widow, was deputised to see Vivienne
home, watch over her and report to Eliot. She was one of a number
of people, friends with the Eliots as a couple, who responded
warmly to Vivienne – the Schiffs for instance, Mary Hutchinson,
Lady Ottoline, Abigail Eliot and Eliot's niece 'Dodo' (Theodora,
daughter of Eliot's dead sister Charlotte) – whose liking was less
reported than Vivienne's wildness. What happened with Alida, as
with these others, is that Vivienne's needs became too exacting, too
self-centred, friends fell away and eventually aligned themselves
with Eliot – the swing in Alida's case was so pronounced that he
rebuffed it.

As the marital situation changed between 1932 and 1934, Emily Hale
had to clarify her own position. Eliot was ambiguous: she was the
love of his life, he told her and then, alternating with that, came
warnings: he meant to go on alone. In this period Emily questioned
him at first indirectly and then directly whether he would do more
than separate.

As an Anglo-Catholic, Eliot held by the rule of St Augustine set
out in *Of the Good of Marriage*: 'The compact of marriage is not done
away by divorce intervening; so that they continue wedded persons one to another, even after separation; and commit adultery

with those, with whom they shall be joined, even after their own divorce.'

The most conspicuous layman in the Church, he put his standing to Emily rather grandly. 'If I had a divorce it would be the greatest misfortune to the Anglican Church since Newman went over to Rome.' He wrote this from Boston on 16 April 1933 as he proposed a separation, not divorce, to his wife's family and a lawyer, Mr Bird.

He put it to Emily once more, six months later, that punishment and disgrace would follow a divorce: excommunication, together with estrangement from the clerics who had welcomed his conversion. He would like nothing more than to marry her, but the rulings of the church must come first. Yet if she was to remain a gift of God, what does this mean for the woman who's the gift? Does she exist in her own right? Emily Hale had no doubt that she did. She took for granted the right to pursue happiness.

Her promise had been to make him happy, yet it soon became clear that Eliot had a Puritanical reservation about happiness itself; sainthood, not happiness, should be the ideal of human existence. Distrust of people who lived oblivious to sainthood made for 'a void' in his relationships, and this tended to drive him 'towards asceticism or sensuality', so he told the Princeton theologian Paul Elmer More. But his love-letters to Emily included confessions of desire, their seductive impact heightened by his struggle to contain it. Surely an eroticised exchange is not the way a celibate should engage with a woman? Still, what he sees as weakness was disarmingly human. Then, too, there was the appeal of his need – however distanced – to hold on to her.

Scripps College was a new institution, founded in 1926. Miss Hale took heart in being wanted to hone speech and build up drama. The lure was a post with professional standing, as Assistant Professor of Oral English. She was also to preside over Toll Hall, where students lived.

Though she knew no one in Claremont, she had one special

contact: Margaret Thorp's distinguished aunt Beatrix Farrand, a
landscape gardener known for her work at the White House and
Dumbarton Oaks in Washington, and the Morgan Library in New
York. A niece of Edith Wharton and friend of Henry James, Farrand
was primed to take to Emily Hale as 'vivacious and ornamental' and
to welcome her to the Huntington, the botanical garden, library
and art museum where Beatrix lived with her husband Max, the
first director there.

Nonetheless, to Eliot, she expressed her fear of loneliness and her
worry to be moving three thousand miles away from her mother.
In view of his troubled wife, Eliot's advice to Emily was to distance
herself emotionally and speak to doctors rather than the patient.
He recommended prayers for her mother instead of upsetting visits
to her asylum. When Hale, wrung by her mother's fate, resisted his
advice, he saw rebellion against God. To her, the situation called for

*Beatrix Farrand, the landscape gardener, in California, 1934. She was aunt to Emily Hale's best
friend, Margaret Farrand Thorp, who arranged for them to meet.*

empathy, not a sermon. Still, he was concerned about her loneliness and offered to give her a dog.

He fancied a blue Bedlington terrier, a fighter bound to 'Growl at strangers' and 'fly at Offensive people'. This breed of dog (looking rather like Eliot himself) would serve as his 'substitute', an 'intimate' companion, who would do everything that he himself, were he a dog, would do. When Emily refused, Eliot capitulates and commits himself to visit her at the end of the year.

Hale stopped tiptoeing and laid him flat with a plan for his visit: should they take a holiday together? They would of course conduct themselves as the moral beings they were.

Eliot had no doubt of her, he replied, it was his own self-control he distrusted.

Would the 'strain' be too much for him?

Not if he could arrange a safety net. If instincts should get the better of him, might he be free to leave suddenly, without causing a problem? He had to be frank with her. Age had not diminished his passions. If anything, they had intensified by concentrating solely on her.

To soothe anxiety, she redefined the holiday as an outing. She planned to have a car and offered a Western tour. Might he like that?

Yes, he would. She proposed Yosemite National Park and didn't put Eliot off by revealing what an expedition that would be. His nervousness now fixed on rattlesnakes and cougars.

Her next initiative was to beckon Eliot towards the Unitarian faith he had rejected. Her uncle, who was minister in Boston's historic King's Chapel, invited Eliot to deliver an address to his congregation, and Hale had a topic ready: 'The Influence of the Bible upon English Literature'. Eliot agreed, and the leaflet of King's Chapel, which she sent, gave him a glimpse of a more formal and beautiful ritual than that of his childhood in St Louis.

But then Emily chanced it: might they go on a retreat together? She had in mind the Unitarian retreat, Senexet, in Woodstock, Connecticut.

Eliot was taken aback. It astonished him to hear that Unitarians accepted people on retreat together. To him, a retreat meant shedding others and praying on one's own. His other objection was sectarian: it would be improper, he argued, for an Anglican to join in non-Anglican practice. The Anglican faithful, he told Emily, would disapprove. But the strictness came from himself. He often called for his adoptive church, born of a *via media* and mild in its minimal demands, to be more strenuous, more exclusive. Lady Ottoline, a devout Anglican, observes in her journal how alien Eliot appeared with 'a temperamental Dislike of Life . . . a very, very odd survival of some Calvinist Ancestor'. To the Calvinist, innate sin is the essence; pleasure, happiness a diversion from the grim truth of human baseness.

'The fact that I am a Trinitarian, and that you are Unitarian, matters very much to me,' Eliot told Emily. 'It means a Fight. Of course I mean to win. Very likely I shan't.' Then he conceded that what seemed to divide them really attached him to her more closely.

Emily was not afraid of Eliot. She was not daunted by his public persona. His forbidding manner, combined with his dominance in the world of letters, meant that few dared criticise him, but Emily Hale cared enough to point out the verbiage that accompanied hesitation in his radio broadcasts. She advised him to talk less slowly – she meant ponderously. When he sent her his preface to *Bubu de Montparnasse*, the French novel whose decadence had appealed to him as a young man in Paris, she expressed her distaste for the book. He felt snubbed, he teased with exclamation marks. It's obvious that he rather enjoyed Hale's courage: sometimes 'my Emily', his 'dear Lady Bird' talks back as 'madam'. He readily concedes Hale's protests about his strangeness and slowness to mature. The Lady of silences no more.

Dante's Beatrice would not have cut her hair, as Emily did in preparation for Scripps, ignoring Eliot's mutter at how barbarous it was. As far as Eliot was concerned, whenever his poems entertain a possibility of love, long hair comes into play, going back to the hair over La Figlia's arms. In *The Waste Land* a speaker dreams of a girl's wet hair after staying out late in a garden, and there's the sweetness of 'brown hair over the mouth blown' in *Ash Wednesday*. Long hair aroused desire, most blatantly in *The Scarlet Letter* when Hester Prynne, meeting her one-time lover in the woods – the frontier (the moral wilderness) is close by in seventeenth-century Boston – takes off her sober cap and shakes down her hair. Eliot is pure Arthur Dimmesdale, the impeccable minister, leaving the woman he has loved to face her hard lot alone. Temperamentally, Eliot is a throwback to Dimmesdale with his hand hiding his heart, who secretes desire, fixates it on one woman – and forbids it.

Like Dimmesdale, Eliot is sublimely eloquent. To read the poet's letters to Emily is to see, and not just to see but to feel, the tug of that eloquence, the beam of his regard, the naked genius when he spells out incipient thoughts for future work, so that it is easy to share her hopes of a happier outcome.

Talking to her more frankly than to anyone, he explained how difficult it was to fight desire when he woke in the morning. When she notes his diminished expressiveness in the spring and summer of 1932, he explains this as inseparable from unsatisfied need. His typewriter stumbles, he crosses out and picks up the thought again with more deliberation, putting companionship before passion, then dependence, reverence and a protective instinct. He decides to label his feeling for her 'respect'. True enough, though only one strand. He was not so earnest that he did not sometimes speculate about her bathing costume and wavy hair.

Unstated was his expectation that she would go along with the sacrifice of personal desire for a greater good.

Sacrifice was a role Emily Hale declined to play in the first half of 1932, and she did so through her work in the theatre. Her letters relayed successes to Eliot without (he complains) telling him anything much. In April 1932 she acted with the Footlight club, America's oldest community theatre, in Jamaica Plain, a part of

Boston. In May she was an aristocratic lady of eighty-five. That this role had something to do with Sir Walter Scott and *The Lady of the Lake* was all she would say. Eliot calls her a secretive minx for not divulging the title of the play, and pleads continually and in vain for photos of her performances. These she withheld, having learnt to avoid his habit of disparagement.

During the month preceding Emily's departure for Scripps and Eliot's departure for Boston, he reverted once more to the lone journey. On 26 July he was dreaming of a monastery with visits to friends, in order to maintain a semblance of normality. In August he tried to wean Hale away from what told against him, her standing by what's natural (herself) versus what's unnatural (Eliot). He recommends her to see, as he does, the natural in relation to the supernatural, rather than merely in relation to an unnatural situation that provoked her resentment.

Just before he sailed for the States, she detects a changed persona in a photograph he sent. This man, she thought, looks alarmingly like a 'crook'.

He was amused and did not disagree. Might she see him as the third-rate actor he supposed he was?

One other person saw him. It was a Russian with Bloomsbury connections, known as Prince Mirsky, who published a piece on Eliot's 'deep phobia of life', which turns into 'biological defeatism' and requires his religion to be *contra mundum* – 'a purity free from vitality'. Eliot thought it perceptive and sent it on to Emily Hale. The 'phobia' can't have appealed to her; nevertheless she had to know. We have to admire his candour.

He revealed also his backward yearning for a world in which his own people had lived and helped to form. There are times, he had told her, when his memories of New England seemed more real than old England, and now with the prospect of being away the whole of his life there could become a dream.

Hearing that Hale had a set of Henry James, Eliot hoped she would sample what he himself was bent on: the fineness of the non-tactile posthumous affair in 'The Altar of the Dead', where a woman devotes herself to lighting candles on a shrine for a dead man who occupies all her life and attention. And in 'The Friends of the Friends', a woman and a man, made for each other, do not meet during their lifetimes. The tale's alternative title is 'The Way It Came'. The woman comes to the man from the afterlife, and this incursion – like the incursion of the Rose – invites 'a rare extension of being'. There is no word for this level of love; it is a 'prodigy' to be inferred. The word 'passion' resonates in the finale: a revelation that the pair continue to give back to each other 'passion for passion'. It was bound up with 'virility', Eliot explained to his protégé, the young poet Stephen Spender, and this particular tale held for him 'the greatest significance'.

So it was that in his distancing of Emily Hale he was not simply too frightened or refined for contact; there was a necessity, an unquenchable desire for parted lovers to commune together. The challenge for Eliot was to wake this chosen woman to the wonder of what he offered.

Aunt Edith, sister to Emily's mother, accompanied her to Scripps to see her settled. She need not have feared. Toll Hall turned out to be a handsome building, approached through well-kept gardens. The students were charmed by their teacher's upright demeanour, the formality of her Boston manners and her beautiful diction, and acted with enthusiasm in the first play she put on, an Italian play by Goldoni called *La Locandiera* (*The Mistress of the Inn*). She endeared herself to them when she broke the heel of her elegant shoe by jumping over the footlights at a rehearsal. The girls visited her continually in her rooms, catching her sometimes in her kimono. Two members of the English faculty made her welcome, Ruth George, an admirer of Virginia Woolf, and a Rhodes scholar, Paul Havens, who taught seventeenth-century literature and had a delightful wife, Lorraine. All three became her permanent friends.

Twelve days after Eliot arrived in America, on 9 October, he put through a long-distance call to California and was eased to hear Emily laugh. He had luxurious rooms (B-II) on the third floor of Eliot House at Harvard, overlooking the Charles River. It embarrassed him that the dining hall was stamped with his family crest in honour of his relative Charles William Eliot, the former president of Harvard. Seventeen years had passed since his fraught visit in 1915. He found himself glad to be back with his family and feel close to his sister Ada once more. When he told her of his misery with Vivienne, she encouraged him to separate, and when he said he'd see Emily Hale after Christmas, she took it matter-of-factly.

In England he was T. S. Eliot; here he was an Eliot. His old circle was still there: his cousin Eleanor Hinkley and Penelope Noyes, both like Emily single in the proper, respected New England manner; his classmate Leon Little; his sailing-mate Harold Peters. The Cambridge Dramatic Club was still active. Fellow-actor Amy Gazzoldi Hall came to see him and said what a loss Emily's departure was. Eliot was aware of the continuity of their friends' lives, unlike his and Emily's. They alone, he told her, had experienced 'discontinuity', and in his case the disjunctions and affinities of a homecoming after years abroad. Whether aware of it or not, he was living out an issue of his future play *The Family Reunion*: the returned exile who has to find out how much he has changed and where he now belongs.

Eliot crossed America by train to visit Emily over New Year. Apart from Ada, he told no one the reason for this journey. Only Virginia Woolf with her quick curiosity questioned him. 'And you are now on the Santa Fe Railway. But why? Where are you off to?' Viewed from the train, the New Mexican desert, he said, 'was one of the most beautiful things that I had ever seen'. He had asked Emily to be at the Claremont depot between six and seven in the morning of 27 December when his train would arrive. She, meanwhile, was preparing her students to meet 'a man of extremes, a man of undoubted faults and highest virtues' – different, as she alone knew, from his neutral disguise and flat, uninflected voice.

Beatrix Farrand and her husband held a party for Eliot. Afterwards Farrand wrote to her niece Margaret to say that Eliot, letting down his guard, had eyes only for Emily Hale.

It didn't take the students long to deduce that there must be a special tie to persuade the poet to cross the continent to their campus. In Miss Hale's room was his framed photograph, inscribed to her. She joked that she spoke only to Eliot while Eliot spoke only to God.

One of her pupils, Marie McSpadden Sands (known as 'McSpad'), drove them to Corona del Mar, where her mother had a house. That day they could walk in privacy on the beach. Not only was this the happiest ten days of his life, Eliot told Emily afterwards, but he had learnt what a kiss is. I like to think the deserted winter beach is where the kiss happened. From this time he began to call her 'riperaspberrymouth'.

Immediately after Eliot's departure, Emily confided to Margaret how happy Eliot's visit had been. In view of the Anglican ban on divorce, Emily said that she would take or leave what he offered, and Margaret applauded the good sense.

'How much does he appreciate of your feelings?' Margaret asked. 'It is a most curious situation and I believe that you are now taking the only attitude that can be taken, given his church convictions. If you can keep yourself in your present state of mind, ready to give what he can accept of sympathy and companionship and understanding and conscious that you can give more if opportunity comes – quite frankly if Vivian [sic] dies – and can yet keep yourself satisfied with that, and as well poised as you seem to be, there is no reason on earth why you should not fall completely in love with someone else – that does seem to be the best solution for all three of you.'

Emily likewise had probed Margaret's marriage. Margaret's reply was unconditionally positive: she enjoys Willard enough to suit Emily's romantic ideals.

After lecturing at Berkeley and UCLA, Eliot began the long train

The beach at Corona del Mar, California, 1934.

journey back to the East Coast. From the first stop, Albuquerque, he
mailed a letter to Emily and then, on 17 January 1933, was overjoyed
to find an unexpected letter from her waiting in St Louis. He told
Emily he was prouder to be the recipient of such a letter than of
anything he'd ever done. There, in his birthplace, he stayed with
his father's youngest sister, Aunt Rose, lectured at Washington
University (founded by his grandfather), and visited the graves of
his parents in Bellafontaine Cemetery.

On 29 January his satisfaction with his West Coast jaunt rose
higher at the sight of a new photograph of Emily in a deck chair.
It was 'perfectly lovely'. He wished he could paper his walls
with the film.

Eliot stopped corresponding with Vivienne while he was with
Emily. He resumed on 11 January 1933, postponing his move to separate until he had delivered a huge number of public lectures as he
re-crossed the country on the return leg: St Louis, St Paul, Chicago,
Buffalo, and then on to Baltimore. He had discussed separation
with Fr Underhill and Geoffrey Faber, and recently with Emily. Late
February Eliot finally effected the decisive wrench. He would never
go back to his wife, never voluntarily see Vivienne again. It came

more easily to release dark emotions about her in an outpouring to
Alida Monro rather than to Emily. He predicted a shallow response
from Vivienne when she heard his decision: emotions only of fear
and vanity, as he saw it, measured against his nightmare of concealed aversion.

He must, he said, 'throw off the poison of uncongeniality and
pretense' and, he went on, 'the whole history has been from the
beginning a hideous farce to me'. In further justification, he adds, 'I
do not believe that it can be good for any woman to live with a man
to whom she is morally, in the larger sense, unpleasant, as well as
physically indifferent.'

It was a bitter spring, when an uncontained animus shot out in
letters to Emily Hale. On the positive side, if there is one, was an
urge to speak openly, without disguise. Might his release remake
him? Might Emily remake him? As 'Emily's Tom', who was he or
who did he wish to be? One trait is clearly stated: he wished to be
less reticent, not only to her, and to wield a blow-like directness in
poems and prose. This meant speaking openly about hateful things.

He ticked Emily off for wanting to write when she was at her best.

No, he said, write at your worst.

The kick of his own worst can be found in these letters to her
during the first half of 1933. It was obsessive against Unitarians of his
own sort and especially Mary May Peabody, who had him to stay
when he lectured at Haverford College. She was married to the
Shakespeare scholar Leslie Hotson, known for his archival discoveries, especially *The Death of Christopher Marlowe* (1925). Like Eliot's Boston
cousins Martha and Abigail Eliot, Mary May Peabody was descended
from the reformer Joseph May, and related to the Alcotts. She
was another Jo March character. Eliot deplored her verve, lack of
make-up and alacrity with Elizabethan airs at the piano. Wanting to
puncture her blitheness, he pictured her to Emily as a woman cut
out to be a stolid housewife trying to be an elephantine butterfly.
Emily had to hear his disgust with these and other well-meaning
hosts and contacts.

Although Eliot's animus was not directed at Emily, she could not like this. It annoyed him when she said so.

'I like to be able to write to you and curse the people I am fondest of,' he told her. 'I think that we all have these feelings but that most people are prudent about what they put into letters, for fear of being misunderstood. I am not afraid of being misunderstood by you, but I would rather be misunderstood than not say exactly what I feel at the moment of writing.'

For him, hatred went with horror at human nature, what he had called 'hatred of life' and 'the nightmare of evil', yet this horror often chose pathetic or easy targets.

She objected in particular to his belittling Eleanor Hinkley, whose three-act play *Dear Jane*, about Jane Austen, was staged in New York by the Broadway star and director Eva Le Gallienne, who herself took the part of Austen's sister, Cassandra, while her lover, Josephine Hutchinson, played Jane, who turns down proposals of marriage. Eliot refused his family's offer of a lift to the opening at the Civic Repertory Theater (popularly known as the 14th Street Theater). He was prepared merely to acknowledge the 'little' bit of celebrity due to Eleanor when the play had good reviews. He discussed with Ada if this appreciation from the left-wing press might change the Hinkleys' politics – implying that self-interest would dictate their convictions. His unfinished *Sweeney Agonistes* was staged a few months later, directed by the talented Hallie Flanagan at Vassar.

Eliot batted back Hale's protests, insisting that, with her, he must be free to strip caution. 'I assure you,' he said later, 'it means more to me to talk thus wildly to you – not even worrying whether I may give you a wrong impression – than to say ... the things ... which I cannot express in words at all.'

Looking back, Eliot admitted that he had been in an 'abnormal state' in the spring of 1933. On 3 April vituperations surfaced in public when he delivered a lecture called 'Two Masters' to the Boston Association of Unitarian Ministers (led by Emily Hale's uncle) in

King's Chapel. Face to face, he upbraided Unitarians in favour of the Catholic ideals of sainthood and celibacy, transcending the human. The higher the ideal, he said, the more men know they are no better than the worst of sinners. He declared allegiance to the true faith and called on his listeners to admit straying by 'their own fault, their own fault, their own most grievous fault', beating down sin as a Puritan might have done. '[I] believe that the supernatural is the greatest reality here and now'. The sermon took its title from the Sermon on the Mount: 'No man can serve two masters' (Matthew 6: 24). Eliot laid out a choice between compromisers – Unitarians – and those like himself who obey the sternest demands of faith. Henry, who was present, was shamed by this 'fanatically intolerant and shocking tirade' in a 'city saturated with associations of your ancestors, immediate and distant'.

When the American critic Edmund Wilson had Eliot to stay in New York, he was struck by his performance. 'He is an actor,' Wilson realised. 'He gives you the creeps a little at first because he is such a completely artificial, or rather, self-invented character . . . but he has done such a perfect job with himself that you often end up admiring him.'

Henry Eliot did not admire the actor. He excused his brother on the grounds of an outsider's 'stage-fright' under English eyes, forced to conform to a caricature thrust upon him by the alien affectations of the Bloomsbury Group. Henry blamed the English for what he could not approve. He deplored his brother's switch to Anglicanism, backed by an 'irresistible, instinctive, more or less unconscious talent for publicity'. Dismissing the public performer, Henry stressed the gift for capturing 'the macabre and gloomy grandeur of the early Fathers'. Yet in mixing Puritan conscience with Catholic doctrine, Eliot took to acting, Henry said, more 'literally than do sophisticated Catholics'.

Hate surged again in his lectures at the University of Virginia in May. His bashing D. H. Lawrence and Thomas Hardy did not go down well, nor his wish to exclude free-thinking Jews from society.

He did not explain his private association of free-thinking Jews with
Unitarianism. After the lectures were published as *After Strange Gods*
he came to regret the intemperateness of his mood at this time and
wished he could suppress them.

While Eliot was in Charlottesville, a cable came from Vivienne
to say she would join him. Eliot replied that it would be impossible
because he was travelling about until mid-June. Her next move was
to warn his brother that Tom's lingering in America was making
his and her position difficult. 'I need not mention the firm of Faber
& Faber.' On 4 June she cabled Henry asking for the date of Tom's
sailing and the name of the ship. Her diary reports buying a model
dress, cream chiffon with black lace, 'for Tom's return'.

When Vivienne first got wind of separation is not known, due to
her policy of denial. Two moves in March 1933 suggest that she acted
quickly. Her first impulse was to shame her husband by letting Lady
Ottoline know she had fallen into a state of 'shocking' neglect,
having taken no more than two or three baths and washed her hair
only twice in all the months Tom had been away. Grime was stuck
under her nails and her teeth were broken. Even though, as Eliot
told Emily, she had a paid attendant as well as one or two servants.

Vivienne's second move was to make a will and name Henry
Ware Eliot executor. It was his family duty, she put it to him. In the
terms of the will she was leaving all her property to her husband.
If she died before his return, he was to have everything. Can this
be a veiled threat of suicide? Safe to say, this letter is extraordinary
in its lucidity, acknowledging that her husband has had a difficult
time, and stating in simple, winning terms her intention to ensure
a trouble-free life for him. The letter is so calm, so unlike Vivienne,
that very likely her family law firm, James & James, collaborated
or checked it. Not a single cry escapes. It's a model of sanity and
generosity.

Eliot tried in vain to persuade Vivienne's mother or brother to
speak for him. Nervous of confrontation, he complained to Emily
of the Haigh-Woods' 'passivity'. Nor would his lawyer consent to

speak for him. He was compelled to write himself, a letter to be delivered by his lawyers, Bird & Bird, after April 1933. The barrister St John Hutchinson, who saw the letter, said it was brutal and that Eliot claimed to have accumulated no money during his stay in America. This was untrue. He had earned about £4,000. But he did have debts to pay, including arrears in taxes. Vivienne's brother Maurice, who looked up to Eliot like an elder brother and at all other times sided with him, found the letter harsh. The fact is Eliot was steeling himself for opposition, aware he had tried and failed to separate in the past. Vivienne's hold was such that he felt if he put a foot into their home he would never escape.

Later that spring Vivienne sent Eliot a reminder, via his brother, that he was to speak in July at the Albert Hall. She was already selling tickets: a warning that she would be there to claim him as her husband.

13

A POSSUMA FOR TOM POSSUM

When the academic year ended, Emily Hale prepared to go East. The intention she gave out was to see her mother and help her aunt prepare for a summer in Seattle. Eliot put a stop to it. He would not be available to see her, he said. She decided instead that she would drive her Ford along the Pacific from southern California up to Seattle. Eliot was against this too; he told her it was foolhardy and exposure to the sun would age her skin.

Meanwhile, in June, he joined his sisters, brother and his brother's wife for a farewell gathering at Mountain View House in Randolph, New Hampshire. There, thinking of Emily, he wrote one of his most uncomplicated and lyrical poems, 'New Hampshire', imagining the voices of unborn children in an apple tree, a blissful scene forecasting the ghostly voices of unborn children in the first of his *Quartets*. He sent Emily a photograph of himself in an old coat on the porch, looking unusually informal and relaxed. This family reunion was the last, for him, of America.

Before sailing back to England on the SS *Letitia* he phoned Emily, contriving to sound steady, though 'afraid of breaking down'.

As always, Hale felt uncertain where she stood. Was this their 'last intercourse', she asked.

Of course not, he said, there were a great many years ahead, but he himself was in the dark.

She brought up his 'intolerance'. This made him bristle; then, in a letter written a day out to sea, on 24 June, and posted from England, he excused his crossness: he had been too upset to know what he was saying.

An issue he returned to was her solo drive to Seattle.

'It seems to me that you take a delight in doing mad things,' he protested.

Praying for her safety, he remembered her lips: 'Dear Bouche-de-Framboise'.

From the time Eliot gave Vivienne a false departure date (the end of June, from Boston), two days *after* he actually sailed from Montreal, he was dodging his wife. Back in England, he went into hiding at creeper-covered Pikes Farm, belonging to his Faber colleague Frank Morley, in Surrey, about twenty miles outside London. His hideaway consisted of two rooms let by Mr Eames, manager of a brick yard. Mrs Eames provided breakfast, lunch and tea, and he dined with the Morleys. The bay window of his study, open in July, looked out on a white gate, a rickety fence with nondescript foliage between the staves and eleven-month-old Sukey Morley in her pram. All correspondence was conducted through his office in Russell Square. Few people knew where he hid: only his solicitor Ernest Bird; his confessor, whom he visited at the Deanery in Rochester; and of course the Morleys.

On 12 July 1933 he and Vivienne finally met, at the office of Ernest Bird, one-armed from the war but no weakling, who had drawn up a deed of separation. Vivienne was purposeful in an angled felt hat and dark suit with a crisp white bow at the throat, unlike the helpless-child image of a neglected, unwashed wife. Two years later she sent Henry and Theresa Eliot a studio photo showing how she had looked at the legal encounter. It was a claim of family connection as well as an assertion of sorts. This is a woman who is not about to take herself conveniently off the scene. Yet the cost to her can be seen in the pained eyes and tense clasp of her hands. There's a sternness to this image and a defensiveness to her expression and posture.

During the proceedings, she held Eliot's hand, and though she pretended he had been somehow entrapped by enemies, he felt that she knew he was making a choice to leave her. His fervent wish was never to see her again; his fear remained that she would 'molest' him if he showed himself.

Abigail Eliot, who had taken to Vivienne, was in London that summer with her lifetime partner Anna Holman. When Abby visited, Vivienne asked, 'Where is Tom?' Abby promised to find out.

She contacted Eliot through his work address and they met in a restaurant. He urged his cousin not to see Vivienne again because it was 'dangerous', but Abby did go, and while Anna waited outside she repeated to Vivienne that it was Tom's free decision not to live with her. Vivienne appeared to accept it.

Meanwhile he wrote regularly to Emily in Seattle, wishing she were with him to make where he was 'home'; at other times wishing she were at least not so far away, though at a safe distance, somewhere on the Continent. One night in August he dreamt she was not at the usual distance but close by and took his hand.

This dream prompted a vision. He recounted it to her as a 'spiritualising' moment that for a few minutes transformed ordinary life. His 'outgoing' feeling for Emily remained with him for two days 'in solitude and silence', reviving the experience in his poem 'Silence', his first poetic record of the transcendent moment.

Hale reflected to a Seattle friend, Sophie Krauss, that it was Eliot's 'exquisite sensibility and moral fibre' that made the relationship 'impossible of fruition'. Her appreciation of his rarity offset her 'frustration'.

After the clamour of celebrity in America, Eliot was on his own at Pikes Farm while the Morleys went to Norway. He liked the mistiness of England, the damp smell of country lanes, the procession of clouds, the changes of light and shade and the solitary old trees on hills. Charmed by a 'radiant' letter from Emily, he composed in return a comic verse in the vein of Edward Lear:

LAST WILL & TESTAMENT

The Description.
> *He had Friends, both Hale and Tubercular;*
> *Rumpuscat was the name of his Cat;*
> *His waistline was perfectly Circular*
> *And he sported a wopsical Hat.*

The Message.

He had Teeth, which were False and Quite Beautiful;
His aspect was Pious & Pale;
And he asked to have sent his most Dutiful
Respects to Miss Emily Hale,

The Bequests.

And bequested her a nice Indian Basket
In which grew a sweet-smelling Fern
And his Ashes, not boxed in a Casket
But contained in a Portable Urn;

And a neat Mourning Brooch, silver-plated
And designed like a small Teddy Bear,
Inside which, as he wished should be stated,
Reposed the last Lock of his Hair. *

The comic verse was a sign he was cheering up after leaving Vivienne. Hale too seems to have brightened over the possibility of a freed admirer and the prospect of a year in England with her aunt and uncle. Eliot assured her that his love was unabated and that he had a new dark red and 'rather immodest' bathing costume, and a new apricot tennis shirt.

Pointing significantly to a nearby rose bush (elsewhere he had called it, rather fancifully, a rose-garden), he fondly confessed that his waking thoughts of her had become 'rather a nuisance'.

As August drew on, it was time for Hale to go back to Scripps. The college, typically exploitative of hard-working untenured faculty, was curtailing her salary during the vacation and might dock it further. Eliot offered 'very special tender and passion-ate solicitude – and it is very often very hard for me to stop at

---

* This final line refers to the fact that the hair on one side of his head had been falling out during his time in America.

that and not go on to a largely selfish fury and rage' at her poor position.

But why stop at passionate phrase-making? At this turning point in his life, when Emily expected some plan of action, Eliot continued to hold back. This was possibly why she stopped writing from 23 August, and her withdrawal continued throughout September.

That month Eliot went on retreat at Kelham in Nottinghamshire, and while there he read a biography of Vicomte Charles de Foucauld, who became a Trappist monk, then a missionary to the Tuareg in Algerian Sahara, where he was murdered. His steadfastness and devotion 'make me very much ashamed of myself', Eliot told Emily. 'A man with such immense stores of spiritual energy, and gifts of grace, so utterly concentrated on the good and on God, makes me feel a very poor thing.' Here is the earliest source for Eliot's play *The Cocktail Party*, where Celia, a discarded mistress, turns missionary and is crucified. Celia's character would be based in some ways on Emily Hale. Curiously, in writing to Emily of Foucauld in his hot landscape, Eliot enters into Emily's return to her Southern California setting: he imagines her 'in blazing heat over baked brown hills and that terrible glare on everything'.

During the weeks of Emily's silence, Eliot cast about for what could have happened. Had he offended her? Or might she be losing interest in him? It occurred to him to suggest her coming to England the following summer, as though it were his idea. It occurred to him also to firm up his commitment.

'I should like you to know, once and for all, that there is nothing in this world that I would not give up without hesitation if I had even the slightest hope that you would accept me as your husband.' The thought excited him. Boldly he confronted the issue of deceit: did she really believe he had established a relationship under false pretences? He did not deceive her deliberately.

When Emily resumed writing, she too was emboldened. She did not want to be an adjunct to his aspiration, his private pilgrimage or *purgatorio*. She did not want a meaning attached to her.

He replied as she would have wished: he loved her for herself. Hale decided to consult Ada, whom she had met at a Hinkley dinner. Ada was clear that her brother would always put religion first.

'If you can continue Tom's dearest friend, giving and receiving confidence and affection, you will be a constant source of happiness and strength to him. For you to suggest anything else would, I believe, merely cause him added suffering,' Ada said. 'Tom will never again be a Unitarian, and he is a man whose nature craves a religion.' Ada, of course, was unaware of her brother's desire for 'riperaspberrymouth' and the kiss out west.

All the time that Eliot was pressing Emily to accept divorce as out of the question, he was beckoning her with overwhelming affirmations of his love. This led her to go on testing the boundaries, so that when she took up the issue once more it annoyed him to find he must excuse himself again.

His position was this: if a marriage had been invalid, the church could annul it. Grounds for annulment could be, firstly, a psychological incapacity to understand the commitment marriage entails. Another ground for annulment was withheld information. Eliot had a case here: he had married with no inkling of Vivienne's state of health.

All the same, he did not seek annulment. It may have comforted him to believe that in the eyes of the church the marriage was void, but were annulment to be granted, he explained to Emily, divorce would still be legally impossible. He said that his wife would have to divorce him for adultery, and she never would. Eliot never revealed to Emily that Vivienne had committed adultery, which did give him legal grounds for divorce. But for Eliot it was never a matter for choice: believing as he did in the sacrament of marriage, he adhered to his faith.

When, eventually, he moved back to London, in November 1933, Eliot kept his address secret: dim-lit, chilly lodgings in Courtfield Gardens, then two only slightly less chilly rooms at St Stephen's clergy-house at 9 Grenville Place, off the Cromwell Road in Kensington. He worshipped at St Stephen's around the corner, and in April 1934 accepted an appointment as vicar's warden, the highest lay position in the parish. When Virginia Woolf challenged him to define belief in God, he did not oblige, staring her down like 'a great toad with jewelled eyes'.

Gloucester Road tube station was handy; the Piccadilly line would take him straight to his office in Russell Square. At Gloucester Road there was a lift to take passengers underground. 'Descend lower', Eliot intones in *Burnt Norton*, and tube scenes, surrounded by vacant commuter faces, would enter the later *Quartets*.

All the while, Hale flourished at Scripps, straight-backed in white linen amid the palms of Southern California. She wore elegant shoes and held her waved dark head a little on one side as she directed her adoring, stage-struck students. Her final production in a College quadrangle in the spring of 1934 was Milton's *Comus*, to commemorate its tercentenary. Though Eliot warned she was overreaching herself, the review she sent him spelt out a triumph.

She remained dissatisfied with his elaborate explanations for inaction. Given her reserve and civil manner, it is surprising to discover how quickly and firmly she brought up the question of divorce when she came to England in the summer of 1934.

As planned, Emily Hale took leave of absence from Scripps and in July joined her uncle and aunt at Stamford House, which they had rented in the Gloucestershire village of Chipping Campden. Hale went straight from the ship to this charming house with old Spode and warming pans. Its owner, Miss Maud Sunderland-Taylor, was a retired headmistress who summered in Dubrovnik. She was a graduate of Newnham College, Cambridge, with a taste for the novels of Virginia Woolf visible among her books.

Emily at once let Eliot know she would not be party to 'dissimulation' as a man's secret woman and that, before leaving Boston, she had disclosed their situation to the Hinkleys.

Eliot admits he had practised too much of dissimulation in the past and had, in truth, 'choked on it', but he believed 'the necessity for dissimulation will grow less in time' and it 'grieved' him that there were actions in the past he could not make intelligible to anyone.

Within days, Eliot was in Campden for a weekend. He found Emily more beautiful than ever. She had a perfect nose, he thought, 'so beautifully moulded to the shape of the eyes that one does not know whether to admire more the shape when half closed under the eyelid or the colour and expression when open'. Most of all, he became aware of 'a strong and positive, even dominating personality'. The really dominating people, he told her, are those who dominate while they are, like her, self-effacing and thoughtful of others.

He left Gloucestershire uncertain how she responded to him. She still held back, it seems. His own feelings were more intense than ever. There was no need to control himself when it came to words. Emotions continued so keen 'that one wonders that one goes on living, that there is anything in one so obtuse and stout as to be able to survive. There. Quite likely I have said things I should not have said . . . But I did suddenly see myself . . . as something that you had made . . . Yours is the only personality of which I have been conscious as more powerful than my own.'

He was due to return at the end of August, and in the course of that month he sent Emily no fewer than nine letters, as her challenge to him came to a head.

On 1 August she confronted him with the damage he was inflicting on their lives.

The following day, he conceded that 'by constantly pressing myself upon your attention, and importuning you with my correspondence, I was really tampering insidiously with your mind'. His self-censure – 'I see myself as a blood-sucker' – was disarmingly honest, though unvoiced was the writer's need to feed off an experience from which he was in retreat.

His answer on 2 August twists about, alternately reassuring Emily then backing off. He would give his eyesight to marry her, he

says. 'But, my love, my love, what do you think I CAN do?' Were he
to seek a divorce it would mean not disfavour for only a time, but
cutting himself off from favour in this world and the next. This, he
groans, 'might break me'. He's 'tormented'.

His plea for pity left her next day 'terribly unhappy at making
your misery more acute'. She took 'responsibility for this last offensive'. All the same, she held him responsible. Her indelicacy, she said,
in having to express her need repeatedly in the face of his inaction
'grows worse in retrospect'.

Stung, he resolved on 6 August to take responsibility for
everything that did or didn't happen and for the 'unhappiness given
to you and harm done to you'. His greatest happiness, he said, would
be to give Emily 'permanent' happiness and 'fullness of life'.

Permanence. Fullness of life. Here we have it: what she was
asking of a man who, a year after leaving his wife, was showing
no sign of moving on, while still holding her to their private
understanding. Yet he did state his position repeatedly and Emily
chose not to walk away, as she was free to do. During stops in their
correspondence, did she think of ending it? Unwilling to give up
hope, she persisted in not hearing what he was telling her: that
marriage, living as a pair, was out of the question. But it was more
complicated, as she felt: his romantic attachment to her light across
the sea bringing back his purity of heart, a poetic consciousness
not to be trammelled by proximity that could diminish or bring
down a God-given gift. The meaning he conferred on her must
have encouraged her waiting, a patience as extraordinary in its way
as Eliot's deathless attachment.

Long ago, Eliot recalls in this letter, Emily had suggested that
they might come to want each other more as time went on. He
now regrets that he had failed to see 'the real importance' of her
expectation. This is introduced with the usual excuse that he is
immature and inexperienced, so it never occurs to him that he
can influence anyone. This is nonsense. No more convincing is his
denial of 'hypocrisy or self-deceit' in trying to persuade Emily that

he wants only *her* happiness. He went so far as to say that he would be happier to see her married to someone else – while admitting he had done everything in his power to prevent it.

After the regrets, affirmation swells. 'I also believe that all the elements that go to make up a "great passion" are here present with us in the right – I might almost presumptuously say ideal – relation.'

Hale did not agree. She brought up two problems: his shyness and his Puritanism. He concedes that 'shyness should have no place; and that "Puritanism" as we knew it, is a negative and unsanctified thing to get rid of'.

But then, despite the ready concessions, he reasserts his attachment to a medieval love: the distant, sublime love of the *Vita Nuova*: 'ecce deus fortior te, ecce amor'.* The correct quote is 'behold a god – love – stronger than me' but Eliot empowers himself by saying to her, 'behold a god stronger than you'.

Now his voice comes from on high. It hardens as he rounds on her. She is too 'ignorant' (though 'innocently', as a Unitarian) to yield to the spirit behind his solitary course. Though desire is there, he will block it. 'However completely I surrendered myself, as I could, I could see no basis for permanent happiness.'

So, no happiness for her after all.

From here on the letter turns to sermon. She has admitted to uncertainty about an afterlife, and he slates this as Unitarianism. He condemns those who feel a 'necessity to snatch what one can, in a world destroying itself'. The uncalled-for 'snatch' – as though she were greedy for pleasure – comes as accusation, formidable, intemperate, despite his agreement that Puritanism was out of place.

After flaying Hale with this accusation, he defers his answer to her crucial question with further prevarication: 'Is there any basis for us? That we must find out this summer if we can.'

Arrangements follow: she is coming to tea with his sister Marian and niece Dodo, so there won't be private conversation. But he

---

* Eliot's misquotation, as Frances Dickey noticed, has 'te' in place of 'me'.

will think of her as a 'shadow' member of his family. Shadow is to remain her place.

Hale did not let this rest. She challenged him for loving 'what I stand for'.

He denied this. 'I don't want you to "stand for" anything but yourself.' To use her in that way is not to be 'in contact'. He worships her for what she is, not for what she 'represents' to him.

She protested too at his being too humble towards her. To this, he assents: humility prevents giving a person whatever one has to give.

Relations that month continued so badly that Eliot had to plead with Emily not to let his words 'inflame your exasperation with me'. Would she at least suspend judgement?

Eliot feared a face-off at the door of Stamford House when he arrived at the end of August, and he asked Emily to assure him in advance that this would not happen.

To his relief, she received him pleasantly. At Stamford House he took two photos of her, one in a 'bacchanalian' pose at the front door.

What awaited Eliot, beyond a commission to write a play for the next Canterbury Festival, was the challenge of Beethoven's late quartets: to rise to the equivalent in verse. He had marked out the A minor quartet in a letter to Emily in March 1931, and then mentioned hearing Beethoven's Razumovsky Quartet while in Boston in the autumn of 1932. 'That's the way I should like to be able to write!' He told Emily of how, when an Italian said to Beethoven that he surely did not consider these works to be music, Beethoven replied, 'Oh, they are not for you, but for a later age.' Eliot heard that in England a Beethoven quartet was said to be 'crazy music' and the audience laughed. A bass player called it 'patchwork by a madman'. In Moscow another bass player stamped on the score as a contemptible mystification. Eliot shared with Hale his like ambition to go beyond his age. It was another naked showing of the poet in the making. She had to be in on his aim to apprehend a similar sublimity to the eerie, other-worldly quickening of the strings in the finale to the A minor quartet.

Roses from Eliot followed Emily to her hotel in Paris when she went there in October with a friend from Scripps, Jeanie McPherrin. On 17 October she returned to London and settled at the Aban Court Hotel in Kensington, within walking distance of Eliot in Grenville Place. There was a rapprochement, with Eliot apologising straightforwardly.

'I know I am a very twisted creature,' he said. 'You mustn't ever expect me to be quite like other people.'

It softened her to hear this. At the bottom of his letter she scrawls a response, not intended for him but for another reader, almost certainly Margaret Thorp. 'I do not mean to sound uncritical about Tom in my letter to you – it is only that as other elements are put out of the way – I see him more and more clearly – which is a good thing – but it is up to me to remember always that he <u>cares</u> for me – and that makes much difference – I know.' Presumably, she enclosed Eliot's letter in a letter of her own on the understanding that Eliot's would be returned.

The rapprochement warmed the day before Hale's birthday, 26 October, when they went shopping and chose extravagant presents for each other. She gave him a Wedgwood tea set, while Eliot picked out a star sapphire ring, hoping it would be blue enough for the blues and greys and pinks she planned to wear on her birthday weekend with her aunt and uncle in Chichester. Eliot proposed to join their party.[*]

Eliot now seemed to capitulate to Hale's refusal to collude in dissimulation. He was ready to appear with Emily at teas with Lady Ottoline Morrell and John Hayward (living near by, who found Hale entertaining and a remarkable mimic), and at the theatre. They saw

---

[*] Either this was postponed, because they were there for a weekend at the end of November, or they went twice.

Hamlet and *Richard II* (with the Morleys) and attended an afternoon rehearsal of *Sweeney Agonistes* so that Hale could give her professional opinion, followed by its opening on 11 November. Aldous Huxley was invited as a guest. The play was produced by Rupert Doone at the Group Theatre Rooms with Sweeney masked as Crippen. He had agreed with her professional opinion that *Sweeney Agonistes* was unsuited to the stage, though still thought it the best thing he had done. There was a Stravinsky concert and a lunch with Mary Hutchinson, where Stephen Spender was another guest. Eliot admired Emily's black dress and red jacket, and resolved to smarten up with the help of a tailor. They dined out in public, and on one occasion Eliot invited her with her uncle and aunt to dine at his club, the Athenaeum on Pall Mall, whose members were men of intellectual distinction. After a lunch alone he assured her that the longer she stayed, the happier he would be.

On 6 November he remarked on her 'unusual fragrance' filling his clergy-house rooms – rather bare, basic rooms near the District line that shook the sherry and glasses he kept on the windowsill. Now teas took place and Eliot admitted other select guests – the Perkinses and on another occasion Virginia Woolf – to his 'Secret' by giving out his address: 'I live in Kensington, if anything in Kensington can be described as Living.' The new tea set was in use, and Virginia Woolf noted his 'respectable' china amid ugly purple decor and meagre dribbles from the hot tap.

Eliot's semi-acquiescence to Emily's claims overlaid feelings so buried that he could bring them to light only by invoking the supernatural. Vivienne's refusal to accept separation turned into a pursuit of her husband, and this gained momentum from 1934. She seemed to him demonic, possessed by a determination to take him with her into a psychic abyss. In February of that year, during Lent, Eliot had conceived a play about a man pursued by Furies. Initially, he saw this as a successor to the unfinished *Sweeney Agonistes*, composed in 1925–26, at the height of his and Vivienne's fight to the death.

The Sweeney drama had come as far as an agony of conscience following a murder, and again, in the new play, the Furies follow a murder that could have been the fantasy of a deranged man. The play would leave this ambiguous.

The hero, Harry, is a man in a marriage not approved by his family. He craves to be rid of his wife and describes her as 'a shivering painted shadow' (recognisably Vivienne to those who knew her). When Harry blurts out that he 'pushed' her overboard, the family suspects a breakdown.

Living with Harry's family is a poor relation, Mary, who makes herself useful. This orphaned dependant is based on the situation of Emily Hale, and Eliot had in mind a plot where a hero was to turn from a woman like Hale to undertake a purgatorial venture. Though the play is set in the present day, in a country house in the north of England, Harry's terror of the diabolic, his sense of sin, his introspection and moral debates and the shame of a cursed nature coming down the generations all emanate from Eliot's own compulsions and deepest roots.

The visible incursion of the Furies explores this inherited frame of mind: the fierceness of its moral judgement. *The Family Reunion* imports the Salem horror over possession and plants it in an English setting that cannot comprehend it. This play stages an interior action, 'the oppressive gravity of mistakes', as Henry James summed up the sternness of the old-fashioned New England conscience. Seen from a woman's point of view, the finished-off wife is peculiarly non-existent in Harry's mind, merely a shadow — a subject for his conscience to debate, just as Eliot's ancestor, confessing wrong-doing after the witch trials, is not concerned with the witches themselves — they remain peripheral to a man's horror at putting himself in the wrong. In Eliot there was this kind of horrified regret, reinforced by Anglo-Catholic doctrine and, only at a superficial level, by English law. In the bones of his twinned self, Eliot remained susceptible to what he called Vivienne's coercive gift of argument. He may have put himself physically out of its range, nevertheless he heard it.

Vivienne too was enmeshed in something more than marriage as a legal contract. In one of her fictional fragments, Sybilla forms the kind of intimacy in which another person became 'a part of herself'. Vivienne told Geoffrey Faber that to sign a deed of separation would be like signing her own death warrant. This statement confirms her husband's earlier understanding that for him to leave would kill her. Faber did his best to calm her down, in his tactful manner, when he put it to Vivienne that she and Eliot got on each other's nerves with serious mental consequences for both. But the problem was not so much the differences others saw: Eliot responsible, Vivienne irresponsible; he reserved, she outspoken; he sane, she insane. No, the problem was that they were too *alike*: a psychic sameness in their intensities.

Letters from Emily, his 'western star', had to be within his sights if Eliot was to escape. He had to envision his star in letters that he could hold in his hand, and he had to send out his own letters like lassoes to hold her fast. That's why, when he set out on his course for leaving Vivienne in the autumn of 1932, he had wanted to write to Emily Hale every day.

She had resisted. His demand had been too much. She would write once a week, she said.

She was being Firm with him, he joked, yet there's a hint of steel. She would find he was not to be stopped. Even if she read only every third letter, he meant to communicate as often as he willed it.

It's as though allegory shaped this poet's life. How strangely his private movement through much of his lifetime re-enacts the grail quests of old: a knight baring himself to moral ordeals. But the poet's medieval dream, distanced by time and carried in poems and letters, was challenged by Hale's efforts at shifting the relationship to the present and future tense. Entering the poetry of the mid-thirties is the Eliot–Hale debate about time. This puts Hale at the centre of Eliot's evolving art as he conceives a great poem about time itself and how we exist in the course of the lifespan with fate in the making, moment by moment. For the poet the 'moment' opens up a vision, what he calls 'reality' or 'silence' or 'light'. It was his experience, not hers, yet he had to have Hale, his intense emotion for her, to bring it on.

Before Hale left London at the beginning of December, Eliot gave her the ring with the sapphire set in white gold, the traditional engagement ring for the English upper classes. To place this ring on her finger was to bind her emotionally. Their last chance for time together was at Chichester cathedral, which they visited on 30 November. Oddly, Eliot made a point of telling Lady Ottoline that after her tea on Thursday 29 November, Emily would be departing from England the following day and that he must leave the tea early in order to catch the 5.50 train for a much-needed weekend away. It's not known why he wished to cover up the time with Hale, unless it felt potentially scandalous.

The same day that Eliot (and presumably Hale) caught the 5.50 from Victoria to Chichester, he wrote to Pound, 'only a POSSUMA can pet a Possum'. Pound identified Eliot as 'Possum' and Eliot took on this character (signing letters 'TP' for 'Tom Possum'). A Possuma, Eliot goes on, is an exceptionally scarce creature, and no ordinary 'ratels [badgers], raccoons or itchneumonia [sic, wasps] need apply'. A coded message that he has taken a mate?

Hale was due to spend the winter in Italy, first in Florence, then in Rome. At a London party, in the presence of Maria Huxley, she and Eliot parted in public 'with a smile and a shake of the hand', as he put it in his next letter. It is a repeat of the parting in 'La Figlia', where the full line is 'As faithless as a smile and the shake of the hand'. Did he forget or did he deliberately omit that dangerous word, 'faithless'? I don't believe Eliot ever forgot anything. To him, parting, the release of his solitary self, still gave priority to art. That winter he was to start what came to be called *Murder in the Cathedral*; the play was to be a close-up of a saint's passage from time into the timeless.

*

Despite the advance in their relationship that autumn, Emily Hale felt far from secure and the silences between her infrequent letters spoke to Eliot of displeasure, provoking an offer or warning – like a red line – to halt contact for several years. If she pressed her case too often, too explicitly, Eliot could quash it with a cold rhetorical question: 'What is the future, I wonder, that you foresee. I never care to think of <u>mine</u>.'

In his draft of *Murder*, he wrote: 'Time present and time past / Are both perhaps present in time future / And time future contained in time past.' Since these words can't be acted, Eliot's director cut the lines, but the poet did not discard them. They would serve as the opening of a great work to come, to be fuelled by further moments with Emily Hale. He needed her.

14

'WE'

'Riven' was how Virginia Woolf saw Eliot when he came to tea in Tavistock Square that November. Could the rift close? This was the challenge for Emily Hale as his partner of choice. Now that he had left Vivienne, could he put that past behind him and heal his nervousness of his wife's claims? He went about London fearful that Vivienne would 'molest' him. So he said when he unburdened to friends: he was the victim of a monstrous pursuit.

Emily, writing from Italy, asked directly: if the obstacle to their future together was his threatening wife, should Vivienne be institutionalised?

Eliot said it would be better, 'but in this country it is very difficult to restrain anyone's liberty'.

Increasingly, Vivienne behaved in erratic ways. In September 1934 she had joined the Fascists, the pro-Nazi party founded by Mosley in 1932, but the nonsense Vivienne bleated about kind and caring Fascists shows more about her feeling abandoned than understanding what the party stood for.

That November she had refused entry to men armed with a court order (secured by Ernest Bird) to collect her husband's property from their flat in Clarence Gate Gardens, where Vivienne still lived.

'I want to put the seriousness of the situation as clearly and forcibly to you as possible,' Eliot said to Maurice Haigh-Wood, 'because it is inconceivable that she should continue to behave as she has been doing, if she realised herself how serious the matter is, and is likely to be for her.' He meant prison for contempt of court. Rather alarmingly, he told Emily, 'I am quite prepared to send her to prison if necessary.'

In December 1934 men broke into the flat (still Eliot's in so far as he paid the rent), wrenching books off shelves and carrying away three bookcases, pictures, a kettle and a bell of sentimental value. A seal ring that had belonged to Eliot's great-grandfather was discovered to be a copy. Vivienne had also stashed assorted silver items belonging to Eliot at the bank, and when he was due to collect these in January she asked the bank manager to conceal her on the pretext of a need to identify him as the owner.

She seemed crazed, but in fairness this was not entirely without reason. Eliot gave her a false sailing date from America and a false port of entry to England, he hid in Sussex and employees at Faber had orders to convey to Vivienne that he was not there. No fool, she questioned the lies that kept her at bay, masterminded by her invisible husband – invisible, that is, to her. Unsurprisingly she believed there was a conspiracy against her. There was.

'Vivienne adopts the attitude that I have simply and unaccountably chosen to absent myself, leaving her in suspense and very much in the dark,' Eliot put it to Mary Hutchinson, 'naturally I have so far thought it fruitless and unnecessary to give her any reasons for my decision.'

Vivienne reproached her brother for colluding in her exclusion. 'If you meet my husband without my knowledge, and without affording me the opportunity to be present, it looks very much like conspiracy.' Maurice was persuaded to add to Vivienne's fears by reinforcing legal threats from Bird & Bird: the firm's series of letters warning Vivienne to return the residue of her husband's property *or else*. It augured physical force. It was not then drugs alone, but this animal fear of being caught, a prescient fear as it turned out, that made Vivienne act in ways that looked irrational. So it was that she took to the streets as a kind of refuge: she felt safer there than in the Clarence Gate flat.

That Vivienne was not violent and meant no bodily harm is a prime fact in the scenes she and her husband played out. His allegation that she would 'molest' him was baseless. Since Eliot was never in physical danger, nothing could be done to constrain his wife. Vivienne, who gave not a hoot for public opinion, knew how to get at him through humiliation, and this led to acts of exposure such as attempting to advertise for him as a missing person in *The Times*.

Emily Hale was not in on much of this, though Eliot did tell her of a 'hideous feeling of contamination' and 'hideous dreams of meeting her [Vivienne], or of being shut up somewhere where I cannot get away from her', and he transformed Vivienne's 'hunting' and 'tracking', into his play about a man hunted by the Furies. On 27 February 1935 Vivienne let Eliot know, 'I take notes of *all things*. These *will be* known in time.'

Twice that March, Vivienne appeared at his office. The drill was for Eliot to slip out of a back door while Miss Swan, the telephonist, and Eliot's secretary, Miss O'Donovan, covered for him. He is not here, they had to say.

'So Mr Eliot is not always here for the Board Meetings?' Vivienne pressed them when she arrived at 4 p.m. in time for the weekly meeting on a Wednesday. 'Of course you know I shall have to *keep* on coming here.'

'Of course it is for you to decide,' said Miss O'Donovan.

'It is *too absurd*,' Vivienne said loudly, 'I have been *frightened* away *too long. I am his wife*.'

These women felt sorry for Vivienne and turned to good-natured Frank Morley, who did like her. He found Vivienne 'a charming, sensitive, affectionate person', yet there was nothing he could do either. She challenged Geoffrey Faber by sending her letters to Eliot through him. Faber assured her that he did deliver the letters, but he refused to act on her behalf, though his wife Enid tried to make up for this by visiting Vivienne and inviting her for dinner. Another time she came to the office with a cardboard box to deliver in person to Eliot. Again, he got away.

Defeated at every turn, effectively silenced when her letters to Eliot were returned unread, she spoke to him in her diary. 'MY dear Tom,' she wrote. 'It almost makes one doubt your sanity, the way you are hiding yourself up as if you have committed a crime.'

Hale hoped that Scripps would ask her to return for the next academic year. Then a blow fell at the end of February 1935. Without so much as a warning, her post had been given away. Eliot tried to console her: it would allow them more time together, an 'interlude' in their lives. For Hale, coming out in hives, a mere interlude was by no means the answer.

In the course of 1935, this prospect of an interlude fused with the prospect of the poem he had had in mind since hearing Beethoven's quartet in March 1931. The poem's first chords sounded in the midst of his current work, a draft of *Murder in the Cathedral*. Eliot set aside nine lines about the losses and gains of time. Loss comes first as a man and woman ('we') enter and take the first steps towards an abandoned rose-garden. The garden is not at first a definite place; it's a dream of love's fulfilment in the course of time: past, present and future. A shared memory of time past can follow unforgotten steps.

Murder in the Cathedral was almost finished at the time Emily Hale was about to leave Rome for England. Eliot's answer to a future for her came straight from the interior drama of the play: Thomas the Archbishop must find the 'right' reason to go forward to martyrdom. Emily must find the 'right way' and seek some 'sanctuary' of her own.

He urged her to accept what she had brought on herself, in his view, and blamed her unfairly for losing her job as a result of trying too hard to please her aunt and her mother. Her aunt, he said, took advantage of her humility. The severity of this hardened even more with astonishing advice not to take virtues and vices too seriously, intimating 'presumption' if she tries to be more than human.

What can only be called misogyny becomes more conspicuous in the first half of 1935. Eliot's letter as editor to a woman writer advised her that though her documentation of seventeenth-century France can't be faulted (he had it checked by a French scholar), to include it in a book was showing off. That spring he also dismissed as freakish a girl who was taken with the writings of St John of the Cross.

There's no way to explain such irrational rulings except as anxiety: unwilling to answer Emily's need for action and unable to control Vivienne's scenes in his workplace, he felt burdened by women. A result of Vivienne's resistance were legal fees climbing from £170 to £300.

Yet his conscience did wake. After blocking Emily's need, his next letter climbs down with a disarming apology. He had been unctuous and preachy. He admits to 'a kind of Olympian hypocrisy – as if I had been pretending to be either above or beyond these troubles myself'. His unwarranted loftiness, he says, had to do with Eliots thinking themselves chosen. It was never taught explicitly, he said, yet all Eliots knew that God preferred them.

Lent over, he cleared his diary for 11 April in anticipation of lunch with Emily, booked weeks in advance at the oldest and best French restaurant in London, L'Escargot Bienvenue at 48 Greek Street.

They met three days after her party landed and settled themselves back in Campden. Hale came up to London to see her doctor and then Eliot. In advance, he warned her not to be vexed with him for shyness. He would wear a new bowler hat in her honour. A sunburnt Emily came looking 'VERY beautiful' in a new blue costume, he told her, and he loved the cigarette case she gave him. The lunch lasted three and a half hours. Afterwards he accompanied her to Thomas Cook & Son to collect her tickets for Guernsey, where, after his weekend in Chipping Campden, she was to join Jeanie McPherrin for a fortnight. Eliot saw her off a week later, with a promise to be at the station and eager to welcome her back on 1 May.

At the very time of Emily's return to England, the first lines for his new poem speak once more to a faceless Emily Hale. 'We', the voice says, imagining their mutual entry into a garden. 'We', his speaker had said to a hyacinth girl who once took him towards the 'heart of light'. Oppressed by the nervy wife, the silent husband had remembered the 'hyacinth garden'. This time, in the spring of 1935, it is to be a rose-garden, and there the poet is about to revisit that pure – undivided – youthful feeling. Emily, in person, was vital to this, and 'we' initiates a new intimacy.

The night Emily came back, Eliot took her to *Henry IV,* and then she and Jeanie stayed in Eliot's room at the clergy-house, while he slept upstairs. He always associated Emily, his 'Rose of memory', with flowers. He put roses in the room and their fragrance – hers, it seemed to him – lingered like the heady scent of *Le Spectre de la rose.*

From then on, Emily was invited to sleep in 'the Bower', as they called Eliot's bedroom. He hoped the communal bathroom would not be too foul. Her evening dress hung behind a screen, awaiting a gala evening at the Ballet. He found better accommodation for himself in the guest room at Faber, done up to Geoffrey Faber's high standard. A night there cost him only eighteen pence. He encouraged Emily to come from Campden as often as she could afford.

When he visited Campden, Eliot made an effort to be cordial for Emily's sake. At her uncle's birthday on 6 June he recited a rhymed toast, 'The Anniversary'. Ostensibly the verse was in honour of Uncle John but on the typescript he has pencilled in 'Miss Emily'.

He mulled over the prospect of the next winter when she would return with her aunt to Boston, minus a position. Since he saw no alternative – he could neither marry nor support a further stay in London – he lit on a solution of sorts in Chekhov's story of 'The Lady with the Dog': a middle-aged married man falls seriously in love with a visitor in town, a lady with a dog. They can't alter their outward lives but their secret selves sustain a narrative of their own, which is their real life. It occurred to Eliot, yet again, to give his Lady a dog, a stand-in for himself, and again she said no.

Once, when she was staying in his rooms — it was just before *Murder in the Cathedral* opened in Canterbury on 15 June — Emily had a headache. Eliot found himself stroking her forehead, looking closely into her face, and she kissed him before he sped out to find a painkiller. Many hours and many days he replayed this scene in 'ecstatic memory'. His fingers touching her face. Her kiss. At the thought of seeing her in a few days, on 18 June, he gave cry, his joy so foreign to his reserve that it came out in Greek.

Little by little, love gained sway that summer.

He did not look forward to a retreat with the Society of the Sacred Mission in early July. On his previous visit to Kelham, in August 1934, he had not taken to austerity in practice, half-cooked potatoes on battered tin plates accompanied by unwanted talk of poetry. The downbeat tone contrasts with his enthusiasm for nursing Emily and for her next impulsive gesture: putting her head on his shoulder. 'My eyes failed again,' he told her, recalling the blinding moment brought on by love for the hyacinth girl.

Another renewal of their past was a concert performance of *Tristan und Isolde* at Covent Garden. The conductor was Wilhelm Furtwängler from the Berlin Philharmonic.

During the last ten days of July, when Eliot stayed at Stamford House, transporting moments led to a sense of 'another world' and yet were 'absolutely normal'. It was a triumph for Emily to have won this admission from her 'abnormal' correspondent, who had distanced her so insistently. One blissful moment happened at the back of a car late at night, returning from a performance of Milton's *Samson Agonistes* at Tewkesbury Abbey. The village is west of Campden — a forty-minute drive. Phrases spring up around them that were to enter *Four Quartets*. The flawed Samson, blinded by his enemies, saying 'O dark dark dark', as he undergoes a transformation as God's agent, and the poet's insistence to Emily, 'I have said this already, and I shall say it again'. That too was to reappear in the second of the *Quartets*, as a need to explore the buried recesses of the soul: 'You say I am repeating / Something I have said before. I shall say it again.'

At Stamford House it was Emily's task each morning to choose flowers her aunt had grown in a three-tiered back garden. She would then arrange them in the house. One morning when they had breakfast in the garden, Eliot took a photograph he called 'a masterpiece'. Emily is crouched beside her can of fresh-cut blooms, smiling up at Eliot, her eyes crinkled and her head characteristically a little on one side as he bends towards her with his camera.

They took long walks, wandering through the small villages of Stanton and Stanway, and stopping in a field for a picnic lunch under a hawthorn tree. Even the horseflies and the grapefruit-ade she drank were memorable. At the Crown in Blockley their tea was on a slanting iron table. When it rained they had to take shelter until it stopped. Was Eliot was totting up their special moments for his poem: 'The moment in the arbour where the rain beat' to add to 'The moment in the draughty church at smokefall'. Moments 'surrounded / By a grace of sense'.

The climax to this series of scenes was 'the summer star-evening under the yew tree'. On the last night of Eliot's stay, 30 July, they lingered in the back garden for an hour before midnight. Emily sat with her head on his shoulder and the finger leaves of the yew tree curved down over them. She bent down to pick a viola and tucked it in his buttonhole.

It was then that Emily voiced what he had longed to hear. He knew she was attached to him, but love was more than he had dared hope.

From the Fabers' country house in Wales, on 1 and 11 August, Eliot wrote the first of a series of stunning love-letters. As a private joke in a lecture on the subject of letter-writing, he had put down love-letters as monotonous. His own in the second half of 1935 are anything but, revealing him a master of the genre. The first two exercise memory, recreating their late-July moments. These letters recall his 'sudden and unexpected sense of glory in having your head on my shoulder for what was either one second or eternity'. His words take on the challenge ahead in his *Quartets*: to find points where time present and eternity intersect.

His letter on 11 August contrasts their enjoyment of minor events, a church fete and a visit from the Thorps, with 'a great experience': seeing *Samson Agonistes*. Afterwards this was capped by half an hour alone in the dark garden at the back of Stamford House. Then, too, there had been the inn yard at Blockley, with its hollyhocks and crooked tea table. These things, he writes, 'are snapshotted on my memory charged with a great significance'.

Reflecting on the last evening in the garden, he relived their words of love. 'I still feel a sort of lowering of the eyes and weakening of the voice in mentioning it. It is still strange that you should have said, what was my craving desire, when you said it. And it is all still the most natural thing in the world, the most right . . . My nightingale!' Sometimes she was 'my mockingbird' because this bird is native to America and its song even better.

As to the photograph, he would have it enlarged. It was to have pride of place in his room, with her 'most charming merry slightly mischievous look which is so becoming'. For many years this favourite image remained there.

To please Emily, Eliot invited the Thorps to join them for a play Emily chose, Shaw at the Cambridge Theatre in London on 3 September. The Thorps offered a pre-theatre dinner at their home. There Eliot conceived a violent antipathy to Willard Thorp, so much so that it was hard to carry a soup spoon to his mouth. He longed to take Emily away and be 'like our real selves'. As a guest, he was at his stiffest, a wax model of himself, for he sensed that Willard found him lacking. Willard, though pleasant enough, appeared to loom ominously like a 'spectre' against the backdrop of books behind glass. There is something strangely prescient in this scene as it played out for Eliot: a fear of losing his hold over Emily.

She stayed that night at 'the Bower', which served as an anteroom to the imaginary garden the poet had in mind. Elizabeth Barrett Browning's poem 'The Lost Bower' suggests an idea of stumbling on a secret garden with bird calls, rose bushes and 'a sense of music, which was rather felt than heard'. Presences 'up-snatched me to the Timeless, then returned me to the Hour'.

Eliot had the room swept in advance and adorned it with a dozen red roses. Once more the fragrance lingered after Emily left. He said, 'I can only tolerate roses when you have been here with them: for myself, the scent is too disturbing.' He counted the flowers the next day, disappointed to find that she had not taken one away as a memento, like the last gesture in *Le Spectre de la rose*, where the awakened girl picks up the rose and holds it to her.

Three days after the Thorps' dinner, Eliot was back at Stamford House. This reunion, from 6 to 8 September, was momentous for Eliot's poetry because it's likely to have been during that visit that he and Emily walked from Campden to Burnt Norton, where Eliot found the setting for the first of *Four Quartets*.

It was a long walk northwards along the Campden road. Not a happy walk. Emily seems to have been rather cross with Eliot that weekend and suppressing it. Eliot glances at this in his letter of 10 September – *not* one of the ardent letters – which mentions, quite matter-of-factly, their visit to Burnt Norton.

An unmarked turn-off took them across bumpy fields and along an avenue of trees to a country house, one of England's hidden places and at this time deserted. There they discovered an actual rose-garden (the roses in their second blooming in late summer), a realisation of the rose-garden metaphor for love in the nine lines Eliot had already written back in March. The poem will lay out the garden as it was – and still is. It's partly a formal garden, with its box hedges and straight alley edged with roses leading towards an oblong pool. In the garden's wilder part with a thicket and birdsong nearby, the pair call up feelings of their youth – so the poet would have it.

Decades later, Eliot would brush off this past as no more than 'the love of a ghost for a ghost'. His statement, after the fact, is like those of the knights in *Murder in the Cathedral*, who address the audience, each with a catchy but distorting story. To witness Eliot and Emily Hale in action is to see a truer story germane to an efflorescence of his art.

15

INTIMACY

Burnt Norton opens as a duet in which each step in the garden is buoyant as a springboard. 'So we moved, and they, in a formal pattern'. 'They' are their former selves or their unborn children moving as lightly as spectres over the dead leaves. That love, called back as it had been in youth, comes to them with the breath of the past. The promise of the past had turned to 'dust on a bowl of rose-leaves' but here it revives, if only for a moment, to hover with its former promise.

Shortly after his return to London Eliot mentions a plan to add a few new poems (as yet vaguely in the plural) to a forthcoming edition of his poems to be published in the spring. *Burnt Norton*, not yet named, was in the offing. That day, 13 September, he also proposed joining Emily for his forty-seventh birthday.

The finest of the love-letters, dated 30 September, followed a four-day weekend in Campden, with flowers from Emily blooming on his table. The letter was partly to thank her for treats beginning on Thursday 26 September, his actual birthday, when he travelled from London. He looked broader these days, bonier and with the old flash of wildness in the eye. At first they were reserved with each other, but then she ventured to ask for a birthday kiss. She stroked his face, 'so lovely', before he went to sleep.

That night between sleep and waking, he had a 'vision' of her. It came to him why she had always affected him: other women might be beautiful but that beauty is outward, while hers comes from within: her goodness, her moral acumen, her taste and, above all, humility – the highest of virtues. In her, this was genuine; in him, a struggle with pride. The vision opens into a pulsing 'I see', and what he sees is a living woman, humorous, tender and vulnerable too because he does see her difficult future and sees as well his own flaws, the difficulties he had made for her over the past year. On the positive side, he sees a man joined to her: to speak of 'us' is more than the sum of their separate selves. Before, human happiness had not been in his agenda. To declare now his happiness grants Emily a union closer to what she had wanted.

On the Friday night they went to *The Yeomen of the Guard* at Stratford-upon-Avon (farther on from Burnt Norton along the Campden–Stratford roads). On the Saturday night, Emily prepared a dinner in honour of her aunt, for whom Eliot wrote a celebratory verse (at Emily's request), 'A Valedictory Forbidding Mourning to the Lady of the House'. Privately it does honour to Emily in that the title comes from a famous love poem, 'A Valediction: Forbidding Mourning'. John Donne wrote it in 1611 or 1612 for his wife, saying ''Twere prophanation of our joyes / To tell the laitie our love', affirming 'a love so much refin'd, / That our selves know not what it is'. He consoles his wife on his departure because their two souls are one.

As a public poem, Eliot's 'Valedictory' offers his gratitude for all the hospitality the poet had enjoyed, but mostly it's a half-humorous elegy for the garden Aunt Edith had tended. For the Perkins party was about to leave Stamford House and would not return the following year. Aunt Edith reciprocated Eliot's appreciation and made him feel as though (as he put it) 'I was almost one of the family'.

Later that night, his last, he and Emily put on macs and stood

shivering in the wind and mist of the dark garden. It is like the
scene of the hyacinth garden: 'we came back late from the hyacinth garden'; 'your hair wet', 'I could not speak'. In 1921 memory
had addressed an invisible and far-off Emily. In 1935 the unutterable
feeling is the same, but the difference now is their proximity. 'So
that you cannot say that I see in you the things that you do not see,
instead of seeing the real human you: because I see them all.' He
assures her that, for him, she is not 'idealised' as she feared, not a
figment of the imagination, though her role in his work has been
part of it. 'I should make you know', he writes, 'how one man's life
and work has been formed about you.'

Fused with the hyacinth garden is his scene of a woman's 'sweet',
brown hair blown over the mouth, an image of fruitful desire,
framed by a window 'bellied like the fig's fruit'. In *Ash Wednesday*,
a celibate turns away from natural love as he climbs a purgatorial
stair; now, thanks to Emily's presence, he admits natural love. In the
back garden, he was so close that her blowing hair brushed his face.

After the four days Eliot returned to London on Sunday 29
September and this letter the following day is a celebration of Emily
and his most poetic letter to her. To address her as his 'nightingale'
recalls the 'immortal Bird' in 'Ode to a Nightingale' (1819) by Keats.
There's some link with birdsong in Eliot's 1935 poem 'Cape Ann',
which he sent to Emily. The 'Sweet sweet sweet' of birds familiar to
him on the New England shore recalls the sweetness of blown hair.

Birdcall, coming from the thicket below the pools at Burnt
Norton, will sound again in the poem he was ready to write. A call
in response to the 'music' in the shrubbery comes at the climactic
moment for two people, 'we', who enter a garden known only to
themselves.

Physical nearness prompts a poet on the brink of writing. On
3 October he asks Emily to participate in this act by confirming on
paper that what took place between them had actually happened,
waiting 'to surrender my memory to its perfection'. To 'surrender',
in his terms, is to shape a memory, making the transition from

life to art. In its actuality, the garden experience had been more intimate in the night garden at Stamford House, with its yew tree, violas and the buttonholes that Emily had picked, than their time at Burnt Norton itself.

In this letter of 3 October, pronouns are in inverted commas indicating selves in a private drama: 'I have stored away in envelopes the various flowers you have given me at Campden for buttonholes, because of their meaning for "me" but I shall treasure still more this bit of austere yew, because it is a part of what you picked for "us".' That bit of yew from the garden of Stamford House will go into *Burnt Norton*: 'Will / . . . Chill / Fingers of yew be curled / Down on us?' We might read these last two letters to Emily Hale as an ur-*Burnt Norton* in so far as Eliot will want her to read it as a love poem. But its coexisting aim was intimacy as the way into a further union. Additions to the typescript look to 'Light of light': to be lit up by nothing less than supernatural intimacy.

It was the happiest birthday he had had since he was a boy, he told Mrs Perkins, and he had 'come to feel "at home" at Campden in a way in which I had not felt at home for some twenty-one years, anywhere'.

Emily, her aunt and uncle then settled for two months in Rosary Gardens in London. The furnished flat was in the same South Kensington area as the Aban Court Hotel, where they'd stayed the year before. When they arrived on 8 October, they found the place tasteless, but Aunt Edith was adept at home-making. Eliot, still within walking distance, had heaps of plans for Emily to renew contact with John Hayward (in Bina Gardens, the next street) and meet his Bloomsbury friends.

The night after they arrived, Eliot dropped by to welcome them. Much later he would remember Emily's face, showing 'the full radiance that belongs to it' when she stood at the top of a short flight of steps to say good night. That scene was repeated over the next two months and he liked to think no one but himself had seen that radiance. Never had Eliot lived so emotionally in the present: gone, in his continued letters, are introspection and records of daily doings. He seems enthralled by her presence, especially her voice, as they sit talking on his sofa.

One outing was to see *Timon of Athens*. In a taxi taking them to a pre-theatre dinner at the Queen's Restaurant in Sloane Square, he remembers they had to switch on the light so that he could help Emily to button up the neck of her dress.

Both of Eliot's plays opened in London that autumn. She went with him to a rehearsal of *Murder in the Cathedral*, due to open on 1 November at the Mercury Theatre, and was suitably impressed. She also accompanied Eliot to a revival of Rupert Doone's production of *Sweeney Agonistes* at the Westminster Theatre (in a double bill with Auden's *The Dance of Death*). To have her with him at rehearsals and theatres seemed like 'collaborating'. His ambition to write plays, he claimed, was chiefly to win her applause, and some day he would like to develop a part for her. And if she were to play the role, it would be his fancy to play opposite her.

What would Emily think of his own performance when she attended a reading for young people on 13 October? He was glad to have measured up. Her presence stimulated him to do his best, and as he read, he felt he was 'living on two planes at once', memorising every contour of her face and shade of expression as she sat in the audience.

On a 'smoky' evening Eliot took her to see Hawksmoor's church, St Magnus Martyr, a likely source for 'The moment in the draughty chapel at smokefall' in *Burnt Norton*. At a Sunday service at St George's Chapel, Windsor, they ran into Lady Ottoline, who offered a lift back to London.

Hale accepted on behalf of Eliot's relatives and said that she and Tom would go by train. She spoke a little louder and more distinctly than most English people, pronouncing each syllable clearly instead of running some together.

Lady Ottoline took against 'the dominating efficient Hales [sic]'.

And again, she could not bear 'that awful American Woman Miss Hales' when Eliot brought her to tea in Gower Street four days later. 'She is like a Sergeant Major quite Intolerable – How can Tom take her about everywhere.'

Eliot still felt the necessity of letters because seeing her with others did not have 'the intimacy of writing'. In a letter he could declare a 'surrender' of a right over himself, which until then he had retained. He liked to be possessed by her and be less free. It was a permanent change 'and can never be undone'. She too yielded herself to become his 'companion' on his journey.

A two-week gap in their correspondence in early November was filled with physical closeness, becoming steadily more 'natural' (Eliot's word) as it came to feel inevitable. To have lunch alone 'domestically' was more 'thrilling' than in a restaurant. That day she was his 'dear Mocking-Bird' – her lovely voice had always appealed to him.

The next masterly letter followed a scene on 18 November, when Vivienne at last ran her husband to ground. There was advance publicity for the *Sunday Times* Book Fair, at which Eliot, Bertrand Russell and Geoffrey Faber were due to speak. Vivienne spotted the news that her husband would be talking at 3.30 in the afternoon at Dorland Hall on Lower Regent Street. Late, as she often was, flurried by the exertion to get there and carrying her dog Polly in her arms, Vivienne rushed into the packed hall – to find Eliot himself entering behind her.

'Oh, Tom!' she cried, turning a face to him of such intimacy that, as she recounts the scene in her diary, no one present could have doubted that here, at long last, was his wife to support him in public.

He made his way to the platform and spoke gravely, in his measured way, on tradition in the practice of poetry, suggesting that tradition should include the revolutionary as well as conformity.

Vivienne signalled her agreement, nodding enthusiastically and holding Polly up for all to see the speaker's pet, as excited as she was.

Literature, he went on, is renewed by cross-fertilisation, by encounters with foreign literature (as in the Tudor period) or with a period far off in the past (as the Middle Ages had been for the Romantics).

When he ended, Vivienne let Polly off the leash. The dog ran straight to Eliot and began jumping up at him. He ignored the dog, but could not ignore Vivienne. She pushed her way through the throng and leapt up beside him on the platform with three of his books under her arm. She placed them in front of him and put her hands on the table.

'Will you come back with me?' she asked quietly.

'I cannot talk to you now,' he replied, signed the books and walked away with the chair of the event.

Bizarrely Vivienne took this to be a public acknowledgement of their marriage and announced to her bank manager that it was all right between them and that from then on Eliot would control her finances.

Emily, who would have been present at Dorland Hall, wrote Eliot a moving letter that very day, which sadly has not survived. She must have disclosed her feelings to him as never before because he read this as her first love-letter and planned to lay a piece of brown paper over the pile of previous letters to mark a new phase. He promised to remember that day, 18 November 1935, for Emily's letter and not for Vivienne's public claim, and he gave Emily his original typescript of the talk with corrections in his hand.

Yet the wish to concentrate on Emily could not wipe out what had happened. Ten days after Vivienne accosted him at Dorland Hall, the New English Weekly published Eliot's bitter words, 'More bitter than the love of youth':

> The tiger in the tiger-pit
> Is not more irritable than I.
> The whipping tail is not more still
> Than when I smell the enemy . . .

Hate hisses over 'the archèd tongue' and the hater's golden eye is 'mad'.

Hale had changed since their first kiss in California nearly three years earlier. Her resolve then, confided to Margaret Thorp, had been to hold back feeling so as to protect herself. But now a freedom to touch came into play. When he wasn't well, she came to sit with him, her arm under his head, twice a day. When he kissed her on her birthday, 27 October, she arched her neck, inviting him to kiss her there. And when they walked arm in arm along the river bank at Greenwich, past the barges, their shoulders brushed. He liked a tall girl, he said, and put his arm around her. Once, when they were due to meet in Dulwich, she was delayed by a November fog. They ran to each other through the murk and he bought her a blue-grey scarf.

Eliot was reticent about 'the most intimate of all' their excursions. It took them furthest from London, to Finchampstead in Berkshire. All he says is that he had liked to see her move about in a pub.

He was not, however, reticent when he remarked how countless kisses were becoming. Once, when she sat on his lap, they fell into a close-wrapped sleep in which he kept part awake to sense their union. He felt the curve of her cheek and soft breath. Eliot told her after she left, he turned out the light and imagined her in his bed, 'with one arm over you holding you closely, a precious rare soul in the most beautiful body'.

The scene of Emily and Eliot enfolded in their waking sleep recalls the centrality of sleep in *Le Spectre de la rose*, even as a solo turns into a duet. Two bodies are in accord, for the woman an extension of sleep because her eyes remain closed while she moves in unison with the Rose as in a dream he has planted. The sleeping union of Emily and Eliot followed their visit to the rose-garden at Burnt Norton, now rising as a poem, and that rose-garden had followed the lingering fragrance of the roses in Eliot's room, after Emily had slept in his bed. His blissful ease resolves 'the torment of love unsatisfied' in his 'Rose of memory' stanza. At the same time, easeful sleep avoids 'The greater torment of love satisfied' (the feeling of 'ashes' after his fling with Nancy Cunard). The sleeping partner owns and keeps desire, like the girl in the ballet with the rose pressed to her face, breathing in its perfume, as the curtain comes down.

So it happened, on the brink of separation towards the end of 1935, that Emily and Eliot entered into their own kind of union as they slept in each other's arms, breathing in each other's breath. It was an aroma they created together, sustained through Eliot's promising words, exquisitely phrased, in love-letters before and after. Suspended in prolonged possibility, it's no wonder that Emily Hale gave herself to this.

Only three weeks remained before she was due to leave with her aunt and uncle. If she wished to stay, she could not afford it. So long as she was in England, she lived as her aunt's guest.

A particular treat Eliot laid on was tea with Virginia Woolf. It took place on 26 November at the Woolfs' home in Tavistock Square. Downstairs in the basement was the Hogarth Press; up two flights was the dining room with murals by Vanessa Bell. Stephen Spender, the young poet whom Eliot published, was present. Hale was a keen reader of Virginia Woolf, unlike Eliot. Woolf had been hurt when Eliot had nothing to say about *On Being Ill*, one of her best essays, she thought, commissioned for the *Criterion* in 1925. *A Room of One's Own*, Eliot had remarked to Hale, was merely 'quite good', and in the early thirties, after Woolf's poetic masterpiece *The Waves*, he had put down her recent work to Lady Ottoline Morrell as 'quite out of date'. The fact was, as Virginia Woolf suspected and as Eliot confirmed in private to Emily, he did not read her, all the while taking it for granted that she read him.

When Hale appeared, Woolf was put out – as put out as Lady Ottoline had been – to find Eliot attached to an unknown woman. Both reduced her to clichés. Where Lady Ottoline thought her a rigid soldier, Woolf thought her 'Eliot's rich American snob lady'. No one in Eliot's London circle was told of her gift; to them, she appeared no more than a hanger-on. Hale behaved in the reserved Boston manner, out of a shyness (she admitted as much to Eliot) and also, it may be, out of her sense of propriety.

She wrote a beautifully observed report of meeting Leonard and Virginia Woolf for her Scripps friend Ruth George, who was introducing her students to Woolf's writings. Hale's readiness for the experience as well as her unassuming alertness shine through the entire letter:

> 19, Rosary Gardens,
> South Kensington, S.W.7
> December 6, 1935.

> Dearest Ruth,
>
> . . . I can think of no Christmas greeting more to your taste, than for me to try inadequately to tell you of my taking tea with Virginia Woolf and Mr Woolf, last week Tuesday. Of course this was done in the company of Tom Eliot, who is one of a closer circle of friends, admitted to their life . . . In the soft light of a small lamp on the square tea table, Mrs Woolf rose to greet me . . . I faced a very tall slender woman, dressed in a dark non-descript dress, over which was worn a short dark velvet coat. The simple dark clothes set off to advantage the small head carrying a wealth of greying hair, thick, but soft, which she wears simply off the forehead, and massed in a great Rossetti like coil at the nape of the very long slender neck. A narrow dark ribbon binds the hair accentuating the pre-Raphaelite impression. The features are delicately modelled, if claiming no regularity of beauty, and although the face is lacking in mobility . . . there appeared to me a sense of the mind's attentiveness and colour, (if I may so put it) traceable under the mask-like expression, mask-like except for the eyes, which register the reaction of each moment. A strong

impression of cool detachment constantly contradicts itself by
an equally strong impression of highly charged concentration.
Her manner is not one to place people at ease, quite frankly
speaking, though with Tom Eliot and Spender she was simple,
friendly and responsive in an almost girlish way. I sat opposite
her at the tea-table, an excellent place in which to listen (yes,
listen, not chatter, Ruth) and to observe. Mr Woolf was at
my right, as thin as she, but much less tall; the face is almost
emaciated, the features very aquiline but not necessarily Hebraic,
the expression warmer than hers, especially the eyes which to
me revealed a number of qualities, such as patience, weariness
and isolation. He carries on his shoulder, not an atlas world of
care, but a tiny marmoset, who lives on this human hill crest, all
day long, peering out at one, first from one side, then the other;
this tiny furry ball has a long tail which hangs down from his
master's neck almost like a short queue, slightly confusing at
first. I found myself getting on very well with Mr Woolf, who
consciously or not puts one soon at ease. After an introductory
theme of marmoset and affectionate spaniel Sally, who was at
our feet, he took up a more serious note of conversation, asking
thoughtful questions about America, question[s] almost naive
such as an inquiry 'whether the American Indian mingled in
our good society'.* ... Tea was simple, but abundant, a comb of
honey from the Woolfs' country place, receiving second place
of honor with Mr Ws. birthday cake which his very old mother
never fails to send to each of her children on the anniversaries;
there is a very odd assortment of furnishing in the dining room
and in the larger drawing room below, whose walls are covered
with decorative panels by Mrs Ws. sister, Vanessa Bell. There is a
slight French flavour in this room, but I had the impression that
their surroundings make little difference to either of the owners,

---

* She does not realise that this question was a test of her own stance and
designed to expose the result of colonisation and racism in America.

or at best are artistic too unconventionally to be admired by the average visitor. Downstairs Mrs W addressed several questions directly to me, suddenly but very carefully, so to speak, as if it really mattered what you answered her, and you found yourself wanting very much to make it matter and were curiously aware of your English as you answered. She sat quite gracefully on a small sofa at the further end from S.S. and me (I had hoped she would be next to me) and smoked languidly but in a very practised way. The impression of cool, half-mocking detachment began to lessen, it became a reserve, a shyness, a husbanding of fine abilities for the moments when they must be used and tested . . . Since then I wrote to tell Mrs W. of how much I had enjoyed her books . . .

Now I must stop, although I have many other things to relate, all making it very difficult to leave London.

Yours,

Emily Hale

P.S. I read to Tom much of your letter and he loved it, too.

With Emily's departure in sight, the emotional temperature rose. On 5 December, Eliot enclosed the opening lines of his new poem, *Burnt Norton*. The nine lines he had written in the spring now extended to seventeen. As the footfalls make their way to the rose-garden, he adds, 'My words echo thus in your mind', addressing Hale as his first reader. Eliot had a genius, his brother said, for infusing intellectual ideas with intense emotion. At the start, the poem speaks to 'you' of what is ephemeral and what holds in the passage of time.

All the while, Vivienne persisted as though the marriage went on. She listed her husband's name with hers in the telephone directory. She sent out joint Christmas cards.

'Why do people stare at me?' she asked her neighbour under a row of steel dryers at a hairdresser. The woman examined Vivienne and couldn't say. But when Vivienne put on her hat, stitched across its brim was the purple wrapper of Eliot's play with the words 'Murder in the Cathedral'. There was madcap comedy as well as pathos in Vivienne's refusal to be dismissed.

Such inescapable facts lie behind another new line for *Burnt Norton*: 'What might have been and what has been'. The past, what has been, points to the present, which cannot, after all, be redeemed. Behind these lines, earlier memories 'gnaw like acid'. This regret for an unredeemable past, the guilt over Vivienne, strikes a different note from the whole-hearted affirmation of the love-letters.

Emily Hale left London together with her aunt and uncle on 11 December. They were to spend the night at the Adelphi Hotel in Liverpool and then embark next day, the 12th, on the *Samaria*, due to sail, bound for Boston, at one o'clock the following morning. Uncle John was excited about the tercentenary of King's Chapel, the oldest Unitarian church in the US, in 1936, and did not plan to return to Campden the following year. So Hale and Eliot were facing a long separation until the late summer of 1936, when Eliot intended to visit her and his family.

They said goodbye at Eliot's place on the eve and morning of the departure day. It's conjectured that she stayed the night, but this did not happen. A letter from Hale to a friend confirms it, as does a public statement from Eliot near the end of his life. This doesn't exclude erotic closeness. Emily took off her stockings and he kissed her bared feet – another scene to be replayed in memory.

Their union did not happen in the clergy-house. A passing remark to Emily that 'the Courtfield rooms belong to us' conveys that they met where they could be together 'without interruption'. Courtfield Gardens makes sense of a detail that at first puzzled me: he could see the Aban Court Hotel from the room where they parted. He could not have seen the hotel from the clergy-house in Grenville Place, but it is only a block away from Courtfield Gardens. They seem to have moved between the two places, and Emily left a letter and a posy of violets for him to find at the clergy-house after she'd left.

In parting, Hale gave him a ring with an elephant seal. 'This ring means to me all that a wedding ring can mean', he promised, 'and I love to wake up and feel it binding my finger, and know that it will always bind that finger.'

His record of their last time together is addressed 'To Emily in whom Tom lives'. It opens with a recent 'release for my pent-up tenderness by holding Her in my arms, on my lap, and pressing my face to Hers to intoxicate myself with the air she breathed out'.

The parting scene is cinematic: how Emily left his room; then ran back to say 'When I'm gone I'm here'; and how he waved a blue handkerchief while his eyes followed her down the street as she walked away and vanished behind a tree. Alone, looking at himself, he sees no longer the same face but a new person coming to birth and signs himself 'the new Emily-Tom'.

He sent the next in this series of farewell letters to her cabin in the *Samaria*, on the day she went aboard, 12 December. He also sent flowers. Though he tried to find her favourite, sweet-peas, none were to be had in winter.

Overwhelmed by what she said in her own farewell letter, and picturing his 'tall girl' with her 'spiritual loveliness', he imagined kissing her as Raspberry Mouth when he went to bed. Can she feel the kiss? Through her he has come to 'know what the touch, the physical contact with a beloved can mean, how it can flood one with a bliss and peace of being alone with the other person . . . there is no substitute for it'. Finally, he bids her 'good night in the Mersey' and signs himself once more 'Emily's Tom'.

Eliot mailed the last of these farewell letters a few hours after the *Samaria* had departed, on 13 December. He was still caught up in their last embrace, her running back for another, watching her walk away, cross diagonally at the Aban corner, then vanish behind a tree. The scene must be sealed in memory. But now he adds a retrospect of his own. Their physical ease with each other has been 'a holy thing'. They had knelt together in the early morning in the pew of his 'rather dismal' church taking in early mass – she had lent herself thus far to his faith. He meant to look back on the intimacy of the last months as a gift of grace.

16

THE WAY DOWN

On board the *Samaria*, Hale was elated. Her chronicle of the voyage in four letters shows her confident and playful, starting conversations with all sorts – a side that women friends and audiences saw, and Eliot too.

She apologised for being 'frivolous and childish', but he read these letters marvelling 'That my Lady should love me so much! Me!'

It led to 'ejaculations of ecstasy' at the thought of times when they had revealed themselves 'so naturally and unashamedly . . . to each other'. It was extraordinary to find himself 'unabashed' with her on his knee, looking into her eyes or seeing her lids over them when she relaxed in his arms, 'and I like to be close and breathe your breath'. A favourite scene was her radiant expression when she would stand at the top of a stair in Rosary Gardens to say goodnight. Another, to be relived, was his brushing her hair, 'beautiful black hair which, when the sun strikes it, is really a very dark brown'. He pictured running his fingers through it, massaging her scalp and bending over to kiss her nose. Why bother with waves when he soon mussed them? 'Your hair will be something to look forward to when I come.'

In his private character as 'Emily's Tom', he calls her 'my Self' at the opening of the new year. It seemed as though they were 'each partly the other' and as such 'fused together'. Memory recapitulates a love scene at *Burnt Norton*'s panting end: 'Quick now, here, now . . .' The climax is at once evanescent and 'always'. Eliot confirmed 'the blessings of intimacy' to Emily on 6 January 1936, intent on taking his poem to its finale.

Meanwhile he warmed to her shipboard play and humour, a return to an American character she'd suppressed with his English friends. Before her stay in Europe, she had let rip in comic roles, as when she'd played a dressmaker delivering a monologue with a mouth full of pins. For a year and a half she had not performed, and this, in Eliot's view, had held her back. The way he put it to her was that in Europe she had been in Boston. Now, going home, her sense of fun came back.

So how did it come about that she plunged into deep depression? Without her side of the correspondence, it's impossible to determine with any confidence the cause of Hale's decline. What happened between the farewell on 12 December 1935 and the altered woman he met in New England just nine months later? In July 1936, before he travelled her way, her aunt cabled Eliot in London to let him know that Emily was breaking down.

It was not passing lowness as before; this time it was serious and prolonged. Her animation vanished. She became numb, flat and unable to speak, except about her faults – a sign that what disturbed her went so deep it could not be uttered.

He was 'puzzled' and made stabs at a cause – though none involving himself. He had continued to write to her as often as before, and with feelings, he declared, unchanged. Or was there something wrong with Hale herself? Henry Ware Eliot came to think so, and of course it was known that her mother was in an asylum. Henry later warned his brother that one mental invalid had been too many; he should not take on another.

A clue to the change in Hale can be found in *Burnt Norton*. During the month after Emily left, in December–January, Eliot is writing one of his greatest poems. He looks on *Burnt Norton*, in five parts, as the start of a 'new period' (along with the huge and unexpected success of *Murder in the Cathedral* on both sides of the Atlantic). On 13 January he calls it a 'new kind of love poem, and it is written for you, and it is fearfully obscure'. Three days later the poem is done and on its way to Eliot's New York editor, Donald Brace. It is 'our' poem, he repeats to Emily on 16 January, with a good deal 'that you and no one else will identify'.

In retrospect the poet calls up the play of light on an empty pool so that it appears filled with water. This grants the visiting pair a moment of 'reality'. It's as ephemeral as sunlight in England. The moment passes: 'Go, go, go, said the bird: human kind / Cannot bear very much reality.' Yet it could last in memory as 'one of the permanent moments'.

An ideal form of art, whether it be a garden or a poem or dance or music, takes the scene beyond the familiar into the timeless: returned to their 'first world', Eliot's pair meet their former selves and move with them ('So we moved, and they, in a formal pattern'), like a dancer whirling *en pointe* ('the still point of the turning world') in tune with the outer edge of sound in Beethoven's late quartets ('while the note lasts'). A feat of this poem is to fuse poetry with arts that reach beyond words.

Stirred though he was by his Dove, Eliot's sense of wrong in relation to his wife – sharpened by the confrontation at Dorland Hall on 18 November – had to countermand his release of desire with Emily. *Burnt Norton* turns away from their light-filled moment in the rose-garden in order for a solitary to 'Descend lower' into his flawed self.

At the command to descend the poem switches from a duo ('we') into a lone state of penitence. Before he reveals this section to Emily, he warns her off. The word 'obscure', in three separate letters, on 13 January, 17 February and 3 March, is peculiarly insistent. He underlines this with an epigraph from Shelley, set down for Emily

Hale alone. 'My song, I fear that thou wilt find but few / Who fitly shall conceive thy reasoning, / Of such hard matter dost thou entertain'. Yet *Burnt Norton* is not all that obscure. So why, with these lines, does Eliot try to persuade Emily to give up on the poem?

Before she sees more than the opening lines, he walls off the poem with dauntingly vague explications of part II (on impersonal patterns in the universe), before the poem's turn to the state of solitude in part III. This section cannot be construed as a love poem and this turn was kept from Emily until Eliot mailed the whole poem in proof on 26 March, a week before its publication in his new *Collected Poems*. The end of March, then, was her first opportunity to take in the poet's detachment from human love. It was certain to shake her trust that this was '<u>our</u>' poem.

Next to the line 'darkness to purify the soul', Eliot gives Hale a clue in ink: 'The Ascent of Mt Carmel'. And next to the passage beginning 'Descend lower', he writes, again in ink, 'The Dark Night of the Soul'. These sixteenth-century treatises by the Spanish monk St John of the Cross preach a solitary discipline: to divest oneself of natural human affections so as to arrive at the love of God.

His poem's swing from human love does not deny the validity of the rose-garden moment. The rationale is that the 'way up' in the rose-garden and the 'way down' of the saint coexist, as in the epigraph from the ancient Greek philosopher Heraclitus: 'the way up and the way down are the same'. These are alternative routes across the frontier of the timeless, and the poem does not lose sight of the route via natural love.

This dual schema is accessible to the religious and non-religious alike. What is 'obscure' lies apart, a claim in a private relationship behind the poem, and concerns only one amongst its myriad readers. For Emily Hale alone, the discipline of St John of the Cross, developed within a monastic order, comes into the poem after physical love has drawn her and the poet into a mutually recognised union. It is the private relationship behind the poem, not the poem itself, that will disturb Hale who, after five years of uncertainty, had at last come to trust Eliot unreservedly and to give him the quality of love his poetry can use. For both, the scene in his Kensington room where Emily took off her stockings had been an act of surrender. Even though Eliot, soon after, felt this was 'holy', Emily felt fulfilled by a human union.

For a proper Bostonian and minister's daughter, who had never before experienced physical love, to touch so freely (for Eliot does remark his amazement at their mutual ease and freedom) would have been to cross a line, and possible only with a man she trusted entirely. So, for him to shun human love would have been more than unexpected; how could it not come as a shock and change her willing surrender to shame and disappointment? The first hint that he will turn away from pleasure comes in an otherwise intimate letter on 6 January when he writes that joy does not lie in the things of this world.

At the same time as bodily trust is betrayed, she cannot find work. On arrival in Boston, she stayed, as before, with elderly Mary Lee Ware in Back Bay. Eliot capped Emily's parting words, 'when I'm gone, I'm here', with a flirtatious tease: 'I am in you at the foot of Beacon Hill.'

There, Emily Hale was a companion and beneficiary, for Miss Ware, the wealthy heir of a leading Boston physician, was inclined to kindness towards a lady without means. It may be that Hale saw herself as helpful friend, but in truth she was again a dependant, a long-term guest, subject to Miss Ware's whims. She might, for instance, invite Miss Hale to summer at her 450-acre estate, a show-piece farm in West Rindge, New Hampshire – or she might not. And she might not make up her mind until the last minute. Miss Ware was absorbed in her glass flower collection, and it seems not all that appreciative of Miss Hale, to whom she left nothing in her will.

At once, Hale looked for a position with help from Margaret Thorp and Penelope Noyes. Margaret must have exercised her connection with Smith College, who offered Miss Hale a post as matron. Eliot foresaw the difficulties: to be a matron would not help

Emily find a social life amongst faculty, and then, too, there was the difficulty of wangling some drama work — he knew how vital it was. An alternative was a post at a girls' school in Richmond, Virginia, and the problem here was the offer: a mere $100 for putting on two plays in the course of the spring semester. Out of that amount she would have to cover the travel cost of $37 and pay in addition for laundry. Eliot advised her not to accept unless she could negotiate better terms. Other proposals came near, then whisked away like scared fish. She was applying from a weak position, with no college degree.

In the end there was nothing for it but to stay on with Miss Ware. There was no question of support from Eliot. Apart from the weekly £5 to Vivienne, he was still paying off a whopping lawyer's fee (in instalments of £50) and making do with his lesser salary as the sole ordinary director on the board at Faber & Faber, in contrast with his colleagues, all of them principal directors.

What Eliot could offer Emily by way of comfort was his able sister Ada. He wanted Emily to form a bond with Ada. At the start of Lent he was about to obey the *Burnt Norton* command to 'Descend lower': a prospect of solitary introspection. It would be helpful for Emily to understand this and not take it personally. To descend lower would be a lone venture, a rigorous act of self-denial, returning Emily to indeterminate waiting.

He asked Ada to receive her with open arms and to let him know if Emily, arriving (his sister reported) in a stylish green costume, was adequately dressed for the Boston winter. He worried about cold houses that faced the river. Eliot had a fussy side when it came to health (his knowing cousin had cast him as that epitome of hypochondria, Mr Woodhouse), wanting to be cosseted, and projected this onto Emily, so that his thought of her silk underwear was anxious, not erotic. He wanted her to wear woollens next to the skin, even if he resisted the scratchiness for himself. He could work himself up over Emily's physical health, and if he sent her a cable (reply-paid because she had no money) it was more likely than not intended to set his mind at rest about a temperature or sore throat.

She wanted to know if his attachment to her was an exercise in memory. It was an astute question. Looking back on his letters of these early months of 1936, it seems that when the poet began *Burnt Norton,* he bathed his imagination in love scenes so as to advance through them towards 'Light' (a revival of the 'heart of light' brought on by the hyacinth girl and by the visit to the rose-garden), a word he added by hand at the end of his typescript of the poem. A blow to human joy in his letter to Emily on 6 January is built into the alternating structure of the poem: another way to advance towards the 'Light' is through the sainthood that cuts off from all that is human, to ready the soul for what is holy. So it happened that even as memory takes in a woman's breath, attention shifts to the conditions for sainthood.

For him it is 'a feeling of being alone – I will not say with God, but alone in the presence and under the observation of God – with the feeling of being stripped, as of one's heredity, one's abilities, and one's name'.

His next move, on 13 February, was to urge Emily to read René Basin's life of Charles de Foucauld, the hermit shot dead in 1916 by Senussi insurgents at Tamanrasset in southern Algeria: 'that was a real saint' – a 'thrilling' life. He was not keen on the lives of men who attained what they did without conflict. Such men fell short of sainthood because conflict was essential to the making of saints. When it came to novels, he fixed on the Russians, *War and Peace* and *The Brothers Karamazov,* where principles conflict with passions.

The saints whose lives the poet had explored in *Murder in the Cathedral* and now in *Burnt Norton* inspired in Eliot a need for 'a *really ascetic* (and from an English point of view, quite *useless*) order'. Lady Ottoline found Eliot decidedly un-English in his strenuousness. When she mulled over his character in her journal, she took issue with his opposition to the humane form of sainthood. 'Tom is an orthodox Churchman – not a Saint. – He is a man who is timid &

needs the backing & *Safety of the Church* . . .' She thought him alien to the 'queer humanity of English people', too rule-bound, too devoid of leniency and 'good old English Compromise' to be an Anglican.

As for Emily, she was beckoned into demonstrative love ('I feel the rhythm of your body,' Eliot said on 10 January), then side-lined as he prepared to cleanse impure desires during Lent.

She tried to take on trust what he had called 'our developing union'. Eliot often repeats this promise. Contradicting Hale's impression, it seemed to her deceptive, but it is only fair to place Eliot's sense of progress in the light of an 'extension of being'. From his point of view this was not incompatible with the way down, and his feeling for her was intact. A letter of 17 February makes an appeal to her first through memory (when he had stroked her forehead and felt shaken by tenderness), and then with a startling admission. It is 'awful', a travesty of love, he says, when it puts a beloved to use.

Encouraged, she mentioned a tribunal to handle cases of unfortunate marriage. She was aware of 'pushing' him. This provoked a severe reply. Not only would nothing alter the position of the church and law, but Eliot accused her of secret resentment against the Anglican church and rebukes her also for selflessness which he regards as narrowing. His target is really the selfless humanism practised by his family, with Hale included as a fellow-Unitarian.

Had she stayed on in London, he now told her, their ways of being together would have changed because the strain on him would have been too much. Their intimacies, 'partly because of their incompleteness', had been exhausting as well as life-giving. It was right, he assures her, to have done what they did: to have been so much together, but his startling conclusion was: 'I think we should behave as if we should never be united.'

The blast was fanned by another – and massive – detonator outside her control: Vivienne's pursuit. On 21 February, the very day he revealed to Hale they could never be united, Eliot took up his new play about a man pursued by Furies.

Meanwhile, there was a new policy about letter-writing. His letters from 24 February switch from intimacy to a chronicle of his doings. He asks her to do the same. On 11 March he worries that he has had her love 'rather under a misunderstanding'.

Two weeks before the publication of *Collected Poems*, Eliot mentions, a third time, the obscurity of *Burnt Norton*. He informs her, for instance, that a reference to the boarhound and the boar stands for war. The meaning is so arbitrary that no one could know.

'There!' he finished, pleased to have called up a fog of explication.

In the past Eliot had thought that Emily didn't care for his poetry and he told her this was as he wished. He had added how little he wanted women to tell him they liked his work. It was not merely irrelevant, it was an irritating presumption.

Penelope Noyes let him know that Emily was less robust than she had been. Previously, he would have leapt to attention at any sign of ill health; it's a sign of how fearful he was of Emily's claim, and how adamant to slough off whatever had been inappropriate to the holiness of Lent, that now he simply put this aside.

Though she was 'forlorn' and thinner, Hale took courage to expose Eliot to a truth about himself. He was intolerant and oppressive, she said. As yet, no one apart from his brother had dared to say this directly to him. Confronting him squarely on his divisive ground, she demanded a definition of Christianity that excluded her and her relatives.

He retorted with the difference between Trinitarian and Unitarian. He was ready to concede that a Unitarian might be more 'Christian' in her conduct, but to him this took second place to belief in the real Presence of the divine. He did concede Emily's purity of heart, her enviable humility and natural goodness.

As she deteriorated further, Eliot disparaged the 'woolly counsels' of the Rev John Carroll Perkins. He was still annoyed by her allegiance to her uncle and aunt, without perceiving how much kinship mattered to a woman who had long been without parents and security.

Having at last received and read the complete poem, Hale had to tell Eliot he was saying things with which she could not agree.

He answered on publication day, 2 April. 'I have been much tormented on your account.'

Five months had passed since they had parted in London, and now he tried to smooth over the buffetings he had delivered. Could he persuade her to accept his version of love? To the news that he had discussed the question of his marriage with Fr Underhill, she sent a 'wan little note' on 9 April and then fell silent.

Eliot begged her to write and sent flowers. But Hale's hope had been dashed too far. At her withdrawal, Eliot turned furious. He spoke of 'an unresolvable element of hostility' between two people, which becomes more important the more intimate the pair. 'A man in love has moments at least when he feels his condition, with resentment, to be one of slavery rather than of self-realisation.' Intimacy, then, means a power struggle. One can't but think of Vivienne.

As spring came on, Hale was still without work. An invitation to stay with Penelope Noyes fell through. Instead, she went to Senexet amid pine woods in north-eastern Connecticut. The retreat did help, reinforced in mid-May by an offer from Smith College, a better one this time, for the coming academic year. As an Assistant Professor of Spoken English, she was to have a salary of $2,000.

Hale was restored enough to take a role in a Footlight play later in May. In the past she had avoided Eliot's critical remarks through the simple expedient of not sending the photos he always requested. For once she succumbed, and he outdid himself in savaging her blond wig and legs looking, he said, like stuffed telegraph poles. As in the past, he disliked her in roles at variance with her gentility. Hale was offered another part with a summer theatre company. This time she kept the details to herself and it's not known if she did perform. The

Footlight play was a success, but from then onwards she was once again in a bad way.

The Perkinses wrote to Eliot in her stead. Emily, they said, felt hopeless from 'waiting for things to happen'. She was finished with patience, and intending to make her life 'anew'. The spiritual heights were not for her. The failure, she decided, was hers, unable to match what Eliot wanted.

In July she took refuge with Aunt Edith and was said to be 'resting'. She could no longer conceal her wretchedness, and this must have been when Aunt Edith sent a cable to Eliot. A letter from Aunt Edith followed, which relieved Eliot because she did not blame him and spoke rather of Emily's unfitness to start at Smith.

Alarmed at last and 'wrung' by her pain, Eliot promised Emily that he was coming and 'we shall be together'. He can and will meet her need 'to straighten things out'.

Before Emily had left England there had been a plan for him to visit the US. More than a week after his arrival he let her know at the last moment that he could not break his journey to see her where she was staying at Fitzwilliam, near Miss Ware's farm in New Hampshire, as he made his way north to join his family at the Mount Crescent Hotel in Randolph.

They were finally to meet in company when they dined at the Hinkleys' on 11 September. While she waited, he contrived to keep hope open by assuring Emily that they will 'lay foundations' (her phrase) of a new life, but for Eliot 'foundations' meant her separate life at Smith: the help he planned was to see her make a good start.

Hale had a friend from the Midwest, Dorothy Olcott Elsmith, who had been at Smith a year ahead of Margaret Thorp. All Emily Hale's lasting friends were of a type: spirited, confident, warmly intelligent and loyal. Kind Mrs Elsmith offered Hale and Eliot seclusion for a week in her oceanfront home, Olcottage,* at Woods Hole on the south-west tip of Cape Cod.

---

* Also called Ros Marinus.

In September 1936 Eliot spent a week with Emily Hale at Woods Hole on the Massachusetts shore, where they took long walks. She was about to start teaching at Smith College.

Eliot pleased Mrs Elsmith's son, a pupil at Milton Academy, by wearing his own Milton tie to breakfast on the first day. At Olcottage, Emily and Eliot were provided with supper on trays in front of the fire when they returned from long walks. These were mostly on the shore and they had one of what Eliot called their 'moments' there, near a grove of pine trees, when the sound of a bell-buoy out at sea struck the ear.

He gave Emily a Bible and amongst the passages she marked was Proverbs chapter 4: 'Forsake her not, and she shall preserve thee; love her, and she shall keep thee. Exalt her; and she shall promote thee; she shall bring thee to honour, when thou dost embrace her.'

Before he departed for England at the end of September, Eliot went to Northampton in western Massachusetts. This was a farewell visit to Emily Hale. By then she was there, teaching at Smith, and he hoped to hearten her in what was a precarious undertaking. She still lacked her former verve and enlivening plans for others. He comforted himself that she was better and that her depression would pass in the course of her work.

On parting that Sunday, they were not alone. F. O. Matthiessen, a one-time colleague at Harvard whose book *The Achievement of T. S. Eliot* came out just then, was travelling back to Boston with the poet. It was similar to the parting at a London party in 1934: nothing much could be said. In silence Emily gave Eliot a rose. Her sad face looked up at the train.

We might ask: why did Emily Hale not walk away?

There's no easy answer. A habitual bond between two people, however fraught, is hard to break, as Eliot had found with Vivienne. Perhaps, at forty-five, she did want his love, even on his shifting terms. She knew he granted her a private share in his poetry and the message he now sent from Boston conveyed a sense of spiritual intimacy deeper than he should have believed possible. She breathed Eliot's rarity.

He did recognise a depression bad enough to leave a mark and he gathered it for his poetry. Emily's insomnia and her unsatisfied questions about past and future find truthful expression four years later in *The Dry Salvages*, with its plangent lines about worried women who lie awake at night trying to piece together past and future 'when the past is all deception, / The future futureless'. Such women ask Emily's question, 'Where is there an end of it', and he, the poet, answers: 'There is no end of it, the voiceless wailing, / No end to the withering of withered flowers.'

Wearing a brown bow tie Emily had given him for his birthday, Eliot boarded a Cunard liner, the *Alaunia*, in Montreal. On the eve of departure, he wrote, 'I shall see your dear sad face at the train window until you give me new images to supersede it.' He adds, 'Your "sweetheart" rose is still in my pocket.' He would use the rose fading in his pocket in *The Dry Salvages*. And he would draw on the shore, the sound of the bell-buoy and 'the soundless wailing'. He would remember the 'rote', a local word for the roar of the sea as the wind changes offshore from Cape Cod.

As the poet vanishes across the horizon, his ship is exposed to the timeless ocean. The vessel and the timelessness will reappear in 1941 as the drumming liner in *The Dry Salvages*. A face relaxes from the sadness of farewell into the relief of non-performance. This space frees an imagination. The crossing invites the poet to 'fare forward' with his dual narrative, an *Ars Amandi* (in love-letters to Emily) and a Sermon on Death (in lines he will write 'not too far from the yew tree').

Eliot landed in high spirits, as observed by the Morleys, whose car fetched him from Plymouth on 10 October. To be back in his eyrie-office in Russell Square reminded Eliot of homecomings to St Louis after summers on the New England shore. There were grapes on the autumn table, and this too, recounted in a letter to Emily ('I almost smelt the grapes'), would enter *The Dry Salvages*, together with the Mississippi, brought back by seeing the 1936 movie of *Show Boat*, with Paul Robeson singing 'Ol' Man River'. Eliot's American quartet will combine St Louis with the New England shore and the bell-buoy out at sea.

'The bell-buoy is still tolling in my ears and calls up the long beaches[,] the seagulls, the pine grove, and the room where we sat on two afternoons,' he told Emily. 'How beautiful that New England country is and how much ours.'

At this stage there was no plan for sequels to *Burnt Norton*, yet the set of poems he would compose in the early forties hovers in the distance. Emotions fix on settings Eliot visited over the late spring and summer of 1936. On 25 May, after Eliot had examined a Cambridge thesis on George Herbert, a fellow of Trinity College had driven him to see Herbert's first parish at Leighton Bromswold, taken on in 1626 when the young poet was still a don at Trinity. Two miles away, down a rough track, was a hidden gem: the small, perfect church of Little Gidding, site of an Anglican community founded in 1626 by Nicholas Ferrar, Herbert's Cambridge friend. On 18 June the poet then visited the Eliots' ancestral village of East Coker in Somerset, gathering more sights and memories for the poems that would form *Four Quartets*.

Once more, with scenes in hand, the poet-dramatist slips away from the woman with whom he had walked the beach. He absconds to a space wholly his own, as writers do. 'Perfection of the life or of the work', Yeats posed the choice. For some writers the work unquestionably comes first.

As the ship drums onward, rhythms sound in the poet's head. Voices in his emerging play, *The Family Reunion*. Harry, the renegade, comes home. Mary enters, her arms full of flowers – an older Figlia in low spirits. Destined for a single life in a women's college, she will be side-lined in favour of a man's solitary pilgrimage. It will take him across 'a whole Thibet of broken stones . . . a lifetime's march'.

17

'BROKEN STONES'

In the summer of 1936 Eliot saw Vivienne on Wigmore Street. To come upon his 'late wife' was a shock. He turned and 'took to my heels', as he pictured the scene an hour later to Pound's wife Dorothy, who had attempted to look after a frenzied Vivienne in Paris ten years before. He doesn't say if Vivienne saw him. The panic was all.

'Only people who have been "wanted" know the sort of life I lead,' he said, still 'rather shaky'.

Vivienne's fear of pursuit mirrored his. From 1936 she feared a danger she could not name. Yet she sensed it coming. Might she disappear for her better safety (as her husband had)? Vivienne decided to give out a story that she had gone to America under the name of Daisy Miller, an American heroine of independence who is damaged by a Europeanised American, a gentleman of the utmost rectitude. In this seasonal allegory by Henry James, the gentleman's chilling name is Winterbourne, and as the narrator of Daisy's story his belittling view of her will take hold. She had loved him and he had disapproved of her by his mannered standards. All his detachment allows him to acknowledge is a minor part in her downfall when he stands, eventually, at her grave. The reader must question his version of events. Vivienne's claim to be Daisy Miller, mad as it may appear, is her coded message as haunting as her image of hornets under the marriage bed.

Eliot never felt safe except in his office, surrounded by pictures of New England ancestors. Vivienne's stalking played on her husband's dread of humiliation, when 'the hidden shall be exposed', going back to the early days of their marriage when, Eliot could not forget, his wife had shamed him as a clunking 'dunce'.

The last of Vivienne's fictions published in the *Criterion* has a recognisable portrait of Eliot as an American financier and poet, who is withdrawn and aloof as though he spoke from a mountain top (as Eliot had done at the end of *The Waste Land*). He has a heavy, slumbering face, powdered white; hooded eyes, leaden, unseeing; a sullen mouth with lips a little reddened; and thin hair plastered tightly down. It's a painted face minus the character projecting it, unlike most English fiction with its premise of truth behind appearance. The foreigner in Vivienne Eliot's sketch is *not* there, and that's the point. And this characterlessness is formidable, not pitiful like hollow men. Power – creative power – inheres here.

The date of the Wigmore Street sighting matters. It was 28 July 1936. At that date Eliot had been further alarmed by Emily's deterioration, following the unprecedented cable from her aunt. To put these dates together is to see convergence of stress. The horror his wife induced tightened its grip, taking precedence and almost obliterating Emily beyond the comfort of possessing her.

Will you come back with me? Vivienne's mirror drama of possession took him over. It reminded Eliot of the Eumenides, the Furies who haunt the killer Orestes in Greek mythology. In Eliot's emerging play, the Furies are part of his hero, Harry, an emanation of his secret self, spectres expected and dreaded.

Eliot installed a heavy lock on the front door of the flat where he moved in May 1937, at 11 Emperor's Gate (across the road from the

clergy-house and still conveniently near to St Stephen's). He said
that the bolt was for the sake of his cleaner-cook, Elizabeth, who
had a room in the flat, but of course it was a safeguard against
'molestation'. Elizabeth's presence helped to guard him, and at the
office he continued to rely on Miss Swan and his secretary. These
loyal women were rather like the guard of grown-up sisters assigned
to protect a not very strong boy.

A parallel fear, more apprehension than terror, was Eliot's anxiety about re-encountering Emily face to face. She was coming once
more to Chipping Campden – following her first academic year at
Smith College – in July–August 1937.

Eliot tried repeatedly to put Emily off coming to Scotland for his
honorary degree from Edinburgh University on 3 July. The excuse
given was that he would have no time for her; the real reason is
likely to have been his old fear of gossip. Hale went all the same,
enjoyed Edinburgh and made friends with the chief reviewer of
poetry for the *Criterion*, Janet Adam Smith, a Scottish intellectual
who did not gibe at her in the manner of Eliot's other friends. John
Hayward, for instance, had nudged Lady Ottoline about the imminent arrival of the 'grim, prim, schoolma'amish female who takes
a dreadful proprietary interest in poor Tom!'

Did they see Hale as a threat to their ties with him? Hayward, for
one, was a brilliant young man who, while still an undergraduate
at King's College, Cambridge, produced an edition of poems by
the Earl of Rochester. Hayward had muscular dystrophy but was
determined to defy fate with his bright eyes, quips and wit. After
he came down in 1927 he settled in London as an editor and bibliophile. Admirable editions of Swift and Donne followed. He was agog
about Eliot and from the time the poet returned to London in 1933,
Hayward in his wheelchair and his flat in Bina Gardens became the
centre of a court forming around him. Members of this circle had a
passion for Sherlock Holmes and exchanged light verse. Each man
had an assigned identity: Geoffrey Faber, who was bald, was the
Coot; Morley, who had served on a whaling ship in his youth, was

the Whale; Eliot was the Elephant who never forgets; and Hayward himself was the Tarantula with a considerable power of stinging, as demonstrated with Emily Hale.

Eliot came to Campden for a weekend, 9–11 July, and then returned (after a conference in Oxford) on 16 July for another week. His packed diary did not leave time to see Emily for the next three weeks. When further commitments came into play, Emily was driven to protest. After all, she was to be in England only a short time. This provoked a quick flare: he knew full well and did not need her to point out that he was extending his absence from three to four weeks. Eventually, they had their serious conversation through letters, which allowed for a subtlety that would have been more difficult in person.

Desire, he judged, was a spur to spiritual development. 'I am sure there is something most precious and invaluable about unsatisfied desires – if they are taken in the right way. Unsatisfied desires can play a most important part in keeping the soul alive and urging one higher – anything is better than just deadening feeling – and can persist and at the same time be combined with a kind of resignation which makes it possible to extract the full value ... out of what definitely is in our mental and spiritual intimacy.'

After Eliot's family reunion in New Hampshire in September 1936, he had returned to the most autobiographical of his plays, *The Family Reunion*, begun in the wake of his separation from Vivienne. Eliot was devising this play all through 1937 and the following year, typing out draft after draft: in all, ten layers of composition. Emily was a prime consultant, the first to be shown an incomplete draft when he came to Campden that summer.

In mid-October he sent her a new draft, with thirty more pages, together with roses for her birthday on the 27th, keeping the Rose impact alive. The rose garden of *Burnt Norton*, visited with Emily two years earlier, reappears in the play but here there is no more than a tantalising glimpse through a small door into a garden, and like

Alice, Harry can put only a longing eye to the aperture. The inaccessibility of the garden has a connotation of virginity that includes the playwright's private backing off from intimacy with Emily Hale.

She passed on this draft of *The Family Reunion* to Frank Morley, and he concurred with her opinion that the role of one of the characters, Mary, was awry. In draft, Mary was like Emily: a character who fires up with a protest about the way her feelings and needs get discounted. In the draft she wants to offer her 'resignation' from the life devised for her. Morley advised Eliot to give Mary more scope so that her fate, as well as Harry's, can touch the audience. (Morley brought up the sadness of innocent, doomed Desdemona's singing her plangent song before Othello sees her off: more of a 'willow, willow' feeling, Morley said, was wanting in this play.)

As the play was re-drafted, Mary's action was now limited to arranging flowers, Morley pointed out. Eliminated are her assertions to Harry, which look continuous with what Eliot did pick up in his letters to Hale. He cut Mary's hope: 'Something should come of this conversation. / It is not too late . . .' In draft, hers is a bracing voice saying Harry takes himself too seriously like many highly sensitive people. The solitary path, she fears, will put Harry in danger, and she makes a panting, urgent speech to his family, pleading with them not to let him go.

Harry's idea is to exile himself from natural life, to go from pole to pole so as to live in perpetual winter. Accept life, Mary counsels. Go with the seasons and their natural transitions. But it seems to Harry a delusive temptation to respond to spring with its subterranean 'crawlings'. The Hale-Eliot division again.

During her spring break in 1938, Hale had a holiday in Charleston. She basked in the warmer climate of the South and mentioned the tropical flowers to Eliot. She hoped not to be plunged back into winter on her return north to Northampton. Her thought, taken up in Eliot's letter to her on 7 April, enters into the metaphoric pattern of his play. Harry's unseasonal, or more emphatically *anti*-seasonal turning back from spring into the winter of his soul's journey parallels the broken stones of the route he is choosing to take.

Martin Browne, the play's director – he specialised in religious plays and previously had directed *Murder in the Cathedral* – asked him to clarify Harry's character. In his reply, Eliot performed a sudden strip. Harry's wife, Eliot said, has contaminated him. The taint goes so deep that it corrodes bone, and this gives him a horror of women as unclean creatures. In Eliot's own past, close to Harry's, women appear unclean before a wife comes on the scene: the yellow feet and soiled hands of the prostitute in 'Preludes', female smells in shuttered rooms and the 'Kuk-Queen' of the Bolo verses.

Harry is partially 'de-sexed', so Eliot tells Browne. The cause of this is Harry's late wife. The part of him that remains 'normal' is attracted to Mary, but she is liable to be subsumed in his shudder at the whole sex.

In the play Mary, the Emily figure who remembers 'what is the real you', appears to offer an alternative, like a door opening on sunlight at the end of a corridor. Her voice speaks of what is natural: water, spring flowers and the onward progress of the seasons. She offers this balm. What puts paid to this course of action is the incursion of the Furies.

In Eliot's first drafts, Mary sees the Furies, as Emily almost certainly saw Vivienne at Dorland Hall. Later, re-drafting the first appearance of the Furies, Mary does *not* see them. She will not acknowledge their existence; in other words, does not consent to their takeover of Harry's life. This infuriates Harry, so much so that abruptly he shuts her up together with the natural life she embodies.

The stones ahead lie 'fang up', an ordeal in Eliot's sights from back when *The Waste Land* looks to 'the agony in stony places'. To walk on sharp stones is a penance for Harry's intention to eliminate his wife. In the play there is a memory of a voyage when she disappeared overboard. Did he or did he not push her overboard one night when she was playing one of her edge-of-life scenes? Eerily, the play forecasts an action in Eliot's own life in which the part he was soon to play in the lifelong committal of Vivienne to an asylum would be obscured.

After reading a complete draft of the play in February–March 1938, Martin Browne points to 'push' as 'that <u>most</u> dangerous word!' His unease with Eliot's draft, as well as advice from Browne's wife Henzie to play up an earlier love for Mary, suggest their awareness that Eliot was working out his own unresolved situation in the play.

Meanwhile Eliot's wife is still at large and acutely apprehensive that something will happen to her.

She rents various hideaways, shifting from place to place: she is still paying £250 a year for 68 Clarence Gate Gardens (Eliot stopped paying the rent two years after he left her), and in 1936 she had taken a house on Edge Street in Notting Hill Gate. At some stage she had taken a flat at 34 Bury Street. There is also a perch in Burleigh Mansions and spells in a hotel, the Constance in Lancaster Gate. Her letters are from the Three Arts Club in Marylebone. She appears to have no home address. She's on the run.

With all these dwellings her debts mount to £700, a very large amount then, so much that her bank manager contacts her brother, who manages the family estate. Maurice Haigh-Wood's own means are limited (he informs Eliot) to feeding his family. One of the Irish properties is sold to cover Vivienne's debts; the bulk of the money is invested and she has £200 in hand, but soon she runs up new debts amounting to £500: multiple rentals, hotel bills, doctors' bills, and a hired piano from Broad & Co.

At the age of forty-eight, Vivienne began singing lessons, and amazingly, after no more than three weeks, was accepted by the Royal College of Music. Exulting in her 'huge' voice, she made herself over as a stylish prima donna topped with red hair. It's like a narrative of a star in the making. Together with voice training she studied the piano. Her diary notes an all-Bach lesson. 'One whole hour of Bach and I loved it.' With this come challenges: she has to acquaint herself with music theory and eventually prepare

for examinations. Like many non-working women of her generation, she is unaccustomed to regular hours, often distracted, and
this common handicap is exacerbated by ills and the forgetfulness
induced by years of drugs.

In *The Family Reunion*, the wife has no voice and her end is off-stage.
Harry says he pushed her, but speaks with such mad insistence that
he is not believed. At issue is his level of mental disturbance and the
question of free will versus predestination. A chorus of Harry's kin
declare that 'the future was long since settled. / And the wings of
the future darken the past'.

Vivienne's future comes swiftly on the heels of the play.

A policeman found Vivienne Eliot wandering in a street at five in the
morning on 14 July 1938. He took her to Marylebone Police Station
and her next of kin, her brother, was phoned. To the inspector at the
police station she appeared confused, which would happen when
she took too large a dose of prescribed medication. Her chemists,
Allen & Hanbury's in Vere Street, had notified her doctor about this
and he had reduced her doses. A new regime was for Vivienne to
collect her medicine each day, and so she did, but it was still open
to her to hoard and dose herself erratically.

This was not the first night that she had wandered the streets (in
the familiar neighbourhood of her chemist), fearing to settle where
captors could find her. It is worth recalling that psychiatric expertise
at Malmaison did *not* find her insane, and did not label her fears as
paranoia. Premonition of a tragic outcome had followed Vivienne's
forced stay in what she'd felt to be a prejudiced sanatorium at the
end of 1925. She sensed that crude thinking at the Stanboroughs had
pitted her against her husband, which is why she asked him to let
it be known that they were not as disunited as the staff might have
thought. Murky though much of Vivienne's history is, given dramatisation on both sides, this particular communication between
them does ring true.

When a worried Maurice Haigh-Wood arrived at the police

station, his sister asked if Tom had been beheaded. Like the hornets under the bed, it sounds mad but could be an imaginative version of truth enhanced by drugs. Everyone she knew was conspiring to keep her husband out of sight. She was, in fact, bewildered by lies. The poet's reciprocal fear of 'molestation' was surreal too. What appeared to be madness in his wife was more like a shared poetic horror. A police officer could have no inkling of this.

Unreported by Maurice is the fact that his sister's clothes, vocabulary and accent would have identified her as middle-class, a 'lady'. This made it unseemly to be roaming in the dark. If Mrs Eliot was left untreated and picked up again, the inspector said, she might come before a magistrate.

Maurice was appalled. He was a decent sort, presentable, well-conducted, a product of a public school. Maurice looked up to men of higher education. He was awed and led by Eliot, who combined brains with a grand background. Tall, lean and dark with a trim moustache, Maurice himself had the social standing of a military officer trained at Sandhurst. He had been in the trenches at the age of nineteen and that experience in the Great War divided the sexes, bonding men and detaching them from unknowing women safely tucked up at home. When it came to his distressed sister, there was a blank in his understanding. Like Eliot he backed away from the spectacle Vivienne made of herself, which does not necessarily mean they did not feel for her. They wished away her embarrassing scenes and deplored her extravagance.

After Maurice collected Vivienne from the police station, he took her home for breakfast with his wife Ahmé, an American dancer. He then escorted her to one of her hideouts, a flat at 21 Burleigh Mansions, the block that had housed the *Criterion* office. She told Maurice that she never slept there, though he suspected she might. She had calmed down by then and reportedly remained so. Yet within a month, Vivienne was committed to an asylum.

18

VIVIENNE'S COMMITTAL

Following Vivienne's run-in with the police, Maurice contacted Dr Reginald Miller in Harley Street. This was his sister's doctor, who accepted responsibility for handling her ups and downs. Dr Miller agreed with Maurice that something must be done. All the same, he was inclined to be conservative in treating her, and explained that when he had checked on her at the Constance Hotel he had found the manageress kind and coping with Mrs Eliot. Dr Miller had been '*fairly* satisfied' and Maurice concurred. This had been his own impression when he had seen his sister there.

Maurice made an appointment for himself and Eliot to confer with the doctor. Finding that Eliot was away, Maurice reported what had happened with the police to a forwarding address: Stamford House in Chipping Campden. Knowing nothing of Emily Hale, he assumed that Eliot was away on holiday.

On receiving the news, Eliot took a measure of comfort, he told Emily, 'in having you by to share these difficulties with. It is a blessing to me that this should have happened just <u>now</u>. And how very appropriate your prayer of Christina Rossetti was!' This was on

18 July. Disturbed about Vivienne, but holding to his humorous 'Old Possum' character, he inscribed an early typescript of *Old Possum's Book of Practical Cats* 'for Miss Emily Hale'.

Meanwhile he instructed Gordon Higginson, a solicitor with Bird & Bird, to stand by when he met Dr Miller. Eliot travelled to London and on 19 July there was a preliminary discussion of Vivienne's situation with Mr Higginson at 5 Gray's Inn Square. Ernest Bird joined them before they set out for Harley Street. Maurice had initiated this meeting and would have explained his dismay over behaviour that had involved the police. It seems on the face of it a minor incident, yet in the doctor's consulting room that day Vivienne's unladylike wanderings, harmless enough, were seen to be so grave that the word 'certification' was in the air. Dr Miller refers to this, not saying who said it, in his cautiously resistant letter two days later to Maurice: 'nor do we want actual certification if it can be avoided'.

What was certain was that no one wanted anything further to do with the police. To avoid a recurrence, Dr Miller favoured voluntary treatment at a sanatorium, possibly a return to Malmaison.*

Eliot offered to increase his £5 a week (about £330 in today's terms) for his wife's support if a permanent solution for her care could be found. It appeared that no one was willing or able to take care of her, and to pay extra for 'some voluntary sequestration' (such as Malmaison), he explained, would be throwing money away. (He was to restate this succinctly on 9 August:

---

* Local doctors could not comprehend Vivienne's crises and recoveries, and she herself liked a Swedish therapist, Dr Anjuta ('Anna') Cyriax (née Kellgren), who had begun by treating Vivienne for colitis in 1924. Her husband, Dr Edgar Cyriax, had treated the nerves in Eliot's neck, head, spine and stomach with manipulation and vibration. Their clinic offered what today would be called alternative therapy, and this suited Vivienne, given the damage inflicted by traditional medicine.

'the supplementing of her income seems inseparable from certification'.)*

On this day, Eliot wrote two letters. One tells Emily Hale that he is exhausted and must now wait. Maurice was to deal with the next step and Eliot himself would 'assume no extra responsibility'.

The other letter, to John Betjeman ('Betje', who had been his pupil at Highgate School), veils his worry in literary quotes. The first is from Othello's speech admitting his guilt for the murder of a wife who loved him. Othello identifies himself as a prominent man who has to confess an unforgivable deed: 'Soft you; a word or two before you go. / I have done the state some service and they know't'. The letter adapts Othello's pain, replacing 'the state' with 'I have done the Shell some service', a reference to Betje's employer, Shell-Mex and BP, since Eliot had agreed to a speech at an exhibition they were devising and the following year Faber & Faber was to take over the publication of Shell guides, co-edited by Betjeman. Eliot's joke looks flippant but the allusion to Othello carries a freight of anxiety over a great man's fall.

Another drift, certain to bewilder poor Betje, is more veiled. Ostensibly Eliot goes on about a Frenchman called Berold, a butcher in medieval Rouen. Berold reports a catastrophe at sea in 'The White Ship', a narrative poem by Dante Gabriel Rossetti about a wreck in the English Channel. Berold is sole surviving witness to

---

* In a letter to Higginson on 9 August, Eliot looks back to what was said: '. . . it was made clear, at the meeting I had with you and Bird, that no increase of payment [his weekly £5] could be contemplated unless my wife's financial affairs were taken completely out of her hands [a practice when a person is certified], and put under the control of some responsible administrator, presumably Haigh-Wood himself. To contribute to the expenses of some voluntary sequestration, as at Malmaison, which she could terminate at will, would be merely to throw money away. In other words, the supplementing of her income seems inseparable from certification.' To supplement her income means an offer to increase what an administrator or her brother would take from her private funds to cover the fee for a private asylum.

the drowning of the heir to the English throne, his half-sister and half-brother, the children of Henry I, in 1120. Death at sea is a disturbing matter for Eliot's hero in *The Family Reunion* as sole witness to his wife's drowning. As we know, Harry thinks he caused her death with a 'push' sending her overboard. The play leaves the truth unclear — or clear only in its image of the wife as a shivering painted shadow who has carried on a dangerous game of tormenting her husband to the point of madness.

Eliot returned to Campden and remained there with Emily for another week or so, returning again in August. He occupied himself with his play, discussing entrances and exits with Emily on a terrace in the back garden of Stamford House. The past had seen him at Stamford House for weekends, a week at most, even at the peak of his love for Emily in 1935. This particular summer of 1938, his stays were longer while events unfolded in London.

Maurice reported again on 21 July that Vivienne 'is now considerably better', staying with their mother in the family home in West Hampstead.

Dr Miller agreed. 'She is apparently better and able to carry on.'

Dr Miller, though, was not an expert on mental illness. He was a consultant at a big general hospital, St Mary's, and wrote on diseases and 'backwardness' in childhood. He suggested that a trusted consultant by the name of R. D. Gillespie should be brought in to assess his patient. Eliot volunteered to pay the fee for an opinion.

Dr Miller considered it reasonable to wait until September, when Dr Gillespie was to return from his summer holiday; on the 21st Miller revised the date of Gillespie's return: it would, in fact, be a month earlier, specifically 15 August. Miller warned against rushing matters and 'running the danger of doing more harm than good'. He was against forcing a critical interview on his patient and put in a word on her behalf.

'It would be difficult for a new man to certify her,' he warned. Two days later he again tried to guard Mrs Eliot in a letter to her husband: 'there is reason to hope that the bad phase is over'.

Dr Miller went on holiday, having arranged for Dr Gillespie to be
called in, should an emergency arise, and then Gillespie too went
away. In view of their absence, there is a question to be asked about
timing. It hadn't taken much for Vivienne to calm down at home
with Maurice and then with her mother. She may have felt more
secure, at least for the present, in family settings. A while back, she
had been sufficiently stable to be accepted at the Royal College of
Music and her fitness for that is apparent in her diary's casual mention of pleasure in Bach during one of her piano lessons. In the long
view periods of rationality alternated with periods of disturbance
when her fretful agitation made it difficult for anyone to be with her;
even friends like Mary Hutchinson, Hope Mirrlees and Alida Monro
came to feel drained. They marvelled that Eliot had borne the marriage for eighteen years, nursed her through crises and collapses,
fetched medicines from pharmacies and returned home during
working days when she made urgent calls to him. He had insisted
that evening invitations include Vivienne. Kind Lady Ottoline, also
wearied by Vivienne going on repeatedly about her woes, thought
Eliot had been angelic – seven-eighths angel to one-eighth not. No
one could be sure what was wrong apart from the addictive effect of
prescribed medications, blurring her medical history.

In the absence of certainty, it is odd to find one persisting fact
over the next three weeks. That fact is haste: some urgency moving
matters on, even though cautious Dr Miller, temporarily off the
scene, had advised a slowdown. It was not long to wait, surely, only
a week or two, before Dr Gillespie would return.

Before leaving, Dr Gillespie had arranged with Dr Miller that
either Dr Bernard Hart or Dr Edward Mapother would fill in for him
in an emergency. Dr Hart was the author of a standard textbook,
The Psychology of Insanity, and a psychiatrist at three London hospitals,
including a psychiatric hospital, the Maudsley. Dr Hart also happened to be the medical superintendent of Northumberland House
Private Asylum in Finsbury Park, designed for the better-off upper
and middle classes. The building, pulled down in the fifties, was a

late Georgian house with three storeys in the central part and two-storey wings, surrounded by extensive grounds and separate villas for less disturbed patients. If Mrs Eliot were to be certified, Dr Hart could arrange for a bed.

The first two days of August saw Eliot back in London, stupefied by the heat and writing to Emily, 'my love'. She came to London, and their excursion to Windsor was to be added to other memories which, Eliot said, were 'very permanent blessings'. After she returned to Campden he promised to re-join her there.

Eliot was a man of conscience; he believed in divine Judgement and damnation; temperamentally he was given to hesitation; yet the five years Vivienne had stalked him provoked a kind of traumatised fear which became ever more intolerable. It was no ordinary apprehension that she would accost him; his word was 'molest'. Since Vivienne was never physically violent, the trauma he was undergoing was in his mind – and real nonetheless.

The depth of his stress is plain in a letter of 4 August, where Eliot performs a verbal jig with six flourishings of a spoon – yes, a spoon – in a letter sent to Frank Morley who had provided a safe hideout when Eliot left Vivienne. The 'spoon' letter, like the Betjeman one, was intended to be incomprehensible, somewhat like the antic disposition of Hamlet facing a deed he must carry through. Eliot chose Morley to witness this performance, a fellow American who knew Eliot's plight, yet could also see the point of Vivienne; alone among Eliot's milieu, he continued to like her despite her bizarre antics. Morley had the intelligence to take in the complexity of the situation: Eliot as a tormented man who yet remained sensible of his bond with Vivienne and nervous of wrong.

At first Eliot teases Morley with his jig. Then the antics pause briefly to let out quaking guilt. Four times a hellish 'abyss' yawns ever deeper to a man pacing its edge. Eliot owns to 'my terror of death' and ends with the plea to the Virgin Mary to 'pray for us sinners now and at the hour of our death'. St John of the Cross, offering an answer to sin, stands by with his severe discipline.

The following day the dreaded ordeal begins: things shift quickly from discussion to purpose. Mr Higginson instructs Maurice to obtain authorisation from Mrs Eliot's husband to go ahead with certifying her insanity. Maurice asks Eliot for a signed agreement.

Two days pass and nothing is heard from Eliot. His silence is audible. On 8 August Mr Higginson chases him, saying that Maurice is now discussing Vivienne with Dr Hart, who cannot proceed with a view to certifying Mrs Eliot unless authorised to do so by her next of kin, her husband as well as her brother. (It is not known if or to what extent her mother colludes. In after years Maurice believed she did, but this cannot be verified. She might not have grasped, or not fully, what authorisation meant.)

'I am hopeful,' Mr Higginson encourages his client, 'that before long we shall arrive at what seems to both Mr Bird and myself the only real solution of this most unhappy business.'

Eliot sent written consent to Vivienne's committal on 9 August: 'I authorise you (if that is possible and you think fit) to write a letter of authorisation to Haigh-Wood on my behalf.'* He thanked Higginson 'for your conduct of the affair'. Eliot would never again refer to the consent he gave that day.

From now on events moved swiftly.

Mr Higginson at once let Eliot know the authorisation would do and that he had the process already in hand: 'Dr Bernard Hart has seen your wife' and 'is satisfied beyond all doubt that she is certifiable'. Dr Hart, though, wanted a second opinion and Eliot

---

* Packed about the authorisation are uneasy 'if's': 'Dear Higginson, Thank you for your letter of 8th instant and for your conduct of the affair. I enclose a letter from Mr Haigh-Wood, forwarded from Russell Square, and my reply to his request for an authorisation to show to Dr Hart. I shall be obliged if you will scrutinise this reply and send it on to Haigh-Wood immediately if you pass it. If you think it should be couched differently, or with more restrictions, I authorise you (if that is possible and you think fit) to write a letter of authorisation to Haigh-Wood on my behalf.'

agreed to pay for this. Dr Hart then called in Dr Mapother, also at the Maudsley and at the top of his profession as medical superintendent as well as being the first Professor of Psychiatry at King's College, London.

But would Mrs Eliot agree to see Mapother, Hart wondered. In his view the case was not urgent. Yet Maurice moved fast. The haste is odd because it would have been in character for Maurice to wish his sister well. She was giving no trouble at this time; in fact, in the past, Maurice himself had never been troubled by her, apart from her imprudent spending. So why, instead of waiting for Dr Gillespie, due back soon, did Maurice offer to arrange for his unsuspecting sister to be ambushed: to have a stranger pounce when she visits Dr Cyriax at 41 Welbeck Street for a massage? For this is what happened. Dr Mapother assessed a suddenly cornered woman whom he had never seen before, and after this one interview, he agreed 'strongly' with Dr Hart that Mrs Eliot was 'of unsound mind'.

Maurice was not callous. He was eager to please, deferential to professionals, with a warm, engaging manner. Perhaps the military had trained him to carry out instructions without thinking too much about them. Maurice lost no time. On the day he received the certificates of the two doctors he took these to a magistrate in Hampstead, who gave the order that delivered Mrs Eliot over to the Masters of Lunacy.

The day's doings were not at an end. Enter again Mr Higginson, that obscure server of clients. He reminds Eliot that the court should appoint a Receiver to take Mrs Eliot's money out of her control.

A cinematic scene. They come as darkness falls on 13 August, two strangers in a car, timed to arrive at about 10 p.m. when the long summer twilight ends. No man Vivienne knows is present at the scene as the net closes: not her brother nor even the doctors. Vivienne and her mother are at home, when there's a knock on the door at this late hour.

The two strangers on the doorstep of 3 Compayne Gardens say

they are nurses. 'After a good deal of discussion' they manoeuvre a helpless woman into their car and drive her away.

Next day, Maurice informs Eliot that Vivienne is safely in Northumberland House and said to be 'fairly cheerful', sleeping and eating well and reading in the garden. This news from the asylum must be misleading. Since this patient, far from tame, is not there voluntarily, she could have been drugged to keep her quiet.

Dr Gillespie returned from his holiday on 15 August, too late to be involved. Two days later, Mr Higginson confirmed for Eliot, still at Stamford House, that certification had been completed. He reassured his client, 'I have no doubt whatever that this is by far the best thing for her in the unhappy circumstances of her case'.

Back in London, Eliot went to see *Richard III* on 22 August. It was the second time, after seeing Emlyn Williams in the title role the previous autumn. Eliot sympathised, he once said, 'with all the extreme failures of life'. He wrote a letter of thanks to Mrs Perkins which shows continued stress; its 'babblings' (as he calls them) are uncommunicative. The hilarity is strained: peace of mind is lost.

After a week as guest of the Fabers in Wales, Eliot had a last weekend with Emily before her return to Smith. Eliot expressed his thankfulness for this particular summer and persuaded her to accept a gift he had long had in mind.

The following Saturday, the day before she sailed, they picked up a Norwegian elkhound called Boerre. At fifteen months, Boerre was not yet full-grown but already formidable. Eliot meant this thick-coated, wolfish dog with gleaming eyes (all too visible in a photo) to be a stand-in for himself as protector. Seeing Emily off at Victoria, he applauded Boerre's clearing their way through the crowd. This dog would take up a lot of Emily's attention, and hopefully distract her from the sadness of parting. He imagined her busy with the dog on board ship.

When he informed Ada and Henry about Vivienne, Henry

approved: 'I am glad that it was Maurice who took this step and that you are relieved of the responsibility,' he replied. 'And I am glad that now you will be able to come and go without fear of annoyance or attack.'

Vivienne escaped from Northumberland House on 15 September. She was caught twenty-four hours later when she tried to draw money from her bank without knowing that her funds had been blocked. Her next and more promising attempt at escape took place with outside help. In the thirties there were Lunacy Law reformers, who realised that some people were wrongly diagnosed as insane. Part of their work was to rescue people who were put away for life only because they were disturbed and difficult. Previously, in the eighteenth century a husband had the power to incarcerate a troublesome wife in a madhouse, the target of Mary Wollstonecraft's novel *The Wrongs of Women*. But in the course of the nineteenth century, legislation did not leave wives entirely helpless. The law in place in the 1930s stated that if a certified person could live undetected in normal society for six weeks, they were automatically de-certified.

A Lunacy Law reformer called Marjorie Saunders had successfully sheltered one such escapee in her London house when she was approached by Louie Purdon, a pharmacist from Allen & Hanbury, to help her one-time customer and friend Vivienne Eliot. Mrs Saunders duly waited for Mrs Eliot at the appointed place in Oxford Street – in vain, for she was caught once more. From then on, Miss Purdon was not able to communicate with Mrs Eliot. Northumberland House did not pass on telephone messages and letters were returned.

Her third attempt to escape was in October and she got no further than the roof. Eliot suggested to his lawyer that Vivienne be moved to a country site to make her 'more docile and less restless'. There ensued a discussion about moving her to an asylum in Dover, but this plan fell through when Dr Frederick Dillon, who

Vivienne Eliot was placed in this mental institution. The photograph was taken after the place shut. While in use, the iron gates were always closed.

ran Northumberland House, said that patients in Dover had greater freedom and Mrs Eliot could escape more easily.

When Vivienne had been in Northumberland House for a few months, the Solicitor General, Alexander Gilchrist, sent his Visitor to see her. Vivienne's first plea was about her Bechstein grand piano, bought while she was at the Royal College of Music. She had been paying for this fine instrument in instalments and £55 was still owing. The Solicitor General felt it would benefit Mrs Eliot if she could be moved to a different asylum, where an instrument would be allowed. A piano, he said, 'would give her some little happiness'. He asked Eliot to pay the £55. Mrs Eliot's other plea to the Solicitor General was to send her husband to see her.

Eliot replied through Mr Higginson on 27 March 1939: 'I trust it is quite clear that I do not wish to see Mrs Eliot now or at any future time.'

And still Vivienne did not give up. According to Eliot's secretary, Linda Benson, Vivienne sent as many as a hundred letters to Eliot, which Miss Benson was told to return unopened and to make no mention when a letter arrived. It would not have been in character for Eliot to close off Vivienne in his mind and feelings, as she well knew. For a sensitive moral being the drastic solution to his and her trauma could not be forgotten.

When Maurice visited his sister late in 1940, he found her 'sensible & normal', though 'extremely wretched'. He reported this to Eliot, then he was sent abroad. Soon after, Mrs Haigh-Wood, who had been in a care home, died. After that Vivienne's sole visitor from her past was Enid Faber, Geoffrey Faber's wife.

Doodlebugs (V-1 flying bombs) launched by the Wehrmacht began to fall on London from 13 June 1944 in retaliation for the Allied landings in France. Eliot's friend Mary Trevelyan asked him if his wife should be moved from Northumberland House to a place of safety. He had already written to his solicitors to ask, he said, but had learnt that he had no 'official status in the matter'. Vivienne's brother did, but Maurice was 'engulfed in AMGOT' (Allied Military Government for Occupied Territories). All Eliot could do, he explained to Mary, would be to press the Solicitor General to speak to the head of the asylum, and then nothing would be done because her brother could not be reached.

After the war, Maurice returned to London. When he visited his sister, he found her, once again, sane. And yet Vivienne was to remain where she was for the rest of her days.

19

WAR YEARS

A year after Vivienne's committal, when Emily returned to Campden for the summer of 1939, Eliot shared with her the high moral ground they had gained in what could have been a risky clamber: 'I don't think that it can be often that two people are able, in such a position, to preserve instinctively and without effort the right order of values and walk surefootedly . . . along the edge of the precipices and heights which most people would be unable to climb, or having climbed might fall from.'

He wrote this before setting out for Campden on his last visit. With Emily's support, reinforced by a 'breathless fortnight' they had spent together that summer, he turns for a while from the abyss he had circled the summer before. His part in obliterating his wife had brought Othello to mind, and in January 1939 he had attended a fancy-dress party as Dr Crippen, who murdered his wife. Then, in March, Henry had appeared, on stage, confessing he 'pushed' his wife overboard. All this suggests Eliot's imaginative proximity to the psychic abyss. The wrong he had authorised continued to rankle, even as he closed with Emily.

It was to be a long goodbye on 3 September, the day that Britain declared war. Well before America joined the war, Hale wanted to stand with the Allies and take on war work in England, but her first duty was to look after her aunt and uncle. At the last minute, with Americans thronging steamship offices, she'd managed to secure berths for the three of them on the *Statendam*, a Dutch ship bound for New York. Eliot told Mrs Perkins that he had urged Emily 'perhaps brutally' to stick to her job at Smith. Before she left she prepared Stamford House for its owner, Miss Sunderland-Taylor, arranging flowers from the garden as well as putting up blackout curtains on the windows.

She and Eliot parted at the door of the house. He had a last glimpse of her face 'screwed up bravely and pitifully'. Then he went back to a London readying itself for bombs, with gas masks, black-outs and torches. Emily, meanwhile, booked a car for Southampton. She packed his parting gift, a circlet of diamonds for her hair.

He mailed her another exquisitely worded affirmation the following day, 4 September, looking back on their last evening,

ending so, with the minutes in the garden and finally and surprisingly our standing together looking out on the moonlight and the yew tree shadow more beautiful than ever before – those last minutes at the window are pictured in my mind with an intensity that can never disappear – that there was a wonderful comfort in the rightness and inevitableness of it all. It will take me a long time to understand fully what has happened – there is a frightening kind of beauty. Part of the time I feel that nothing that can happen now can matter; and at present I am divided between this queer bliss and worrying about your getting to Southampton: but I do not doubt that there will come a deep rheumatic ache in the heart before very long, which will have to be accepted and mingled with the other feeling. It seems now that ... this strange happiness had come to me quite in spite of myself.

... Let a growing realisation of what you have done for me, of

the perfect rightness with which everything has fallen into place
this summer, and of the growth, both of identity of feeling and of
our knowledge of the extraordinary degree to which we already
felt in the same way — and of how our so different experiences
had left us both with the same knowledge and innocence — keep
you in the radiance that we have known.

    Your adoring
    Tom

    The yew tree in the garden of Stamford House, whose fingers curl
down on mortals who place themselves under it in the first of the
quartets, was to reappear: a yew rooted in 'significant soil', in the
elegiac close to Eliot's third quartet. On parting he comforts Emily
that they will remain part of Campden and Campden will remain
part of them. This mark of their encounters on English soil ends
this American quartet, *The Dry Salvages*, completed early in 1941 at a
time when the poet's dual ties criss-cross the distance between an
England cut off by Hitler's conquests and a still-neutral America.
The yew is at once a private marker and the tree of graveyards. At
the close of this quartet, lives passing through time to their mortal
ends live on in the soil significant to them.

    Eliot and Emily Hale had a pact sustained across what he called a
'gulf of years' parting them for the duration of the war. She speaks
of the pact towards the end of the war, on 26 April 1945, in a letter to
him that survives in a copy — the sole letter among the thousand
or so she sent that she copied for herself to keep. And here it is that
she spells out the 'very complimentary, rather grave responsibility
you have placed upon me — and which I have always consented
to accept — since 1934 — when we came together in those thrilling
London days'.

    Her 'responsibility' conveys an agreement active while Eliot was
writing his masterworks. In his letters 'our' testifies to her presence in their duet. Sealing the pact the poet repeats 'our', not in

the ordinary way, and not as mere courtesy, but in the firing of art. *Burnt Norton* is '<u>our</u>' poem. Another letter speaks of 'our communion'. Words and phrases for poems rise in their exchange. Hale had 'a grace of sense' to move with Eliot, 'still moving / Into a further union, a deeper communion', he puts it in *East Coker*, the first of the wartime *Quartets*, composed in January–February 1940. 'Moving' confirms what Eliot had told Emily of a developing union destined for the afterlife. The mortal end will be the 'beginning' of an endless hereafter.

Her own high-minded nature and ambitions as a performer and director of plays suggest another motive for accepting the pact: to play an everlasting role in lines like 'The moment of the rose and the moment of the yew-tree', when the finale to *Four Quartets* brings together these scenes they had inhabited. So then: '<u>our</u>' love poem; 'our communion'; 'our Quartets'; and, yet to come, '<u>our</u> next play!' This play was to be lighter and less introspective, for she had been right, he said, to divine that the dark matter of *The Family Reunion* was something he had 'to get rid of'. Eventually, '<u>our</u> play' will go on stage as *The Cocktail Party*, with the Emily character as its leading lady, a woman in the grip of destiny, driven by a distinction beyond her social set.

Eliot was taken with Hale's advice to write the play for a sophisticated New York audience, with an American actor taking the lead: either Katharine Cornell – able at verse speaking, Hale said – or Helen Hayes. She also mailed him a collection of twenty modern American plays. Her encouragement assured him that they would go on growing together.

To accompany the pact, Eliot devised a plan for her single life, and here she proved less cooperative. She was to fill her life with a career in educational institutions, upheld (as he was) by letters and reunions.

Since he could not contravene Anglican rules, she saw these as barring her. In September 1938 she'd repeated the accusation she had made two years before: he was 'narrow' and 'intolerant'. Her own tolerance was manifest in the rosary she gave him for his fiftieth birthday, which hung at the head of his bed.

She favoured 'diversities of forms of worship' and considered it arrogant to insist on more truth in one religion than another. Spiritual reality is 'common to all religions'.

'Broadmindedness', he retorted, is a serious error. There is a point beyond which difference of forms means difference of belief. How could she not think difference important? Since she did think Trinitarian beliefs were superstitions, he felt justified in calling her 'just a little bigoted!' though he signs himself disarmingly, 'Ever your lover and bondsman'.

Now, surely, she thought, with Vivienne certified, there must be some change – some action Anglicans could sanction? She mulled over this after she sailed in 1939.

The Church did not recognise insanity as a ground for dissolving a marriage, Eliot explained again. That she should make a claim raised the temperature that autumn, and by November provoked a blast. It compelled him to ask himself, he said, 'why it is so difficult for me to discuss it with you at all. It is part of the difficulty, of which I have been very much aware, of discussing matters of the Christian Faith.' Her persistence made him 'miserable', he complained.

While Eliot saw out the war as a rooftop fire-watcher at an Air Raid Precautions post in Kensington two or three times a week, alternating with retreats to the safety of Surrey, Emily Hale cooperated up to a point with the idea that she would exercise her gift, her voice, in academe and in this manner support herself.

At Smith, theatre was the fiefdom of a long-time member of the English department, who happened to be Eliot's relation. Samuel Eliot was a mediocrity who found some agency in extending his power. Instead of nurturing talent, such a character guards his territory from a newcomer who might outdo him. Eliot acknowledged how frustrating it must be to see Sam putting on productions she could do better.

Miss Hale made the best of the situation. Her students, for instance, worked on the chorus from *Electra*. One of her finest efforts was to advise a student from New York, Maria de Blasio, writing a thesis on Eliot. Miss Hale made sure that the poet himself read it. Eliot responded with an extraordinarily generous letter. He did not, of course, tell Maria that Miss Hale had actually worked with him on his recent play in the garden of Stamford House.

She told Eliot that she did not meet people in other departments. And instead of mitigating loneliness, her hunting dog, by now full grown, was unmanageable on the loose in Northampton. He even managed to injure one of her teeth. She sent Eliot a photograph of the huge creature planted on her lap. She looks uneasy, holding off while gamely trying to placate him. Eliot regarded it as 'one of the worst photographs of you I have, unfortunately'.

In September 1938 Eliot gave Emily this elkhound as a substitute companion. Boerre proved rough and difficult. She looks daunted in this photo of 1939.

Eliot advised her on the ways of the world. 'In a large college you don't get on unless you push, an art, my dear, for which I do not think you have ever shown much natural aptitude. You have an indomitable will and a strong personality, and I know that you could push anyone or anything that you believed in, except your-self: a combination of conscience, pride and refinement is I believe the formula that stands in your light!'

In fact, the following month, March 1940, the acting president of the college, Elizabeth Cutter Morrow, renewed her contract: two more years with an increase in salary. Miss Hale then gave a talk on the value of speech training to the Alumnae Council. An unqual-ified success, the talk was published in the *Smith Alumnae Quarterly*. She argued that good speech was not an added grace like a curtsy; it was integral to character and spirit. She was against ruling out differences with standard pronunciation.

Eliot thought this 'first rate' and, with that, warned of jealousy from her colleagues, 'one of the most violent emotions which can drive people to unexpected behaviour'. He himself took care not to get too close to another poet.

In 1941 Eliot joked to the Bloomsbury art historian Clive Bell that he still planned a scholarly edition of his Bolo and Columbo verses. His father would have called these jingles nasty, and it's peculiarly so in a man of fifty-three, the need to disseminate sadism to pleasure men – a celibate's quirk? Of course, Emily Hale continued to know nothing of this strand in the poet.

Eliot sustained celibacy for much of his life, and from the late thirties his practice became stricter. Until then, he had experienced unfulfilled desire as a spur to a higher life and Emily had been caught up in that intention. Then he chose a new and austere con-fessor in the Reverend P. G. Bacon. Eliot confided to John Hayward in 1939 that he no longer regretted desire and intended to live out the rest of his life as a 'rather fanatical Catholic'. This period in war-time London saw a swing away from the rose narrative. In the final

quartet the poet must not write 'To summon the spectre of a Rose'.*
('I was thinking of the Ballet,' he told Hayward.) The post-freeze
challenge was to expand love 'beyond desire'. This is to liberate the
soul from attachment to past and future. Emily, however, remained
attached to the future in the way most of us are.

Their letters cross the space between their different positions,
moving apart and back in their duet. These wartime letters are
like an adagio, a slow unfolding of partners who cannot attain
each other. When she comments on the darkness of his poetry,
he defends the second and third *Quartets* as 'serene'. It may seem a
surprising answer in view of the section of *East Coker* that begins:
'O dark, dark, dark . . .' Eliot applies the dark to the stripping-away
of human emotion and identity in the course of the 'way down'.
Implied is the hope of becoming an agent of the Lord, but Eliot
guards against 'hope of the wrong thing', in the same way that
the saint in the making in *Murder in the Cathedral* must guard against
spiritual ambition: *not* the lifetime of the saints 'burning in every
moment'; rather a reliance on 'trying' through the habits of the
religious life: 'prayer, observance, discipline', the watchwords of the
third quartet. The humility of climbing down from the perceived
and longed-for heights of the spirit could be what Eliot means by
'serene'. He says 'humility is endless'. This is very fine, in line with
the ideal that the meek shall inherit the earth. Yet it's not the end:
a fourth quartet was under way in the spring of 1941.

Eliot hoped, he told Emily, for more 'light' (as a counter to darkness) in *Little Gidding*, the last of the *Quartets*. He tried this out in his first
draft of the poem. After an air raid, the poet, leaving his Kensington
post, encounters his other self moving towards him through the
lingering smoke. It is his timeless self, joining the 'compound ghost'
of the immortals, the poets of the past. The poet points to a Dantean
encounter (adapting Dante's *terza rima*) on a route that should end in

---

* In the first draft of 1941 this is a 'ghost' of a rose. An alternative to 'summon'
is 'raise up' the ghost.

paradise. Eliot tries to affirm this in his first draft: he has light come as sunrise, a ray of grace; 'and the sun had risen'.

It was perfunctory, unfelt.

He admitted to Emily he was 'stuck'.

That spring of 1941 he had another reason to feel at a loss: the death of Virginia Woolf in March. For over twenty years she had been first his publisher, then his friend, and this tie had attached him to English literary society. Yet, he now saw, she had meant even more. He said to Emily: 'She was to me like a member of my own family, somehow.' At her death he reverted to feeling an expatriate, 'a ghost in an alien, plebeian and formless society'.

Emily worried about her post at Smith, and wondering if she could secure herself with credentials she enrolled in three summer courses at the University of Wisconsin in Madison (near Milwaukee, where she had been in the twenties). She obtained an A in all her courses, but this did not impress the new college president, an Englishman called Herbert Davis who had taken office in the fall of 1940. Nor did Davis appreciate Miss Hale's help with extra-mural courses and, in the spring semester of 1942, co-chairing of the Speakers' Bureau. After Pearl Harbor, this was an organisation of faculty members who volunteered their services for the war effort. In the ongoing tug between speech and drama, Davis sided with drama – that is, with Sam Eliot. Davis transferred to him a fund that his predecessor, President Neilson, had granted to Miss Hale for recordings of poetry and plays. He inveighed against 'frills', meaning faculty including Miss Hale, and added that he had to 'clear the deck'. He announced the appointment of a stellar figure from a federal drama project, Hallie Flanagan, to head a new Department of Theater.

This was the theatre director who had mounted the outstanding Vassar production of *Sweeney Agonistes* in 1933. Eliot remained friendly with Flanagan, and in London the following year they had met for lunch and tea and talked in Sweeney-ese.

Miss Hale was vulnerable because her contract had just run out. The blow fell in July, brutally late, after the end of the academic year and too late for her to apply elsewhere. Abruptly, she found herself with no income. What Eliot did *not* do is surprising. He did not write to the congenial Flanagan. Little would have been necessary, merely praise for a teacher whose gift was going unrecognised.

Emily asked him to intervene with Sam Eliot. He waved this off, saying the family connection was too remote. Soon after, on 24 July, Emily sent what Eliot called a 'brave' letter, together with socks in 'lovely wool' which she had knitted for him.

Her need for support had never been so pressing and other friends rallied round. Margaret and Willard Thorp made a plan for Eliot to come over and Professor Thorp undertook to fund this through his renewed offer of a visiting position at Princeton, advising students on creative writing. When Thorp had made the original offer in 1939, Eliot had been taken with the idea and had left the possibility open. This time Eliot turned it down. He gave Emily two reasons. The first was that he already had plenty of young men requiring advice. The second was patriotic: 'I belong to England'.

The Thorps then had another idea. They knew of the trove of Eliot letters. Hundreds. Might Princeton acquire them? If the university made an offer for the letters, Hale would have something to live on. Accordingly, she brought up the question with Eliot and had a reasoned reply: it was for her to do as she wished. He would only caution her that living people were mentioned in the letters and he would therefore ask for an embargo of fifty years. He caricatures the Thorps' eagerness, sharpening pencils and filling fountain pens – too bent on editing and annotation for the likes of two people who meant to shield their privacy.

'I do confess some hesitation about the Thorps,' Eliot said, 'not that I do not like them personally very much but I fear the ruling passion of the academic mind, especially when seated in a chair of English literature – the craving to publicise.'

Writing from his wartime perch in Shamley Green, he explained further, 'I want to continue to feel that I am writing to you alone, and not with the Thorps or anyone else in the background: for otherwise I should feel a kind of invisible censorship, and would be hampered in speaking freely in the future – I should always be thinking of some future curious reader.'

Emily did not then take up the Thorps' suggestion.

That July and August, Eliot packed his letters with details of his jaunts. While she reeled from the blow to her career, his diary-letters, regular as ever, regaled her with his holiday in the New Forest, followed by a trip to Scotland and then a wartime mission to Sweden. His letters continued to send her a few commiserating words before turning to his own doings.

After struggling through eighteen drafts of *Little Gidding*, in the summer of 1942 he was completing his revision of the poem, the finale to *Four Quartets* as a whole. Only seven more lines to write, he tells her on 27 August. The lines included the memory of the rose-garden moment, 'Quick, now, here now – always'. This is the illuminating way and the other, the purgatorial trial, follows Dante waiting for Beatrice to bring him 'the fire wherewith I ever burn'. It's the sublime fire itself, the creative fire. This forms the 'crowned knot' of fire at the end of Eliot's *Quartets*. 'And the fire and the rose are one' is the last line.

He had written the first three *Quartets* swiftly, each in about three weeks. The fourth took a year. To Emily he ascribed this to 'spiritual aridity'. Yet to be abandoned is almost a condition for the greatest religious poetry: for Donne crying to his Maker, 'Except you enthral me never shall be free / Nor ever chaste except you ravish me'; Eliot's pain – 'the intolerable shirt of flame' – is in this tradition. He is, after all, a purgatorial poet rather than among visionaries like Henry Vaughan, Emily Brontë or Emily Dickinson. In *Little Gidding* he resorts to the words of a thirteenth-century visionary of divine love, Julian of Norwich, saying 'all shall be well and all manner of thing shall be well'. Not his own words, not his own vision. In place of his own flawed attainment, the *Quartets* offer instead the form of the higher life, a vessel for the divine spirit.

To watch the poet as he joins the immortals is not to excuse his human faults. 'Fools' approval stings' is the self-lashing the poet administers in his final draft when grace does not come to him. In the end he has to fall back on the fierce power of confession to beat up the poetry with an admission of 'things' done to others' harm. The sinner can contrive an approved public image, and he can slash it.

The poet does not want the adulation of fans who believe he can do no wrong. In the next century, do we baulk at being among those 'fools'? Might it be truer to see that stripping himself of humanity proved, in Eliot's case, self-defeating? The assurance of immortality comes to Eliot the poet, not the man.

In the meantime, Hale deteriorates. She awaits hospital observation. It's delayed. If her illness is, as it seems, a reactive depression, it's not treated as an emergency. She makes two moves to wake Eliot to her condition. She cables him about the delay and, throwing caution away, blurts out that his 'self-centred' oblivion (in her letter of 28 August) had revealed a man who differs from the person she'd believed him to be. He has proved selfish and two-faced.

This silences him. She must be muddled, he replies finally. All people are multi-sided; no one sees all facets of another person. Further, he assures her of his consistency. 'I was certainly not repudiating the past or anything that I have felt, or the reality of the communion.'

He goes so far as to concede that words are no substitute for <u>presence</u>. He knows that she is 'very, very lonely'. If he were in her place, he admits, 'I should want you to be near me'. But 'should', the conditional, is tricky; his grammar leaves him uncommitted.

As to his flaws, he offers a strange defence: he is no more self-centred than a man who has moral scruples about murder in getting an inconvenient person out of the way.

A torrential self-justification in October turns to reproach, in particular for putting him in the position of 'an unwilling lover, whose slowness and hesitancy, perhaps whose cowardice, make it necessary to face a decision: a decision which, had I been free to make, I would have been the first to urge as speedily as possible.' Though she seems to have asked him for career support and then for his presence in an hour of need, he turns this into the old issue about marriage, telling her that she has left him with 'an intolerable and terrifying sense of guilt' which he cannot escape. Once he brings up this debate, he can claim the moral high ground and, from there, grants a 'misunderstanding' on her part, saying that he had explained this over and over. To violate a religious law would violate himself. It exasperates him that she will not take in what she has been told.

This self-defence shifts the issue from selfishness to his sense of injury. He reinforces this grievance with another on New Year's Day 1943, warning Emily that if she will not grant that he gave as much as he took, she will hurt their relationship: 'the fountain dries and the flowers fade', he says, as though this were her fault, forgetting that it was he who foresaw 'dust on a bowl of rose-leaves'. At this time, Eliot disparaged Burnt Norton (to the scholar Helen Gardner) as a 'mediocre' garden, merely 'wandered into'. This is untrue; it was a residue of the confrontation with Emily.

Unbowed, Emily stood by her view of his self-centredness, and still Eliot believed himself no more immune to that fault than anyone else. If there was in him a strain of egotism, he saw it as a religious trait. Because his nature was 'sombre', his faith took a 'sombre tinge', belonging perhaps 'more to the faith of my seventeenth century ancestors than to the form of Christianity to which I adhere!'

In the meantime, Emily took herself to remote Grand Manan Island in the Bay of Fundy, between New Brunswick and Nova Scotia, where she could live at the Anchorage Inn at off-season rates. Eliot deplored the lack of amenities, reading matter and company – as though without money she had much choice. She stayed on the island until the end of November 1942.

*

In 1943, the year Eliot put the *Quartets* together as a book, he returned to the issue of their papers, declaring his sole motive was to archive her letters 'as a kind of monument to you'.

Emily seems now to entertain the idea, for that summer she asks him to go through her letters with a view to making a selection for eventual publication. He baulks, expecting this task to give him 'more heartaches than happiness'. Why so is unclear, but their activity in building up an archive leads him ten days later to repeat his warning not to write in future 'as if for publication, or for the perusal of future Willard Thorps!'

The following month, August 1943, Eliot makes a crucial statement to Emily. What he says is consistent with a curious motive, evident earlier, that it was *her* letters, not his, that mattered for his posthumous plan. Here is the telling sentence, prefaced by a playfully formal 'Madam', an address used when he sensed Emily's independence from his control.

'Madam, may I say firmly … that, for my purposes, it is quite sufficient that a selection of your letters should be preserved'.

His own letters are dispensable, he says. Since he wrote them only for her, they could be destroyed at her death, if she so instructs. It is *Emily's* letters that must remain for posterity and a selection would suffice. At the foot of this letter he adds, 'Your letters would go in a box, not to be opened, to the Bodleian.' There is a plan here, active from the start and somewhat opaque. While Emily began writing to Eliot in answer to a declaration of love, his concern with preservation complicates, even alters, the relationship.

The effect is of a correspondent as a work of art: a Pygmalion of sorts chiselling a statue of a woman with whom he falls in love. It is as if Eliot were writing letters in order to elicit hers for the purpose of a posthumous record that is to surprise the world, catch attention and reinvigorate future readers. Could this even be his prime purpose? If so, it fits Henry's astute portrait of a brother with a 'talent for publicity'.

The parallel between the mythical Pygmalion and the Eliot of the Hale letters is an imaginative stir in an artist inspired by love. Neither artist trusts women, but when Pygmalion kisses his lovely statue, she warms with the breath of life. This is exactly what happened with Emily in 1935 when Eliot's kisses – at this point they lose count – wake her to love. Pygmalion married his work of art whereas Eliot held by the solitude an artist needs if he is to soar.

1943 was the annus mirabilis of his poetic career rather than the public honours that came later, for in that year the great work of his maturity *Four Quartets* was published: first in the US and a year later in England because of a paper shortage during the war. When Eliot turned fifty-five in September, Emily hailed him with Shakespeare's sonnet CXXII: his achievement in 'my brain / Full character'd with lasting memory', a gift destined to go 'beyond all date'. Her praise fits his climactic scene where, in the smoke after an air-raid, the poet joins the compound ghost of the immortals. He said of the *Quartets*, 'I rest on those.'

At length, at the end of 1943 Hale managed to find a temporary post for one semester at Bennett Junior College in Millbrook, New York. She was pleased with what she accomplished there and played a minor role in one of John Van Druten's witty plays. She also acted in *The Merchant of Venice*, taking pride in her improved delivery of Shakespeare's lines (and attributing her progress to Eliot). He thought the part of Hermione in *A Winter's Tale* would suit her: a once-loved outcast, a good wife maligned unjustly, who will make a comeback. During the spring semester in 1944, her spirits lifted with an offer of work at Concord Academy, a high school in Massachusetts. Accommodation in Concord proved prohibitively expensive. Tired by a futile search, her belongings in storage, she lodged in one room or another, longing for a home of her own.

'Poor child', Eliot writes and, deploying the passive verb, wishes something might be settled.

Eliot was President of Books Across the Sea, a flourishing international operation with a branch in New York. Its London base was a library in South Audley Street in Mayfair. When Emily asked about a job that summer, Eliot said that he already had volunteers with means of their own.

Emily could not overlook such persistent unhelpfulness. She asked if he had become more self-centred.

'I confess I <u>seem</u> to myself rather less self-centred than I was,' came the reply, 'but perhaps what you mean is more encased in a shell. I do believe that these five years [of war] have had a withering effect – as well as ageing one more rapidly.'

Eliot often commented on Boerre, sounding hurt when Emily decided to part with him. When the dog died in July, Eliot was 'deeply grieved'. Boerre, he said, had 'symbolic value' for him and he might be jealous and resentful of a less troublesome replacement.

On her fifty-third birthday in October, his cable arrived, punctual as ever: 'AM OBSERVING 27TH LOVE AND KISSES THOMAS ELIOT'. He had actually written 'love and wishes'. When he heard, he said that the operator had 'interpreted' the message. It was not all that easy to resist the charm of humour.

Responsible to the pact, Emily continued to reply as expected. His letters are domestic, chatty and humorous about his cosy berth with Mrs Mirrlees, aged eighty-one, in Shamley Wood near Guildford in Surrey. From there he relays his host's operatic lament over the gardener's mistreatment of the cauliflowers. Their amusing yap in Eliot's wartime letters to Emily rehearses the chat of characters in his postwar comedy *The Cocktail Party*. Mrs Mirrlees (or 'Mappie'), the mother of Eliot's friend Hope, was grand, lovable, a Scottish Christian Scientist in an otherwise devoutly Catholic household. Hope and her mother's sister Miss Moncrieff were 'Papists'; this aged and irritable aunt, 'Cockie', was often away at her club in London, having an orgy of bridge and Masses at the Jesuits (so Eliot reports to Emily). Then there was Mrs Behrens ('the Field-Marshal' in charge of the hens), another Scot, who had married into a well-known Jewish family. She too visited London, in her case to see her daughter Mrs Blumenfeld, referred to affectionately as

'Brutal Behrens'. Muddle Hall, otherwise known as The Shambles, felt like home to Eliot.

He caricatures himself as an incorrigible worrier over petty arrangements, his family neurosis. Emily was to lend an ear. He could pour out upon her the whole story of his day with its plaints and duties. How little, for instance, he looked forward to three able women who were coming for tea. One of these was Lady Rhondda, editor of *Time and Tide*. There was no Lord Rhondda. The title had been held by her Welsh father, and inheritance was not reserved for the male line. She was to be accompanied by her friend Theodora Bosanquet, who had been Henry James's amanuensis. The Rondabouts, as Eliot called the pair, were to come with Eliot's new and younger friend Mary Trevelyan, an adviser to foreign students, who sometimes invited Eliot to read for her charges. These visitors took their turn in the comedy of that time when Eliot lived surrounded by the humorous talk of women who made much of him as the sole man in a female household. He was in his element among women who looked after things; it was like the watchfulness of his chattering grown-up sisters back home, far, far back, in St Louis.

As Emily took in the social pages of Eliot's letters, she could see the impression he made, and she understood how indissolubly bad and good blended in him. Had he married her, he would have had to share her setbacks. As it was, he could safely turn away, averse as ever to female claims. He did know Emily was thinner and did wonder if she had enough to eat. Unwarmed by bodily contact, her physical presence appears to fade, so that while she remained full-blooded to her friends and to the girls she taught, Eliot was writing to a communicative ghost of his own creation – what it seems he had always meant her to be.

20

MISS HALE IN HER PRIME

Towards the end of the war, in the fall of 1944, Miss Hale put on a Bethlehem play in verse with the small girls at Concord Academy and she directed the older girls in *Quality Street* by J. M. Barrie. Sarah ('Fanny') Tomaino played the lead, and recalled: 'Miss Hale's presence during that short time in my life has always remained with me — every detail — how she costumed me in her own Empire-cut, satin peignoir. How, after the performance, when the material was hopelessly stained with perspiration, she said, "Of course it can never be worn again." Then seeing the anxiety on my face, either said something or smiled in a way that said, "Never mind, it is worth it to *both* of us."'

Because the teacher seemed old to a schoolgirl, she called her Mrs Hale until she was taken aside and told 'Miss Hale, if you please, Fanny. As yet I have not accepted the hand of any man in matrimony.'

Early the next year, Miss Hale staged *Dear Brutus*, also by Barrie. It was a risky choice, she feared, a little-known play about a second chance, a fantasy of a life that might have been, and she confided to Eliot that this particular production might finish off her career. But it proved a terrific triumph, and the school asked her to stay on.

It pleased Eliot to hear that she gave her girls an informal talk on *The Family Reunion* and that she liked a local production of 'our "Quartets"'.

Concord is a historic place both for its part in the Revolution and as the home of Emerson, Thoreau and the Alcott family, as well as Nathaniel Hawthorne. Then too, one of Hale's lifelong friends lived in Concord, Mary Foss, once Mary Walker Parker. They had been girls at Miss Porter's School in Farmington, Connecticut, and they remained laughing and sisterly. I remember the flavour of friendship between women of the generation or two before Women's Liberation reset womanhood in the seventies. Looking on as a child, I saw how they stuck together throughout their lives. Mary had a confident, lively daughter, Sally, at Concord Academy, who in her last terms took part in Miss Hale's plays.

Sally Foss found her a born teacher, a listener attentive to what a girl was thinking as well as to what she was saying. 'She liked learning, she liked sharing,' Sally recalled, at ninety-six. 'She was very relaxed, very open, very honest, very genuine. And funny. We laughed a lot.'

During lunch hour Miss Hale would come by and say to the girls, 'if anyone wants to talk about speech or travel or poetry or anything like that, I'd love to fill you in with this'. It was inviting. 'She liked interpreting what you said or what you meant or asking how else to say it. She could have been a psychologist actually.'

Like her mother, Sally loved acting, and she and her twin brother tried to write dialogues. Miss Hale taught them how to express the pain of loss, a father or mother or boyfriend. 'She taught us how to get into a specific emotional place and then write about it, which I hadn't done before.' She told them that, with a play, 'you're telling a story, but you're also talking about feeling, you're talking about experiences that are new. You've never had them before, so you're either scared or you're joyful. Whatever. That's the kind of conversation we had with her. I remember feeling very grateful to talk with an older person so easily.'

Whenever Emily stayed with the Foss family she would play games with the children. 'We'd make up words, or [find] new words', Sally remembered. 'I'd look for a word that I'd read and hadn't used before. She used to say "el-oh-cution". Everything had a sort of rhythm to it, a pattern to it.' She would raise her hand and conduct as Sally or other pupils spoke, so that they felt the rhythms of language. 'She was on stage in a way, but genuine. I mean it was Emily talking. She could get you to laugh or she could get you to understand something that was questionable.'

Fresh from hearing her voice through Eliot's letters, it was a delight to hear this and lit up this Miss Jean Brodie-style teacher and generous woman.

Near the end of the war, Eliot accepted invitations to Paris, Sweden, Iceland and North Africa. He never went to America. His excuse was that he could not afford it, though he must have saved a fair amount of money, having lived rent-free as the prize pet in Mrs Mirrlees' pet-filled household. All he had to cover was food and incidental expenses. When he was driven up to London, usually on a Wednesday, for a night or two a week, he had stayed at first with the Fabers in Frognal Road, Hampstead, then in a house owned by Faber & Faber at 23 Russell Square, which the firm took over in 1942. Then, too, *Murder in the Cathedral* went on playing in improvised theatres throughout the war: Eliot had ten years of accumulating royalties.

There was no urgency to be with Emily (though he might cable her if she neglected to write punctually every week). He would come after the war, he told her. He would wait for regular passenger shipping to be resumed. He would wait for the end of the Japanese war.

During the long separation, intensity faded, weakened further by the crisis in 1942 when Emily lost her post at Smith College and Eliot did not support her. By 1945 her letters were more infrequent and seemed to Eliot 'like reports from the past'. That March, he regrets

being prevented from coming to the help of anyone in America: a
'deprivation' to him not to be able to do anything for her. At last,
in April 1945, Emily Hale resolved to clarify where she stood, even if
it meant the end of the pact. Here in full is the letter she copied in
pencil in her barely legible scrawl:

April 26th

What I want most of all in this letter, to say — is to re-align relations between us once again, after now nearly six years separation.
Changes of personality naturally take place constantly — influ-
enced by all manner of inner and outer conditions — and we
both have changed, I am sure, since we parted in 1939. You have
lived under the terrific pressure of war and its attendant stresses
outwardly and inwardly — to you, poet and unusual man that
you are, the results must be incalculable in effect. I have also lived
thro' diverse new personal experiences and attendant adjust-
ments. Naturally, some of these are tied to my relations with
you — present and past. After my illness, I wanted most strongly
to feel I could marry you and so wrote you. As your answer told
me again, that was impossible under existing conditions I wondered whether I might not be happy with someone else instead,
and whether our love for each other would remain always a rare
thing to hold close, but of a nature to be unfulfilled; and whether
it would be wronging that relation to live [in a way that is] more
normal. (There was no one actually asking me.) Unconsciously,
this has been in my mind and heart for these two years past — and
I felt it only honest to give you suggestions of my bewilderment.
Since you may have sensed this, but have never referred to any
possible change in me or you, and since your letters are usually
so very undemonstrative and impersonal, it is hard for me to
tell from them just what you consider yourself to me, or myself
to you. As the possibility of a cessation of war in Europe draws
closer — not a return to normal, — such cessation would bring

changes of all sorts into the open, so to speak. Do you still feel
that if you were free you wish to marry me? That you would love
me as you have these many years, I do not doubt, but that love is
so far apart from other great facts and truths of life, that in these
five to six years, I have no way of knowing whether you are as
you were or not. I now wish to say that if you do wish to marry
me ever, I shall keep myself always waiting and ready for you. But
I would rather the truth from you, in case you feel differently,
and I should understand, and still want to try to be what I could,
to you – to try to carry the usual, very complimentary, rather
grave responsibility you have placed upon me – and which I have
always consented to accept – since 1934 – when we came together
in those thrilling London days.

Emily did not mention to Eliot that she kept a copy. At the top,
slanted to one side, is an instruction in ink to a future reader: 'Copy
of Private Letter to be destroyed without reading.' She underscores
'reading' with two lines. There was a mixed impulse to preserve
privacy and at the same time to have it on record that she did offer
to walk away.

Eliot agreed to destroy the letter after he mulled over it, and he
took a month to do so. It troubled his conscience, he confessed, that
he had wronged her.

An answer, she was saying, must turn on his *present* feeling.
What, she asks, has happened to him since those summer reunions
warmed by embraces in the shadow of the yew? In a sense, he himself had brought out (in *East Coker*) what was at issue: what Emily
called the 'ascetic theology' of the 'way down', numbing desire.
'The chill ascends from feet to knees' as the penitent undergoes
'frigid purgatorial fires / Of which the flame is roses . . .' This was
the future way in the winter of his being as he had laid it out, five
years earlier, in the darkest months of 1939–40, darkened further by
the blackout and braced for trial – in public terms, a national trial
in war. He would never speak of desire to her again.

From the time of bodily freeze, Eliot's letters to Hale had been less endearing. The freeze, of course, was his doing, welcoming pain on the scale of an operation without anaesthetic. *East Coker* does not mention the private guilt about Vivienne, a prime element in the act of penitence. This one section in *East Coker* comes over as cruelly severe, compared with the moderate approach to self-abnegation in the fourteenth-century *Cloud of Unknowing*. That treatise, quoted briefly in *Little Gidding*, has a no-nonsense tone, eminently English: there's to be no self-inflicted pain, nothing contrived, in the monastery run by this anonymous spiritual director. Holiness, he was saying, cannot be forced.

After Eliot's freeze – its creep upward through the body had coincided with the message from Maurice that his sister was normal – come admissions of flatness. His letters to Emily drone on about his doings. No indication that the way down – the celibate treading the broken stones of penitence – brought on divine communion. Not for the poet, or only at a remove, the vision of Dame Julian that all shall be well. The glimpse of a rose-garden fades from sight as the years pass (though the memory is called up momentarily at the close of the *Quartets*). In February 1945 he tried to picture Emily walking in snow boots to and from the school.

At length, that spring, she posed her question about ending their pact. Here is the missing piece in the puzzle of their attachment. If she had not copied out this letter, her acceptance of responsibility would have remained unknown.

His answer, when it came on 22 May, was non-committal. It was for her to decide whether she wished to go on. A week later he took a sterner line: only Vivienne's death could release him, and a wish for that, 'to be put away with constant effort', would be sinful. 'In plain words, I should never want to marry anyone else: that would be for me as impossible a change of personality as abandoning my Christian beliefs and principles.'

In the interim she pressed him yet again about 'finding the beautiful, the divine in this life'. He bats this back. Her position leaves him in the dark: she implies he should 'do something about it, and, if so, what should I do?' Characteristically, he offers a confession: he had proceeded only a certain distance along 'the "purgative" way' and was 'yet a stranger to the "illuminative" way'.

The existence of their pact compelled him to admit that he was haunted by 'the fear that I have interfered with your life far more than I was aware of or had any right to do'.

Then, in June, Eliot breaks the news to Emily that he has agreed to share a flat with John Hayward, who offered a haven: John would furnish the flat and see to all domestic arrangements. This new set-up would be for the rest of his life, Eliot told Emily rather apologetically, knowing it would come as a further blow to hope. It was, he said, a prospect 'of a future nothing better than which can happen. It would be the same even if John and I agreed in a few years to separate. One knew all this, with the reason, before, but the heart evades longer than the mind can. I am sure, my dear, that you will understand all that this means to me without my saying more.' Then he adds: 'At moments my regret over this becomes passionate.'

About the impersonal diarising in letters to her, he says that 'a simple spontaneity' was impossible: 'To speak of my own feelings towards yourself might have been to make a greater claim upon you than was right'.

He proceeds to shift the pact onto a footing of 'a very peculiar kind of "friendship"', though admitting this definition is inadequate. A shuffling conditional clause insists on consistency: she can trust in his love developing 'only' as it would have done 'as if we could have come together, many years ago'. The outcome of Emily's offer to end it was to re-lock her in the if-clause.

Trying still to understand, Emily wondered if his state of being over the last years had made him 'withdraw from life'. It's an astute reading of his character but her mistake was to see this as a consequence of the war, rather than a longer dance of possession and withdrawal.

Can there be some link between Emily's move in bringing up

marriage, even hypothetically, and Eliot's moving in with Hayward?
This effectively displaced Emily, shutting off any residual hope of
a future together, but without ending the pact, for Eliot always
wanted her letters. In February 1946, Eliot joined Hayward at 19
Carlyle Mansions, a third-floor flat on Cheyne Walk in Chelsea
(Henry James had lived in the same block, at number 21). Hayward
was to have a large front room with a bay window overlooking the
Thames, and the other front room next to it was to be for seeing
others. Eliot took possession of three smaller rooms off a passage
towards the back.

Hayward was the most sociable of men. The flat was the centre
of Tarantula's web of bibliographers that by now extended across
Europe and America. His visitors were continuous; as one left, the
next would arrive. His world was dispensing advice, judgements
and hilariously funny stings (provided you were not the victim).
The flatmates lived separate lives, an arrangement that secured
Eliot's privacy. Sometimes he might accompany Hayward to the
literary parties of the capital: it would create a stir when he arrived,
pushing Hayward's wheelchair. But he was free to shut his door
whenever he chose.

The move left him too fatigued to plan a forthcoming visit to
America, he told Emily. The feeling behind this dance is hard to
name. Call it the will to possess her with no ensuing claim.

At last he crossed the Atlantic in June 1946. He could not afford a long
stay, he said and warned it would be crowded with family visits. For
the first four or five weeks he would be occupied with Frank Morley,
now with Harcourt, Brace in New York. Eliot stayed with Morley
on East 66th Street while Emily Hale was completing the summer
term at Concord Academy.

Fanny Tomaino, the actor among Miss Hale's girls, recalled forty
years later sharing a seat with her on a train from Concord to Boston.
Miss Hale 'looked more dressed up than I'd seen her, in a blouse with
a ruffle. She said, "I am going to the zoo with Tom." What a thrill

to have her share this confidence! The school grapevine had it that Miss Hale had some secret connection with the famous poet T. S. Eliot. Also, I was the only member of my English class who felt that she "understood" *Ash Wednesday*. Thus my fantasy connection with Mr Eliot was already in place. And there, as the train pulled into the platform, stood "Tom" himself, in his dark clothes, leaning on an umbrella. The train passed him before it stopped and I heard Miss Hale's voice calling "Taum, Taum" down the platform.'

Eliot visited Emily at her lodgings in Humbert Street. After that, in July, she was in Dorset, Vermont, a rural spot with a playhouse on a lake north of Bennington. A summer theatre company, the Dorset Players, revived after the war, had invited her to accept the part of the eccentric medium, Madame Arcati, in Noël Coward's comedy of ghosts, *Blithe Spirit*.

Young Sally Foss offered to drive Eliot to Vermont to meet up with her mother and Emily Hale. Sally had not seen him in his London outfit, so didn't realise, as they spoke on the phone, how amusingly incongruous his wish to wade in the lake would be: a Foss photograph shows him with his trousers rolled at a lakeside picnic with Emily Hale, Mary Foss, Sally and some friends. Eliot unbent enough to join in a game of Red Rover.

In another photograph, Emily and Eliot stand under a tree. She is easy, smiling, head cocked, as it often was, her hands casually in the pockets of her shirtwaist dress, while Eliot stands rather stiffly to attention in his suit, embellished with a white handkerchief in the breast pocket. He looks out of place, a visitor from another world, in that rural setting. And so he said he felt at times during that particular return to America: like a ghost from the ruins of London.

When Eliot looked forward to seeing Emily that evening, she said, 'Yes, but I'll be different. I'll be in costume.'

To be with her when she was acting, to see her in her element, was a return to the earliest basis of their relationship. For Eliot, it was an ideal way to be with Emily, occupied with her own role on stage and making no claims on him. Lowness vanished in her

Eliot wading with 'trousers rolled'. A picnic near Dorset, Vermont, July 1946.

company. She appeared a blithe spirit indeed in the lively, admiring Foss circle. It was as though, all through the 'gulf of years', he had been in deep freeze and was now reanimated. He told the Thorps of 'four very happy days', and afterwards affirmed for Emily that he had been happier those days with her in Vermont than he had ever been. On leaving in early August, he lets loose the soaring note of farewell letters in the thirties.

'Beloved my Female,' he began, asking her not to leave him for more than a week without a letter: 'the truth is that I am insatiable, and two days after a letter begin to feel as if I had not heard from you for weeks'. She was to write often and her letters must uphold him. 'But what I most need, day by day, is the constant reassurance of your love, which always seems such an incredible gift that I sometimes tend to fear that I have merely dreamt it, and now I crave always more and more of your spiritual gifts to me.'

For the first week after his return to London he was 'still in a state of exaltation', he told her on 2 September, and then during the following weeks had gone through an agony of missing her. Being with her in person had dispelled his flatness. 'It seems to me that what I am in love with is now much more you and less merely my idea of you.'

The fixity of this anxious obsession with her letters left poor Emily uneasier than ever in times gone by when Eliot had exercised verbal sway. Perhaps this is why, a month after he left, she defied him. Repeatedly, Eliot had warned her off the sacrament of communion since she had not converted to Trinitarian belief. But Emily took communion in September 1946. And she wanted him to know.

His response was furious. Firstly, he demanded that she ask permission of the vicar or else he would have the disagreeable duty of telling on her. Then he prodded the authenticity of her Unitarianism: his parents would have shunned communion. Finally, he tried to shame her with impropriety: it was like barging into a club where she was not a member.

His ruling only served to straighten her spirited back.

'Now, my very dear,' he said, 'it is no use avoiding the fact that this refusal is going to make a serious difference to our relations.'

'My whole nature cries out against limiting attendance at the communion table,' she insisted.

Why did she rile him? Without her side of the correspondence, this has to be a guess. I think her flare-up was not as sudden as it seems. It was in character for her to be gentle and tactful. In former days, he had urged her to be less polite, 'an Emily of fire and violence'. Her report now would not have been so deliberate had she not suppressed a slow burn. Her outburst is like lava forcing its way through layers of habitual restraint: a cumulative rebellion at his entitlement to exact letters while remaining oblivious to the needs of his correspondent. There had been his backing away from the blow to her in 1942; there had been his evasive reply to her plea for clarity in 1945; and now, in 1946, there had been little time to be together. Fun, yes. A thaw of the freeze, yes. Verbal love to bring on another year of letters – that too, as always.

Was this confrontation a way of setting fire to a prison in which her life had been locked for so long? Eliot caught fire. He fanned the flame higher by declaring her wilfulness a flaw in their pact. He told her that if she flouted the sacredness of communion he could not marry her even if he were free.

And then suddenly, quite unexpectedly, he did find himself free.

21

THE PLAY'S THE THING

Vivienne Eliot died of heart failure early in the morning of 22 January 1947. She was fifty-eight and had been shut away for over eight years. When he heard, Eliot put his face in his hands. He wrote to Emily that day: the 'nightmare' of Vivienne's 'tormented and tormenting life' took him over and yet plans came quickly, set out in that first letter.

He decided to wear half-mourning for six months (although the clothing of grief had gone out after the First World War). His public line would be that it had been a marriage of 'normal' affection until Vivienne's 'increasing dementia' caused 'inevitable alienation and inevitable separation when cohabitation made my life impossible'. This would preserve 'decorum' – for the dead as well as for himself. He asks Emily to keep their 'plans and deliberations' secret. They will talk 'about the future, for a year hence' when he comes to America in April. He signs himself 'Lovingly Tom'.

The torment, rectitude and secrecy were all in keeping with the past. But new in this letter is the future. The future belongs to the human dimension of time (dismissed in *Four Quartets* as 'waste sad time'), not the higher dream of the timeless, the dimension of lasting art and what is divine. Eliot's masterpiece seeks points of intersection between time and the timeless: the garden; the bell-buoy out at sea, sounded by the groundswell that began in the Beginning; and the yew tree in the 'significant soil' of a place haunted by their lives whose spirit will stay always. An invisible Emily Hale shared moments that had crossed the frontier of the timeless. But Vivienne's death brought home to the poet how trapped in time he could be: the past marriage, the present end to it, 'time present' that brings on a limiting future.

Eliot's letter to Emily on the day of Vivienne's death looks ahead to this future. The word 'marry' is not there, yet is implied in the plan to wait a year. Twelve days later, after Vivienne's funeral on 3 February, a second letter shows a change of mind. Over these days it came to him: he could not bring himself to marry her.

The turnaround happened at Vivienne's funeral. It took place at Pinner cemetery, north of London, with Fr Cheetham of St Stephen's officiating and otherwise only Maurice Haigh-Wood and his wife, Enid Faber, and Eliot present. Enid Faber recorded vividly the chilling scene of five people 'in a funeral chapel with blasted windows on a freezing day'. She adds, 'Tom's flowers were missing.'

As Vivienne's coffin went into the ground, Eliot changed, he said, into an old man. From that day, he pictures for Emily a man who does not know who he is or what he wants – to his great distress. Or does he, consciously or unconsciously, play up the distress as an excuse? This is a poet with a divided self, given to shifts and turns. How much he feels and how much dramatised is obscured, even it may be from himself. The facts of his life, slow to emerge from his secrecy, make it possible to pinpoint one trait: the extraordinary speed of Eliot's imagination, how immediately the events of his life fed his work or, coming closer still, how his work forecasts the life. The only unforeseen part of his plan was that his wife died too soon, because it brought on a problem he never intended to solve: marriage to Emily Hale.

For all his hesitation, Eliot was consistent in his focus on ordeals in the lives of saints and martyrs. Three days before Vivienne died, he told Emily that he was about to write a play. In fact, he had spoken of this to her long before, in 1939, as 'our next play'.

A little more than a month after Vivienne's death, Eliot was in touch with Martin Browne to discuss the play. His previous play *The Family Reunion* had mystified audiences in 1939 and had a run of only three weeks. This time Eliot was determined to write a popular play, strong on plot and action. It opens with the disappearance of an unloved wife.

So long as Vivienne had been alive, his hidden involvement with Hale went on, fortified by intensive correspondence and the rectitude of Eliot's position on the permanence of marriage, but once Vivienne died obligations to Emily Hale erupted in his path.

For Hale, of course, marriage was the answer to the years of waiting. Imagine, then, her shock to receive Eliot's letter of 3 February.

Bad conscience, the letter tells her, brings on 'an intense dislike of sex in any form'.

It could be tempting to simplify this as absence of attraction were there no evidence to the contrary. To bring up sex so baldly was to detach from his habitual language of desire. In the first year of their tie he had said 'there are times when I desire you so much that neither religion, nor work, nor distraction, and certainly not dissipation could relieve it – it is like a pain that no sedative will deaden, or an operation without anaesthetic'. In 1935 their contact had become intimate enough for Hale to be shaken when he withdrew. The swing away from sex in 1947 was a repeat of that earlier stance and led to a warning shot in Hale's direction.

'I cannot at this moment, face or think of any future except just going on.' What Emily will have to bear is acknowledged only in passing as part of his own moral drama: 'all I do by mentioning them [his sufferings] is to inflict suffering, as I have always done in my life. Yet if I didn't speak of them, I should ... simply be guilty of deception.'

But is this not deception itself? The virtuous wish not to deceive is designed to muffle the shot he is readying to fire at Emily: his resolve to put an end to a claim she refrains from making.

She replies considerately, too much so for Eliot's comfort. Her patience makes him uneasy. To shoot down her trust he sees as his ordeal. He tells his brother that if Emily does not give up, he will have to commit suicide.

The disturbance he felt in February swells further to a 'cataclysm' so devastating that it blocks the future.

Each successive letter takes a step towards what must happen face to face. On 14 February he positions her as outsider with no access to his state of mind. After needing regular letters from her for the last sixteen years, he shuts the door on communication, no matter how sympathetic, from her side. It's not that he is unfeeling but anxiety commands: a force mustered by a sensitive person who quails at confrontation. There's a position to be gained and he's impatient to get it over. A semblance of discussion required by civility will hold up but not deflect this. The severance must be carried out whatever the consequences for Emily because he has to protect the solitude his gift must have if it is to flourish.

So it is that the less she engages with him the simpler it will be to do what must be done. An effective block is to tell her that she cannot understand him because he cannot understand himself. As yet he has no words, and is 'strangely impelled to quote my own dramatic character [Harry], in the belief that I was there expressing something which I had not yet come to experience, when I made him say "it goes a great deal deeper / Than what people call their conscience". For it goes deeper than a sense of guilt for specific . . . acts.'

There had been, he concedes, 'a kind of flowering' as a result of their pact. In the summers he regards as 'the happiest of my life, when I came constantly to Campden, I was escaping from my life and getting through the little door, and while I was in the garden I became a young man again'. But then, on a chill winter day in the graveyard, he comes to as an aged man.

Eliot was only fifty-eight when he sees himself as an old man who lacks resilience for fresh adaptation. There was a physical reason: his hernia, which had been repaired at nineteen, now needed repair again. Age, though, is an old excuse. 'I grow old . . . I grow old . . .' Prufrock says to himself as he goes among the women. It's a weary voice Eliot invented when he was twenty-one. In 1947, he creates a man 'meeting himself as a stranger face to face'. Instead of the poet's encounter with his timeless self in the *Quartets*, he meets a victim of time: a crumpling man. Eliot wants to convince Emily that 'while I still love you . . . as much as ever, it is this previously unknown man whom I . . . will have to get to know'.

His imagination then invents a macabre scene of dis-embalming: 'when the body is exposed and unwrapped, we see it for a moment as it had been in life before it crumbles to dust'. A lover is preserved in mummified youth until the moment Vivienne is buried, when he becomes a decrepit old man.

In April, just before he will see Emily in America, he is more explicit. 'I recoiled violently from the prospect of marriage, when I came to realise it as possible. This is what we have to face.'

He argues further that physical intimacy without entire spiritual intimacy would be 'a nightmare'. In case this might leave a loophole for hope, he insists that this is not now just a matter of exorcising 'the demons of the past'. This denies the 'reality' of their shared moments and relegates Emily to a category that includes Vivienne, underlined by his claim not to be made for marriage.

It's hard to know what to think of the contradictory man behind the positioning. In his mid-twenties, before he married, Eliot spoke of inhibition and refinement to Conrad Aiken. That was genuine, reinforced by his hernia and his father's prohibition against carriers of syphilis. The uninhibited and unrefined Bolo rhymes imagine violent sex not far from Sweeney's conviction that 'every man' wants to do a woman in. Problems with marital sex Eliot blamed on Vivienne who, he said, didn't want it.

A characteristic of the wife, Lavinia, in a draft of his new play is to see through her husband's guises: '. . . you'll find yourself another little part to play, / Make up another face, to take people in.' When she asks what role he is now going to play, the husband replies resentfully: it's the role you impose upon me.

Just as marriage to Vivienne had made it possible for the poet to 'live through material' for poems, so Vivienne's death and its life-changing consequences released in him a creative phase driven by confession about the parts the husband plays.

Among the roles and contradictions there is one constant. It's the single-minded trajectory of a destined life derived from Charlotte Eliot's poems and reinforced by her son's reading during his graduate years at Harvard. For certain seekers the religious life begins in negation, in closing off every other alternative, Eliot said in his most self-revealing essay (on the Jansenism of Pascal, a seventeenth-century stand-in for Eliot's Puritan forebears). *The Cocktail Party* identifies a 'kind of faith that issues from despair', negating normal life, including wedded life, as a makeshift. The Dove hidden ('Oh hidden') in the hero's breast was done for once she became a candidate for marriage.

Emily Hale responded mildly, kindly. He interpreted her sympathy as a sign that she did not as yet take in his intention to minimise their conveniently unmarked bond. To put it more strongly, he feared, might impress her as 'insane' or 'dishonest'. When he remarks to Emily that what men chiefly want in a woman is the Blessed Virgin Mary, he puts this in the past tense as something he 'had'.

Still, could her existence go on in his work? He had fancied at times Emily was a saint and in the drafts he used the word 'sanctification' until Martin Browne advised him to drop it. The saintliness of Eliot's poetic imagination and Emily Hale performing as an actor were to come together as the most promising woman Eliot ever conceived in a play he soon began to write. In the play this is a woman who is admired by a film director and could have acted in Hollywood. Hale was in her element in a moral comedy, and this too' may have stirred Eliot's plan for a comedy of manners, or more to the point, spoofing the genre.

When the wife vanishes in *The Cocktail Party*, her husband, who has been enjoying an affair with a desirable woman, more well-conducted and loving than his wife, discovers that he does not want another marriage. What he wants is not to be disturbed, to go on as before. In fact, he wants his wife back, assertive and contradicting though she is. He is so disturbed by this reaction that he sees a psychiatrist, who doesn't regard him as disturbed. It's a legitimate choice for the mediocre to plod on with marriage.

Of course, to be troubled was not disabling for Eliot – not for his works. On the contrary it could be fertile, as with his breakdown in the course of creating *The Waste Land*. His 'crumbling' early in 1947 is similarly fertile, rehearsing phrases for the clash in *The Cocktail Party* where the husband, Edward, must find the words to explain to the woman he has loved that he is done with her.

'But how can you say you understand what has happened?' Edward says to his mistress, Celia. '*I* don't know what has happened, or what is going to happen'.

He wants to 'be alone', he goes on.

Celia thinks his angst 'is just a moment of surrender / To fatigue. And panic. You can't face the trouble.' This comes close to hearing the lost voice of Hale's letters to a man like this.

Then Edward ends it with Celia. 'I think you are a very rare person. / But it was too late.' He has met himself as 'a man / Beginning to know what it is to feel old.'

A question in the Eliot–Hale letters surfaces in this scene when Edward retorts, 'What future had you ever thought there could be?' It had been Eliot's own rhetorical question when, long before, he had brushed off one of Emily's many attempts to shift their relationship.

Celia wants to hold her lover to 'a private world of *ours*', recalling the letters' private language of 'our' and 'us', a compound different from its separate elements. Eliot gives his mummy image to her:

CELIA.   *I looked at your face: and I thought that I knew*
          And loved every contour; and as I looked
          It withered, as if I had unwrapped a mummy.

Eliot reshapes Emily as a woman disconcerted up to a point but fairly quickly in agreement with his own position. Celia longs to be alone, unlike the lonely Emily, and she comes to the same conclusion as Edward that their love affair had to end. The whole thing had been 'make-believe'. Edward voices Eliot's spin on his past with Emily so as to justify what would otherwise have been a betrayal.

EDWARD.   *I see that my life was determined long ago*
          And that the struggle to escape from it
          Is only make-believe . . .

In this way the scene reframes Emily's story to fit the play's transmutation of her fate. Cast out of the marital narrative, she will embrace loneliness and sacrifice as a holy destiny. Guiding Celia towards this vocation is the psychiatrist Harcourt-Reilly, who is in the business of seeing patients into the life destined for them. The wise doctor is really a divine agent. In his consulting room Celia chooses the way of a saint. Literally, she moves out of sight, no longer on stage. What befalls her in an unimaginably distant setting reaches the cocktail crowd only as news.

As with *Burnt Norton*, a great work of art has integrity in its own terms but can be at variance with a truth *outside* the work in so far as it feeds, as in this case, on a private relationship. Eliot resolves a disjunction between the rarity of Emily (as his source for Celia) and his own need to shed a physical attachment by creating parts for two very different men: the disturbed husband who wants to be rid of Celia and an artist who turns up at the cocktail party – a film-maker called Peter Quilpe who adores Celia for her potential as an actor. He is drawn to the purity of her voice, as he puts it in an early draft of the play: 'the one pure note' that stands out from 'chaotic noise'.

Both Quilpe and Edward are spokesmen for a fictional image of Emily as a woman whose lovability is unsuited to marriage in the humdrum way the play presents it: a couple's stale thoughts, vanities and discreditable motives mirroring each other. Quilpe's veneration serves to confirm Edward's conviction that marriage to Celia would be the ruin of her loveliness. When, eventually, Geoffrey Faber saw the play, he was frank enough to say that this was not marriage as he was so fortunate as to experience it.

It's weird to re-read the play in the light of Eliot's letters to Emily Hale because the play draws so directly on a turning point in their lives. But in other ways it is Eliot's design to recast Emily in quite another mould as a woman who responds to the break-up of human love by departing from the human condition and, 'Transhumanised', undergoes crucifixion. This is an unassuming woman, with genuine humility, who unexpectedly outstrips her society, but she is no longer the Emily Hale we have come to know.

All the same, the play does stage something of the visionary element that Emily shared or called out in Eliot, which he detaches from the natural woman and distils as a visionary ideal when Celia says

> ... *what happened is remembered like a dream*
> *In which one is exalted by an intensity of loving*
> *In the spirit, a vibration of delight*
> *Without desire, for desire is fulfilled*
> *In the delight of loving.*

She chooses to take herself away — beyond sight both literally and spiritually — by embarking on a journey into the unknown that will try her to the utmost. Celia journeys to the East to join a nursing order. The transformation from ordinary to destined is wonderfully convincing. The play, like *Murder in the Cathedral*, invites the audience to contemplate a development of a full-blown soul as it reaches beyond human limits.

Eliot flew to the US on 22 April 1947, intending to stay until June. His purpose was to see his brother, who was dying of leukaemia, and also to have it out with Emily Hale. He warned her that it was to be a grim visit, different from their last time together in Vermont. This time, he said, he was approaching America like a ghost who has lived among the 'ruins' of post-war London, a visitant from another world with a panic-stricken craving to vanish back into his habitat. All he wanted, he said, was to get the visit over.

Henry Ware Eliot died on 5 May. Theresa Eliot, assuming that Tom would want to marry Emily, invited her to the flat at 84 Prescott Street, across the way from Harvard in Cambridge. He turned on the well-meaning Theresa in a white fury. The next move was to explain, in Emily's presence, his course of action to Aunt Edith and Uncle John, on holiday in Petersham, a woodland setting with a lake in rural Massachusetts. Whatever he said managed to conceal his blow to Emily from her protectors. He left them, she said, bemused.

Emily and Eliot spoke in the privacy Dorothy Elsmith offered them at Woods Hole. We can't know what was said, but a hesitant vulnerability made itself felt when Eliot told Emily afterwards that he had been 'pretty well numbed . . . – a semi-anaesthesia by which . . . an organism tries to defend itself'. She had to hear quite a lot about Eliot's paralysis, his numbed nerves and his 'agony' when he thought of her.

They spoke further at Emily's lodgings in Hubbard Street, Concord, when Eliot came in June to deliver the Commencement address at Concord Academy. Crossed out in his notes are thoughts on marriage. He makes an analogy to writing poetry: you can't be sure if you can do it, and the same goes for a man and a woman. Married people might think they know all about each other, but 'every moment is a new problem'.

He regarded it as his hardest performance during this period (harder, then, than his address on Milton at the Frick Collection in New York and a poetry reading at the National Gallery in Washington DC). The assembled schoolgirls wore regulation long white dresses. He spoke to them keeping his head down, a lanky figure stooped over the lectern looking, it was said, like an aged eagle. Patty Wolcott remembered 'shaking hands with him, his hand already withdrawing as mine took the grasp'. Fanny Tomaino recalled a 'praying mantis' handshake and his studied pronunciation of 'po-et-treh'. She was bored and disappointed by his 'cool, dry tone' – she had wanted him to sound like a poet. After his return to England on 19 June, his mind fixed on a last memory of Emily 'framed in the doorway'.

This time there was no ardour on parting. The letters Hale wrote from now on refer to 'the change'. She now took on a passionless role as dear old friend. Lending herself to his wish, her letters are confined to ordinary doings, relayed in a natural voice but without the resistance that had provoked Eliot in the past. Her measured, carefully matter-of-fact manner conveys her sense of him as no longer the person she had thought.

He kept these letters – they were not burnt with the rest – only because they were *not* love-letters. To anyone who did not know of the hundreds of earlier letters they would appear tame, which was the intention: to erase what had been, even though the poet maintained a husk of loyalty and the habit of correspondence. He still depended on the exchange of letters. But the emotion in their previous correspondence disappears, apart from an occasional reminiscence on Hale's part, haunting her letters like a sudden and swift visitation from their past.

A window for hope was left in an afterthought that he was not 'unified' in his decision not to marry. It did trouble him that he was throwing away 'something most valuable' and he spoke 'tenderly' to the woman he still called 'my only love'. Yet this was by the way, not meant to sway a resolve.

A month after his return to London, Eliot was due for surgery on his double hernia. The further prospect of losing his teeth later in 1947 reinforced the image of an ageing man. His letters focus on the immediate ordeal of his operation and poor food at the London Clinic at a time when postwar rationing was at its peak.

It was legitimate for Emily to reach out to him with an old friend's concern, and his diary-mode invites this with details of his operations. The first operation was so long and complex that the surgeon decided to leave sewing up the hernia on the other side for a second round of surgery. Recovery was slow: Eliot mentions his sagging belly. He would stoop his way along the Chelsea Embankment, grateful for benches, some with slats missing in the wrong places.

He recovered with the Fabers at their new country home, Minsted House at Midhurst in Sussex. From there Eliot made a strange communication to Emily, weirder even than the mummy, when his thoughts turned yet again to *Richard III*, the play he had chosen to see on 22 August 1938. This date matters: it's the anniversary of Richard's downfall, and only a few days after the dark deed of Vivienne's committal, a fortnight after Eliot authorised this. On 22 August 1947 he marks the 462nd anniversary of the Battle of Bosworth Field in 1485. Why should he tell Emily, and what does he expect her to make of it?

In a BBC TV documentary called *The Mysterious Mr Eliot*, broadcast in 1971, only six years after Eliot died, a number who had known him personally were on screen, among them Hope Mirrlees. She related how each year on this date Eliot would wear a white rose in his lapel in memory of Richard III, signalling allegiance to the House of York in the Wars of the Roses. Hope was amused by the absurdity and put it down to Eliot's being a foreigner. No Englishman, she said, would have made such a gesture.

Eliot's mention of Bosworth Field shortly after putting an end to Hale's future suggests that his white rose had more to do with Shakespeare than history: the scene when, the night before the battle, the ghosts of those Richard had wronged come back to haunt him. One of the ghosts is Richard's wretched wife, who had died that same year. Though condemned by the judgements of his victims, the king stands his ground until the end.

After Eliot ended their pact, Emily found refuge with Penelope Noyes, on holiday in New Hampshire. Then she went to tend her aunt and uncle in Petersham, and from there returned to the Dorset Players, in order to take the lead in a thriller, *Kind Lady*. Eliot thought it a terrible play, but expected Emily to make a bloodcurdling job of it, and Dorothy Elsmith reported that Emily had indeed excelled. Eliot's comeback was that Emily's 'theatrical art' was wasted on summer visitors.

Her next role was in *Dangerous Corner*. Eliot dismissed J. B. Priestley (themes pretentious, beyond his limited powers) with his old abrasiveness. Earlier that year, in the midst of the shock he was delivering to Emily, he'd reproached her for putting on *Richard II* during Lent. The harshness and tenderness fire at will, as in the poetry.

Emily recounted the change in a letter to her friend Lorraine Havens, whom she had met at Scripps and who had been there when Eliot came to the campus. Her voice is sensible. Her eye for character saw from start to finish that this genius was erratic and difficult and at this point she did not permit herself to be shaken. Her poise is impressive in accepting the poet's make-up, not blaming him or herself for his turns and twists.

> ... he loves me – I believe that wholly – but apparently not in the way usual to men less gifted i. e. with complete love thro' a married relationship. I have not completely given up hope that he may yet recover from this – to me – abnormal reaction, but on the other hand I cannot allow myself to hold on to anything so delicately uncertain ...

Ten years later, when Emily reflected again on this, she remained sensible, not accusatory. It's painful to read the way she absorbed this terrible blow. To her, Vivienne's death made possible 'the anticipated life together, which could now be rightfully ours', but instead 'something too personal, too obscurely emotional for me to understand, decided TSE against marrying again. This was both a shock and a sorrow, though looking back on the story, perhaps I could not have been the companion in marriage I hoped to be, perhaps the decision saved us both from great unhappiness – I cannot ever know.'

Miss Hale's post at Concord Academy turned out to be as unsatisfactory as were other temporary posts after she lost her place at Smith College. There's a 'prime of Miss Jean Brodie' situation wherever she went, a born teacher who left an imprint on her special girls but was insufficiently appreciated by the head. She was underpaid, even though all of the productions she put on appear to have been triumphs, especially *Richard II* – like *Comus* at Scripps, a high-flying venture. Miss Tucker, the headmistress, wrote about it in the local newspaper but neglected to mention Miss Hale.

As a sweetener, Miss Tucker offered her accommodation attached to the school. At first she was jubilant, but then dashed to see the uninhabitable quarters, not even winterised. Then too the status of a woman who worked for her living was low. When Miss Hale brought the greatest poet of the age to the school, Miss Tucker was not quite as appreciative as she could have been. All this added up to Miss Hale's decision to resign her post at the end of the school year in 1947. This coincided with the stress of Eliot's visit.

Eliot was uneasy about how Emily would support herself. He thought she might lean on him financially, though she never did. Her idea was to offer recitals of poetry, mainly for schools, confident in her ability to introduce poems. He suggested to her a list of poems read on the BBC.

In January 1948 she approached Scripps with a proposal to give a reading of Eliot's works. President Hard, uninterested in the fact that Eliot himself had visited the college back in 1933, turned this down.

A more workable plan was to join the drama society in Concord. Eliot's high regard for Emily's art led him to warn her of jealousy: the same warning he gave when she was at Smith. It proved unnecessary. She was soon running the society. Happily too she found a new berth in three upstairs rooms at 9 Lexington Road and for the first time this seemed a home of her own. Her rooms looked out on the meeting house of First Parish Unitarian church on Lexington Road, where she gave a programme of Christmas readings, including Eliot's *Journey of the Magi*. Some poems she performed from memory. Two young teachers at Concord Academy, delightful Australians, rented the rooms below and Miss Hale dined with them about once a week. Another night she would dine (as a paying guest) with a friend and she had couples for tea. It was possible to fit in six. Then, she told Eliot, she attended 'Bee' evenings in Boston: a circle that went back to their youth. Of course she was dutiful to her uncle and aunt, both of whom were ailing. She spent weekends with them in Boston, did their shopping, mending and other errands, and offered what consolation she could.

She joined the League of Women Voters and the Concord Women's Club. A newspaper cutting (sent to Eliot) reports on Miss Emily Hale's 'inspired' reading of a play, *The Dover Road*, by A. A. Milne to a good-sized audience. 'Her deep understanding of the humor and drama of the play was revealed in every slight variation of her flexible voice.'

After extensive war work, Jeanie McPherrin had become a dean at Wellesley College (where later she taught French). She asked Emily for a night in her pleasant house. Seven women academics were invited to meet Miss Hale at dinner, including Eliot's relation Miss Mainwaring. Emily wore a grey crêpe dress and beautiful old French pearl earrings, a gift from Eliot.

She describes what she wore in a letter to Eliot, which he retained, along with all her letters to him from this time. After the change, the two-way correspondence can be seen. Her 1947 Christmas letter smooths over their differences. It is selfless in its courage and kindness:

I am sure you wrote after consideration and evaluation as truly
and as fairly as you could. I think the matter from your point of
view is wholly clear to me now . . . It may be after a longer period
of adjustment on my part, I shall ask you [to] correspond more
often again . . . May you have some Peace I pray – some comfort
to your soul and strength to your body. The New Year is indeed
dark for all of us unless we pray for Light – Light – Light. Your
loving Emily

The last words reflect back to him the flashes of light at the close
of the draft of *Burnt Norton* he had sent to her twelve years earlier.

Once, on New Year's Day 1948, she drops again into intimacy
when she confides the strain 'of my family's attitude about the
whole affair which seems to leave me out of the picture entirely,
which of course, is not yet the state of mind I feel!' For a moment
she permits their former selves to surface, inviting the comfort of
empathy. There is no reproach in this hint to him to think of her.

In the New Year Honours for 1948, he was to receive the Order of
Merit, Britain's highest award in the arts, science and armed forces,
with only twenty-four living recipients. In America the previous
June he had delayed his flight back for the sake of accepting an honorary degree from Princeton, where he had been one of thirty-six
recipients including President Truman, General Eisenhower and
the Secretary of State George Marshall, who that month gave an
address at Harvard urging what became known as the Marshall
Plan for the post-war recovery of Europe. For Eliot this was one of
thirteen honorary degrees, each of which mattered to him. 'One
can hardly refuse an honorary degree.' Can't one? Virginia Woolf
had refused, thinking them merely 'the baubles of the brain-
selling trade', and in her diary she writes 'it is an utterly corrupt
society'. Eliot believed the same. To sail to America was to be on
his way to Gomorrah. Why should Gomorrah's accolades matter?
Yet they did.

The downside was to fear that such accolades were a sign his career was over. As it happened, the King reinforced this. When George VI presented Eliot with the Order of Merit, he remarked, 'Poets, when they become Laureates, never write again.'

Emily's advice was to look on it as a challenge, not the end of him. She urged him to use his experience. 'The emotional content of your day to day existence, may not be recovered from ever – but should go towards new deeper sources of understanding and creative work.' She had no idea he was creating a play using his refusal of her to propel the plot.

Aunt Edith was donating some four hundred lantern slides of English gardens to the Royal Horticultural Society in London. She asked Eliot to represent her at a celebration on 2 March 1948, and to speak about his visits to Cotswold gardens. Lord Aberconway, the President of the Society, would introduce him. The event was to take place in the lecture hall above an exhibition of early spring blooms from Cornwall and the Scilly Isles. Eliot was bound to draw a crowd, and friends from Campden would be there. It came to Hale that she could use her savings to fly to London as a surprise.

In the end she did not go, but the fantasy was still alive when she recounts it to him.

Miss Emily Hale 9 Lexington Road Concord Massachusetts

February 29th, 1948

Dear Tom,

... When I last wrote you [4 February] I almost told you that you were probably to see me on March 2nd, as I have for a long time felt the pleasurable urge of thinking I shall be, as well as wanting to be, present to represent her, and bring home a very personal account of Tuesday's occasion. I was going to stay about a month, visit Meg and Doreen [Eliot and

Emily had often visited Meg Nason's teashop in Broadway, a village not far from Campden], and other friends and fly both ways ... But for several reasons, I gave up this little fairy-tale scheme – tho' as Tuesday draws near I find myself wishing I had gone over! I think my <u>chief</u> reason for not going was the thought that I could not have really ... found satisfaction in the plan – because of the condition now of the Ps [Perkinses] – tho' I think they may live for months more ... But, being myself, I could not do it ...

I imagine, looking facts straight in the face, that you will be very glad I did not come, whether I saw much of you or not. In time, I suppose, we can meet on some new basis fairly securely, but now, within a year still of last summer at Woods Hole and Hubbard St. the occasion might have been more difficult than we could realize – but it is strange not to write that my chief regret at changing my plan is because I cannot have an unaccustomed chance to be with you!! And, just as I left yesterday ... someone sent Aunt Edith a box of lovely fresh sweet-peas – and what memories they awakened which haven't quieted themselves to-day! Funny, isn't it – what starts the dumbness and the numbness quivering again.

... For so many weeks this event of March 2nd has so completely filled the thoughts of the Ps. that I only hope the aftermath will be compensation enough for the long long anticipation. And you saw the pictures last at Petersham – well, I guess it is as well I shall not be present to hear your reference to that occasion ...

I am <u>delighted</u> to learn you are beginning a new play, Tom, and shall love to hear anything about it you care to tell me. ...

I'll be thinking of you on Tuesday, and perhaps you'll be thinking too of

Yours lovingly,

<u>Emily Hale</u>

Eliot responded with 'very poignant memories' of Petersham, where he had seen many of the sixty-five slides shown at the London event. In his report for Aunt Edith he pictured a crowded hall, with some people standing.

'It would have been very surprising to have had you appear suddenly in London' was all Eliot said of Emily's fantasy, together with advice always to make advance plans in case accommodation should prove difficult.

Not having gone to England meant that Hale was at hand when a girlhood acquaintance, Marguerite Hearsey, approached her to fill a vacancy at a top girls' boarding school, Abbot Academy in Andover, Massachusetts. The speech and drama teacher had suddenly died and the post on offer was for the rest of the school year. The salary was double what Concord Academy had paid. An added attraction was comfortable accommodation with a school trustee, a widow named Mrs Clingman, who treated Miss Hale 'most considerately'. She had breakfast with Mrs Clingman and took her other meals at the school. The food was good for so big an institution (180 girls).

Her letters present a new containment, rather like the resolute single woman in *Washington Square* by Henry James, a favourite of Eliot's. Disappointed in the exploitative character of her only suitor, Catherine Sloper takes up her singleness 'for life'. People might think her negligible, but the story invites us to see an invincible integrity. Like her, Emily Hale remains herself, even as she plays the role Eliot expected. She writes without effort or contrivance, with an instinct for loving kindness active already in the child who looked after her infant brother when their mother was ill.

She filled Eliot in on her pleasing new job. 'It is a large boarding school – 119 yrs. old – close to Phillips Andover boys' school – and has a fine reputation.' At first she was there from Wednesday evening until Saturday, doing speech for beginners and advanced dramatic work and readings with older girls of some ability, teaching sometimes seven or eight hours at a stretch. During her first two weeks at the school she prepared them for 'a reading of *Outward Bound* as a complete play – a novelty to try'.* It was due to be presented to the student body and faculty. The nine girls in the cast were 'very friendly and responsive'.

She embraced her girls' enthusiasm for acting, she told Eliot, 'their obvious affection towards me is very sweet and comforting'. Heartened by this, she risked directness, summing up where he had left her with admirable resolve to go on in her own way. 'Since the future is not to give me, anyway, what at one time I thought it was going to[,] a little larger place in the spot-light of worldly affairs – I am grateful I can be very useful still to young people and to an art which I think has become pretty much a part of me – and there is a real chance to develop the work at Abbot.'

She chose to stage *The Swan* for Commencement on 29 May. This was a 1914 play about the challenge for a princess of swanlike dignity in attracting a suitable prince, who shows no awareness of her as a woman.† The play was by a Hungarian refugee, Ferenc Molnár (Franz Molnar), who fled to New York in 1940. Miss Hale was proud of her girls' 'very fine' performance and their 'loyalty' to what she chose to try. The Molnár play turned out another triumph, she was glad to report to Eliot.

The following year she staged works by American women, Edna St Vincent Millay and Amy Lowell. Though Eliot did not 'relish' them, Emily stood up for what she chose.

---

* *Outward Bound* (1923) is by Sutton Vane, about seven people on a ship who don't know why they are there and where they are bound. It turns out that they are dead and bound for Judgement. (Sylvia Plath had a similar idea in her marvellous story 'Mary Ventura and the Ninth Kingdom', about people on a train bound for the frontier of mortality.)

† In time *The Swan* would be the basis for a Grace Kelly movie with Alec Guinness, released in 1956 to coincide with Kelly's marriage to Prince Rainier.

Appreciative Miss Hearsey offered Miss Hale a permanent post. She also offered a newly renovated duplex in School Street to compensate Miss Hale for giving up her rooms in Concord. Eliot promised a visit to Andover in October or November 1948, when he would be at the Princeton Institute for Advanced Studies. The offer to him was handsome: $1,000 for travel and $2,000 from the Rockefeller Foundation for two months. In Princeton he was certain to see Margaret Thorp, whose successful book, *America at the Movies*, had recently been published by Faber & Faber. Despite this, Eliot expressed a reservation: 'Margaret is so very serious.'

Oxford granted Eliot an honorary degree. Though he might have liked Emily to be there, he said, no ladies could attend luncheon at All Souls College nor dinner at Christ Church. The favour Emily really wanted was for him to join her on Grand Manan Island in Canadian waters beyond Maine. She drove north with her Scottie dog, Rag Doll, for company, stopping over in Augustus, Maine, at the home of a student in her senior class.

Careful though she was to be no more than a chatty old friend, she did allow herself to touch on memories. In late August Eliot was about to stay with the Brocklebanks, whose 'lovely house and setting' recalled, for her, 'very pleasant occasions' in the past. She writes: 'This visit will bring you the closest to Campden since 1939 that you have been – I wonder how such a return to the region . . . will affect you? . . . I cannot quite accustom myself to the change.' She was honest again about present feelings when she wrote from Boston a year later:

My spirit I confess sinks very low at times, and I am learning to try to deal with the most subtle of all deviltries – loneliness and not complete happiness after my first year of work. But the former will always be with me, I imagine – and the latter is naturally a comparison and must be dealt with quietly and patiently and submissively. I have to put all my thoughts in my work, the standards to keep among the students, and the fortune of my pretty rooms – and the chance to help others as the opportunity comes. [She then mentions his sister Marian and niece Theodora sailing for England.] Their going evokes memories which as yet I cannot live among.

There was this delicacy in her hold on truth. Innate goodness is not a quality much talked of but she had it.

Eliot's project in Princeton was to revise a first draft of *The Cocktail Party*. He reported to Emily on his progress with the play, but only in terms of Acts and scenes. In the meantime, Martin Browne encouraged him to expand the scene where Edward, having been abandoned by his unlovable wife, casts off his mistress, Celia, who expects to marry him.

Eliot's visit to Andover was not a success. He felt that he did not read well, but the problem may have been his mood: an embarrassed and guilty reluctance to see Emily despite her efforts to set his mind at rest.

While at Princeton, Eliot was announced as winner of the Nobel Prize for Literature. He left America earlier than planned, bound for Sweden, and from then on the gap widened between him and an obscure schoolmistress.

Eliot kept *The Cocktail Party* from Emily until the play went into rehearsal on 25 July 1949. He writes only about Henzie Raeburn, Martin's wife, as an unsuitable understudy for three parts; he doesn't reveal them. Emily, meanwhile, was preoccupied with her own productions, including Sheridan's *School for Scandal*.

'My dear, it is a very long time that I am without news of you,' Eliot wrote. 'Do you not like to write any more?'

When he finally sent the script to Emily in late July, she was astonished. Here she found her pain displayed in the rejected mistress with the rejecter speaking words written to her in private. Then, in Act III, she came upon the details of Celia's terrible end: how hostile tribesmen liked to 'smear the victims / With a juice that is attractive to the ants'. This will torture Celia further during her crucifixion.

These scenes silenced her.

After two weeks she protested. It was usual for her letters to Eliot to run on smoothly with one clause unfolding out of another, but her intakes of breath are palpable in uncharacteristic dashes. On the page is a panting dismay:

> I wish I could be enthusiastic about it, my dear, but I can't be. In the first place, you never gave me a hint of the nature of the play, and it is its content which has so taken me aback – I fear – much as in "Family Reunion." It is in other words, too personal to many things I know – if no one else – for me to be very objective about it – did you realize this yourself – its extremely personal element – of your own thought – your own experiences, lately? [She concedes the skill of his characterisations] – except Celia – who remains nebulous to me – and oh, Tom, how could you so brutally destroy Celia at the last? That description of her immolation (is that the word?) seems beyond the canon of dramatic laws of restraint. I cannot be anything but honest with you, Tom you would not wish me to be, I know. I think you have given your cast a very stiff assignment and I hope they and Martin prove equal to it. I wish the best for you for its sake as much as I can – I hope to hear from you how rehearsals go etc before too long.
>
> Yours always, with friendship's love
> Emily Hale

Eliot's answer was flat denial. *The Cocktail Party* had not used their private story, he said. The play was fiction.

Emily's integrity held. She did not accept that he had not used her. She still saw, and all too keenly, her private situation ready to go on view to all the world. Nor could she accept immolation as a divine plan.

For an audience, unaware of the personal source, *The Cocktail Party* is about spiritual promise as an alternative to marriage; it drama- tises a quality Eliot recognised in a person he had loved. For the first and last time in his career, he created a woman who acts in her own right, not as a foil to a man's self-realisation as artist, convert or sinner. Celia is the focus for sympathy. Never did Eliot conceive so lovable a woman, at once assured and sensitive. But then – he kills her in a sensationally cruel way.

By the time Emily read the script it was too late.

During the play's previews in Edinburgh, she was far off on Grand Manan, where she succumbed to an attack of gastric flu. The star sapphire, the ring Eliot had given her in Chichester in 1934, disap- peared down the lavatory.

'I miss the ring,' she said, 'not only for the beauty of it, but for the long and precious association, as intimate to me as almost anything else you ever gave me, because it was the first gift of such personal character. By a strange chance I had, the day before I lost the stone, sent in an order to a jeweler who is making over into a new setting the diamond circlet you gave me in the last summer at Campden. I could never wear it since the change of two years ago . . . Ordering this one day, and losing the sapphire the next was indeed like an allegorical illustration of "The King is dead. Long live the King."' Did the dead king mean the Eliot who had loved her, replaced by the rising playwright?

Eliot reported to Emily what a success the play had been. In October she re-read it, tight-lipped, her protest about her usage effectively silenced. 'As for the "personal" allusions – I referred to them in my second G[rand] M[anan] letter, and shall not speak of them again, since you so thoroughly deny them.'

The Edinburgh audience took against the biting ants. Henry Sherek, due to produce the play in the West End and New York, demanded a cut. 'There is universal distaste & criticism of the juice line. Surely the horror is enough without this? It seems unnecessary to me & why fight <u>everybody</u>.'

The flippancy does come over as voyeuristic, a relish of aggression rather than a window on sanctity. Celia's murder reminds us of the violence done to the lady in white with her head bent between a strangler's knees in 'The Love Song of Saint Sebastian', succeeded by the Lysol bath for the prostitute in *Sweeney Agonistes*.

Eventually Eliot did yield to opinion, and on 25 October let Emily know he had toned down the martyrdom because he did not want to be accused of indulging in sadism. It was 'alarmingly common' in brutal films and fiction emanating from New York he said. The finger of blame points there.

The Cocktail Party opened at Henry Miller's Theatre on Broadway on 21 January 1950, with the Duke and Duchess of Windsor in the audience. The opening was threatened by aversion to Eliot's anti-semitism aired in the *Saturday Review of Literature*, which linked him with Ezra Pound's fascism, condemned in his post-war trial for treason. Eliot brushed this off as mass hysteria provoked by a possible campaign to stimulate the circulation of the magazine. He saw himself as a victim of 'violent defamation'.

Emily played fair in praising Eliot for the other leads in the play, the so-called Guardians, Alex and Julia ('Julia is excellently drawn I think'). Their comic turns as gossiping busybodies disguise their serious roles as guardian angels. In the latter capacity they are in league with the Unidentified Guest at the party, who reappears in Act II as the wise doctor. It was played superbly by Alec Guinness, keen-eyed behind his glasses.

Julia was based on Mary Trevelyan, six years younger than Emily. In 1949, when Eliot bumped into Mary at a chemist shop in Southampton Row, he greeted her with a line from the play: 'Oh, it's YOU again, Julia!' The published play acknowledges Miss Trevelyan for scoring the jolly song the doctor sings as he downs a cocktail, and in her copy of the play is a note from the playwright thanking her for her contribution to Julia, a party guest given to insistent interruption which turns out to be the social disguise of an angel. In the course of the forties, Eliot became increasingly dependent on brisk, practical Mary Trevelyan and she fell increasingly in love with him.

22

ENTER A GUARDIAN

Mary Trevelyan had made the first move back in November 1934. She was then a single woman of thirty-seven with a liking for travel and adventure, who had recently settled down to be Warden of the Student Movement House. This was a grand house with Adam fire-places in Russell Square, a club and hostel for students from Africa, Asia and the Caribbean who had come to one of the University of London's sixty colleges. It was known to be a place safe from dis-crimination, maintained by the Students' Christian Movement. Miss Trevelyan invited Eliot to read his poems there.

Born into a Church of England family, Mary was the devout eldest daughter of George Philip Trevelyan, who had built churches of his own high church persuasion. Miss Trevelyan contacted Eliot after he lent his voice to a drive to build churches in London. In this he was something of a throwback to his grandfather who, in 1837, had built an elegantly proportioned, four-square church, with ped-iment and columns like the Parthenon, on a bend in the untamed Mississippi. His grandson's contribution to church-building was a pageant he called *The Rock*, put on at Sadler's Wells. A 'God-shaken' Stranger, come amongst the English, speaks in a prophetic voice, denouncing hollow humanity seated next to him in a tube train, and warning of the way the world ends. The only answer to the imminent end of the world is to build a holy place. It is not then surprising that the Stranger should call for 'Nehemiah the Prophet'.

As leader of the Israelites exiled in Babylon in the fifth century BC, Nehemiah speaks with a view to rebuilding the temple in Jerusalem and he leads a devout few who keep faith with the ancestors. Eliot's dramatisation comes straight from the Bible: Nehemiah is an expatriate who, unusually, achieved high office at the imperial Persian court as pourer of Artaxerxes' wine — this job comes into Eliot's version. But despite the king's support he finds his work opposed by men in the province of Judea — Eliot names them — who impede the Lord's work. So Nehemiah and co-builders have a trowel in one hand and a weapon in the other. In Eliot's pageant, the weapon turns out to be a gun rather loose in the Prophet's holster. The holster adds a comic Western touch to the tension.

This was the very note Eliot brought to his tie with Miss Trevelyan: comedy infusing their commitment to a place of prayer — kneeling together where prayer has been valid. Mary would always connect Psalm 51, 'Have mercy upon me . . . blot out my transgressions', with Eliot kneeling beside her in the darkness at Tenebrae, their favourite of all the services they attended together.

Her true-blue character as a Guardian called out a new role in Eliot: neither the adult carer he had been with Vivienne nor the poetic lover with Emily, he offered Miss Trevelyan the child in him: a nursery rhyme child who can be angelic or fractious, sure that nanny will dote on him even if a rebuke is in order. It became his habit to phone Mary and announce himself as 'Badboy' or 'Goodchild', according to the mood of the hour. She was ready to be amused by her charge when he was *not* being the great poet, only playing up as a 'silly old boy'. Her briskness was not analytic: she took little notice of Eliot's antics except as antics, but his Nehemiah character — slid into an apparently idle exchange on the phone — meant more than a tease.

Nehemiah was the prime model for seventeenth-century Puritans migrating to the New World in order to found a city on a hill, a new Jerusalem. Nehemiah, teller of his own story, a man who takes a journey to build a holy place, dominates spiritual biographies and sermons in Puritan New England. To 'Fare forward', Eliot's refrain in his American quartet, was a phrase he repeated to Mary Trevelyan whenever he went away.

The migrant was an aspect that Mary, a professional handler of foreigners, was quick to note: the 'distraught refugee face' of Nehemiah Eliot. He allowed her to see this, as Henry Ware Eliot had done long before. In Henry's opinion, Bloomsbury had induced stage-fright and compelled his brother to mutate, at least outwardly, if he was to be one of us. Where Henry looked on in pity, Mary Trevelyan found this rather funny but in a sympathetic manner.

The stranger in Eliot had taken shape in the period when London had been a 'tough nut' for an American to crack. The refugee face was self-protective: it asked Mary to look after him in a way that left him alone. As with Emily Hale, he preserved a strictly guarded relationship, controlling the time he spent with any one person. Mary did not have the raspberry mouth and curly-haired grace of Emily nor, thankfully, the desperate adhesiveness of Vivienne. She had more a look of George Eliot: her face long and oval, with a steady gaze, chin on her hand as she looked at him. Hers was an inquiring, not intrusive look, though its knowingness, now and then, discomfited him. All the same, her ready helpfulness brought peace: her memoir about him often records restful drives and evenings at her flat.

Mary didn't bother with her appearance or clothe herself to make a statement. She had cheek-length brown hair, un-waved and a little rumpled, accompanied by the large directness of the Trevelyan nose. Her casual look would fit our present day, but men of Eliot's traditional view expected women to be sleek, to have their hair done and carry themselves elegantly, as Emily did, or dress with style like Vivienne, whose flounced skirt and scarf wound about her head and tied behind the neck had fitted her for the dash of Bloomsbury and Garsington.

Though Mary was nine years his junior, Eliot cast her as older – a full generation older. What he wanted was to be Mary's adoptive nephew, and from that peculiar stance to join in her Englishness: the forthright eccentricity of people who take it as a birthright not to succumb to norms. Mary Trevelyan's actual nephew, Humphrey Carpenter, explained the Englishness of their ilk: 'If you're eccentric, you're all right.'

Humphrey defined his aunt as a type who no longer exists: daughters of the Victorian vicarage. They spoke in the accents of the 1880s: they said 'gel' for 'girl' and 'crorse' for 'cross'. Miss Trevelyan's kindness to her student charges contrasts with Eliot's formal courtesy and patience with the would-be authors who approached him in his capacity as Faber editor. Mary put people at ease. Her straightforwardness, lightened with humour, sparked others, and she was genuinely caring in her practical way. With no children of her own, her charges mattered all the more.

Eliot duly read to her students in October 1935, and on that occasion he brought with him a 'mysterious lady', so Mary recorded in her diary. It's likely to have been Emily Hale, who was in London for October and November that year, and accompanied Eliot everywhere during an interlude of visibility in their otherwise secret attachment.

The following summer Miss Trevelyan was running music events at a 'hallelujah' camp for Christian students at Swanwick in Derbyshire. Because she was 'tough' (her word), she was deputed to look after Eliot when he came there to read. It proved awkward, for the poet arrived out of sorts, with a stiff neck. He read *The Waste Land* and 'The Hollow Men' in a harsh voice with his head on one side. Mary dared to send him her parody of his performance, stiff neck and all, which she devised for the students. She was proud to receive an amused reply.

She had him back for another London reading in October 1940,

after the Blitz had begun. The students were edgy. Eliot's measured voice calmed them, Mary noted. She was impressed by the
fact that he had fire-watched (with other older men posted on
roofs to spot outbreaks of fires during bombing raids) the previous night and was to do so again the following night. She then
invited him to her adaptation of a medieval Nativity play. In spare
moments, mainly in shelters during bombing raids, she wrote a
book about her charges called *From the Ends of the Earth*. (Her own
far-flung travels are part of it, including a flight to Beijing 'in a
tiny plane which appeared to be tied together with string'. She
sent her manuscript to Eliot and it was published by Faber & Faber
early in 1942.)

As an editor, Eliot himself had foreign protégés. One was a Tamil
poet from Ceylon, Meary James Tambimuttu. For another, an
unnamed Indian poet unhappily married to an Englishwoman.
One night when Mary fetched this poet from hospital, following
a drunken crash into a lamp post, the young man lolled back in
the taxi reciting yards of *The Waste Land*. His fantasy was for Miss
Trevelyan to be his mother and Eliot his father. This she reported
on the phone to Eliot, who said, 'I think we could have done better
than that.'

As 'a mainstay for her waifs', Mary proved tolerant and sturdy,
appealing to the waif in Eliot himself. Sometimes, she recalled, he
held her hand for a very long time. He did so at a university event,
claiming to be afraid of the chancellor's wife. Teasingly, he signs
a letter to her in the most limp and flaccid tones of which he is
capable. It's the flirtatious comedy of a man trying his best to be
impotent but not naturally so.

Their first lunch, a long one, was at Viani's in Charlotte Street.

'What were you like as a child?' she asked as they strolled back to
work in the spring sunshine.

'Born on the Mississippi,' Eliot began. He was in full flood, for he had just then completed *The Dry Salvages*, recalling the Mississippi bursting its banks and the purple grapes on the autumn table when the family returned to St Louis after their Cape Ann summers.

That long lunch *à deux* seems to have taken place after Virginia Woolf died in late March 1941. Her death left Eliot bereft and 'alien' once more. He signed a letter to an editor 'Metoikos' (a resident alien in ancient Greece). In a way, Mary Trevelyan replaced Virginia Woolf as arch-insider in Eliot's adoptive country.

Confident Englishwomen of his generation looked on his propriety as comic. Like Virginia Woolf, Mary Trevelyan joked about Eliot's clothes, especially his attachment to the too-small bowler hat atop his head. As churchwarden at St Stephen's, he would hang the bowler carefully in the vestry, in case someone sat on it while he went about the collection. Mary relished the oddity of his get-up when the Bishop of London attended a dedication ceremony at St Stephen's. Eliot's galoshes were an incongruous addition to a tail-coat. Inherited from his brother, these galoshes were too big, and he lost one under his seat during the service. Mary pictures him 'plunging about in his pew, trying to retrieve the galosh'.

Eliot did not overlook her connections: an uncle was the eminent historian G. M. Trevelyan, Master of Trinity College, Cambridge; her brother Humphrey was a diplomat; her brother-in-law Harry Carpenter was Warden of Keble College, Oxford. Her grandmother on her mother's side had played the violin under the baton of Elgar in her Worcestershire girlhood. Mary herself had won a scholarship to the Royal College of Music and there studied the organ and conducting under Sir Adrian Boult. She had taken a post as organist and choir-trainer at St Barnabas' church in Oxford and then taught music at public schools, Radley and Marlborough.

She had a weekly slot on the wireless as a member of a religious brains trust called the Anvil: amongst a set of theologians, Mary was meant to represent 'the ordinary person'. In this role, she consulted Eliot on answers to questions sent in by listeners. His disquisitions were lengthy, and since notes were not permitted in the studio she was content – not without a hint of triumph – to forget everything he'd said the minute she went on air.

Eliot began to attend church with Mary, and the Anglican calendar marked their days. The dating of his letters to her recall martyrs and saints. While Emily Hale was depressed during 1942 and writing less often, Eliot took to dining out with Mary of an evening. Even war-torn London offered his favourite French restaurant, L'Etoile on Charlotte Street, or the Garrick Club. Alternatively, they might dine at the Oxford and Cambridge Club and, later on, the Athenaeum. Mary's base in Russell Square was only a few steps away from Faber & Faber, and then when the Student Movement House moved to 103 Gower Street her office was not very far from Eliot's; it was easy to meet for sherry or gin at the bar of the Russell Hotel.

At the age of forty-three, then at forty-four and forty-five, Mary found herself stirred. His humour had a flirtatious undertow. It showed itself in displays of piffle, the verbal equivalent of a peacock's tail, or when he shoved his hat to the back of his head and sang a tune about a date in Harlem. On a much later occasion, in Mary's bathroom, he hummed, 'Say gal, I'm certainly glad to know you' – calling up Gatsby's romantic fixation on Daisy, who says 'I certainly am awfully glad to see you'.

Towards the end of 1942 Mary admitted to herself that she was in love. Sounding faintly in the background was an alarm bell: his humorous admission that he was mad. Yes, 'dotty', Mary concurred. And he gave another warning: a habit of 'dropping everything and everybody'. Of course she knew nothing of Eliot's Beatrice who failed to interest him, just then, when she lost her job.

Each of the women in Eliot's life brought out a facet of the enigma he presented. Vivienne Eliot had enacted the 'horror of life': the poet's stabs at the heart of darkness. Where Eliot delivers assaults on paper, Vivienne had had the nerve – some called it madness – to make this blatant. She had no fear of vulgarity: her accusations, collapses and shamelessness were draining, yes, and also riveting.

Onlookers had pitied Eliot, yet his wife had spoken to a beat of flagrant emotion in poems written between 'Hysteria' in 1915 and ragtime in *The Waste Land* with its syncopated rhythm in the mind of the put-upon husband.

Emily Hale spoke to the refined seeker after virtue, the man of faith treading in the footsteps of his mother's pilgrim soul.

Mary Trevelyan, the woman visible at Eliot's side, endorsed his public character as Anglican churchman all through the forties and into the fifties. It would be easy to assume this was more superficial than the poet's phantasmagorical bonds with Vivienne and Emily, yet the tie to Mary had its own profundity. When sainthood proved out of reach, his *Quartets* resort to prayer, observance and discipline. Prayer comes first, and with Mary there were shared prayers, including prayers for each other.

Eliot prayed for Mary daily and was glad to hear that she did the same for him. Whenever they parted, each said 'Bless you' to the other, and 'God be with you'. Mary told him that she often prayed *The Cocktail Party* prayer for him.

> *Protect him from the Voices*
> *Protect him from the Visions*
> *Protect him in the tumult*
> *Protect him in the silence.*

These were the words of Julia in Act II. She speaks as the Guardian of Celia (the prayer speaks of 'her', not 'him'), who earlier in that scene has resolved to transform herself as a single woman dedicated to a selfless higher life. We know that Emily Hale had not approved this scene, and at the same time she warned Eliot that Julia's transformation from comic busybody to prayerful Guardian, popping up in the doctor's consulting room, might provoke an unwanted laugh. John Gielgud had issued a similar warning about the incursion of the Furies in *The Family Reunion*. Eliot had been so angry with Gielgud that he would not have him play Harry; as then, Eliot closed off

Hale's critique. His touchiness had to do with his commitment to figures from a timeless realm who make incursions into time-bound lives. Eliot took these warnings from experienced actors to be misunderstandings of his faith, whereas Gielgud and Hale were concerned with staging a supernatural entrance in a drawing-room scene or doctor's office.

When Eliot invited Mary, along with some twenty-four others, to attend the London dress rehearsal of *The Cocktail Party*, she admired the American actor and screen star Constance Cummings, playing Julia, and Mary added (but then crossed out) in her memoir, 'so much of her is me!' Emily's distress over Celia contrasts with Mary's apparently happy identification with Julia. In the play's first scenes Julia is variously described by herself and others as 'a silly old woman', a 'dreadful old woman' and a 'maiden aunt', who turns up 'when she's least wanted'. The editor of Mary's memoir, Erica Wagner, suggests that these phrases cast 'a painful light on Mary's remark that she had to spend so many years loving him [Eliot] – and being hurt often. Hurt which could be seen to include very public humiliation in the form of this play.'

In the divergence between Emily's and Mary's responses lies the difference between a woman who is beginning to see she is a has-been and a woman with hopes on the rise. Emily's resistance to one aspect of Eliot's adopted faith – its insistence on marriage as a sacrament – differs from Mary's rootedness in a religion that retains much of its Catholic origins. Eliot told Mary that, had he not left America, he would have converted to Catholicism. He said that his choice of Anglo-Catholicism had to do with his choice of nationality, embracing England's church.

Mary Trevelyan's finest hour took her away from Eliot. Following the D-Day landings in June 1944, the Allies freed Brussels from German occupation on 3 September. Later that month, Mary set out in a relief convoy from Great Russell Street. From Normandy, Mary drove through mud and wreckage, bound for Belgium. Her first night was in a room abandoned by German troops, with swastikas and Hitler slogans of conquest scrawled on the walls. Slowly, over three days, she crawled north-east in a vehicle with no lights nor rear-view mirror, her purpose being to set up a relief station for front-line troops. On arrival in Brussels, she commissioned a hotel called the Albert and turned it into 'heaven' for soldiers on short leave. Mary Trevelyan was brilliant with disturbed men who could confide how appalled they felt at themselves for following orders to kill; they were eased by tea in bed, quiet corners filled with books and dances by night. But never for a moment did she forget that these men had to climb again onto trucks that would take them back to the front. Her briskness offset the sympathy she knew could shake them.

All this she relayed to Eliot in a series of vividly moving letters. These must be preserved for posterity, he said. Longmans published them in 1946, without Eliot's name, under the title of a popular song, *I'll Walk Beside You*. The book gives an intimate sense of the final stages of the European war. This is a woman who seemed to know what men need in desperate times. She arrived just as the Allies reached the German border and tragically lost the Battle of Arnhem. Had they won, the war could have ended much sooner. After Arnhem, she was at an airfield to comfort the wounded in transit to England.

In March 1945 she travelled north-east in a jeep to take in the Rhineland Offensive. At the Dutch border, she stayed overnight at the town of Nijmegen. Shells sounded and bombs fell. Next day their jeep crossed the German border. A sign read THIS IS GERMANY. YOU HAVE BEEN WARNED. The horror of what Mary witnessed is a counterpart to *The Waste Land* – she writes with the same sort of hallucinatory power:

> At first it seemed as though we were in a dead country. Every tree along each side of the road had been blasted, every farm or cottage by the roadside had been razed to the ground ... There

was no sign of a human being, no birds to be seen or heard – it was just a wilderness, a land over which the hand of death had passed, and we seemed the only living creatures.

There was the ruin of a church, a shelled fish shop, and crosses by the side of the road to mark the graves of men who had died to gain this ground. 'I felt that all the world was wrecked and this could not be real.'

Back in Brussels in April 1945, Mary received released prisoners of war. Many had been interned for the five years following the defeat at Dunkirk. They were brought to the Albert in a ragged state, some wearing cast-off German uniforms or pyjamas. Covered from head to foot in white delousing powder, the survivors looked like dazed ghosts. It was odd for them to meet an Englishwoman; they seemed unresponsive, hardly knowing how to behave. But Mary Trevelyan found ways to restore them: to take in what they had to say when speech came; to encourage a little joke; to have a local band play tunes of five years earlier.

Eliot cheered Mary on from the side-lines, his refuge amidst the overfed pets of The Shambles. He joked over his preoccupation with cat-concerns: 'In the year that King Uzziah died, / Rumpuscat felt bad inside.' From that vantage point Mary appeared a 'Man of Action', though in fact her letters are strikingly maternal: nurturing, practical, matter-of-fact, yet heartening. She reflected how much easier it was to deal with fifty thousand soldiers than one moody poet.

She renewed the friendship with Eliot on her return to London in 1945. He was pleased when she brought back a crucifix, which she had rescued from a bombed German church, and liked her giving him a rosary. Typically, he did not mention his one from Emily.

While she had been away, Eliot had been troubled by clerical appointments and it was a comfort to confide his doubts to Mary, whose insider status freed fearless opinions. She rejoiced in her own private 'scum list', including members of the Students' Christian

Movement, who sacked her in 1946. An ally, Ann Stokes, said it was
because she displeased them by not promoting conversion. It was
part of her tolerance to enjoy the otherness of the overseas students,
who brought with them their own forms of faith. She lent herself
to others without losing a jot of what she was.

While Eliot buried Vivienne and detached from Emily, Mary took
off on her next venture, an intrepid expedition to the East. She
joined UNESCO, spent a while at its headquarters on the avenue
Kléber in Paris, and in 1947–8 was posted to Burma, Singapore, North
Borneo and the Philippines, in order to survey educational needs
in war-devastated countries. Her title was Head of the Field Survey
Bureau in the UNESCO Department of Reconstruction in Paris.
Eliot was inclined to match her with the high-flier in his family, his
cousin Martha May Eliot, whom he described to Mary as 'the boss
of children's health in America'; she was president of the American
Public Health Association, the first woman to hold that post. She
was also the only woman to sign the founding document of the
World Health Organization.

In London, Eliot was conceiving *The Cocktail Party*. He prodded
Mary for information about cockroaches and local treatment of
tribal enemies with a view to Celia's end. On 5 January 1948 he looked
forward to 'the next instalment of your adventures among the
wilder tribes'. His letters refer repeatedly to his 'seven imaginary
characters', stressing they were fictitious, though all three women
derive from women in his life: Celia, the charming one-time
mistress; Lavinia, the unlovable wife; and the guardian angel he
called Julia. 'He seems attached to a lady called Julia', Mary noted
on 15 March 1949. She recognised herself as one of the play's three
'immortals', as Eliot called them.

From the beginning of 1949, Mary and Eliot met so often that
it occurred to her that they 'might come to some clear "working
relationship" . . . I really didn't know where I was at all.' It's reminiscent of Emily Hale repeatedly asking Eliot for clarification. Mary

explains her grounds for thinking there was more than friendship: 'Tom gave me many indications that he reciprocated my feelings for him', not only a continuous stream of presents, and 'in such ways as holding my hand for an almost embarrassingly long time on saying good-bye'. She had no inkling of Emily Hale and what she had meant to him.

During Holy Week, they attended their favourite Tenebrae service, feeling its drama, as Mary describes in her diary: 'many psalms and the candles put out one by one until the church is in complete darkness – then there is a loud bang (which made me jump) and silence'. A silence, at once holy and tired, suffused a late dinner at a restaurant in South Kensington.

Five days later, on Easter Monday, there was a heat wave and Eliot in his shirt sleeves sat in Mary's flat with long, cold drinks. Mary brought out a domestic side to Eliot, which his readers would not have suspected. He liked to help cook their simple supper and take out the rubbish.

After their time together on Easter Monday, Mary sent a letter to Eliot before she set out for a holiday in France and Switzerland. The following is her report of what she wrote, later crossed out in pencil. Her brackets are aptly described by Erica Wagner as 'a kind of typographic shelter, one almost feels, a kind of half-concealment. Almost as if her pain – agony is the word she uses – could be contained.'

(Before leaving I wrote to Tom, having come to the conclusion that I could no longer go on with our increasing intimacy without the assurance that he knew my feelings. It was characteristic of Tom that he sent NO reply to Paris, in spite of my urgent request that he should do so – one glance at my letter and he had put it on one side until 'the burden of the unwritten letter became greater than the pain of writing'. And he will never know the agony he caused me.)

His reply awaited her return. For him it was a 'showdown'. He
told Mary that Vivienne's death had left him too burnt out to contemplate marriage, but he withheld mention of Emily. He admitted
it had crossed his mind that things might have developed had he not
become a man haunted by the past. He thought he and Mary had
found a stable friendship. This he would be sad to lose – it would
leave a big gap – but this was for her to decide. He assures her there
is nothing on his side to cause her embarrassment and considerately
asks if he might call for her on a particular evening and take her
out for dinner.

When she opened the door they both spoke hastily to get past
this moment of meeting and had a slow, poor dinner at the Russell
Hotel, dreading the talk to come. Catching sight of Eliot's 'distraught refugee' face, Mary's determination to be firm and cheerful
carried them through.

So the friendship went on as before with prayers, early mass,
Sunday mornings in church, and after church, exploratory drives
in Mary's car. Their favourite excursion was to Paddington and the
pub close to where the Eliots had lived from 1916, which appears in
The Waste Land. The climax to one Paddington outing was to drive the
whole length of the Portobello Road. For all those drives, lifts and
other constant acts of assistance, and for all Mary's resolute cheer,
the depths of her feeling for Eliot were not unvisited.

Mary attempted a second proposal just over a year later, in June
1950. She hoped that Eliot had had more time to get over the effect of
Vivienne. As Wagner perceives, Mary 'felt that he was sending her
signals which he himself was not willing to recognise' and that his
reliance on her 'meant that they must be more than simply friends'.
She reasoned to herself, 'Why should we both be lonely?'

Eliot did not want Mary's second proposal to survive. He told
her, 'I read it through . . . then tore it into strips, then burnt it.' The
move finally necessitated an explanation of his prior commitment
to Emily Hale. He still did not mention her by name when they
had it out in Mary's flat on 5 June 1950, but he did explain that he

had never been in love with any but this one woman, 'and still am', though he no longer wished to marry or even see her because he felt guilty when he did.

He said, 'I have never told anyone else and I am very grateful to you for forcing the truth from me.' He left Mary in the dark about Emily's story, implying her limited grasp of a religious drama in which she had acted.

'I don't suppose the lady will ever understand what it was all about. She, and others no doubt, would say I ought to have seen a psychologist.'

Mary leapt at once to the broken love life of Celia and Edward in *The Cocktail Party*, which takes both into the consulting room of the psychiatrist. Mary kept this to herself; her memoir puts it in brackets. Her tact and acceptance of a nurturing family role were rewarded with a beaming smile as Eliot raised a toast 'TO THE GUARDIANS'.

He believed, he told both Mary and Emily, that he was under-going a psychological change of life. In her no-nonsense way Mary put Eliot down as a hypochondriac. He could never see her on a Tuesday, his day for visiting his doctor. She, together with John Hayward, decided that he overdid illness as an excuse not to see them. Put upon but resigned, these two 'Guardians' joked about the extent to which Eliot took refuge in the London Clinic for a problem as minor as athlete's foot. He lay in bed with a huge cage over the offending foot. But he did need privacy if he was to write, and then too he began to suffer from an irregular heartbeat. In his early sixties he became the old man he had always claimed to be.

The American poet Donald Hall often recalled Eliot as he had been in the autumn of 1951. Hall, a New Englander, had arrived in London as a diffident young Harvard poet, as Eliot himself had been. Hall too was about to go up to Oxford as a graduate stu-dent. He cherished his meeting with Eliot, its sense of kinship, all the keener for the fact that Hall asked nothing for himself. 'Eliot was only sixty-three ... but he looked at least seventy-five,' he recalled. 'His face was pale as baker's bread. He stooped as he sat at his desk . . . He smoked, and between inhalations he hacked a dry, deathly smoker's hack. His speech – while precise, exact, perfect – was slow to move, as if he stood behind the boulder of each word, pushing it into view.'

When members of the Eliot family came to London each summer, his sister Marian and niece Theodora delighted in Mary Trevelyan and approved the ready care she gave. Marian confided to Mary how much she wished Eliot would marry her, though she admitted her brother could be difficult. She was kind enough to add that Mary might be better off alone.

When control was at stake, he would go white (as when his well-meaning sister-in-law had invited Emily Hale to meet him in 1947). He was angry when he thought Mary had muddled an arrangement he himself had made. He willed her to agree with his version of events, so as to validate his rebuke.

Mary did not capitulate. 'I won't be put in a corner for something I didn't do.'

Another time, when she dropped him off at home, she said on parting that she hoped he would enjoy himself during a forthcoming publicity visit to Paris. At which he suddenly shouted, 'DON'T say that! It's what people always say when you've got to do something you don't want to do.' He retrieved his case and umbrella from the car and repeated 'DON'T say things like that,' banged the door and shot into the Carlyle Mansions at a run.

'Well, well!' Mary said to herself. Sometimes she vents a 'tiens!' or 'Oh la!' or 'Strike me pink.' The last was in response to an unexpected bolt following what had seemed idle chat. Eliot had remarked that John Hayward was afraid of Hope Mirrlees. Mary had replied that she too found Hope 'formidable'. Eliot was outraged on Hope's behalf, while Mary regarded the comment as 'mild'. Her protests are always brief and jokey, like a mother with a cross child.

On the phone she asked him not to be so sudden, but, if he must, to run up a red flag of warning 'to save my nerves'.

Though her nephew's memory of her lionising Eliot can't be ignored, Mary was unfazed by fame. She was clear-eyed, sensible and chockful of goodwill, and she had to deal with a common problem of genius: the selfishness that often serves it. Seeing it simply, Mary knew him in the way his sisters did.

Mary was alert to 'Badboy' (as he could jokingly call himself to her in private), even if she did not know the wrongs that pained his conscience. She had the confidence to insist on truth. Her feeling, though, was benevolent and forgiving. She told John Hayward that it was hard for a man to be a classic in his lifetime.

Eliot had explained to Mary that he could not marry again because he could not allow more than limited time to any one person, nor, as a solitary, could he bear prolonged proximity to others – even John, who was the most considerate of flatmates. She told herself to accept this, and yet she did occasionally push at the barriers.

'Women always get me in the wrong,' he said over drinks at the Russell Hotel.

'That's what you always say,' she replied. 'I knew that would come.'

'You must make allowances for a neurotic.' And then he would give her the name of a priest to summon to his deathbed.

In the early years of their attachment, he would disappear for up to three months after they'd had a particularly congenial time. He astounded her with a pretence, willing her to agree, that they saw each other no more than once a fortnight even though they may have met two or three times a week. To see more of *anyone*, he said, would get on his nerves.

Contact became more frequent after Mary moved from Bloomsbury to Chelsea in February 1953: a top-floor flat at 23 Chelsea Embankment, between the Physic Garden and Ranelagh Gardens. She now lived within walking distance of Carlyle Mansions, and her car was conveniently at hand. It was tempting for him to 'drop by' for a drink or meal, quiet evenings together as a comfortable couple who shared habits, tastes, beliefs and prayers.

Often, when he visited, they had music. One evening she played 'The Arrival of the Queen of Sheba' on the piano. Mary said what fun it must have been for Handel to write that, and Eliot replied, 'But what fun to be able to play like that – you sound like a spirit released!' Another evening they listened to a recording of Beethoven's Quartet op. 132, an inspiration for *Four Quartets*. Or they might browse through a Faber book on Degas's dancers, which Eliot had brought.

On the phone he would start speaking as though continuing their conversation. Once, very late, she heard a husky voice saying, 'I just rang up to say good-night.'

In the course of their attachment, he expressed 'a relief that, with understanding, we can both say what we really mean to each other. I wouldn't say what I say to anyone but you, nor would I allow anyone else to say what you say to me!'

He enjoyed disclosing the odd intimate fact, as when he told her that his confessions (three times a year) were not really confessional and that part of his penance was to accept his confessor's invitation to lunch. It was like putting himself through an English ritual stressing good form. He would confess much the same minor matter as on the previous occasion. It might be that his attention wandered during prayers. The confessor never seemed to notice the repetitions, and Eliot was content to furnish him with trivial, made-up sins, so as to 'cover up' what was too subtle or complicated to explain. The confessor would then shake hands, say 'How are you?' and then they would share a meal.

Mary's memoir relays this matter-of-factly. She accepted Eliot's confession ritual. If she had thought it questionable, she would have said so. He was getting it right, it seems, in not expecting too much. Or was he fostering Englishness? Might a Catholic priest have probed so slight a confession? Eliot did once say that he found Anglicans too lenient and would prefer something more 'Ignatian' (Ignatius of Loyola founded the strict, intellectual Jesuit order). For Ignatian read the Calvinist rigour Eliot craved, knowing hell in his bones. Anglicanism was really too mild and tolerant for a man of his extremist temper. Too much *via media*.

His confession-talk with Mary shows an unreserved Eliot. Relatively unreserved. Where Vivienne had shared his fierceness, Emily and Mary were averse to slurs. How did Emily feel when he went so far as to cast a slur on Margaret Thorp, whose book *America at the Movies* did Faber & Faber proud? And how did Mary Trevelyan feel when Eliot adapted a nursery rhyme to punish Dorothy Sayers, ostensibly for talking too much, 'poor soul', but really for her annoying popularity as a writer and for her rival prominence at an Anglican conference:

> *Wee Dolly Sayers*
> *Wouldn't say her prayers,*
> *Take her by the hind leg*
> *And throw her down stairs.*

When the *Quartets* accept the need for humility – 'humility is endless' – it was not hypocrisy. Eliot's ancestors, looking into the mirror of election, knew the chief sins were pride and despair. He was aware how fallible he was. In the autumn of 1948, aboard the SS *America*, Eliot found himself among 'the usual representation of Central European ghettos and the lower middle classes of every-where'. Sixteen years after his critique of arrogance in his Coriolan poems, his own pride is unmistakable. Hitting out verbally was bound up with his gift and the gift could not be dissociated from his neuroses, he excused himself to Mary, who nevertheless protests about his 'intolerance' in her diary.

In a letter to Emily, he refers to a child taken in by Eliot's friends the Tandy family. The mother, whom Eliot called affectionately 'Pollytandy', was a witty warm-hearted woman whose domestic affection he enjoyed. Geoffrey Tandy was a marine biologist and broadcaster for the BBC. He was the first to broadcast Eliot's *Old Possum's Book of Practical Cats* for a Christmas programme in 1937. Eliot tested his delightfully humorous cat poems on the three Tandy children, and one of them, Alison, known as Pooney – Eliot's god-child – was a dedicatee when the poet published *Old Possum's Book of Practical Cats* in the autumn of 1939. Bearing well-chosen presents, Eliot was at his jolliest and most fatherly with the Tandy children, but he was not quite pleased that autumn when he happened to visit the family at Hope Cottage in Dorset and found 'it' there. An unfamiliar little girl: a refugee from Nazi Germany. It. The pronoun leaps off the page in a letter to Hale. Eliot was told what a nice child this newcomer was and how eager to learn English. Yet this did not deter him from turning her into an object.

During the Holocaust, in 1942 and again in 1945, he remarked on Martin Browne's two 'very Jewish looking' sons, the point being that their mother Henzie had been Jewish before she'd converted to Christianity. The Brownes had sent their boys to America during the war. Does their safety there make Eliot's exposure – often fatal in countries under Occupation – less disturbing?

The women in Eliot's life appear separate. In Mary Trevelyan's memoir or in his letters to Emily Hale each seems the prime attach-ment. Humphrey Carpenter said that when Eliot confided to his aunt about Vivienne, as they drove around old haunts, he revealed nothing beyond what a reader could have imagined. This came with excuses: they had married 'very young' and there was 'some insanity' in Vivienne's family, which he'd come to know only when she broke down.

Then too his story of Emily Hale (in response to Mary's second proposal in June 1950) omits two thousand letters: the thousand-plus letters on each side. Eliot pictured for Mary a love sustained by his exemplary though unenthusiastic faithfulness. The insubstantial story was reinforced in August 1953 when Eliot said he must meet an American arriving by boat train.

'This,' Mary thought, 'is, undoubtedly, Miss Emily Hale – to whom T. was engaged for so long – his conscience about her and the way he "jilted" her must be very bad — he hardly ever meets trains!'

What reached Mary was a report of a faded woman, 'poor Miss Hale', paying Eliot an unwanted visit in his box at the theatre during the first interval at the opening of his new play, *The Confidential Clerk*, in Edinburgh. Eliot's niece Theodora, with him in the box, had this impression — duly passed on to Mary — of a has-been chasing a celebrity. This role for Emily Hale, in contrast to her former parts, the elevated rarity of Beatrice and Celia, was already in the wings in August 1953, to go on stage in 1958 in Eliot's last play, *The Elder Statesman*.

As Eliot's letters to Emily dwindled in the early fifties, his letters to Mary also dropped off into postcards, mainly greetings from abroad and minor arrangements. These are humorous, chummy, not designed to deepen friendship. He was becoming a postcard person, Mary realised, as she became ever more solidly at hand, given his need for support. In March 1956, after a morning at Buckingham Palace, where the Queen awarded her an OBE (for services to overseas students), she was 'thankful' to collect Tom at his office to do a little food shopping and then cook supper together, with music to follow for the rest of the evening. Aware, as John Hayward pointed out, that he had no other close friends, Mary saw herself functioning as his 'next of kin' in England, appointed to inform his American family about his flagging health and to keep a check during his spells at the London Clinic. He depended on Mary more and more, especially for the lifts — so much so that he bought her a better car and would not accept the sum she gained from trading in her old one.

In the summer of 1954, Mary's reliable car carried him, together with his sister and niece, to stay at Tennyson's one-time home, Farringford, by then a hotel, at Freshwater on the Isle of Wight. Mary took care of arrangements, ensured Eliot was seated in the dining room with his back to other diners, walked with him and lay back side by side after climbing the cliffs known as the Needles.

On another occasion, when she fetched Eliot from a stay in Sussex, they passed a keen-eyed Julian Huxley and his wife Juliette on the road. Eliot joined Mary in a laugh at the gossip the Huxleys were bound to circulate around the capital.

From 1954 to the end of 1956 they saw a lot of each other: drives, dinners out or at Mary's flat where they listened to music. He gave her a new recording of Mozart's Clarinet Quintet, saying, 'I love the *economy* of Mozart.' They listened to the Coriolan Overture, which Eliot said he would have liked for his funeral but thought too grand for him. Instead he planned the second movement of Beethoven's seventh symphony, hardly less grand with its throbbing crescendo. Mary was to oversee his funeral. He spoke of a grave at St Stephen's or, better still, East Coker.

When Mary and Eliot met at the 8 a.m. service on 2 August 1956, Mary suggested a drink that evening, 'if you'd *like* to see me'.

'You know quite well that I never *want* to see *anybody*,' he replied.

'Proposal cancelled,' Mary said cheerfully.

'Oh no – you are different,' he tried to say. It was one of what Mary describes as strained attempts to make amends.

From September 1956, Eliot appeared edgy and nervous. If Mary contradicted him he brushed it off, 'My *dear* lady . . .' It was suggested that he write 'The Education of T. S. Eliot', on the model of *The Education of Henry Adams*. He was 'really tempted'. Yet he would never do an autobiography: 'There is too much I can't say.' On walks with Mary, he was breathless, emphysema adding to heart palpitations, and he moved slowly. Mary noticed he was becoming increasingly melancholic, with lapses into silence. She noted his gloom on 18, 25 and 27 November, and then again on 2 and 3 December when he accused Mary of 'impertinence' for asking why Faber & Faber didn't do more for their books. There may be more to Eliot's touchiness: he perhaps picked up an implied criticism that he did not look after Mary's first book. She had taken her next, the wartime memoir, elsewhere.

Of late he had said that people called him neurotic, and when

Mary had said 'I know', he burst out, 'You DON'T know.' Talk turned to the characters he was devising for a new play.

'Well, *do* make them human beings this time,' Mary said.

'Don't I always?' he replied. 'They seem human to *me* – but perhaps I don't know much about human beings.'

'How can you? You dislike them so much.'

'Well, I'm sorry for them,' Eliot said, 'they seem to me pathetic.'

Mary added, 'You only like them at a distance – so long as they don't come near you – so how can you know them? But the odd thing is that you *do* seem to know a lot about them, one way and other – you've an eye for their *little* failings!'

He mulled over this, not hearing the Mozart on Mary's gramophone.

One time, after a tiff, Eliot sent a rebuke. While the letter was in the post, the two met and had a jolly time. The bolt, when it arrived, took Mary by surprise. She was too forthright not to confront Eliot. How could he have acted as usual when he knew what was coming? He waved this away, but a more annihilating message lay in wait.

At the end of December 1956, looking rather better, Eliot mentioned a plan for a three-week stay with Margaret Behrens, his fellow guest at the Shambles, who had a home at Menton in the South of France. On 2 January 1957, Eliot came to Mary's flat for sherry. His friendship seemed just as Mary took it to be. She was leaving the next day on a short holiday in France and Switzerland. Unusually, she did not hear from him, but a letter awaited her return on 9 January. It was late in the day and she read it the following morning.

It told her that Eliot was to be married to his secretary, Miss Fletcher, early that very day, 10 January. By the time Mary Trevelyan read the letter, the new Mrs Eliot and her husband were flying to Menton for their honeymoon.

23

THE POSTERITY PLAN

When he found himself ready, marital love came as an entrancing gift and it brought a special benefit to him as poet. For this union with a woman a generation younger offered a chance to firm up a future for what he would leave. This entailed rewriting the past so as to take Emily out of his story and centre his new wife as the one and only partner and chosen carrier of his works. To see the replacement of one story by another, we need to compare the plan Eliot had devised years earlier for Emily Hale.

Fame did not worry him. So Eliot had told Emily. In some sense he believed it, for he was retiring and inward. But the claim was untrue. He did want the topmost recognition, the Order of Merit, and another ambition along the way was to be the King Edward VII Professor of English at Cambridge University. Honorary degree ceremonies at Harvard, Yale or Princeton necessitated putting off plans with Emily. The poet's reasoning, 'I have to . . .', took him onto platforms, the much-photographed figure of a reluctant, well-combed elder in a dark suit and glasses with round, black frames, obliged to appear before the public.

A younger generation did not detect the tiger eye, though that eye, burning through his subjects, and the whipping tail, ominously still, did show in 'Lines for an Old Man'. Where Virginia Woolf had marked 'the wild eye', his expanding public admired his restraint and heard, from on high, the virtue that could transform the world: 'humility is endless'.

Earlier women in his life had access to this divided man: to Vivienne, to Emily, and to Mary Trevelyan, he allowed himself to utter bursts of antipathy. Then, as his eminence grew in the late forties and early fifties, propriety hardened as a carapace warding off others. In later life he came to suspect his mother and brother, and even, in the end, Emily, of wanting to share his fame without regard for his poetry.

How does a poet document 'the unattended / Moment' that shapes a life, like 'the awful daring of a moment's surrender'? His own imaginative surrender to a particular woman was inscribed in poems for all time. Only their private letters serve as documentation of what had been: Emily as participant in the actual experience that had validated encounters in poems and plays.

Among the issues between them – strict versus lenient faith; the permanence of marriage versus divorce; and Eliot's belief in the superiority of the 'unnatural' over the natural – there was the question of preservation. To take in the priority he gave to preservation in his relations with Hale, and to discover where she stood at first and then later, we have to go back briefly to the poet's plan as it emerged.

Initially, Emily Hale had resisted Eliot's intention to preserve her letters amongst the papers he planned to hand over to the Bodleian Library. He had wished to share his posthumous reputation with her, he had argued; through her letters to him posterity would learn 'the truth' about a man who had been compelled to wear a mask all through his life.

Uneasy about this plan and disconcerted by Eliot's secrecy, she had consulted Margaret Thorp and her husband. Over the years, Eliot grew wary of Willard Thorp, especially that evening when they dined with the Thorps in London and Willard loomed as a 'spectre'.

*

After 'the change' in 1947 Eliot looked on further letters as separate from the love-letters. The better Hale played her role as dear
old friend, the guiltier he felt and the less he looked forward to
seeing her.

The Cocktail Party was having its long run on Broadway when he
saw Hale in 1950. He felt awkward and told Mary Trevelyan that he
no longer wished to see this unnamed love of his life. A man does
not like to feel guilty, he explained (while telling Emily that Mary
herself was a thorn in his flesh). It's tempting to forget this but it's
part of a pattern.

In the period between 1947 and 1956, nothing was said to Emily
about preserving letters. To follow a conflict that blew up at the end
of this period, it is necessary to take in the nature of the 'change'
as it unfolded.

Emily went along with Eliot's desire that letters between them
remain private so that he could express unfettered opinions. On
8 June 1948, after Eliot confided adverse views on his family, she
promised to be 'dumb as an oyster'. So it shocked her to discover
that, while she maintained a faithful silence, he was putting on
stage the very words he had used to reject her, spoken in the early
scene (Act 1, scene ii) of *The Cocktail Party* where Celia's lover ends
their affair.

In December 1947, Emily suggested they limit themselves to
writing once a month. Eliot agreed and the number of letters drops
sharply. Emily understood that she must make no claim on him;
loving friendship and no more was to be the residue of their pact.
Emily complied, not because she was all that compliant by nature
but because she felt sorry for Eliot. While she was playing the role
asked of her, Eliot reverted to a role reminiscent of Prufrock among
the women, muttering, 'I grow old . . . I grow old . . .'

It was not only his sense of ageing as he reached sixty, nor his
guilt over Emily, that eroded or altered his long-held idea of shaping
her to a posthumous plan. The wider context was Eliot's celebrity.

Vivienne (*right*) with close friend Lucy Thayer in 1924. She was publishing stories in the *Criterion*.

Eliot sent Emily this photo in Nice in December 1925. At the height of marital stress, he had taken a rest and did not give his wife his address.

Eliot in his Faber office early in 1926, at a time when his marriage was most fraught.

Emily (*middle, front row*) with members of faculty at Scripps College in California. Next to her, *seated right*, is her friend, Ruth George. Standing, *left*, is Paul Havens, married to Emily's confidante Lorraine Havens.

'The new photograph of you in the deck chair [in Claremont, California] is perfectly lovely'. Eliot wished he could paper his walls with her sleeping figure.

Emily smiling at Eliot at Stamford House, summer 1935. His poetry associates her with flowers. He called his photograph 'a masterpiece'.

Emily accompanied Eliot to Burnt Norton (*below*), unoccupied in 1935. In his poem *Burnt Norton*, the garden is haunted by the voices of unborn children ('the leaves were full of children / Hidden excitedly, containing laughter.')

Emily and Eliot walked the aisle of rose-bushes (*below right*) towards the pool.

Mary Trevelyan welcomes the Queen, Princess Elizabeth and Princess Margaret to the Student Movement House on 17 December 1942. At this date she was surprised to find herself in love with Eliot.

'Four very happy days.' Post-war reunion. Dorset, Vermont, 1946.

Eliot chose Helen Gardner to interview him for the *Sunday Times* in 1957. He liked her book, *The Art of T. S. Eliot*.

John Hayward oversaw the drafts of *Four Quartets*.

Eliot looked on his new wife, Valerie, as the one and only love of his life.
At the opening night of *The Elder Statesman*, September 1958.

Hale returned to Campden, planning
to re-connect with Eliot.

Eliot's final play stages a faded actress
threatening a public figure with old love-
letters in her possession.

Emily Hale resolved to preserve her Eliot collection. She wished
she could be there when the letters 'burst upon the world'.

On 6 March 1950 he had appeared on the cover of *Time* magazine, but his public presence surpassed his time. Both the public and the poet-dramatist perceived a lasting achievement, a classic in his lifetime, and this prompted him to shed Emily for a more exclusive hold on posthumous fame.

Emily's fourteen letters around that time, from 1947 to 1949, survive, as do a further nine written in 1956–7, and two more, in 1961 and 1963. In the first batch, Emily soothes a flagging man and takes care to avoid the issues of the past. Now and then her feelings rise to the surface, allowing Eliot to glimpse how she holds her own. She admits to the prospect of a long 'adjustment' to 'moving forward as bravely, as trustfully, as possible, from day to day merely'. That 'merely' says enough to touch him, were he so disposed. Moving forward meant renewing herself through plays and readings which included Eliot's *Journey of the Magi* for a Christmas recital. She stands up for her attachment to Margaret Thorp, 'the intimacy of our long years'.

Though she accepts that loneliness would always be with her, her thoughts for Eliot are generous, filled with concern for joyless duties, like his acceptance of yet another honorary degree at Aix-en-Provence. He does not conceal from her how exhausting it was to pursue his public role. The extent of his visibility reinforced his fear that the recognition coming his way was a terminal sign.

Emily witnessed this public figure on display in Edinburgh at the opening of his next play, *The Confidential Clerk* (with Margaret Leighton and Denholm Elliott) on 24 and 25 August 1953. Eliot did not invite Emily to join him in his box where he sat with his niece, Theodora, and his producer, Henry Sherek. Full houses for the play's London run were ensured by a celebrity linked with moral prestige. Even the Queen and Princess Margaret attended a performance.

Emily was ready to discuss the deadening effect of fame. 'Dearest Tom', she urged, should resist any obligation apart from creating for the world at large. Her advice picked up one of the issues from the past: personal confidences versus his impersonal manner:

... don't, don't become a 'public symbol' my dear. What tragic words. It is just from that, I must add, that I had hoped to keep you from becoming. Perhaps I still may if you will first help yourself to keep as personal as you can in your own thoughts of your life, and other private lives.

Always your
Emily

Raising this in November 1953, she provoked an 'outburst' (Eliot's word). He was seeking fame solely for his work, not for himself, he said. It was horrid to be inspected like a beast at the zoo. Celebrities who accept themselves at the public valuation are hollow. He would not lose 'the real me' and felt no different from the person he had been before his fame, nor indeed different from the child of early photographs.

Emily kept him informed of the plays she directed, including Sheridan's *School for Scandal* (which she thought equalled her successful production of *Richard II*). Having always adored Shaw, she put on *Pygmalion*. When Eliot heard, he disparaged the play for its premise that speech determines class – Shaw's socialist view of class as a construct rather than a birthright.

Eliot complained about press reports that he was making a fortune from his writings – the wealthiest poet on the planet, according to *Time* magazine in March 1950, including $1,600 a week from *The Cocktail Party*. And indeed, in 1951, after the play had completed its London run that February, he had to pay income tax of £25,000, he told Hale.

She, in contrast, could not afford to keep her dog, Rag Doll. That is, if she kept him, she would have to give up something else. It was a hard choice. The Scottie had been a devoted alternative to the elkhound who'd plagued not only Emily herself but, on the loose, Northampton at large. If Eliot did not take up the cause of Doll, he gave Emily many gifts – earrings, a hat box, an evening bag – and worried about her thinness. He suspected that she saved on food.

He was concerned enough to say that were he free to come her way, he would like to watch her eating a steak.

When he did visit America in 1955, he saw her one time only. Travelling now with heart palpitations, his exacting schedule of readings was, he told her, hardly a rest cure. In New York, the adulation was so insistent that he had to escape through a back door of an auditorium. Fans phoned his cabin on board the ship returning to England. This was decidedly not a rest cure, he said again. His heart raced and when his ship docked at dawn, he was taken straight to the London Clinic. A partial cure in itself to be left alone.

Emily spent Christmas 1955 with the Thorps at 142 Nassau Street. They revived the question of what she would do with her letters. Willard promised her that Princeton would keep them safe for the future.

By December 1955 Eliot had drafted the first act of a new play about a celebrity whose powers are failing. This distinguished statesman is increasingly unwell, and the provisional title is the phrase lodging in his mind which he had used in writing to Emily earlier in the year, 'The Rest Cure'. The eventual title was *The Elder Statesman*. The play picks up Emily's question about the effect of fame on character, which had provoked the outburst in November 1953. His ageing hero is the focus of public adulation but hollow of heart. He is to be saved by a daughter figure, 'a peach of a girl' who is 'too good to be true', as Eliot described his new heroine to Mary Trevelyan. The loyalty of this lovely young woman will fill the Elder with love.

By 9 January, Eliot had a rough draft of the second act, in which two people from the Elder's shady past return to haunt him with threats of exposure; one of these is an actress. In terms of character and social position this is a caricature: a coarse, lowlife woman, Maisie Mountjoy, who is set on blackmail. So far, so distant from Emily Hale. And yet elements in her situation do draw on Emily's life. The public figure has once loved a woman he has set aside; she has his letters in her possession; and she wants to revive their attachment. Maisie's signature song is 'It's Never Too Late for You to Love Me', adapted from an American song of the fifties 'It's Never Too Late to Say I Love You'.

Just then, Emily was considering whether she might secure the past by placing Eliot's letters in a vault designed to preserve them for all time. In resolving to act independently, she did not mean to contravene Eliot's interests, since he had often said his letters were hers to do with as she wished. His own intention had been to preserve the truth for posterity.

Amongst the twenty-six[*] surviving letters from Emily Hale to Eliot are four that are torn. These are dated from October to December 1956 and coincide with another turning point in Eliot's life. All four have been pieced together with tape that has darkened over the decades, partially obscuring the words. If it was the recipient who tore these letters, why did he? And then, who fitted the fragments together? And that's not all: the most important question is what, if anything, connects the tearing of these letters with the fact that, between October and December 1956, Eliot proposed to Valerie Fletcher.

Where does a story start? Eliot was a poet of beginnings and endings. But any beginning is an arbitrary point. Could tearing the letters be part of a process of discarding Emily Hale when Eliot recoiled from marriage in 1947? Or did this go back to interventions by the Thorps, whom Eliot had long distrusted?

Emily understood from the Thorps that donating the letters to Princeton had to be done before she died. It was an oral discussion and Emily, perpetually poor and unused to dealings with assets (she had never owned property apart from a sofa and two or three bits of furniture), may have misunderstood. Why the urgency? Why could she not leave a bequest in her will? Conceivably, the Thorps urged the advantage of making this gift while she could allow herself a foretaste of its reception. Emily considered the proposal over the next few months.

---

[*] The number includes her copy of her letter to Eliot in 1945.

Meanwhile, Eliot's health was failing. There were frightening attacks of tachycardia; coughing from chronic bronchitis exacerbated by emphysema brought on by smoking; and colds and flu during the damp English winter. He spent three weeks in the London Clinic in February 1956. When he came home to Carlyle Mansions, he could not sit up without his back aching.

In April he sailed to New York, and then travelled to Chicago and from there to the University of Minnesota, where he delivered a lecture on literary criticism to a stadium of twelve thousand. Dismissing the overly clever critiques, he said all that is wanted in a reader is to be intelligent. Afterwards he stayed in Cambridge with family: Theresa Eliot, then Eleanor Hinkley. He tried in vain to see his ailing sister Margaret. He had long disliked her. Their mother had favoured her, but after leaving her home in St Louis, Margaret became reclusive and neglectful – too depressed to function. Although she was dying, she went on postponing her brother's attempts to visit. He told himself that she couldn't take in the fact that he was in her vicinity for only a time.

On 26 May he went north to Abbot Academy – his third visit to Emily's school (he had been in 1948 and 1952) – where he read Cat poems from *Old Possum*. To the young French teacher there, Marjon Ornstein, Miss Hale appeared elegant and 'elegant in mind'. There was no indication that Eliot already had an eye to a peach of a girl; in his physical condition, a new relationship would have seemed unthinkable and his visit kept up the ritual of devotion.

Emily again asked Eliot if he had any preference for the deposit of their correspondence.

No, was the answer. Nevertheless, the continued need for privacy was understood: any gift she made must be confidential until both of them were dead.

In June, Eliot returned home by sea. On his way to the pier, his pulse rate doubled. When the RMS *Queen Mary* docked at Southampton at 2 a.m. on 12 June, he was taken off the ship in a wheelchair, with newsmen and cameras ready on the quay. An ambulance took him to the French Hospital in London, and as he arrived at 5 a.m. a hunched, shivering journalist, who must have waited for hours, let off a flashbulb in his face. News followed of Margaret's death, and cousin Frederick's taking charge in his effective way. Emily reported fully to Eliot on Margaret's cremation. It mattered to him that Emily had attended this event in the absence of his sister-in-law Theresa. Though his own relations with Margaret had been almost non-existent, he was annoyed with Theresa.

Emily Hale came to a decision in July. Her letter to Willard Thorp begins, 'In both a small way, and a very large way, this letter washes the shores of the literary future beyond our imaginings.' She has gathered together all Eliot's letters, and in the autumn would send them to Princeton 'in your custody'.

Her announcement invites Willard to 'lick his whiskers' and adds, 'naturally you will realize this decision is due mainly to my years of friendship with you both'. The letter ends 'Wishing I could be present to see your face and <u>hear</u> you, when you read this.'

After the exhausting trip to America, Eliot planned to rest in Switzerland for a month, from 14 August, yet he did want letters from Emily because he gave her the address where he would be staying in Geneva. On 15 August she wrote to inform him of her Princeton plan. She asked if he might prefer Harvard (the main repository of the Eliot papers, collected by his brother). Eliot repeated calmly that he had no preference. He promises that he will think more about it but relies on a long understanding that his letters would be sealed for fifty years after his death.

The Swiss holiday was disappointing. It rained most of the time. Eliot flew back to London with an abscess on his hip. On 12 September, at Heathrow airport, Mary Trevelyan, stopping there on impulse to offer a lift, watched from a distance as he was wheeled to an ambulance. She left quietly. Not being family, she had no rights. Throughout these months before he married, she had no idea that the peach of a girl could be eligible. Emily was equally unknowing when she acted on her plan for the letters in September–October 1956.

More than a month of silence followed Emily's letter of 9 September, which has not survived. It is uncertain whether or not she knew that Eliot had been admitted to the London Clinic, worried by further evidence of physical decline. During this time, she assembled the letters and agreed to send them in a trunk to the librarian at Princeton, William S. Dix. He was to store it, sealed, until she visited in the autumn, when he, she and Willard were to work out the terms of access.

On 6 October Eliot wrote to Emily, asking for confirmation of the fifty-year embargo. His literary executors were Bird & Bird, who would oversee his legal right to protect the privacy of the letters.

By 14 October Eliot became nervous over the continued silence from Emily. He was anxious that she was liable to cede control and that the avid recipients of the letters, Willard Thorp amongst them, would read them and disseminate his secrets, eroding the posthumous plan. This disposition of his papers made him feel as though he were already dead.

Eliot shot off another letter to Emily the following day, 15 October, in a state of alarm. The fear came upon him that he could no longer trust her secrecy, a fear commingled with guilt.

If he suspected everyone, should he suspect her too? Whom, then, might he trust?

A candidate was at hand: his trusted secretary, physically present every day and slipping on high heels whenever she entered his office to take dictation. It would not have taken much to turn to willing, devoted Valerie Fletcher in the way he had turned to other sympathetic women in the past, Mary Hutchinson and Alida Monro. Only now he was more helpless. The more he thought of the letters, the more he feared having placed himself in Hale's power. For a man accustomed to control, it was an intolerable situation.

Eliot's message of 15 October took only three days to reach Hale,

who replied by return. Since 1947 she had been careful not to distress the broken-down man Eliot had presented. But in this letter
of 19 October, her feisty side reappears, restored by the excitement
the untold story aroused amongst the few in the know. In place of
loss, there was a growing confidence that her life had mattered. It
sounds in her independent decision to shorten the release date of
the letters by making it fifty years from 'now', 1956. Not exactly what
Eliot had intended.

Defending her action, she reminds him how he had impressed
upon her his standing as a 'Public Figure'. Her capitals take a teasing
liberty. She was mindful of Eliot's immortality as a poet and also of
the poet's plan to preserve letters. Every letter, she dares to say, had
been designed for the future.

This comeback so infuriated Eliot that he tore up the aerogramme. Who else had reason to do this? If Eliot read the letter
at Carlyle Mansions, it could have been John Hayward, self-styled
keeper of Eliot's works, who pasted them back together. If Eliot read
the letter at the office, or took it there, the repairer could have been
his secretary, if by that date he was confiding in her. It is not difficult
to imagine her piecing the torn letters together, needing to know.
After 6 October there is no further mention of Bird & Bird as literary
executors; once Eliot turned to his willing and effective secretary,
she was well able to care for his interests.

That month, October 1956, Eliot composed a preface to a collection of essays, *On Poetry and Poets*, due for publication the following
year. This book is dedicated 'TO Valerie'.

Following another letter from Eliot to Hale on 27 October (her
birthday) – the fourth letter that month – there fell another silence.
It was not until 12 November that she broke this with reproaches for
ignoring two requests: one had been for a personal message on her
birthday instead of a routine cable. This was an old grievance and
Eliot had explained how he had been taught to be frugal with the
number of words.

The other was a reminder that he had not written a Cotswold

poem promised in the heyday of their romance. It went without saying that she would be visible in such a poem. To this, Eliot retorted: what was *Burnt Norton* if not a Cotswold poem? Lurking in her modest politeness is a rebuke, and Eliot was too alert not to hear it: a reminder of his semi-deception in assuring her – as he had drawn her to him – that *Burnt Norton* was to be a love poem. It is, in its way, but a way subsidiary to a solitary's commanding narrative. Hale was making it clear that she had not forgotten: she had been deployed for a poetic purpose and then discarded.

The chief matter of the 12 November letter was to announce a 'Red Letter' day about to happen: a celebration on the 17th to mark the handing over of the letters. She would travel from Andover to Princeton and stay with the Thorps from Friday to Monday. Her thank-you letter to Margaret Thorp afterwards recalls an 'historic' occasion, heightened by 'the courtesies of Willard'. On this day of all days, she was granted her due for all she had undertaken with Eliot.

> I enjoyed every minute of my visit ... faced with the signifi-cance ... as you all naturally gave me to understand – I had to recognize that there is an undercurrent of exciting challenge – which I hope and pray quite literally – I may meet wisely. I find the pain of returning to the past is softened a little by remember-ing ... the fact that innocently and unpredictably I am involved so closely with this Personality is part of the wonder which I never can get accustomed to.

She informed the Thorps that she had written to Eliot (on 23 November), 'so his reply will be the next chapter in this biog-raphy which as yet has no author, except ourselves!' This one was a more considered letter on notepaper, so as to free up her hand to impress on Eliot how responsible and honourable the Princeton recipients were and how entirely he could trust them. Unfortunately, in her concern to ease him she quoted William

S. Dix, saying he was gaining 'a progressively clearer idea' of the letters' 'richness', and incautiously too, she filled Eliot in on her plan to visit Princeton after the letters had been catalogued. Quite reasonably, Eliot deduced that the librarian was reading the letters instead of sealing them. His distrust only sharpened. He believed, correctly no doubt, that if anyone at all read the letters, their contents would get about. One concern was what he had said about living people.

As bad, from Eliot's point of view, was that Thorp and Dix leaned on Emily to intervene on Princeton's behalf, hoping to persuade Eliot to alter his stipulations so that present scholars might have access to some of the material during their lifetimes. So it was that Hale asked Eliot to shorten his embargo to ten years, and to allow his current letters to her to be made immediately available to readers in the library. Unfortunately, again, Emily said the two Princeton representatives 'disapproved' of the long embargo. This word was like a red rag to Eliot. It was 'impertinent'.

On 27 November he tried a last-ditch protest.* Since rational argument did not dent Emily's intention, he tried an emotional appeal.

I had assumed that the letters of mine which you are giving to Princeton University would be sealed up at once ... My God! does this mean that a complete stranger, a professional librarian, is already reading letters which were composed for your eye alone? I seem to have heard of dying travelers in a desert, with the vultures starting to dismember them before the end. I feel somewhat like that.

To position Emily with predators torturing him to death was a blow but she took it coolly. During similar pleas for pity in 1947, she had put his need before her own and kept up her kindness;

---

* It was the same night that he gave a reading for Mary Trevelyan's Goats Club for students at London University who had come from all over.

this time, she stepped back. His 'tone' gave her to understand that nothing personal could be said. Her next communication, on 3 December, had to be impersonal, she explains, because the preservation of letters was now a matter of business.

The aim was to clear up a misunderstanding. No one, she assured him, was reading his letters, and she would of course follow his stipulations, including an extension of the embargo to whatever date their deaths would dictate. An excuse follows: she was a 'novice' at negotiation and had approached him only at the suggestion of guides whom she respected – educated gentlemen. She would now ask Dix to write to him directly, to confirm the arrangement, which would be just as he would wish.

Eliot's probing had to do with fear, she saw. This made her sorry for him and she hoped that he would allow her, as a friend, to say so.

Such 'condescension' was in bad taste, he said, fuming at this turn from compliance.

In a politely firm voice, Emily Hale divests herself of the ghostly role, the invisibility imposed upon her. She has decided that what her life has been must become visible to the future. Her answer reverts to an aerogramme because she had to be economical. These are hard to read because her scrawl is tightly packed, using every inch of the space. But this one is typed so as to be businesslike. Here a side-lined woman grants herself permission to enter a public arena and take control.

Of course, what Emily Hale did not at this point know is that Eliot's emotive plea came from a move of his own. His secretary was wearing his engagement ring under a finger stall as she typed in a room with other secretaries at Faber & Faber. Preparations were under way for a secret marriage. With this in prospect, he did have reason to fear the record of his declarations to Emily which she, with help from Dix and Thorp, meant to preserve. These two decent men – Willard was 'Sir Guide' or 'my tutor in Public Affairs' – understood what would matter to the future.

Emily's letter asks what Eliot was planning to do with her side of the correspondence. The negotiators at her end had asked if her letters too should be at Princeton. She trusted that he would leave instructions.

Finally, she assures him that nothing personal about him was ever discussed with his family or friends. She ends, 'I hope you will be somewhat calmed, my man, by this answer.'

Her words failed to calm him. He tore up the letter.

Mary Trevelyan, knowing nothing of what Emily called the 'tempest', noticed a change in Eliot. He turned silent. Mary thought she might have annoyed him and owned to herself 'how very little I understand of what is going on in that very disturbed brain of his'.

Emily, meanwhile, feeling drained by the row, found relief in 'an absolutely jellyfish existence' with friends during the school holidays. In New Bedford and Woods Hole, she mulled over 'the very difficult correspondence' and Tom's disfavour.

'His attitude over the whole matter has been "formidable" as the French say,' she reflected to Margaret Thorp. 'I did what I could . . . for the literary world's sake – but, oh boy, what a reaction!!'

After Eliot's brief encounter with Emily in Eccleston Square, he had sent her his poems, hoping (in Dante's words in the mouth of his master Brunetto) that his work, his 'treasure', will outlast his life: *nel qual io vivo ancora*. This message in 1923, even more crucial to the poet than lasting love, was lasting art: 'where I live on'. When he and Emily came together in 1930, how bent he had been on curating his archive. How bent he still was. She had been the poet's invisible intimate ('O hidden'), lending herself to the poetry of spiritual trial. But now, at the close of 1956, Eliot made a decisive switch. Gone was the rose of memory and the penitential solitude in stony places. The new scene was to be domestic. Just as his health seemed to give out at the age of sixty-eight, he found himself rejuvenated by a young woman of thirty. She found him ready.

24

THE DISCIPLE'S STORY

From the age of fourteen, Esmé Valerie Fletcher had been an Eliot fan. During the war her father, an insurance manager at the State Assurance Company in Leeds, sent her south to boarding school, Queen Anne's at Caversham, in the country near Reading. It was not as safe as the Fletchers would have hoped. A German bomber, spotting the red cloak of her school uniform, strafed the grounds. The Messerschmitt swooped low enough for the girl to see the pilot's face 'distinctly' as he fired on a bridge she was crossing. She looked back on her escape not as luck but as 'spared' for Eliot.

At school Valerie (as she was called) mixed with sporty girls not expected to go to university. Her love of poetry did not dim her exertions in the lacrosse team, but in 1940 she was struck – famously – by a recording. It was *Journey of the Magi*, Eliot's 1927 poem, read by John Gielgud. The 'coming' of holiness, its witness – the wordless vision and the uncertainty that follows a return to the world – pierced her soul. This girl heard words that reach towards the Word, and found herself committed to follow the poet as a disciple.

At seventeen, in 1943, she extracted reluctant permission from her parents to go on her own to London. Her purpose was

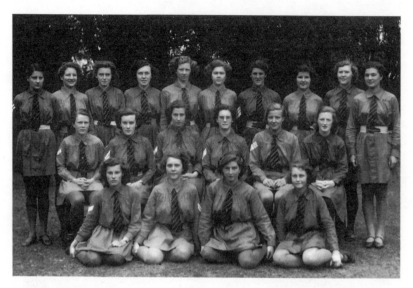

The Scarlet Runners (lacrosse players) in 1943, at Queen Anne's School, Caversham. Valerie Fletcher, top row, far right.

to hear Eliot read at the Albert Hall. His carefully articulated monotone was disappointing yet did not deter her sense of destiny. It came to her, as she put it later, she 'had to get to Tom, to work with him'.

To prepare herself, she trained as a secretary. There was a six-month stint in the Brotherton Library at the University of Leeds, then a none-too-appealing practice run as private secretary to a novelist, Charles Morgan, and, by good fortune, some work with Dylan Thomas on film scripts. Dylan Thomas was getting her closer; he had an appointment to see Tom Eliot (and was so unkempt that Valerie had to borrow a shirt and trousers for him to wear).

He asked, knowing her ambition to work for Eliot, 'What's it worth to you if I push his present secretary downstairs?'

One Sunday she took herself to St Stephen's to see Eliot coming towards her in person, as the churchwarden taking round the collection box. While she waited for an opening, she began to

Miss Fletcher.

Valerie Fletcher in a Faber staff photo album.

amass his first editions, a collection that was to equal, if not better, his own.

An offer came her way from a friend of her father, Collin Brooks, a journalist who knew Eliot as a fellow member of a newly founded Tory dining club. When Valerie was twenty, Brooks had Eliot inscribe her copy of *Poems 1909–1925*, published by Faber & Gwyer soon after Eliot had joined the firm. She wrote to thank him and received a civil reply.

In due course, Brooks let her know of a vacancy at Faber. The night before her first proper encounter with Eliot, she was so nervous that she cut her hand and arrived for the interview wearing a bandage. There were other women after the job. Eliot chain-smoked, as nervous as she. They discussed poetry, and as she left the office he put his chin around the door and hoped her hand would be ready for typing – a way of telling her that she was chosen. So it was that at the age of twenty-two she became Eliot's secretary. Her appointment (on a salary of six pounds, ten shillings a week) was on 31 August 1949, the day after the opening run of *The Cocktail Party* ended in Edinburgh.

Miss Fletcher entered the scene neatly dressed, with her hair in a tight roll and pinned back; her fresh-faced readiness trailed no emotional baggage. Level-headed, comfortable in her own skin, she stepped out in the role she longed to play as his protector. When a visitor for Eliot arrived in the office, she stood up and her arms swung back and forth in an urge to shield him. Dazzled by the poet, she saw no reason to hide it. The other secretaries teased her, and she took it in good part.

Seven years passed. Throughout her twenties she treated 'Mr Eliot' formally. He called her 'Miss Fletcher' and spoke of her as such to others. He could not get to know her, he remarked to Mary; she shut up like a clam and this suited him. But he did notice how dutiful Miss Fletcher was, to a fault when she stayed on after hours. At such times he shrugged off devotion as 'tiresome'. It gave him the 'creeps'. Or so he said to Mary, and pictured his dodge into the lavatory to avoid having to walk with Miss Fletcher down the street. All the same, this was a man of habit. He grew accustomed to her face, her daily presence, participating in his work and clearing his way while making no claim on his attention.

After the quick decisiveness of her appointment, we might surmise that he had an eye for her, even though he claimed to Mary that secretaries were more or less interchangeable. When he left for a three-month visit to America in September 1950, he asked Mary to report on various people, and Miss Fletcher's name was on the list. News came that she had dined out with a protégé of Eliot's, a Bengali literary scholar, Dr J. Ghosh, who wrote Eliot appeals for help and whom Eliot tried his best to place in academic posts. Eliot wished Mary had boxed Miss Fletcher's ears. Was it jealousy? Protectiveness? He takes her date to be improper for a woman under forty and he gives Mary an odd reason. He can't have his secretaries consort with his waifs and strays, he explains. What this suggests is that inadvertently Miss Fletcher had crossed a boundary. People were in compartments, a means of control so that information did not pass from one part of his life to another.

Early in 1955, Eliot was laid low with flu, first in the London Clinic then at home in a state of 'severe' depression. Towards the end of February, Miss Fletcher came to the Chelsea flat each day, Monday to Thursday, at five, to take dictation. This may have been when John Hayward began to suspect 'somewhat more to that flower of the Yorkshire marches than meets the eye'. If Eliot's health should deteriorate further, should he be in need of a nurse, Hayward detected a candidate ready to be a Lady with the Lamp. This much he perceived in his acid manner, distancing Valerie Fletcher as a presuming outlier. He closed ranks with Mary Trevelyan as Eliot's appropriate choice: devout, classy, connected to the aristocracy and to the uppermost echelons of the church, diplomatic service and Oxbridge. But Eliot thought otherwise. Here was a pretty young woman in daily attendance, her ease and warmth thawing the freeze of his unused body. Trained as a secretary, she did not contradict him, as Mary did, and her deep respect, enhanced by a generation gap, meant she did not question his apartness as Emily had done. Miss Fletcher proved neither restless nor dissatisfied with a subordinate job, unlike some previous assistants: brainy Miss O'Donovan in the thirties, who preferred the BBC, or, in the forties, Miss Melton, who left in order to farm and then, when she did not succeed, asked for a reference with a view to a job he regarded as 'too big for her boots'. If he could safely rely on Miss Fletcher in the office, might she expand her brief and take on the posthumous affinity once reserved for Emily?

The benefit of a devoted young woman was certainly in his mind at the end of 1955 and into 1956 when, at sixty-seven, he was drafting 'The Rest Cure'. It was partly through writing this play that Eliot woke to Valerie Fletcher, who, like Monica, the daughter in the play, could offer a public man unconditional love. Valerie made the offer through her new friend and go-between, Margaret Behrens, who invited her to stay at Menton. There Valerie confided her feelings for Eliot and Mrs Behrens encouraged them. Valerie had never wavered in her determination to marry Eliot or no one at all, and Mrs Behrens broke this to Eliot. The message emboldened him to propose by letter: 'Dear Miss Fletcher . . .'

So little did they know each other outside the office and so unsure was he of her response, that he took the precaution of offering a way out: they need never mention this again and would go on as before.

Miss Fletcher of course said yes.

Newly engaged, they met behind a pillar in the Russell Hotel. Other secretaries at Faber & Faber did spot 'the socking great emerald' under the finger stall, and pressed questions in vain. According to Rosemary Goad (later the first woman to be a director of the company), no one suspected Eliot was the man.

They married secretly, to avoid the press, at 6.15 a.m. on 10 January 1957, not in his own church but in St Barnabas' on Addison Road, Kensington, the same church, it turned out, where his old poetic model Jules Laforgue had married an English girl. The priest was a friend of Eliot's solicitor Gordon Higginson, who had helped to certify Vivienne. Mr Higginson himself was best man.

The certainty this union, brought to Eliot in the last eight years of his life, seemed to change him completely. Erotic poems to his second wife reverse his disgust for the flesh in poems like 'Sweeney Erect' and most palpable in *The Waste Land* manuscript: the 'hearty female stench' and the clerk and typist coupling 'like crawling bugs'. It appears nothing short of metamorphosis that Valerie Eliot restored the poet to what, she claimed, he always was: a domestic man 'made for love'.

The marital poems belong neither with the degraded flesh nor with a purified tie to a Lady of silences. Fair copies of three poems in 'Valerie's Own Book' (actually two exercise books) are of a piece with the final poem in Eliot's 1963 *Collected Poems*, 'A Dedication to My Wife' (originally the dedication to *The Elder Statesman*, completed after they married), which speaks of sleeping lovers whose bodies smell of each other. In the same way, 'Sleeping Together', 'How the Tall Girl and I Play Together' and 'How the Tall Girl's Breasts Are' affirm physical love based on trust and commitment.

We are invited to witness how the poet and his wife 'play together', taking off clothes. Because she's so tall, her nipples touch his and their tongues meet evenly. The stimulus is as much in looking as in touch: we are invited to see the tall girl's breasts from below, from above and from the side, where the cleavage invites the lover's hand. Eliot's poems have an awakened freshness, as he observes – after twenty years, for he had said this before to Emily – a woman's body as a thing of beauty. But, as poetry, it can't compare with, say, Donne's lover whose roving hands, licensed to 'go / Before, behind, between, above, below', are likened to voyages of discovery: 'O my America! my new-found-land.'

The poet's simplicity is sweet when he repeats, 'I love a tall girl', and nice too, the tenderness when he strokes his wife's back and long white legs as she 'sits astraddle' on his lap. Explicitness, though, is less erotic than suggestion. It is no match for the overwhelming theatricality of Yeats's lover, with his 'mask of burning gold / With emerald eyes'. Eliot's words of love were designed to please his wife and to sustain her through a future without him. For readers, they are meant as a sign of sorts and their message is layered. Overtly there is a message about male potency: erection and emission. The change is startling. Does human love now replace this poet's journey towards divine love? What role is assigned to the woman who succeeds Beatrice?

Before, in crossing broken stones that 'lie, fang up, a lifetime's march', Eliot had looked to paradise as unlikely, undeserved. He could revere the perfect lifetime, 'burning in every moment', but had remained imperfect himself, and out of this abjection had come the great poems of his middle years. But then, in 1955–6, when he conceived 'The Rest Cure', he began to imagine a cure in the possibility of forgiveness.

At that turning point, when Eliot's health was failing and he asked himself how to prepare for death, he found a rejuvenating alternative. As always, there were moral issues: the shift led him to cast off others. The row with Emily in the last months of 1956 coincides with his embrace of Valerie. But what else drove the daring of a third surrender to a woman, a wife, when he was sixty-eight? It had to be a powerful need to countermand hesitation. Up to a point, Mary was of course right to fix on attraction. But we might also guess that the turn to Valerie was a turn *from* Emily, so closely are these acts linked, and further, that the turn from Emily had to do with a dream that had served its purpose and was now at an end.

As Eliot lost control of what he would leave to posterity or, rather, feared loss of control to Princeton men in league with an Emily he no longer trusted, the unquestioning loyalty of a disciple turned him to a new dream. Valerie gave the dream substance as they held hands in company and danced together at a charity ball. It was the New Bridge Ball on 28 May 1957, at the Mayfair Hotel, where other dancers were Lord and Lady Pakenham and Thomas Pakenham and Lord and Lady Pethick-Lawrence (the latter pair famous for their imprisonment during the fight for women's suffrage).

Eliot, immaculate in evening dress, said, 'This is my "coming-out" tonight. I haven't danced for years.'

Mrs Eliot, knowing he was nervous, waited for a waltz. 'This is the first time we've ever danced together in public.'

The Eliots celebrated their marriage with formal photographs and the poet gave out statement after statement about his newfound happiness. In this way he imprinted his marital union on the public mind, on their joint bookplate and joint coat of arms, on the flyleaves of the books they owned, and on the minds of his colleagues and friends. When he took his wife to New York, he called his editor, Robert Giroux, to say the hotel was fine but they would like a double bed.

His love poems tell us nothing about Valerie, except that she has long white legs and delights to see him roused by her beauty as she stands naked in high heels. It's easy to guess the elation for her, to be chosen by an immortal, knowing she could stir him. All the same, Eliot's picture of such scenes remains to tell us something else, and a clue lies in an obscure publication, the last serious work he wrote.

A sign of the grace coming to Eliot unexpectedly through human love is laid out in a British Council booklet on George Herbert (1962). It is a spiritual biography in which Eliot speaks in unison with the seventeenth-century poet, moody, snobbish, meticulous of dress, who turned aside from the world. Like Eliot, after suffering divine absence Herbert had a happy marriage in his last years. The booklet explores a belated turn to natural happiness, like Eliot's own, and it concludes movingly by quoting in full Herbert's poem 'Love: III', with its blessed sense of forgiveness. It starts, 'Love bade me welcome: yet my soul drew back, / Guiltie of dust and sinne.' Every part suggests a parallel with Eliot's life, especially the grace of the last two lines: 'You must sit down, sayes Love, and taste my meat: / So I did sit and eat.'

Eliot once remarked that however intimate a love poem may be, it is meant to be overheard. An addition to his marital poems is a teasing limerick (in 'Valerie's Own Book'): 'The Blameless Sister of Publicola', dated 16 September 1959 and alluding to 'The noble sister of Publicola', Valeria, who is reported as icicle-pure in *Coriolanus*:

I know a nice girl named Valeria
Who has a delicious posterior

And beautiful thighs
Where her true lover lies
While his penis explores her interior.

Before their marriage, Eliot resisted — so he told Conrad Aiken — Valerie's appeals to him to 'burst into Bolovian song'. But afterwards he copied out assorted stanzas, previously reserved for men, in 'Valerie's Own Book': twelve stanzas in one exercise book and two in the other.

He distinguished between a rhyme designed to entertain and what is said to a lover in private, which must be 'in prose'. Many of his letters to Emily Hale show him to have been a master of the private love-letter, one of the most eloquent who ever lived. It was Eliot's charming custom to write letters to his wife when she went out. Often of a Sunday he would put an envelope for Mrs T. S. Eliot on the mantelpiece.

'He was my darling,' she said. She treasured these and, long after, when she was ill, she took a few to keep under her pillow in hospital.

Compelling her further were messages left on their magnetic Scrabble set. In 1994, nearly thirty years after Eliot's death, she told an interviewer that a message she had yet to read was still there — his private words still hovering in the air between them.

Valerie Eliot entered the poet's life at so very late a stage that she had to be somewhat in the dark about his earlier ties. How much did she come to see beyond what she had known? And how was a loving disciple to cope with facts that could emerge after Eliot's death? There can be no sure answer to these questions, yet not to pose them would collude in myths that gather around great lives. Eliot's venture to centre Valerie biographically, however belated, together with the need to protect her, is sufficient reason for his anger at losing control of his letters to Emily Hale.

Like Emily, Mary expected a continued friendship, but from Eliot's point of view each presented the threat of a third party in the marriage. For each had been more than a tame 'friend'. These women trailed long and complicated relationships short of marriage but with marriage on the radar. Each woman was an unexploded mine in the path of a new narrative. It would not do for either to come too close to Valerie.

All this hovered in the shadow of the bridegroom when Valerie herself was only thirty. She looks young, creamy, palely gleaming in a pillbox hat in the photographs newsmen caught of her about to board a plane at the end of their honeymoon on the Côte d'Azur, eyes startled in a sudden flash of publicity. By her side Eliot, recovering from flu and thickly wrapped under an old man's hat, looks a little hunched, like a Puritan burdened by secrets.

His announcement to Mary Trevelyan on the eve of his marriage had told her that the move was not sudden. He and his wife-to-be loved each other very much. Mary's first thought was that Eliot 'had gone out of his mind'. He had kept to himself the way his heart could open to Miss Fletcher's dedication, her feeling for his poetry and the clean appeal of an able young woman who did not trouble him with expectations. Before, his desire for a particular woman – for Emily – had been an exception to his fear of womanly flesh as tainting, unclean. In the light of this, his attraction to Valerie was a 'conversion' to her youthful physical ease and ready acceptance of his own failing body. Then too, and wondrously reassuring, was that in her eyes he could do no wrong.

When he was younger, he had liked 'a tall girl', as Emily was, and Miss Fletcher too stood tall in heels. Where Vivienne had been 'Wee' and Emily elegantly thin (Eliot had urged her to fill out), and Mary had the 'Man of Action' go required of women in the war-torn

forties, Valerie Fletcher stood with more feminine women of the fifties, who dressed to enhance curves and breasts.

Mary reasoned in her sensible way, 'I am inclined to think, that Tom is a man whose strong sexual impulses have been deliberately frustrated for many years – some of his early (unpublished) poems give some indication of this. He has married again almost exactly ten years after the death of his first wife and it is possible to suppose that he may have set himself a period of "expiation" (see *Family Reunion*) of ten years for his real, or imagined part in the mental derangement that befell her.'

But then reason gave way to bewilderment at secrecy that put friends in a false position. Trying to make sense of his character, she adds, 'Tom has always been a great "runner-away" – he is extremely deceitful when it suits him and he would willingly sacrifice anybody and anything to get himself out of something which he doesn't want to face up to. I used to wonder sometimes how far he was aware of this.'

Shaken, Mary fell back on manners, and on 13 January 1957 she sent a note of good wishes to his office to await his return from honeymoon. She claimed that the note was 'as kind as I could make it', not realising how her shock spilt out. 'Perhaps you and I mean rather different things by friendship. I sometimes think I have too simple a faith in very simple things,' she typed. 'And I cannot change, as I have told you before.' A postscript announced, tellingly, that the clock in the car had stopped. It recalls a prediction in *The Family Reunion* that a clock will stop in the dark, a stop to a ticking life.

When she heard nothing back, she wrote again, this time by hand, on 14 February, owning her shock. It unseated the sturdiness she had shown in the war and the capable person she was with students. His move, she tells Eliot, left her 'quite helpless' and 'quite lost without you'. She doesn't spell out her reliance on what he'd told her: 'our friendship over these last fifteen years is too firmly rooted now to be destroyed'. What she does say is that she hopes to see him, but will understand if it is not possible.

'Very dear Tom,' she goes on, 'I look on our long friendship, with all its ups and downs, as a very deeply valued possession – please understand this – & <u>nobody</u> can take it away from me.'

Her voice comes down on '<u>nobody</u>'. Valerie didn't like her, Mary believed, and it's easy to see why: another efficient woman close to Eliot. The hearty casualness of Mary's manner could have added to Valerie's dislike, as well as the north–south divide. Mary was taken aback to hear that Eliot's secretary had been allowed to open her letters marked confidential. Again, then, a crossover of stories with women not staying in assigned compartments.

Eliot replied to Mary three days later. Stung by her bluntness, he retorts that his idea of friendship does indeed differ from hers. Her letter seemed to him 'a very gross breach of good manners. There should have been no need to remind you that I cannot accept your profession of friendship which ignores my wife and the fact that I am married.'

Mary had offered to slip out of church quickly to avoid the embarrassment of an encounter.

He misreads this and gives her to understand that rectitude must forbid a clandestine tie. This slam of the door, recalling past slams of her car door, carried finality.

She tried writing once more, on 23 February, saying she was 'puzzled' and must clarify his misunderstanding about embarrassment. The embarrassment between them had to do with *his* strange behaviour. 'Since you both returned to England you have not got in touch with me, nor let me know where you were staying, and it seemed that you did not wish to see me.' Including 'both' makes it clear that she held his wife responsible for cutting her.

Eliot let a month elapse before making an excuse that he had been ill and 'occupied' with finding a flat. When they were settled, the couple intended to ask friends, a few at a time, for tea or sherry. The formal tone and the corralling of Mary with others denies their special tie as though it had never been. The fierceness of Mary's response, her outspoken sense of betrayal and influential connections in the church made her dangerous.

Months went by until, in late July, he invited Mary at the last minute to join his sister and niece for dinner. Hurt by months of silence, she claimed a prior engagement and said that, given the length of time that had elapsed, it might be better not to meet for another while.

It was their last contact.

Mary commiserated with John Hayward, another surprised and hurt old friend. The fact is the two had come to know too much. Both had witnessed the streak of sadism. Hayward believed that Eliot fought against it. Hayward had been told of the marriage only two days before it took place, while Valerie had waited outside the room. It came to Hayward that his flatmate was leaving to spend the two nights before his wedding elsewhere, with people little known to him. Eliot looked on his hosts, Collin Brooks and his wife Lillian, as providing refuge – it would have been refuge from Hayward's astonishment and the doubt he might have raised. The secrecy is curiously similar to his previous marriage.

'I am still, like Othello, puzzled in the extreme,'* Hayward said to Mary a month later. 'I feel, after eleven years, as if Tom had suddenly died – at least to me.'

Eliot paid Hayward an extra month's rent. Later he returned to the flat to collect his belongings, and then for one stilted tea. Mary, for her part, spoke of what happened as 'my jilting'. Her fair-minded nephew, Humphrey Carpenter, confirms her conclusion. 'It is understandable that she interpreted his marriage – whether or not he meant her to – as the final rejection.'

The severing of these ties did not heal in Mary and Hayward. Eliot left, she said, 'so great a sadness in the hearts of his friends',

---

* *Othello*, V, ii: 'Perplexed in the extreme'. ('Perplexed' is derived from the Latin *plectere*, to entwine. The word came to mean entangled. Coming from Othello, it means deceived.)

begging a question: 'Have John and I known and loved the real man?' A year later, in 1958, Mary put together a memoir, 'The Pope of Russell Square', drawing on Eliot's letters and a rougher diary of their conversations, recorded since 1949. The memoir ends with the *Cocktail Party* prayer by the two Guardians, which Mary had said for Eliot each night and which she continued to say:

> *Protector of travellers*
> *Bless the road.*
> *Watch over him in the desert . . .*
> *Watch over him in the labyrinth . . .*
> *Protect him from the Voices*
> *Protect him from the Visions*
> *Protect him in the tumult*
> *Protect him in the silence.*

25

CURATING THE PAST

How much could one tell a young wife about the past? In the play Eliot completed after his marriage, two people pursue an ailing old man. They bear witness to wrongs he did earlier in his life and kept under wraps. Confronted by accusers, this man looks to me like a modern re-creation of Shakespeare's wonderfully theatrical scene where Richard III's victims, one by one, return to haunt him – that play Eliot saw after authorising Vivienne's committal to an asylum. The effect of Richard's encounters with these ghosts is more than creepy: the apparitions wake his soul to guilt, granting this villain a tragic dimension on the brink of death.

The confessional element in much of Eliot's work is blatant in *The Elder Statesman*, a play about confession as the means to forgiveness. The challenge for the playwright is to imagine how someone young and admiring – a daughter in the play – might take disillusioning facts. Lord Claverton has to confess to his daughter Monica how much a poseur he has been: 'How could I be sure that she would love the actor / If she saw him, off the stage, without his costume and make-up'.

In the play, Maisie Mountjoy, the stage star he once loved, arrives at Claverton's rest home with photostats of the love-letters he sent her. The originals, she tells him, are safely locked in her lawyer's cabinet. Claverton had been her first lover and she'd expected him to marry her. When, 'slippery' and 'sly', he did not, she sued him for breach of promise. Exposure would have wrecked Claverton's political career, and so there was an out-of-court settlement.

The letters are drawn, of course, from Eliot's situation with Emily Hale: a threat to his wife's trust in his newfound simplicity of heart. To put it bluntly, a wrong was done to Emily Hale, which the law could term breach of promise. The poet had declared how keen he was to marry her if only he were free.

Hale's resolve to archive his letters coincides with Eliot's resolve to replace her as the love of his life. 'Coincides' cannot be entirely accurate, for there's no knowing the germ of a scene. It's enough to recall that in the new play, the feeling of a peach of a girl for an elderly man, her father, took root in Eliot's imagination as he drafted the first two acts in the winter of 1955–6. Curiously, this is precisely the time that the Thorps pressed a still undecided Emily to preserve the letters.

For a man contemplating marriage to a woman thirty-eight years younger, the danger lay with the letters, which explains what was unclear to Hale herself and to her Princeton associates: why Eliot, his engagement still secret, became exercised to the point of rage late in 1956. Thwarted rage. For he feared the future: a time to come when his wife could live long enough to read those letters. Would the voice of his intimacy with Emily Hale shake Valerie's faith in him?

Lord Claverton confesses and dies in the final act. The climax of Act III is to shame and topple the public statue, as it were, and do so himself. It's a testimony to match that of 'things ill-done and done to others' harm' in *Little Gidding*. Eliot's poetry and drama have their greatest impact when he is most daring; that is, when he risks exposure.

Everything the Elder says in Act III is by way of baring himself to his wife: his avoiding his accusers; the gravity of his sins as distinct from crimes; and, fascinatingly, his confession of a continued tie to the actress — 'she knows that the ghost of the man I was / Still clings to the ghost of the woman who was Maisie' who 'hasn't forgotten or forgiven me'.

Valerie's imaginary stand-in, Monica, had thought that the Elder suffered from 'morbid conscience', but now, happily, she can affirm it is 'the real you I love — the man you are, / Not the man I thought you were'. The celebrity she had adored stands before her — and before his audience of course, and now before us in the next century — stripped of masks and vulnerable to dislike.

The play's message to Valerie confers on her the 'real' love. In fact, Eliot had declared the same in a farewell letter to Emily in December 1935. Then too, the 'Dedication' of the play to 'My Wife', saying 'The roses in the rose-garden which is ours and ours only', transfers the rose narrative to her. Along with 'reality' and the rose-garden, the Dedication's tribute to lovers 'Who think the same thoughts' transfers exactly the words he had used to Emily in his letter of 24 December 1930: the strange new bliss 'to find another person thinking the same thoughts and having the same feelings as oneself at the same time'.

Above all, the Dedication's stress on sleeping together repurposes his sleep enfolding Emily in 1935, saying to her afterwards that nothing can wholly express his tenderness: 'I believe that to go to sleep in each other's arms would be the only complete expression.'

The Elder Statesman ends with words of love between Monica and her fiancé, Charles Hemington. Their consciousness of a new person emerging from their union reuses what Eliot had said in letters to Hale signed by the composite 'Emily-Tom'. It is impossible to know how consciously he revised the record to wipe out that composite, as though it had never been.

It happened that Emily Hale stood ready to make a comeback in a drama of her own devising. She would sail to England and seek Eliot and Valerie out. Her intention was to be accepted and accepting.

Emily Hale was restrained over the news of Eliot's marriage. What blew apart their pact in 1947 had resigned her to friendship.

On 11 January, writing from Abbot Academy, she told Margaret Thorp, 'I know nothing & nor can I say anything, nor think it all through. How strangely this fits into the pattern of my giving over the collection of letters – the friendship – the earlier love of the years – in its intimacy – is also sealed now for all future time.'

Over the next days she was 'touched' by 'very dear' expressions of loyalty from the few close friends in the know. Margaret wondered if there could be 'mitigating circumstances'.

Emily was not inclined to think so. 'What "mitigating circumstances" there may be – I know not of – except that a great writer has behaved like a very usual human being: in his older years found a very young and attractive woman to take care of him, putting aside all else.'

Unlike John Hayward and Mary Trevelyan, Hale expressed no surprise. Instead, four days after the wedding, she wrote what Eliot called a 'very fine letter' of gracious wishes and a separate one to Valerie, who was said to be 'very much pleased by your writing to her'. Emily continued to write to Eliot as though nothing much had happened: she fills him in about Aunt Edith's stroke and deteriorating condition, and she commiserates with the newlyweds' travails in furnishing a flat of their own. These letters exclude anything to jar Eliot, so successfully that on 10 February 1957 a relieved Eliot hoped that Emily might come to England and meet Valerie.

That same month, Emily pencilled her introduction to the letters. It's a largely factual draft, honest but not revealing and, with exquisite manners, refraining from blame. Her story goes like this: Eliot, a 'gifted' and 'groping' young man, had been in love, and so long as he was with Vivienne, Emily held back. Their five summer reunions in Chipping Campden in the 1930s were the happiest of Eliot's life until his second marriage. For herself, there had been 'much kindness and happiness . . . as well as inevitable pain'. While she accepted Eliot's decision not to marry her, she could not understand what remained for her still a 'mystery'. The conclusion is imbued with the Thorps' urgings: her duty to posterity in preserving these papers. 'I bequeath this collection to a public perhaps yet unborn.' Her last sentence refrains from comment: 'May the record speak'.

At sixty-five, she was due to retire at the end of that school year and once again anxious about money. Aunt Edith had been moved to a nursing home in Newton. The costs were draining what her aunt had set aside as Emily's inheritance. Emily would now need to support her aunt, and she looked in vain for a new post. She considered offering herself to some corporation as a hostess, personal trainer or greeter.

'Is this a crazy idea?' she asked Margaret. 'Can you help "sell" me anywhere?'

She let Dix know she was at a loss. Did it cross her mind that he might offer her some sort of work in return for the priceless treasure she had handed to Princeton? Might the university find some speech and drama work for her in her time of need? Nothing whatever came her way. Her self-effaced letters to Eliot between January and March mention the money worry to him too, which he notes without offering help; otherwise she holds back in the polite old friend role, leaving him unafraid to sign a reply 'With much love'.

And then, with no explanation, he stopped writing. (It would be in character for caution to set in after inviting Emily to meet his wife.) He did however send a copy of his new collection of essays, *On Poetry and Poets*.

'Your critical writing has always been my especial pleasure,' she responded, 'delighted to see how many "favorite" essays are included.' Despite her civility, she found herself in the same excluded position as Mary and Hayward.

Over the summer of 1957, Emily Hale packed up her belongings in preparation for leaving Abbot Academy. As she sorted her things she came upon the draft of her introduction to the Eliot letters, and she sent it, as promised, to William S. Dix on 15 July. She also sent the typescript of *The Cocktail Party* (received from Eliot in July 1949) to Scripps College.

Retirement freed her for a new venture: she booked a passage to England. On 2 October she broke the news to Eliot that she was coming to 'live' in their old haunt, Chipping Campden. Her letter tells him that she's in excellent health and will move into Garth Cottage on the 11th. One incautious line hints how abnormally he could behave – not a testimony he would wish his wife to read. 'Nothing seems natural these days – but if you care for me to meet Valerie and continue a long <u>friendship</u> normally, I think the moment has come perhaps.' She underlines friendship to assure him there would be no stronger claim.

Eliot excused himself as a 'minor' casualty of Asian flu. Emily could let them know when she might come to London. Encouragement, though, was wanting.

She held on for about ten days, to allow for recovery, but nothing further came. Garth Cottage proved unwelcoming and cold. The shock of Eliot's coolness was compounded by acute loneliness, and she had to admit to herself that she had made a mistake. She fell ill and the local doctor advised her to fly back to Boston without delay.

On 23 October she wrote again to Eliot to inform him of her departure. Though she was to be in London before catching her plane, she did not give him her address. It would not have done to press herself upon him. Her letter ends on a note of finality.

Dear Tom,

I was pleased to have your note, tho' sorry to learn you were a 'minor' casualty of the 'Asian flu'. I hope you have wholly recovered. Yes, my coming here must have surprised you, and it is not the right choice for a number of reasons. Furthermore my leaving Abbot and Andover has been more of a 'break' than I realized apparently, for I am not in good health, and the excellent doctor here (for whose presence I can be grateful indeed) is ready to let me go 'home' rather than try to carry on under abnormal physical conditions.

This is naturally very unwelcome and difficult, but I do not think unnatural, considering everything of the last thirty-eight years of teaching and being a happy member of a community. So, I shall be flying back I trust, early next week, and unable to meet Valerie – to whom give my sincere regrets please. I may stay for a time with a kind older friend of the last few years intimacy, in her apartment in Boston before finding my feet again. With God's help I shall, I know.

... It is all very unexpected, but some lesson will come from it later I believe. Good wishes to you for your life and work as always.

Your friend

Emily Hale

Confronted with her abrupt departure, Eliot justified himself to cousin Eleanor on 26 October. He was 'puzzled' by her 'strange behaviour': why did Emily come to Campden and why did she not tell him where she would stay in London? 'It all seems very odd and unnatural, and makes one rather apprehensive about her state.' Nor did she give an address in Boston. The fact that he cannot communicate with her is a relief, he admits.

Without informing Eleanor that he had cut off Emily Hale after a correspondence of twenty-six years, his letter quotes her protest that nothing seemed 'natural'.

At this time his old bond with Eleanor revived over her well-chosen wedding gift. It was a first edition of *The House of the Seven Gables*, Hawthorne's novel about a New England family curse blighting the descendants of a man who had perpetrated murder during the witchcraft frenzy in the seventeenth century. A 'Bull's Eye', Eliot said, 'exactly right'. A young woman in the novel, Phoebe, a ray of sun, transforms the gloom of the old Puritan house (Hawthorne's model, which still stands in Salem, with its dark corners emblematic of dark minds). 'The dry-rot of the old timbers of the skeleton frame was stayed'. The young woman kindles 'the heart's household fire' of the forlorn inhabitant.

Eliot's follow-up on 12 December says how sorry he was not to have seen Emily. There's head-shaking over Eleanor's report of what sounds like depression. He feared that Emily must have wasted a good deal of money on her *recherche du temps perdu*, and then he goes on to exonerate himself. Emily, he alleges, was inclined to complain of her old friends neglecting her. This led to unwarranted blame. How convincingly he becomes a victim. Easy to hint at mental problems, given her mother's history.

In this manner, he belittles Emily to her old friend. It was fair to say she was pained by retirement and neglect, but here he switches from pity to side-lining the situation as her problem – an 'obsession', he says – by seeing himself as merely one of Emily's well-intentioned friends who stand wrongly accused.

A third letter to Eleanor, on 2 February 1958, continues the disparagement with a fresh claim that Emily lacks 'resources' for retirement because she has never been much of a reader. This belies the record: the wide range of her reading in serious and popular drama; the many Shakespeare plays she put on; and, not least, her public readings, including as they did poems by Eliot himself.

The three letters add up to a character assassination. Cloaked in pity, they are persuasive. And he was not done with this campaign against a woman he had once revered.

Emily could not have been as disturbed as Eliot thought, or not in a seriously prolonged way, because in March 1958 she took up a temporary post at Oak Grove School in Vassalboro, Maine. It was 'an endurance test' but she got through it.

However restrained and civil Emily took care to be, her very existence presented a danger. For she was familiar with the hidden ardent Eliot. She knew too much, even if she damped it down in her soothing, post-change letters. Though she carried discretion over into his new marriage, his past with Emily presented too much of a threat to his new role: the new normal, a man made for marriage. It was inevitable that sooner or later, given the changed situation, he would resort to a common action: to wrong-foot the predecessor of the woman now in favour.

In 1960 Eliot heard of Emily's biographical introduction to the Princeton bequest. The prospect shook him, reversing the indulgence with which he had greeted Emily's idea of writing a short memoir back in 1938. 'Well, my dear, why shouldn't you write anything about me that you like!' Eliot had responded at that time. 'So long as you keep it strictly private – as private as our letters – for unfortunately the interesting things cannot be said until everyone is dead.' But now, with circumstances changed and in the fourth year of his marriage, he dealt his past with Emily an all-out blow in a letter to posterity, typed on 25 November 1960.

> Emily Hale would have killed the poet in me; Vivienne nearly was the death of me, but she kept the poet alive. In retrospect, the nightmare agony of my seventeen years with Vivienne seems to me preferable to the dull misery of the mediocre teacher of philosophy which would have been the alternative.
>
> [When Vivienne died] I suddenly realised that I was not in love with Emily Hale. Gradually I came to see that I had been in love only with a memory, with the memory of the experience of having been in love with her in my youth . . . I might mention at this point that I never at any time had any sexual relations with Emily Hale.

To validate Valerie as the love of his life meant invalidating Emily and reinventing that past. The letter alleges Emily's 'insensitiveness' and 'bad taste', that she was not a lover of poetry and that her primary interest in him lay in his reputation. Propriety dictates that instead of 1930, the starting date of the Eliot–Hale correspondence, he puts forward 1932, the date he separated from Vivienne.

To a poet, these were not lies. Filled with apprehension over what Emily might say, he recreates their relationship, and in doing so wipes the slate clean for his wife. After a lifetime of withholding personal information, Eliot was determined to protect Valerie for the future. The letter's conclusion testifies to 'what it was to love a woman who truly, selflessly and whole-heartedly loves me'. This is a woman who professes no inconvenient needs or ambitions of her own, other than togetherness. That this letter is really for his wife becomes clear when he adds 'I find it hard to believe that the equal of Valerie ever has been or will be again; I cannot believe that there has ever been a woman with whom I could have felt so completely at one as with Valerie.'

Eliot instructed his executors to publicise this testimony when his letters to Hale were released. In 1968, three years after his death, his wife, retaining a copy, duly passed it on to William Bond, then the librarian and curator of the Eliot family collection in the Houghton Library at Harvard. This detonated according to plan soon after 9 a.m. on Thursday 2 January 2020, as six of us sat down to read the Eliot–Hale letters in Princeton's Firestone Library. I had barely read a line of Emily Hale's memoir when Eliot's unexpected statement dropped into my inbox, sent on the dot by Leslie Morris, the curator at the Houghton Library.

Eliot's strike against Hale did not foresee the feminist revolution of the 1970s. By 2020 his letter was bound to backfire in a world now alert to the common tactic of the empowered: character assassination of the victim. But two memorable phrases survive the blast. One is 'the love of a ghost for a ghost'. In so far as he had resisted Hale's effort to bring the poet out of the phantasmagoria and into actual life, he felt justified in saying that his letters came from 'an hallucinated man'. This relationship was a delusion, he wants his wife and readers to believe. The word 'ghost' in fact goes back to his dismissal of the 'ghost of a rose', specifying his past attachment to the ballet, in his 1941 draft of *Little Gidding*.

The other phrase is more obscure. Eliot alleged that Hale took the wrong view of the papers, and then goes on to say 'The Aspern Papers in reverse'. In preserving the Eliot letters, Hale reversed what Miss Tita does in Henry James's tale when she burns the letters of the great American poet Jeffrey Aspern to the woman he loved. Miss Tita, her niece, companion and heir, a faded single woman, does this in revenge against the narrator, who is after her papers but will not pay the price: marriage. Eliot implies that Hale's motive, too, was revenge on a man who would not marry her.

Undeniably, there's gallantry in the elderly Eliot's attempt to protect his young wife. But then, too, there's cruelty. The letter to posterity betrays his long pact with a woman whose love he had urged. And it was this strike, not the gallantry, that reverberated in news reports.

Emily Hale did not teach after the stint in Maine. She continued to take an active part in public affairs, particularly women's issues, first in Northampton, where she returned in 1958 and stayed at 83 Crescent Street for six years. For two of those years she served as president of the Women's Club. She acted in a comedy, *The Solid Gold Cadillac*, at Smith College. In April 1961, taking up the role of 'old friend', she wrote to Eliot on the death of Geoffrey Faber, saying no reply was needed.

Northampton did not relieve her loneliness. It proved difficult to return to the past and retrieve a sense of belonging. So, in May 1963, she moved back to Concord, to a small house, 9 Church Green, built during the Revolution. That summer saw a wave of reminiscence stirred by Willard Thorp. By 15 July she had recorded a spoken memoir on tape. Whatever she said left 'revulsion against the whole story – so personal – so painful in many ways of T.S.E. and E.H. – becoming public property in years long after we both are gone'. In August, Willard worked to win her back for their joint project. He persuaded her to answer questions he would put to her for the benefit of future scholars, and gave her to understand that this would be more valuable than her reminiscence of 1957 (to introduce the letters), which gave little away. Pressed by the Thorps, she swung between generosity and privacy.

Margaret suggested that she might identify personal details in Eliot's work.

'There is *mighty little* of me in any poetry!' she said. At the same time, she yielded to a reading from the letters to be stored on tape.

Yielding further, risking a hard-won peace of mind, she approached Eliot once more, this time to ask what he proposed to do with her own letters. A copy survives, sent to Willard Thorp in Princeton.

September 12, 1963

Dear Tom,

It is difficult to break the silence which has existed between us for the last several years, but you would be the first to admit I think that the changing circumstances of our lives and increasing years necessitate that we both face certain facts and problems with courage and objectiveness.

. . . [Professor Thorp and Mr Dix] asked me to ask you if you cannot reconsider the time limit set by you for public access to the letters to a much shorter period than the one you have already named. I concur wholly to this request myself . . .

Closely connected to the disposition of the Princeton letters are my letters to you which long ago you planned to place in the Bodleian at Oxford. The question has also been asked in Princeton if these two collections should not be under the same roof . . . It would seem to me if you are still preserving my letters, that your consent to placing them in this country would be the only correct practical solution, don't you think? And do you or I have legal claim to them?

Remembering your scrupulous attention and care in all legal aspects relating to literary material, writers' rights, etc. I am sure I can count upon you to leave specific directions in all matters regarding our past correspondence which assumes very different implications today than earlier. I think you will be aware that for me to consider my life as important because of its relationship to you – a noted world figure – is very difficult. I must as now act impersonally for the sake of the future in raising these questions, equally difficult for both of us but wholly professionally and historically correct. I do hope you will accept what is thrust upon us – shall we say – because you are you.

Further, I hope your health is better than I know it to have been lately. I learn of you from time to time from the Cambridge relatives.

In thoughts of past friendship,
Emily Hale

This move on Princeton's behalf firmed up Eliot's intention to silence his one-time 'Lady of silences' once and for all. Since her letters were his property, he had the right to ask an editorial colleague at Faber, Peter du Sautoy, to burn those from 1930 to 1947. He did not say who the correspondent was, though du Sautoy guessed it was Emily Hale. He said to me, over lunch at the Russell Hotel in 1986, that the letters were tight-packed in a large metal box. It had been a matter of honour not look at them. I believed him, but there were others, he said, who did not.

Why did Eliot not burn the letters himself? The reason he gave du Sautoy was that there was no coal-burning stove in his flat. Other motives can be guessed: the Macavity habit, the calculating cat who leaves no trace of harm; and then too a wish to protect his wife from involvement in the erasure of Emily.

The du Sautoys invited Eliot and his wife to dine in Bedford Square to celebrate Eliot's birthday on 26 September. By 30 September 1963 Hale's letters to Eliot were destroyed, and on that day he put the finishing touches to his 1960 letter repudiating 'the love of a ghost for a ghost'. He also typed the following reply to Hale's query:

I have the greatest dislike to revealing my private affairs to the public now or at any time merely because of my importance in the world of letters, whatever that may be. I have indeed no desire to give information about my private life to the scholars and biographers who have nothing better to do than pry into the biographies of men of letters, and I am afraid that in the same spirit I have destroyed your letters to myself. The thought that posterity may be interested in my work naturally gives me some pleasure but not the thought of posterity being interested in my private life.

Mislaid or unsent, this never reached Emily. On 15 October 1963 she said to Margaret, 'I wonder sometimes if he *ever* will answer. Courtesy at least should have sent an acknowledgement of my request, don't you think?'

Two weeks later she began to wonder if 'something has changed his mind about keeping my letters'. Meanwhile, the Thorps edited a transcript of a tape, probably her responses to Willard's questions.

Early in 1964 she remarked to Willard, 'I have *almost* a suspicion that my letters may have been destroyed! Having re-read "The Cocktail Party" lately I find many a passage which *could* have hidden meaning for me and for him. But his *apparent* discourtesy is hard to take.'

Eliot died on 4 January 1965. Emily Hale described her feelings in a letter to Margaret seven days later, catching her breath at the thought of his turn from her.

9 Church Green
Concord, Mass 01742
January 11, 1965.

Margaret my dear,

Your short note . . . was very welcome on Saturday. I thought naturally, a great deal of you, Willard and Bill Dix, since we four are so very intimately concerned with what is now a future – as well as a past – mystery and remarkable personal story.

I had not known until last autumn – and then not in great detail from E.H.H. [Eleanor Hinkley] how terribly ill he has been for two or three years – the old bronchial weaknesses, plus many complications, so an oxygen tent seems to have been in constant attendance, Poor Man. The family report that Valerie has been *very* remarkable in her nursing as well as other wifely duties – her life has indeed been devoted to his wants – perhaps I could not have fulfilled this requirement as she has done – perhaps – only perhaps – the decision to marry her was the right one.

I had gone ... from New Bedford to Woods Hole ... so that I was with Dorothy E[lsmith] who knew both T.S.E. and our relationship as intimately as anyone. I can't answer you very closely as how I 'feel' – some of it has come back so vividly, it has not been easy; and having the public know *nothing* is at once a blessing and a burden ...

I try hard to take this all dispassionately but it is a little hard ...
Lovingly
Emily

Immediately, her revulsion against disclosure came back. Allegiance to Eliot took precedence over scholarship, she told the Thorps firmly, and asked them to return her tapes so that she could destroy them. A friend undertook to incinerate 'miles' of tape. Her chief feeling was to eliminate intimate details, not only for Valerie Eliot's sake, 'but from my *own* feeling for shielding the association with a man I loved, and who, I think, did not respond as he should have to my long trust, friendship and love'. She told Willard that she should not underline 'the miscarriage of what seemed so perfect a solution to the long years of waiting for happiness. It might <u>not</u> have been happy or right, had the relationship been consummated.'

Only her introduction to the letters remained. In March and April 1965 she revised it, adding, at Margaret's suggestion, that Eliot had called *Burnt Norton* a love poem for her. It had been a quiet and deep bond, kept 'as honorable . . . as we could'. During the Campden years her aunt and uncle had been uneasy. 'My relatives knew the circumstances of T.S.E.'s life, and perhaps regretted that he and I became so close to each other under conditions so abnormal, for I found by now that I had in turn grown very fond of him.' She 'accepted conditions as they were offered under the unnatural code which surrounded us'. It was in many ways 'a strange story'.

This 1965 version of the introduction recounts the later setbacks. After 1947, she goes on, 'We met under these new and difficult circumstances on each of the visits he continued to make to this country . . . the question of his changed attitude was discussed, but nothing was gained by any further conversation.'

She is candid too about what happened after her stay in Campden in October 1957: when, later, Eliot brought his wife to Boston, he never contacted her. At least the memory of their being together was hers, she said, 'and I am grateful that this period brought some of his best writing'.

She tried not to be sorry that he had probably destroyed her letters and told herself that he had done so to protect her, not himself or Valerie alone. Mingling with her gratitude was hurt at being wiped out from the record. It was consistent with 'how terribly secretive he was about our "affair"'. She did regret that she would not be around when Eliot's letters 'burst upon the world'.

After Eliot died, Hale renewed an old association with the theatre director Martin Browne while he was writing *The Making of Eliot's Plays*. He accepted her request to remain 'in the background, without personal mention'. He writes warmly about her 'very good letter' in which 'you hardly spoke of yourself' and approves her idea of stretching a hand of friendship to Valerie Eliot. This she did in an aerogramme from Concord dated November 6, 1966:

Dear Valerie,

Our mutually dear friend (and your cousin) Eleanor Hinkley has been anxious for a long while that I should get in touch with you. This I am very happy to do; I have wanted always to know you, when Tom was with you, and since I am sure you'll remember I wrote you when the news of your marriage to him came to me, so that I trust in these years you have realized I was your friend, as well as his. I cared for him, as you know, and he cared for me through many years before and after his first marriage. We had many happy experiences together, especially in the summers when my aunt, uncle and I were in Campden, England.

Tom's natural reserve, and my own, kept the public, and even some of our friends, unaware of the closer friendship between us. When certain hopes I had could not be fulfilled I tried always to be loyal and very much the friend he could trust.

Since his marriage again and his death, this reserve about the past I have scrupulously kept for all our sakes . . . I have played the role as I felt was the only one for his sake & yours — if not my own . . .

The devoted care you gave Tom and your living for his every wish must give you the strong comfort and reassurance of how life can be lived on a high plane of fine-ness.

Most sincerely yours

Emily Hale

The two women met in America, most likely in 1968 when Valerie Eliot visited the Berg Collection at the New York Public Library where a new curator Lola Szladits had uncovered the *Waste Land* manuscript. Emily refers to their meeting as 'a good memory for the future' in a Christmas card she sent to Valerie that year. It's a card printed for her quoting St Theresa's sayings, among them that 'Patient endurance attaineth to all things.' She adds a hope that Valerie's technical problems have not been too heavy. That polite wish is not empty: it marks an excuse that Emily did not fail to take in: was it that Valerie put on the brakes, aware that her husband would not have liked the contact? Decades on, Valerie told a confidante, Clare Reihill, that she understood the important role Emily Hale played in Eliot's life.

Emily's passion for the stage held to the last. After nine years' absence from directing, in 1967 she put on Lady Gregory's one-act comedy *Spreading the News*, with a congenial cast of ten.[*] In Concord, in December 1967 and at the age of seventy-seven, she performed with aplomb as the mother of Henry Higgins in *My Fair Lady*. When

'Do you mean that my son is coming to Ascot today? What a disagreeable surprise!' Emily Hale as Mrs Higgins in My Fair Lady *with the Concord Players.*

---

[*] Lady Gregory wrote this play for the opening night of the Abbey Theatre, Dublin, in 1904. Hale's interest in Irish drama – particularly the Yeats and Shaw plays she staged over the course of her career – went back to her exploratory visit to Dublin and meeting with Micheál Mac Liammóir in 1929.

Mrs Higgins, in her picture hat, long lace gown and parasol, made an entrance with ease and style, she took over the stage and received an ovation.

Emily Hale died, aged seventy-eight, on 12 October 1969; her life-long ally and confidante, Margaret Thorp, died in 1970.

Despite Eliot's effort to separate the story of Emily Hale from that of Valerie Eliot, a convergence could not be avoided. Over the years, as Mrs Eliot put together a complete edition of her husband's letters, she did not forget those sequestered at Princeton. Initially, Eliot had let it go when Hale had set the release date at fifty years from 1956, which would have made the letters available in 2006. By then, Valerie Eliot would be eighty and likely still to be alive. Once engaged to Valerie, he insisted on his previous stipulation that the embargo be longer: fifty years from the death of whoever survived the other. By the time this longest of all his embargoes came to an end, his prospective wife would be in her late eighties or nineties. Or she might no longer be alive, which is what happened. Valerie Eliot died, aged eighty-six, in November 2012, eight years before the letters were unsealed. She had appealed to the curator at Princeton to be allowed to see them, but Don Skemer had to refuse. When we spoke in the reading room in February 2019, Mr Skemer explained that he had no choice: Princeton had to abide by the conditions of a bequest.

Valerie Eliot gave her all to her husband. With her, he found perfect happiness during his last years and she said that she would not have missed any part of them. The extraordinary transformation she effected through their domestic union was, it turned out, a high point in her continuing role as his disciple. As a girl, she had heard the voice of a traveller along a cold road to Bethlehem. She gave herself body and soul to a man who bore witness to a vision at the heart of his poems. The spontaneity and openness of her meeting with the beating 'tom tom' held firm for the rest of her long life.

Valerie Eliot had a mission to guard the poet's papers and image. She believed it Hale's fault that Eliot did not marry her after declaring his love in 1914. She defended him too against Stephen

Spender's opinion that he was sexually bad for Vivienne, by explain-
ing Vivienne's reluctance because she feared having children. 'On
medical advice they ceased relations.' It's unlikely that she knew of
Vivienne's joy in an 'affair' with her husband in the summer of 1919.
This fact was buried for a long time amongst the papers of Mary
Hutchinson, not readily available to Mrs Eliot. In the matter of
Vivienne's committal, she stood by Eliot's claim to have been unin-
volved; also that he didn't visit her because doctors told him not to.
Vivienne, she said, was in the 'nicest part' of the asylum until she
upset other patients. Valerie sustained Eliot's closeness to Maurice
Haigh-Wood, sympathised with his continued financial straits and
need to sell manuscripts and she took him regularly out to dinner.

Valerie Eliot had to walk a difficult path after the poet died. With
this in prospect, she said in 1969, 'I live in terror of failing Tom.' A
widow at the age of only thirty-eight, her commitment to her husband's oeuvre, the source of her feeling for him, was intensified by
her pity for his sufferings. Before they married, he had confessed
to abnormality in terms of what it cost to be a poet. It came back
to her after he died, how he had said that his life had been like a
Dostoevsky novel. Bitterly, he would quote from Elizabeth Barrett
Browning's poem about the making of a poet as a warped thing:

> Yet half a beast is the great god Pan,
>   To laugh as he sits by the river,
> Making a poet out of a man:
> The true gods sigh for the cost and pain —
> For the reed which grows nevermore again
>   As a reed with the reeds of the river.

Valerie Eliot became a director and supporter of Faber & Faber; a
philanthropist after the worldwide success of the musical *Cats*; and
a backer of the London Library, following her husband's stint as
President (1952–65). She set up Old Possum's Practical Trust, a well-
funded foundation for the promotion of the arts, including the

Book Trade Charity. Yet her greatest challenge was to restore Eliot to 'normality', ending the 'cost and pain' of being a poet. She had loved to have him at home where she could 'pet' him. Eliot would read aloud from Boswell's *Life of Johnson* while she darned. After decades of craving solitude, he wanted most to be with her. She never left his side as his heart gave way to the emphysema brought on by the smoking rife in his generation. In a coma at the last, he came to the surface like a diver, only to say her name. She never left his side and, with her there, death came gently.

Once he was gone she felt, she told Eleanor, 'utterly unreal and short-circuited and achingly aware of "the presence of his absence". He wrote me a wonderful letter in which he said we would be together always, together when one was living and the other dead, and that he would be waiting for me.'

For a long time she changed nothing in their ground-floor flat in Kensington. Even the oxygen bottles Eliot had needed for breathing remained. In the flat with its blue plaque his photographs still cover the walls, his portrait looms in the sitting-room, and in his study the stacked and neatly labelled boxes of his papers remain. Did it comfort Valerie to feel his presence, to hear his voice in the inscriptions of books to 'beloved Valerie', their validations of their union, or was it a lonely life? She did say it was hard to bear the pressures: all the begging letters and the noise of comment. She detested a fake image of her as a nurse, carrying Eliot bodily into their home. Such an act was physically impossible, she said.

In his last eight years, Eliot invited his wife to engage in his posthumous existence. Valerie Eliot lived the long afterlife guarding the poet's reputation. Her story is poignant because everything of importance to his greatness had happened by the time she took her place at his side. She was to clear the way towards a lasting belief that Eliot had been an innocent with a childlike heart, who could do no wrong. What she couldn't know was the farewell relationship he devised for Emily Hale, the twinned relationship with Vivienne and the complex past that lay behind his rejections of Hale, John Hayward and Mary Trevelyan.

With Valerie, to be love's dream come true is a *simple* role but to those, like his brother, who knew him far back, nothing was simple. He had carped at his nearest and dearest, ignored his brother's insight and good marriage, and fixed instead on Henry's collecting of family papers as a substitute for living. This stab could be a delayed answer to Henry's extraordinarily knowing letter of September 1935 piercing the façades because Henry was genuinely anxious for his brother. As the poet grew older, he minimised as lionisers the people who loved and helped him.

There in shadow was the other Eliot from whom the married Eliot had been saved, an astonishing rescue by Valerie for all the world to see. Where Emily had once watched with him for his poetic moment, Valerie was to tend his altar – a new posthumous plan. 'The Altar of the Dead' was an unforgettable prediction of her role by the Eliot scholar Walt Litz, when I visited him at Princeton in 1972. How much he would have liked to know that Eliot shared with Hale the appeal of that very Henry James tale where a woman lives to tend the shrine of a man she has loved.

Valerie Eliot was faithful to an Eliot in whom she found and brought out 'the simple soul' of the child he had been before he became 'misshapen', fearful of human warmth and 'the importunity of the blood'. To his brother, his simplicity would have seemed another self-dramatisation, marking the flair for publicity. To be an ideal husband was as surprising as the preceding roles: the renegade from his American family who turns into an Englishman; the convert who falls short of sainthood; the ascetic turned potent lover. The poet, like a great actor, could enter into what he imagined so convincingly that the women he drew into these scenes became part of them. Valerie proved the perfect wife, so much so that Emily Hale, hearing of this, concedes that she might not have matched it.

Apart from remaking a man, Valerie Eliot's two other magnificent achievements were her editions of *The Waste Land Manuscript* (1971) and *The Letters of T. S. Eliot*, the first volume in 1988, the centenary of his birth. This volume was revised to include additional letters in 2009, followed by successive volumes.

The annotations to *The Waste Land Manuscript* provide a lasting work of scholarship, not overloading readers with the kind of superfluous information that Eliot's obscurities make all too tempting.

The *Letters* are built on her determination not to make do with carbons and to find the top copies with their inked additions. She worked seven days a week. It pleased her 'to recover him in this way', even if occasionally it was 'rather desolating' when she found him troubled: 'one cries too over this anguish in certain periods'.

A far-sighted decision was to include letters from Eliot's correspondents. The edition therefore preserves telling letters from Vivienne, Henry Ware Eliot and many more. Eliot had tried to obliterate Vivienne – he had wanted no letters before 1933 to survive – but Valerie Eliot, with exemplary fair-mindedness, brought her forward. Eliot's will appointed his wife as sole handler of his papers and asked her to destroy as she saw fit. But this she resolved not to do. Her aim was completeness. Nothing was to be concealed.

An even bolder decision had to do with her notes to the letters. In January 1966, a year after Eliot's death, she told Eliot's friend Aurelia (Bolliger) Hodgson, 'Although Tom has forbidden a biography, I hope to incorporate interesting biographical facts', and later that year, in August, she told Robert Giroux, 'I cannot go against his wishes', however 'the letters will make a most marvellous autobiography, and will be a valuable quarry for biographers fifty years hence!' Indeed, her abundant, accurate, intelligent and informative notes 'bypass his directive' by providing 'the best building blocks of a biography', as her co-editor, John Haffenden, has said.

The multi-volume *Letters of T. S. Eliot* is a match for Mary Shelley's collected edition of Shelley's *Poems* in 1838. As the poet's widow, forbidden by the Shelley family to produce a biography, she too had offered a treasure of biographical data in her notes. Valerie Eliot's long widowhood is a story of growing character and attainment in her own right. Her ashes lie with Eliot's, as he planned, in St Michael's Church in his ancestral village of East Coker.

EPILOGUE

Eliot's letter to posterity left no opening for debate: the future must forget Emily Hale. His statement is designed to reduce the Eliot–Hale correspondence to nothing. But letters that in time would brush off the cobwebs clinging to dead celebrities – in Eliot's case the myth of poetic 'impersonality' imprinted on readers of his day – now surface. I remember Helen Gardner, in her last lectures on Eliot, telling students to focus on lines when emotion breaks through the erudite cover. The Eliot–Hale letters show him to have been intensely emotional in an actual relationship with his hyacinth girl.

Proof of Emily Hale as the hyacinth girl came in his second letter to her, on 3 November 1930. Frances Dickey, reporting for the Eliot Society, was next to me at a long table, and as we read that extraordinary letter we jumped up to hug. For this letter confirmed what had been in the past risky links with Hale provoking annoyed reviews from men who put Hale in her place as a female of no importance. The risk, starting in the seventies, had been to fill out an impression as a schoolgirl, reading Eliot with my mother, a poet and Bible teacher 'at the bottom of Africa' (she would joke). My mother's attuned reading had sensed the private trials between the lines.

'The love of a ghost for a ghost' is both true and untrue: it is true, as Eliot saw it, that once a poet is visited by a muse he is haunted ever after, but the phrase used to dismiss Emily Hale is untrue, flagrantly so: their pact had involved the touch of living bodies when they had slept in each other's arms in a state of bliss. Emily Hale did not exist solely as a figment of a poet's imagination.

This troubling ambiguity stayed with me in January and February 2020 as I read through the whole collection of letters, before the pandemic took hold. In March the archives were closed to visitors and remained mostly closed while I tried to understand the nature of Eliot's long obsession with Hale in relation to his spiritual journey and to ties with other women in his life.

His candour to Emily offers a close-up of his dark side but this in no way diminishes the poetry. On the contrary, it becomes clearer than ever that his greatest poetry was forged in the gap between a deeply imperfect nature and the perfection he could conceive and convey: the lives of the saints 'burning in every moment'. Tantalisingly for him, he had sightings of perfection and then had to tread a stony path. There was much for a man of conscience to suffer.

Emily Hale came to be the heroine of this story, along with other women who gave themselves to the poet in their different ways. I admired the sense and grace with which Hale met Eliot's 'abnormality'. The letters show how fine she was in her passage through a hard life, how spirited in her readings, staging of plays and readiness to perform and direct in her seventies. Her letters to Eliot after the 'change' rise to steady compassion, containment and resignation, bearing out his sense of her goodness. A similar selflessness is evident in Mary Trevelyan and Valerie Eliot. Vivienne recognised his genius before it was plain to others, including his family. Elated, she trumped his family with this boast: her certainty, more certain than even he could be at that point.

As Hale points out in her introduction to the letters, she shared the poet's creative years, and for this she came to feel grateful. By the time he married Valerie Fletcher, his life's work was done. That single fact – not love alone, nor forgiveness – made it possible to restore the uncomplicated soul he had once been.

Emily Hale was the first and foremost of the four women who recognised in the poet a sensitivity so acute as to be 'frightened'; each wished to protect him. Even the needy Vivienne, after he left her, thought her 'protection' vital to his longed-for return. Mary Trevelyan, the Guardian, offered the practical protection at which she excelled with foreigners. She responded cheeringly to Eliot's 'refugee face'. Emily, the Rose of memory, protected his sensitivities, referring only delicately and at long intervals to his intolerance and self-absorption. Valerie became his final protector as keeper of his papers.

These women came closer to him than any man, even though his professional life as bank clerk and editor was among men. As writer, he belonged to Ezra Pound's set, the Men of 1914, and to the men-only circle that met at John Hayward's flat in the thirties. There were monthly *Criterion* dinners for his chief contributors, none of them women, and there were also the recipients of men-only rhymes. After his conversion, he joined the all-male enclaves of the church, made retreats at Kelham, conferred with a group called the Moot, lunched with his confessor and wished to retire to a monastery. Then too he was a clubman: the Tory dining club; the Garrick; the Oxford and Cambridge; the Athenaeum. Yet for all this, including jokes, men were somehow kept at bay.

With women it was different. He looked to certain women for transformation: Vivienne with her gutsy flair was to make him into an English poet, while Emily was to ease the way towards divine grace. Valerie was to turn an ailing, fastidious man into a lover, eager, even earthy. With her, Eliot found a late-blooming capacity for married love, through Valerie's unstinting generosity. She adored an elderly man game for parties, even dancing, who willingly abandoned the costs of creativity. Each of the women created her own version of Eliot. Mary Trevelyan chummed up to an Anglican wit. Emily respected a fellow Bostonian whose propriety fought against desire.

For her it was a pattern of closeness and withdrawal. The

letters mark Emily's face skewed in pain: on a railroad platform at Northampton, Massachusetts in 1936; framed in the doorway of Stamford House in 1939; and in Concord, the most painful of all their partings, in 1947. Each time (except the last), the wrench she endures generates a poet's flight of eloquence. There is, though, one indisputable fact: Emily Hale chose to stay with Eliot. She would not want our pity. Though the relationship was more in his control than hers, his letters do bring out her bravery in challenging the dark places Eliot revealed. She understood who she was. She knew her worth to him and his poetry. In her sixties she refused to hide her role for all time, and in the end came to understand that a great writer could behave like a 'very usual human being', so that marriage to him might not have done after all – not for her.

In the run-up to *Four Quartets*, he exposed to Emily the source of his inspiration behind his protective façades. On New Year's Eve, December 1931, he tells her

> I get flashes of perception of a kind of 'pattern' ... flashes which do not give peace 'as the world gives' but which, while they last, reconcile one to all the mystery of ... suffering in the past. Just as still more rarely, at other times, I have a kind of flash of anticipation of my future ...

And then again, some eighteen months later, in the intimacy of their faceless communing, he finally finds words for his most profound and private experience.

> Occasionally, very rarely, the periods of heightened life pass for a moment into a mood of peace and reconciliation, a momentary perception of a pattern in life, which one just accepts. This never lasts more than a few minutes, with me. At present I have rather an awareness of the possibilities of spiritualising my ordinary daily life a little more, and of how far I have to go.

To participate in this inspiration and the masterpiece that followed was an extraordinary calling for Emily Hale, and though
she kept that calling to herself, her pupils felt the glow when she
spoke of the poet.

The strictness of Eliot's privacy had a counterpart in the erudition
on the surface of his poems, shielding the confessional core. He
explains his distrust of record in the line 'our own past is covered by
the currents of action.' To decipher a life through its public doings
was, he judged, as misleading as the 'Pastimes' of psychoanalysis,
palm-reading and fortune-tellers raking over entrails or tea leaves.
He asks us to see how futile it would be to put together a compen-
dium of the poet's acts, because too much detail obscures both the
sense of destiny driving so willed a life and its distinctive pattern.
The challenge set out in essays on other writers is to discern the
pattern in the carpet of a great oeuvre.

His lifelong venture was to fit a flawed self – in need of remaking – to the model of saints and seekers who perfect their souls.
There is a mission to revive their tried and tested pattern laid down
in the wilderness of Exodus; in the 'dark, dark, dark' of Samson's
blinding; and in the ordeals of the grail quest. For a sinner, the way
had to be purgatorial: 'To be redeemed from fire by fire.'

Eliot was drawn to the medieval mind for its openness to visions.
In the modern mind, he said, dreams replace visions – low or
mediocre dreams. The very movement of his poetry is the glimpse
of 'reality' followed by the drop into the 'waste sad time' before
and after. When his wary character ventures 'among the women'
the gift for vision fades. But then Emily enters to quicken the
poetic moment. 'Quick now . . .' He tests it on the pulse, moment
by moment, and seals it in words. She has her part to play in the
sequence which culminates in faith. His part is to make it his own,
to take on the ancestral journey in his own time and renew it for
generations to come, '. . . here, now, always – '.

NOTES

ABBREVIATIONS

AW	Eliot, *Ash Wednesday*
BN	Eliot, *Burnt Norton*
C	*The Criterion*, ed. Eliot 1922–39
CCE	Charlotte Champe Eliot (mother)
CFQ	Helen Gardner, *The Composition of* Four Quartets
CPy	Eliot, *The Cocktail Party*
DS	Eliot, *The Dry Salvages*
EC	Eliot, *East Coker*
EH	Emily Hale
EH to TSE	EH's letters to TSE, 1947–57. Eliot Estate
EMB	E. Martin Browne, director of TSE's plays
ES	Eliot, *The Elder Statesman*
EVE	Esmé Valerie Eliot (née Fletcher)
f	folder or folio in manuscript collections
FQ	Eliot, *Four Quartets*
FR	Eliot, *The Family Reunion*
GF	Geoffrey Faber
Houghton	Houghton Library, Harvard University. Eliot Family Collection
HWE	Henry Ware Eliot, Jr (brother)
IL	Lyndall Gordon, *The Imperfect Life of T. S. Eliot*
IMH	TSE's early notebook and loose poems in the Berg collection, New York Public Library. *Inventions of the March Hare*, ed. Christopher Ricks
JDH	John Davy Hayward
L, i–ii	*The Letters of T. S. Eliot*, ed. Valerie Eliot and Hugh Haughton
L, iii–ix	*The Letters of T. S. Eliot*, ed. Valerie Eliot and John Haffenden
LG	Eliot, *Little Gidding*
LW	Leonard Woolf
MC	Eliot, *Murder in the Cathedral*
MH	Mary Hutchinson

MHW	Maurice Haigh-Wood (brother-in-law)
MME	Mary Trevelyan and Erica Wagner, *Mary and Mr Eliot: A Sort of Love Story*. Substantial selection from a memoir (PRS, below) with narrative
MT	Mary Trevelyan
NWEH	*Narrative Written by Emily Hale* (drafted 1957, revised 1965) to accompany Emily Hale's letters from Eliot. Published online, ed. Frances Dickey and Sara Fitzgerald (Princeton Special Collections, 2020)
OM	Lady Ottoline Morrell
OPP	Eliot, *On Poetry and Poets*. Eliot's edition
Plays	Eliot, *Collected Plays*. Eliot's edition
Poems/R&M	*The Poems of T. S. Eliot*, vols i–ii, with notes and commentaries, and including verse unpublished during TSE's lifetime, ed. Christopher Ricks and Jim McCue
Poems/TSE	Eliot, *Collected Poems 1909–1962*. Eliot's final edition
Prose	*The Complete Prose of T. S. Eliot: The Critical Edition*, i–viii, ed. Ronald Schuchard et al
PRS	Mary Trevelyan, 'The Pope of Russell Square'. Typescript memoir of TSE, with extracts from his letters to MT. PRS is the full, original typescript, with its addition of photographs and reviews, now in the Bodleian Library, Oxford. See *MME*, above
SA	Eliot, *Sweeney Agonistes*
SE	Eliot, *Selected Essays*. TSE's own selection
Sparrow	Ann Pasternak Slater, *The Fall of a Sparrow*
Thorp Papers	Manuscripts Division, Department of Special Collections: C0292, Firestone Library, Princeton University
TSE	T. S. Eliot
TSE to EH	Emily Hale's letters from T. S. Eliot, 1930–57, in Manuscripts Division, Department of Special Collections: C0686, Firestone Library, Princeton University
VHE	Vivienne Haigh-Wood Eliot
VW	Virginia Woolf
VW/*Diary*	*The Diary of Virginia Woolf*, vols i–v, ed. Anne Olivier Bell
VW/*Letters*	*The Letters of Virginia Woolf*, vols i–vi, ed. Nigel Nicolson and Joanna Trautmann
WL	Eliot, *The Waste Land*
WL/facs	Valerie Eliot, facsimile edition of *The Waste Land*
WT	Willard Thorp

1: HOME WOMEN

5   *'impersonality'*: E. M. Forster challenged the poet's claim to impersonality in 'TSE and his Difficulties', *Life & Letters*, ii (May 1929), repr. *Abinger Harvest*. TSE's reply (10 Aug 1929) in *L*, iv, 573, admitted that 'the "impersonality" doctrine . . . has its personal motives of course'.

5   *'memory and desire'*: *WL*: I.

7   *people 'not wholly commendable'*: *LG*: III. *Poems/TSE*, 206.

7   *'common genius'*: Ibid.

7   *TSE met EH in 1905*: Approximate date of meeting in TSE to EH (18 Aug 1932),

box 3, f. 5. He does not give the year but says it was when he came to Boston.

7   *Eleanor Hinkley:* 1891–1971, an exact contemporary of EH. See *Plays of 47 Workshop* (NY, 1920), *A Flitch of Bacon* (1919), *Dear Jane* (written 1919 and produced in 1932) and *Mrs Aphra Behn* (1933).

7   *Cat Morgan's tribute to EH:* 'Morgan Tries Again', *Poems/R&M*, i, 308–9 (in a section of Uncollected Poems. 'Miss 'ale' is 'one that old Morgan would most like to see' in the office at Faber & Faber.

8   *voice, one in millions:* TSE to EH (July 1942).

8   *As 'children':* TSE to EH (18 Aug 1932), box 3, f. 5.

8   *white toes:* 'A Cooking Egg', *Poems/R&M*, i, 344 has an excised stanza about an innocent 'Pipit', whom TSE would identify to EH as herself. See below, chapter 6.

8   *the Berkeley Street School:* This was among the other preparatory schools EH attended in Boston: Miss Ingalls's school in Cambridge and Miss May's school in Boston. EH's curriculum vitae, *c.* 1930, in Smith College archives. Thanks to Sara Fitzgerald for finding two schoolgirl photos of EH.

8   *EH tells her aunt and uncle of her dedication to theatre:* On 5 October 1946 TSE acknowledges receipt of a letter Hale had forwarded, written by her to her aunt and uncle on 9 June 1905. He tells Hale that he was impressed with thirteen-year-old Emily's writing and her dedication to the theatre. She sent TSE the 1905 enclosure after he saw her perform in Vermont.

8   *Edward Hale to Edith Milliken Perkins:* TSE to EH, box 14. Edward Hale wrote from 40 Evergreen Place, East Orange, NJ.

9   *'came forth':* L, i, xxxvii.

9   *TSE in the family:* TSE to EH (7 Sept 31), box 2, f. 2, relays his position at home.

9   *HWE's weaknesses more 'tolerable':* TSE to EH (16 Oct 1943), box 12, f. 3.

9   *'coloured by domestic bitterness':* TSE to EH (19 Feb 1936), box 6, f. 6. See TSE's impression of Ada, expressed to JDH (20 Feb 1943), cited *L*, vii, 878n.

10   *TSE's reserve:* He wrote to EH: 'I wish to have no reserves . . . ', TSE to EH, box 2, f. 1.

10   *'disgust':* TSE to MT (19 Dec 1944), Houghton. Letter quoted in *MME*, 57.

11   *'stole':* TSE to CCE (10 July 1919), *L*, i, 376.

11   *dodged another party:* Recalled 6 Aug 1953 while talking to MT. PRS.

12   *TSE's poem about his cousins' camp:* L, i, 2–3.

12   *'a terror of excessive community . . . ':* TSE to EH, box 11, f. 1, EH was about to go on a communal summer holiday to Grand Manan Island in Canadian waters just north of Maine.

12   *'First Debate between the Body and Soul':* IMH, 64. *Poems/R&M*, i, 239.

13   *'a lifelong affliction':* TSE to Richard Aldington (6 Nov 1921, during a breakdown), *L*, i, 603.

13   *'I had to find out . . . ':* TSE to EH (Feb 1933), box 4, f. 2.

13   *Columbo, Bolo, and his 'Big Black Kween', etc:* Poems/R&M, ii, 247–85. The editors' heading is 'Improper Rhymes'. A number are in *IMH*, 311–21.

13   *'bum is big as a soup tureen':* Poems/R&M, ii, 270.

14   *'from my cunt to my navel':* 'Fragments', *IMH*, 314. *Poems/R&M*, ii, 285.

14   *'unctuous'; 'preachy':* TSE to EH (2 Apr 1935), box 5, f. 2.

14   *exchange with GF:* This view on 25? Aug comes two months after TSE's conversion in June 1927. *L*, iii, 660.

15 *None of the women . . . would see these rhymes:* EVE was not shown these before she married TSE. (Afterwards he copied fourteen assorted stanzas into two exercise books, which they called 'Valerie's Own Book'.)

15 *'Circe's Palace':* Harvard Advocate (25 Nov 1908), lxxxvi, 9. *Poems Written in Early Youth,* 20. *Poems/R&M,* i, 231. The sluggish python is TSE's invention, but it interprets Odysseus's report that to enter Circe's bed drains manly energy. (*The Odyssey,* Book X.) With thanks to Isobel Dixon for the Hawthorne link.

15 *'Came Christ the tiger':* 'Gerontion', *Poems/TSE,* 29.

15 *'How unpleasant to meet Mr. Eliot!':* 'Lines for Cuscuscaraway . . . ', *Poems/TSE,* 137.

15 *'I am by temperament . . . Calvinist':* TSE to GF (28 Dec 1934), *L,* vii, 428. See *L,* viii, 811n: Peter Quennell recorded in *The Wanton Chase: An Autobiography from 1939* (1980) that when he once suggested, in exchange of letters with TSE, 'that the author of *WL* was still a Puritan at heart, [TSE] had asserted that he was proud of his Puritan ancestry, and that a long line of studious clergymen and judges had firmly fixed his mental pattern'.

16 *'my great etc. gnd.father used to hang witches . . . ':* TSE to GF (28 Dec 1934), *L,* vii, 428.

16 *Andrew Eliott's date of migration:* TSE gives this date in a letter but he also gives the date as 1671 in a letter to Jean de Menasce (31 May 1940), *L,* ix, 542. It is unusual for his excellent memory to falter, which suggests some uncertainty about the actual date.

16–17 *TSE on his grandfather:* TSE to EH (2 Apr 1935), box 5, f. 2 and again (11 Jan 1937), box 7, f. 4.

17 *Easter Songs:* In Geneva Series of small white booklets by three women and seventeen men, praised by the *Journal of Education* as an 'inspiration to higher thinking and nobler living'. The publisher was James West of Boston. CCE had three poems in the thirteen pages: 'At Easter-Tide'; 'Ring Easter Bells!'; 'Be Glad and Gay'. Copy in Houghton.

17 *TSE confidences about his mother:* TSE to EH (9 Jan 1931), box 1.

17 *'affirm before the world and deny . . . ':* AW: V.

17 *'or some shadowy personality behind her':* TSE to EH (2 Apr 1935), box 5, f. 2. See dream figures from his past compelling the speaker in *AW:* VI.

18 *'Suffer me not to be separated':* AW: VI.

18 *'Silence':* IMH, 18, and *Poems/R&M,* i, 243.

18 *'wires':* Transcribed as 'waves' in *IMH* and *Poems/R&M.* But voices over the 'garrulous wires', as in telegraph wires, makes sense in the context of human noise obliterating 'Silence'.

2: SCENES IN PARIS

19 *'listless discouragement':* Verdenal to TSE (5 Feb 1912), *L,* i 35.

20 *'Portrait of a Lady':* TSE's began with what became part II, drafted in Feb 1910. Henry James was the American par excellence who made a life in Europe. He began his European life by settling for a year in Paris.

20 *Adeleine Moffat:* Douglass Shand-Tucci, the authority on Boston architecture (blogging on the Back Bay site he founded, www.backbayhistorical.org), contradicts the effete lady TSE invents. Sapphist meant lesbian, after the poet Sappho who lived on the island of Lesbos. Virginia Woolf and her circle spoke of Sapphists, while TSE uses the shortened 'Saph' in a letter to his cousin Eleanor.

21 *lethal pen:* Part III, written after an interval in 1911.

21 *'what if she should die . . . ':* George Eliot condones murderous fancy in a work of literature as distinct from murder in her correspondence with her publisher about 'Mr Gilfil's Love Story' in *Scenes of Clerical Life.*

21 *J of J. Alfred Prufrock:* TSE told this to Aurelia Bolliger (c. 1931–2) and said Prufrock would have been ashamed of the name and suppressed it. Bolliger, together with Ralph Hodgson, stayed with the Eliots at their flat early in 1932. She kept a wire-bound notebook recording her impressions and what she learnt. Bolliger papers, Bryn Mawr College.

21 Mona Lisa *smile:* Wyndham Lewis called this a 'Giaconda' smile when he met TSE in Pound's flat in Kensington in 1914–15. Recalled in *Blasting and Bombadiering* (1937).

21 *Matthew Stewart Prichard:* TSE confided this to EH (24 Mar 1931) and again on 6 Mar 1933, box 4, f. 4. That day TSE was lecturing on Henry James, *The Turn of the Screw,* with its question whether two children were possessed. The other text that day was Conrad's *Heart of Darkness.* After TSE left Paris, Verdenal continued to see Prichard and relayed his lukewarm opinion to TSE at the end of 1911, *L,* i, 28, 32. Prichard's dates are 1865–1936. He became secretary to the Director of the Boston Museum of Fine Arts in 1902 and Assistant Director from 1904. In the *Edinburgh Companion to TSE,* Jewel Spears Brooker says that Prichard also lodged with Mme Casaubon.

23 *father and 'nastiness':* Henry Ware Eliot Sr to his elder brother, Thomas Lamb Eliot (7 Mar 1914), *L,* i, 41. Syphilis was God's punishment and he hoped a cure would never be found.

23 *'Purge . . . ' and 'immortal gifts':* CCE, 'The Present Hour', *Christian Register.* Copy with Eliot family papers, Houghton.

24 *'Suppressed Complex':* Poems/*R&M,* i, 1149. Undated. Enclosed in letter to Pound on 2 Feb 1915.

24 *the girl's sleep:* Susan Jones (email, 2022) explained: 'When I danced this role with Scottish Ballet (we were taught by Alicia Markova, who got it from Karsavina), I understood that the essential mood – and the difficulty – of performing this apparently slight role is that the girl is asleep, and appears to be asleep (with gaze cast downwards to give this impression) throughout the dance. She is dreaming, she is guided, transported by the spirit of the Rose until she wakes fully at the end.'

26 *Nijinsky on his role as the Rose:* Romola Nijinsky's version, *Nijinsky* (1933; repr. Penguin, 1960), 113.

26 *cerebral anaemia:* Recalled in TSE to JDH (8 Feb 1940), *L,* ix, 422.

27 *TSE on 'Marie' in* WL: TSE to EH (2 Mar 1931), box 1, f. 3.

3: A CHANCE OF LOVE

29 *'Hidden under the heron's wing':* In *IMH,* 82, and in Poems/*R&M,* i, 275, this poem unpublished in TSE's lifetime, follows a suicidal poem with post-mortem, 'Do I know how I feel?', *IMH,* 80. 'Under the heron's wing' is in pencil on the verso, and I've assumed it's a continuation, i.e. one poem, because, after the diversionary thought of a lovely girl, the poem returns to suicide.

29 *TSE in the Stillman Infirmary:* Receipt (with TSE's Ash Street address) on his payment for medication from the Infirmary, with dates, in Houghton.

If this was indeed one of his bouts of shingles, the medication is likely to
have been for pain since this illness, lasting typically for about a fortnight,
would not have been treatable.

29   *TSE's view of shingles:* TSE to EH (19 Apr 1938), box 8, f. 6.

30   *date of 'The Death of St Narcissus':* Eliot refers to this poem in a letter to his new,
      influential mentor, Ezra Pound, on 2 Feb 1915, *L*, i, 94. Writing on Valéry's
      narcissism in 1958, TSE spoke of Narcissus as an aloof and frigid 'spiritual
      celibate'.

30   *'deeper degrees . . .':* 'Dante' (1929), *SE*, 214.

30   *TSE reading Dante from 1911:* In 'Eliot's Emilia' (Burnt Norton lecture in July
      2022), Frances Dickey suggests that he started reading Dante from 1909,
      encouraged by the poetry, art and translations of Dante Gabriel Rossetti
      and by George Santayana in the philosophy department at Harvard.

30   *TSE's student copy of Dante:* Tricky to locate in Houghton. Traceable via
      acquisition no: *AC9.El464.Zz91ot (assigned in 1951 after transfer from the
      Eliot House library). The Temple Classics edition was edited by Israel
      Gollancz and published by J. M. Dent in London. The *Commedia* was first
      printed in 1472, soon after Johannes Gutenberg invented the printing press.
      TSE's copy has a faded and frayed beige ribbon as marker for the *Inferno* and
      a pink frayed and faded ribbon for the *Paradiso*. The *Purgatorio*, later central to
      TSE's oeuvre, looks little read compared with the *Inferno*. His marginal lines
      are invariably alongside the Italian text, not the English translation on the
      facing page.

31   *'is transmuted . . .':* Canto XXIII, ll.1–4.

31   *'with the fire wherewith I ever burn':* Canto XXVI, ll.28–30.

31–2 *TSE acting:* He took the role of Lord Bantock opposite Amy de Gozzaldi in
      Jerome K. Jerome's *Fanny and the Servant Problem* in the Cambridge Dramatic
      Society's production in 1912–13.

32   *'thrill & excitement':* TSE to EH (18 Oct 1932), box 3, f. 6.

32   *TSE recalled charade at the Hinkleys' party:* TSE to EH (21 July 1931).

32–3 *stunt show:* Programme in Houghton. Repr. *L*, i, 40.

33   *EH recalled TSE playing Mr Woodhouse:* NWEH (draft, 1957), box 14, f. 8.

33   *EH's dresses:* TSE shows how observant he was of her dresses in letters to EH
      (3 Feb 1931, 2 March 1931 and early Oct 1935).

33   *TSE as mollusc:* TSE to EH (Jan 1931).

33   *EH's party at the opera:* Puzzlingly TSE mentions EH's 'parents' as present.
      Unlikely that her mother could have been released from the Boston
      asylum. Was TSE referring mistakenly to her Aunt Edith and her husband
      Dr John Carroll Perkins, or to her uncle, Philip Hale, and his wife? Since EH
      had little money, it's possible that she was given the tickets (for a Monday
      night) by Philip Hale (1854–1934), a music critic.

34   *TSE's recollection of* Tristan und Isolde: TSE to EH (20 Jan 1931), box 1, f. 1–2. Also
      15 Jan 1932. TSE kept the programme, with the cast and date. Houghton:
      HWE collection, box 3, bMS Am 2560 (103). TSE published 'The Legend of
      Tristan and Isolde' side by side with *WL* in first issue of *C*.

34.*   poem 'Opera': Poems/*R&M*, 236.

34   *'his heart swells . . . pulses in his breast':* Tristan und Isolde, Act III.

34   *'After that night at the opera':* TSE to EH (23 July 1931).

35 *Clement Circle:* EH was staying in west Cambridge, walking distance from Harvard. Her home with her father was at 5 Circuit Road in his parish of Chestnut Hill, near Newton.

35 *love that goes beyond its object:* Helen Gardner's marvellous accuracy in *The Art of T. S. Eliot.*

35 *'no mention of marriage' etc:* N WEH, first drafted in 1957 as introduction to the Eliot–Hale letters, box 14. f. 8.

35 *'When I first knew you . . . ':* TSE to EH (Dec 1930), box 1, f. 1.

36 *date of Weeping Girl poem, 'La Figlia':* In a letter from TSE to Evdo Mason (21 Feb 1936) he said it was 1912. Texas. (Letter omitted from *L*, viii.) JDH, advising the French translator of TSE in 1947, thought the date was 1911. JDH was living with TSE at the time.

36 *director and scene-making:* Anthony Cuda in lecture on 'Belatedness' at the TSE summer school, July 2019.

37 *prefers art to life:* In 'The Lesson of the Master' by Henry James, a seasoned writer instructs a young writer on the verge of greatness to elicit emotional intensity and then leave it. His lesson is to avoid commitment to a woman, or else her needs will spoil his art.

37 *novelistic scene:* See Megan Quigley for ground-breaking work on TSE's poetic fictions.

37 *Bolo and Colombo verses copied into notebook:* TSE made a full, fair copy in a neat hand in a small black hardcover notebook. Donald Gallup, Eliot's bibliographer, saw this in the Pound archive in the Beinecke Library, Yale. He reported it no longer there from 1994. *Poems/R&M*, ii, 270.

37 *'raped her':* IMH, 317.

38 *St Sebastian dies on the woman's breast:* This scene is close to Gautier's Rose poem, the source of the ballet, where the Rose says to the girl, 'I have your breast as my tomb.'

39 *Vera Brittain's generation:* Brittain went up to Somerville College in 1914, at the same time as TSE entered Merton College.

39 *'No one looks at them':* (14 Oct 1914), *L*, i, 70.

39 *'nervous sexual attacks' and 'wall' of refinement:* To Aiken (31 Dec 1914), *L*, i, 82.

39 *desires and 'very sorry' for women:* TSE to Aiken (30 Sept 1914), *L*, i, 64.

40 *'ending in -Uck . . . ':* Lewis to Pound (Jan 1915), *L*, i, 94n. IMH, Appendix A, 305. It has been argued that the attempt at publication was merely a joke. Yet TSE did take the time and trouble to copy out his entire corpus to date – on sexual assaults, the threat of an extended penis and piles of excrement – in a separate notebook (see note on Bolo and Colombo above) designed for that purpose.

40 *date of 'Suppressed Complex':* After TSE sent this to Pound, he sent it to Aiken on 25 Feb 1915. *L*, i, 96.

40 Le Martyre de Saint Sébastien: A blend of poetry and dance in Paris in late May 1911 at same theatre as the Ballets Russes, preceding their arrival. To cast the saint as a woman was erotic: the Italian poet d'Annunzio, who wrote the spoken words (in French), was in love with her. Her ecstatic dance was choreographed by Fokine and performed by Rubenstein to the music of a polyphonic chorus composed by Debussy.

40 *found its way into Eliot's Narcissus:* Nancy Hargrove, *T. S. Eliot's Parisian Year*, 34–6.

40   *Rubenstein:* What Henri Ghéon called Rubinstein's 'hyacinth hair' was
      possibly to find its way, years later, into the hyacinth girl in *WL*. Ghéon
      used the image in his review of *Le Martyre de Saint Sébastien* in the July 1911 issue
      of *La Nouvelle Revue Française*. According to John Morgenstern, TSE read this
      journal avidly. With thanks to Susan Jones, author of *Literature, Modernism
      and Dance.*

41   *'I heard often from him':* NWEH, draft 1957, TSE-EH letters, box 14, f. 8. Sara
      Fitzgerald has discovered that EH performed in the following: *Through the
      Looking Glass* (1912); Olivia in *Twelfth Night* (1914); Roxane in *Cyrano de Bergerac*
      (1915); a farce, *Eliza Comes to Stay* (May 1915); and directed Yeats's *Land of Hearts
      Desire* and a play by Lady Gregory in association with Lucia Briggs in the
      department of English at Simmons College.

4: 'THE POET'S BRIDE'

42   *'complete surprise':* NWEH (revised after TSE's death, 1965).
42   *'did not love you after all':* TSE to EH, box 1, f. 1.
43   *lunch party in Magdalen College: L,* i, 105n.
44   *Dublin properties owned by the Haigh-Woods:* Seven houses in the Dublin suburb of
      Kingstown (now Dún Laoghaire): 1, 3, 4 and 5 Haigh Terrace; 16 Tivoli Road;
      1–10 Eglington Park; and Eglington House.
45   *'Can it be . . . ':* (7 May 1916), *L,* i, 150.
45   *Boston caricatures:* 'Cousin Nancy', 'Aunt Helen' and 'The *Boston Evening
      Transcript*'. *Poems/TSE,* 20–2.
46   *not blood shaking the heart: WL:* V. TSE to EH (3 Nov 1930), box 1, f. 1: the lines
      beginning with 'blood shaking my heart' in *WL* were written with
      EH in mind.
47   *wish to shed virginity:* TSE to Aiken (31 Dec 1914), *L,* i, 82.
47   *'I could have danced like a faun':* VHE to Thayer (15 June 1915), *Sparrow,* 18–19. (The
      date of the letter shows Vivienne making up to Thayer eleven days before
      she married TSE.) She pictured herself as a gem, a diamond or a white flame,
      with golden eyes, who will be lost to him when he goes back to his 'savage
      land'. She was not shy to boast 'you will never meet with such another'. If
      he hadn't stood her and Lucy up for a night out at the Savoy in London, she
      reproached him, 'I could have danced like a faun'. Bronislava Nijinska said
      that *Prélude à l'après-midi d'un faune* was to be part of her brother's two-week
      programme in London in March 1914, but whether or not he did stage it is
      unconfirmed. According to VHE's diary, she saw Nijinsky dance on 12 March.
47   *chloral hydrate:* Ann Pasternak Slater, in *Sparrow,* notes the belated date, Nov
      1925, when VHE's chloral addiction was finally diagnosed.
48   *'Hysteria':* Dated Oxford 1915. Published Nov 1915 in *The Catholic Anthology.*
48   *set story of needing to escape from America:* TSE to EH (1 Aug 1931), box 2, f. 1.
48   *less 'suppressed':* (2 July 1915), *L,* i, 113.
49   *'Rosa Buckle':* Text in *Sparrow,* 595–7.
49–50 *VHE's private means:* VHE's annual allowance in *Sparrow,* 28. Some years later,
      in 1922, VHE mentions having a sum of £1,000 in hand. After her father's
      death in 1927, she became entitled to a third of the rentals, amounting to
      £569 3s. 4d between 1927 and 1933. Bodleian MS Eng let. B.22. Cited *L,* vii, 459n.
51   *'Ode': Ara Vos Prec.* TSE eliminated 'Ode' from the American edition (Knopf)

of his second volume of poems (1920), and he worried that 'Sweeney Erect' would shock his mother. TSE to HWE (15 Feb 1920), *L*, i, 441.

51   *'knocked out':* TSE to HWE (2 July 1915), *L*, i, 114.

52   *war horribly futile:* TSE at tea with Abigail, who was pleased with TSE's political radicalism and describes the talk in letters to her parents. Abigail Eliot Papers, Schlesinger Library, Radcliffe College, Cambridge, MA.

52   *china and brass in Haigh-Wood home:* Observed later by Aurelia Bolliger.

52   *'clodhopper':* TSE to HWE (1 Jan 1936), *L*, viii, 10.

53   *'She has everything to give' and 'the one person for me':* TSE to his father (23 July 1915) *L*, i, 119.

53   *Haigh-Woods 'outsiders socially':* TSE to EH (8 July 1932), box 3, f. 4.

54   *Fred Eliot's success as Unitarian minister:* Led TSE to write one more acid family poem. 'Mr. Eliot's Sunday Morning Service' (1918) foregrounds pimply flunkeys handing round the collection box, in contrast with martyrs of old, 'invisible and dim'. In private, for years to come, he dismissed Fred as 'an ass' (TSE to MT, 1948).

55   *'blunder':* (10 Sept 1915), *L*, i, 125.

55–6 *Russell to OM:* Sept 1915. Ray Monk, *Bertrand Russell: The Spirit of Solitude*, 440.

56   *possibility that VHE's condition was self-induced:* Munchausen syndrome is suggested by Ann Pasternak Slater, *Sparrow*, 115. Might the psychology be similar to the effect of the African *sangoma* (witch doctor), who can induce people to fall ill and even die through the power of suggestion? A highly suggestible person like VHE might bring on actual illness. Her Harley Street physician, Dr Miller, thought a lot was put on. See also p. 252n.

56   *'I did try . . . ':* TSE to EH (c. Sept 1931), when EH asked if he was protecting VHE.

57   *Russell's exchanges with Lady Ottoline:* Cited by Seymour, *Ottoline Morrell: Life on the Grand Scale* (1992; repr. Faber 2009), 332–3.

57   *'force':* TSE's first letter after his marriage, to HWE (2 July 1915), *L*, i, 113.

57   *'I have lived . . . ':* *L*, i, 138, from VHE's parents' home, 3 Compayne Gardens.

59   *'Tom knows . . . ':* VHE to HWE (11 Oct 1916), *L*, i, 171.

59   *'I do shove':* (11 Oct 1916), *L*, i, 169–72.

59   *orange . . . fad for this colour:* Stephen Calloway, 'The Wider Influence of the Russian Ballet' in *Diaghilev and the Golden Age of the Ballets Russes*, ed. Jane Pritchard (London: V&A Publishing, 2010), 126–7.

60   *last rag':* VHE to HWE (21 Nov 1918), *L*, i, 302.

60   *'practically starving':* VHE to CCE (28 June 1917), *L*, i, 207.

61   *'Will you do that?':* (5 Nov 1916), *L*, i, 174.

61   *VHE's ploys over money:* She brings it to the Eliots' attention that that their son's pyjamas are old and that he tears them 'mercilessly'. Another letter explains at length how poor they are, how dutifully she darns away at Tom's worn underwear – and by the way, she's travelling to the north to visit a childhood friend and had to have a new outfit for this trip. One Christmas, CCE sent £3. Vivienne thanks her profusely before letting her mother-in-law know that a winter coat for TSE had cost ten guineas.

61   *failure to compose new poems would disappoint VHE more:* TSE to HWE (6 Sept 1916), *L*, i, 166.

61   *'a constant canker . . . ':* (11 Oct 1916), *L*, i, 171.

62 *'hatred of life':* 'Cyril Tourneur' (1930), *SE*, 166.

63 *to the point of madness:* TSE to EH (July 1932), box 3, f. 4.

63 *'off our heads all the summer':* VHE to HWE (21 Nov 1918), *L*, i, 304.

63 *'awful nightmare':* (6 Sept 1916), *L*, i, 166.

63 *'Tell me . . . Emily':* *L*, i, 162.

64 *'dazed and numbed':* The door between him and Emily seemed closed for good, TSE recalled to EH (7 Apr 1931). EH had confided this to TSE.

64 *father would have to fund two homes:* TSE to EH (1 Aug 1931), box 2, f. 1.

64 *The possum plays dead:* Richard Mabey, cited by Frances Wilson, *The Ballad of Dorothy Wordsworth* (London: Faber, 2009), 213.

64 *date of 'Elegy':* This undated fragment fits TSE's quatrain period, 1917–19, See Lyndall Gordon, *Eliot's Early Years* (OUP, 1977) and *IL*: Appendix II. In form and content, 'Elegy' looks like a variation on drafted stanzas of a quatrain poem, 'Whispers of Immortality' (late May–early June 1918): 'Our sighs pursue the vanished shade / And breathe a sanctified amen . . . ', also 'And when the Female Soul departs / The Sons of Men turn up their eyes . . . '

64 *'as in a tale by Poe':* *WL/facs*, 116–17.

65 *'And when the Female Soul departs . . . ':* *IMH*, 368.

66 *house in West Street, Marlow:* The same street where Shelley had lived at Albion House in 1817.

66 *TSE's essays on Henry James:* 'In Memory of Henry James' (Jan 1918), the lead piece in the James number of the *Egoist*, repr. *Prose*, i, 648–52. TSE did an additional essay, 'The Hawthorne Aspect', after reading James's book on Hawthorne (1879), in June 1918 and published in the *Little Review* that August. Repr. *Prose*, i, 736–44.

66 *'the deeper psychology':* 'Henry James: The Hawthorne Aspect', *Little Review* (1918).

5: UNDER ENGLISH EYES

67 *'a great strain . . . ':* (2 July 1919), *L*, i, 370.

67 *dependent on VHE:* TSE to CCE (29 June 1919), *L*, i, 370.

68 *'dress parade':* To HWE (2 July 1919), *L*, i, 370.

68 *'everywhere a foreigner':* 'Henry James: In Memory', *Little Review* (August 1918). Susan Mizruchi, *A Very Short Introduction to Henry James*, 9, quotes William James: Henry James lived 'hidden in the midst of alien manners – assumed as "protective resemblances"'. TSE's sense of being a foreigner was repeated to HWE (2 July 1919), *L*, i, 370 and yet again to Max Bodenheim: 'I have got used to being a foreigner everywhere' (2 Jan 1921), *L*, i, 532.

68 *'preyed':* TSE, 'Henry James: In Memory', *The Shock of Recognition*, ed. Edmund Wilson (NY: Random House/The Modern Library, 1943, repr. 1955), 856.

69 *'out of the frying pan . . . ':* *L*, i, 222.

69 *'a sort of fairy tale farm':* VHE to CCE (22 Oct 1917), *L*, i, 226–7.

70 *VHE not keen on sex:* Confided to OM. Miranda Seymour, *Life on the Grand Scale*, 425.

70 *'done Evil':* TSE to OM (14 Mar 1933). *L*, vi, 562. TSE later wrote to Alida Monro: 'The spectacle of Bertie was an element in my conversion.'

70 *first visit to Garsington:* Seymour, 347–8, notes OM's attempt to get through to TSE in French, and quotes from OM's journal (British Library Add Ms 88886/04/03): 'I felt him monotonous without and within. Where does his

queer neurasthenic poetry come from, I wonder. From his New England
Puritan inheritance and upbringing?'

71 *OM's appearance:* VW/*Diary* (16 May 1919), i, 272.

72 *'sensitive'; 'chaotic erudition':* TSE to MH (11? July 1919), *L*, i, 377–8.

73 *'very American and obstinate!':* VHE to MH (13 Mar 1918), *L*, i, 256.

73 *not Fun:* VHE to MH (29 Oct 1919), *L*, i, 410.

73 *'I can be seduced':* To MH (16 May 1919), *L*, i, 349–50.

73 *'provincial amours':* TSE to MH (1 June 1919), *L*, i, 356.

73–4 *TSE's list for MH:* (11? July 1919), *L*, i, 378.

74 *Russian ballet as model:* 'To obtain, with verse, an effect as immediate and
direct as that of the best ballet' comes from his review 'The Duchess of
Malfi at the Lyric', *Prose*, ii, 173.

74 *'War' in* The Egoist: Dec 1917.

74 *'I love you . . . ':* VHE to MH (18? May 1919), *L*, i, 351.

74 *'Yr. lover':* (8 June 1932), *L*, vi, 277.

74 *some women fall in love with their own sex:* (Jan 1920). *L*, i, 437n.

75 *Lady Ottoline's list of women:* Seymour, 416.

75 *OM cut her hair:* Ibid.

75 *'cinema acting':* VHE to MH (13 Mar 1918), *L*, i, 254.

76 *'there was a civilisation here':* To Max Bodenheim (2 Jan 1921), *L*, i, 532.

76 *'to understand you':* TSE to MH (11? July 1919), *L*, i, 379.

76 *'the heights':* Very near the end of TSE's life, on 11 Nov 1964, LW sent TSE a
beautiful statement including this observation. *The Letters of Leonard Woolf*, ed.
Frederic Spotts, 534.

77 *an explorer, not an expounder:* CFQ, 15.

78 *'irremovable mask':* A. N. Wilson's striking phrase in *The Mystery of Charles Dickens*
is 'irremovable carapace', 34.

78 *'I have acquired . . . ':* TSE to J. H. Woods at Harvard (21 Apr 1919), *L*, i, 339.

78 *Aiken on the changed TSE:* Ushant (Boston: Little, Brown, 1952), 215.

78 *TSE concurred with criticism of VW:* He confided the ensuing Bloomsbury
drama to his cousin Eleanor Hinkley, with himself cast as an unknowing
American drawn comically into the fearsome intricacies of this foreign set.
(17 June 1919), *L*, i, 363–4.

78 *'a stick':* VW/*Diary* (10 Apr 1919), i, 262.

79 *'the driving power':* VW/*Diary* (5 Dec 1920), ii, 77.

79 *TSE's faint praise of VW: After Strange Gods.* See also 'The Contemporary Novel',
Houghton: bMS 1691.14 (35). Commissioned in 1926, this was written in
English and then translated as 'Le roman anglais contemporain' for the
Nouvelle revue française (1927), repr. *Prose*, iii, with the unpublished original essay
in English, 83–94.

80 *VW noticed TSE's eyes, etc:* VW/*Diary* (19 Sept 1920), ii, 67. Later, *Diary*, iv, describes
the jewelled eyes of a toad.

80 *TSE neglected VW as writer:* VW/*Diary* (20 Sept 1920), ii, 67.

80 *'I do not in my heart admire her work':* TSE to EH (7 Apr 1931), box 2.

80 *'scimitar keenness':* VW/*Diary* (10 Sept 1933), iv, 178.

80 *'as I never had a favour from that man . . . ':* VW to Quentin Bell (26 July 1933), VW/
Letters, v, 207.

80 *'well-water in him . . . ':* VW/*Diary* (10 Sept 1933), iv, 178.

81   *'happiest with the Woolfs'*: TSE to EH (7 Apr 1931). He spoke further of the
      Bloomsbury Group as his own set. TSE to EH (26 Jan 1932).
81   *'Tom . . . is very like myself'*. VW/*Diary* (26 Sept 1937), v, 112.

6: CONFIDING LINES

82   *'rather lovely'*: TSE reminiscing to EH (12 May 1931). He does not say when
      Noyes's visit took place.
82   *'I hope it was a nice letter'*: (17 June 1919), *L*, i, 365.
83   *discarded stanza*: *IMH*, 365. 'Whispers of Immortality' was published in 1918.
83   *Pipit as a little songbird*: *Poems/R&M*, i, 507. Jewel Spears Brooker (email on 15
      Jan 2021) links the songbird with TSE's calling EH 'Bird' or 'Birdie'. He also
      calls her 'dove' (linked to the hidden dove of 'Difficulties of a Statesman')
      and 'my nightingale'. There is the hermit thrush of *WL* and the thrush of
      BN. Pipits are monogamous, unlike Lucretia Borgia. Epigraph to this poem
      from Villon refers to shame in the thirtieth year of the poet's life. This may
      allude to the thirtieth year of TSE's life, which had just begun when his
      wife committed adultery in October 1917.
84   *Pipit's identity coming to light*: TSE to EH (3 Nov 1930), box 1, f. 1.
85   *'my love for you . . . '*: TSE to EH (3 Nov 1930), box 1, f. 1.
85   *the Borgias*: Lucrezia Borgia's first husband proved impotent, which allowed
      that marriage to be annulled; another of her husbands died in suspicious
      circumstances. There's little point in tracking facts about Lucrezia
      because, like most of Eliot's allusions, it's twisted to fit his purpose. No one
      knows for sure about the actual Lucrezia who died in 1519, except that her
      father was a cardinal who became pope and, though illegitimate, she was
      regarded as a prize in the European marriage market of the late fifteenth
      and early sixteenth century.
85   *Piccarda*: With thanks to Isobel Dixon for relevant facts. Also for 'three big
      alluring nouns' in our collaborative reading of 'A Cooking Egg'.
86   *title of the music for* Spectre: *Invitation to the Dance*, Op. 65, is a piano piece in rondo
      form written by Carl Maria von Weber in 1819. It is also well known in the
      1841 orchestration by Hector Berlioz. See Chapter 3, above.
86   *1919 date of 'A Cooking Egg'*: TSE did not date this poem, and *Poems/R&M*, i,
      510, was under the impression that TSE read 'A Cooking Egg' on 12 Dec
      1917 at Lady Colefax's fundraising event. The source for this was Richard
      Aldington's memoir, *Life for Life's Sake*, but this states, p. 204, that TSE's
      reading of this poem in fact took place *after* the war, during an event
      arranged by the Sitwells. Since TSE usually published new poems fairly
      quickly, I was surprised by the apparent gap between Dec 1917 (or earlier
      that year) and the *Coterie* publication of 'A Cooking Egg' in May 1919. If it
      already existed, why not include it with the poems printed in March 1919
      by the Hogarth Press? This suggests the poem was written too late for
      inclusion, some time between Feb and Mar 1919.
87   *'I tried to pretend . . . '*: TSE to EH later, 1930–1.
88   *'an affair'*: VHE to MH (27 Aug 1919), while TSE was in France. Ann Pasternak
      Slater has re-dated this sole record of the Eliots making love, *Sparrow*, 87–8,
      during what VHE calls 'the Peace weekend', 18–20 July 1919, with a public
      holiday on 19th to celebrate the Versailles Treaty.

88 *'natural sincerity'*: Schiff to VHE (9 Dec 1921), *L*, i, 612.

89 *VHE 'a dear'*: So Abigail Eliot wrote to her mother Mary May Eliot (4 Jan 1920). Abigail Eliot Papers, Schlesinger Library: MC327, f. 17. In 1926, TSE's niece Dodo (Charlotte Eliot Smith's daughter) took to VHE in the same way, and she too called her a dear.

89 *Mansfield's report on the Eliots:* To Violet Schiff (14 May 1920), *L*, i, 473, n.1. and quoted in *Sparrow*, 104–5.

90 *VHE to TSE while he was in France:* (16 and 20 Aug 1920), *L*, i, 492–3.

90 *line cut from exchange in WL:* II: *WL/facs*, 12.

90 *like the La Figlia poem:* Anthony Cuda points out in his lecture, 'Back, late, from the hyacinth garden' (11 July 2022) that the hyacinth garden echoes a scene TSE had tried to write several times, going back to 'Song' in 1907 and 'La Figlia' in 1912. Cuda showed how repeatedly Eliot's grammar counters a possible future with the conditional perfect, so that what might have been would never have happened.

91 *song when love was about to take off:* Tristan und Isolde, Act I.

91 *"Oed und leer das Meer':* Tristan und Isolde, Act III.

91 *early in 1921:* Wyndham Lewis reported to Schiff (7 Feb 1921) that TSE had completed four parts of the poem he'd had in mind. Seamus Perry (lecture on 'Eliot in Margate', 2022) surmised that it would have been the four sections of *WL*: I.

91 *inability to speak:* The personal link with *WL* is made by Frances Dickey, 'Let the Record Speak', *Twentieth-Century Literature* (Dec 2020), 436.

92 *'put so much of his life into it':* CCE to Thomas Lamb Eliot (7 May 1923), *L* ii, 124. (TSE's letter to CCE has not survived.)

92 *'my life and work will be misunderstood . . .':* TSE to EH (15 Mar 1932), box 2, f. 8.

7: A PRIVATE WASTELAND

93 *VHE on WL as part of her:* To Sydney Schiff (16 Oct 1922), *L*, i, 765.

93–4 *TSE's dependence on VHE in editing WL:* Jewel Spears Brooker, 'Dialectical Collaboration: Editing *WL*' in *The Cambridge Companion to The Waste Land*, 106–7, excels on the opposite tugs between VHE's and Pound's editing. VHE's input, she says, came nine months before. Citing VHE's summer outburst to HWE, 'be personal', she brings out the autobiographical elements, reinforced by 'WONDERFUL', whereas Pound depersonalises and cuts what's too close to the Prufrock-Portrait of a Lady phase of personal writing.

94 *'horror' of politics:* TSE to Richard Aldington (7 Apr 1921), *L*, i, 550.

94 *Eliot family reunion in London:* See Abigail Eliot Papers, Schlesinger Library, MC 327, box 2. f. 20.

96 *Nancy Cunard:* her identity can't be verified without a doubt, but her biographers have collected circumstantial evidence. Anne Chisholm's suggestion has been substantiated by Lois Gordon, *Nancy Cunard* and Anne de Courcy, *Five Love Affairs and a Friendship*.

96 *biographical details of Cunard, including dates:* Generously shared by Anne de Courcy in Nov 2020, before publication. De Courcy, *Five Love Affairs and a Friendship*, 80–1.

96 *TSE's green powder:* TSE to EH (14 July 1932), box 3, f. 4. The date of the Cunard

parties is not mentioned, only that TSE was young at the time. He wore the
powder to Lady Rothermere's parties as well.

96   *'Burbank with a Baedeker': Poems/TSE*, 32–3.

96   *Fresca as Cleopatra:* 'The barge she sat in, like a burnish'd throne, / Burned on
the water . . .'. Shakespeare, *Antony and Cleopatra*, Act II, ii.

96   *interrupted grail quest:* 'The Tale of the Sankgreal' (from French sources), tale
III of Sir Perceval in Sir Thomas Malory's *Works*, ed. Eugène Vinaver (OUP,
1971), 550.

97   *re-done portrait of Fresca.* VHE's 'Letters of the Moment: II', *C* (1924). John
Haffenden discovered an early, 27-line draft of the Fresca couplets in TSE's
hand amongst VHE's papers in the Bodleian Library, *PN Review*, 175, vol. 33/5
(May–June 2007), 18–23. There is no conclusive answer to the question who
wrote this. Collaboration with TSE is plausible at a time when he touched
up VHE's writings. Haffenden brings out VHE's independence, lightness
of touch, geniality and tact; also her avoidance of TSE's misogyny and
distaste for the female body. 'I think it's almost certain that Vivien tinkered
with the verses by herself – precisely in order to modify their purport and
tone.' Ann Pasternak Slater prints the *C* couplets (*Sparrow*, 522), and suggests
(p. 631) 'Vivien had no hand in them'. They were published with VHE's
pseudonymous and genderless initials, FM, certainly with TSE's assent
as editor.

98   *VHE to MH from Paris:* (20? Dec 1921), *L*, i, 618–19.

99   *alternative to the Unreal City:* TSE to Russell (15 Oct 1923), *L*, ii, 257. 'Part V which
in my opinion is not only the best part, but the only part that justifies the
whole, at all.' In the finale TSE, in his trance, reaches towards an unstated
reality. He spoke about this absence from reality to MT (22 Jan 1953):
'sometimes, because I cannot express the reality I have to take refuge in
unrealities'. *MME*, 154.

99   *TSE's grateful thoughts of VHE:* TSE to HWE (13 Dec 1921) from Lausanne, *L*, i, 614.

100 *Cunard's version of what happened with TSE:* To JDH (3 March 1965), Humanities
Research Center, Texas, box 6, f. 4. Cited by Lois Gordon. After TSE's death
Cunard sent a prose poem to JDH. 'The Letter', cited by Anne de Courcy.

101 *'Not every life's moment . . .':* With thanks again to Anne de Courcy.

101 *TSE's version:* TSE to EH, box 1, f. 1. He offered a somewhat different version to
GF (18 Sept 1927), *L*, iii, 712. No name mentioned. Reportedly, he had enjoyed
'adultery' and had repented.

101 *'The Life of a Great Sinner: The Plan of the Novel':* VW and S. S. Koteliansky,
Translations from the Russian, ed. Stuart N. Clarke (Virginia Woolf Society of
Great Britain, 2006), 53–72.

101 *TSE's belief that Dostoevsky's Sinner outdid WL:* TSE to Kot (11 Jan 1923), *L*, ii, 10.

102 *TSE living in a novel by Dostoevsky:* TSE to Eleanor Hinkley (23 July 1917), *L*, i, 210.

103 *WL as grail quest:* CCE to Thomas Lamb Eliot (7 May 1923), *L*, ii, 124.

103 *TSE read WL to the Woolfs:* VW/*Diary*, ii, 178.

104 *VW on his 'eel' quality:* Ibid., 170–1.

104 *Quinn's support for TSE:* In return, TSE gave Quinn the *WL* manuscript and
a notebook of early poems with some laid in typescript drafts of poems.
It was thought these had disappeared, but were discovered in the Berg
Collection by a new curator, Lola Szladits, in the late sixties.

104   '– *just* mad *to see it*': VHE to TSE, *L*, iii, 8–9.
105   *VHE 'utterly worn out*': TSE to MH (26 Aug 1923, *L*, ii, 199.
106   '*still gasping*': (20 May 1923), *L*, ii, 140.
106   '*Medicine à la Mode*': *Sparrow*, 618, 730.
106   '*crumbling*': CCE reporting TSE to HWE (29 Mar 1923), *L*, ii, 95.

8: A SIGHTING IN ECCLESTON SQUARE

108   *EH's drama courses*: Curriculum vitae (*c.* 1930). Copy in Smith College Archives.
109   *1923 date of meeting of EH and TSE in London*: This date can't be verified. *NWEH*
        gives the date as 1922. EH's memory for dates is less accurate than Eliot's.
        Without stating a date, he recalls in a letter of 1930 to EH that their last
        meeting had been six years earlier. This would make the date 1924, but
        there is evidence for 1923 as the date EH went to London in an article by Phil
        Hanrahan, 'T. S. Eliot in Love', *Milwaukee* (Nov 1989), cited in *IL*, 571.
109   *EH reminded TSE of the unanswered question*: TSE to EH (18 Sept 1931), box 2. Eliot
        quotes her words back to her.
110   *Passages from Arnaut Daniel in the* Purgatorio *and Brunetto Latini in the* Inferno: TSE
        repeated these Dantean passages. Brunetto Latini speaks of *Il Tesoro* (*The*
        Treasure), Dante, *Inferno*, Canto XV, 119–20. TSE repeated the inscription in
        a copy of *WL* he gave to GF (27 May 1925) and in a letter of thanks for books
        given to him by MH (27 Sept 1928). In his future poetry he would return
        repeatedly to the *Ara vos prec* plea for pity in *Purgatorio*, Canto XXXVI.
111   '*hell*': TSE to Pound (20 and *c.* 27 May 1923), *L*, ii, 140, 141.
111   *conducting 'a conversation with spectres*': *Prose*, ii, 503–12. Unpublished in TSE's
        lifetime, this significant eight-page typescript is ostensibly on the
        seventeenth-century dramatist Chapman, intended as a preface to a book
        on Elizabethan dramatists. TSE began planning a series on Elizabethan
        drama in Sept 1923, when he told VW, as his publisher, that he hoped to
        work solely on it and his verse play over the winter (*L*, ii, 214). He rewrote
        this piece twice before the end of 1923, then scrapped it. It was then
        reconceived as a paper read to the Cambridge Literary Society in Nov 1924.
        See also TSE's explanatory letter to OM on 30 Nov 1924.

9: FIGHTS TO THE DEATH

112   '*we could die with less effort in London*': (6 Apr 1923), *L*, ii, 103.
112   *VHE's story, 'The Paralysed Woman*': *Sparrow*, 579–88, 658–60. Ann Pasternak Slater
        shows that the story was conceived when the Eliots rented a high-up flat
        in Eastbourne in 1924. Assistants Irene Pearl Fassett and Jack Culpin were
        there, both of whom appear in the story. TSE commuted from London for
        weekends, as André does in the story.
112   Holy Dying: By Jeremy Taylor (1651).
112   '*I am useless and better dead*': TSE recalled VHE's words to MT (28 Oct 1954 and
        again in Dec 1955), *MME*, 190, 215.
113   *VHE 'nearly was the death of me*': 'Statement by TSE on the opening of the
        Emily Hale Letters at Princeton' (written 25 Nov 1960), released to the public
        2 Jan 2020.
113   '*fireside*' *journal*: GF to TSE (9 Mar 1925) *L*, ii, 599.
113   *VHE's sketches in the manner of Mansfield*: VHE deplored Mansfield, following

her husband's cue, yet VHE's slice-of-life treatment of domestic scenes, showing the futility of lives going nowhere, as developed by Chekhov and his follower, Mansfield, shows an influence, even if unconscious. The difference is that VHE is more subjective, in the manner of TSE. (*Sparrow*, 592).

113   *VHE's unpublished fragment:* 'Sibylla's Fear of a Tête a Tête', *Sparrow*, 669.

114   *'the damage that people have done her';* 'has killed *V*'; *etc:* TSE to Murry (Apr 1925), *L*, ii, 627–8. 'I have deliberately killed my senses' repeats the confiding line at the close of 'Gerontion' in 1919.

115   *Murry advised TSE:* (16? Apr 1925), *L*, ii, 631.

115   *'I know I have killed her':* To Murry (mid-Apr 1925), *L*, ii, 632.

116   *'I have championed you . . . ':* TSE to Marianne Moore (18 June 1925), *L*, ii, 682. Ann Pasternak Slater makes a plausible case for VHE writing this confrontational letter, not TSE. There is no proof, but it's likely that TSE shared VHE's feeling and that the letter is infused with it.

116   *VHE's allegation about Lucy Thayer:* VHE to Pound, *L*, ii, 684–5.

116   Sweeney Agonistes: TSE had had this verse drama in mind from 1920 when he mentioned to VW his wish to do a play involving the four characters of Sweeney. He had begun it in Sept 1923. Two scenes were published in *C* (Nov 1926 and Jan 1927).

116   *VHE on 'good' marriage, including 'sexual relations':* *L*, ii, 772–3.

117   *'imprisonment', 'oubliette':* (25 Nov 1925), *L*, ii, 787–8.

117   *TSE feared friends believed VHE:* Recalled to MT (28 Oct 954), PRS.

117   *VHE's threat to sue:* OM heard this from Russell. OM's Journal (3 Mar 1926), Goodman Papers, British Library Add Ms 88886/04/034. Cited by Carole Seymour-Jones, *Painted Shadow*, 416–17 and *L*, iii, 98n.

118   *Dickens performing Sikes:* A. N. Wilson, *The Mystery of Charles Dickens*, recreates this vividly.

119   *'menace':* VHE to Murry (July 1926), *L*, iii, 223–4.

120   *'perque domos ditis vacuas':* By 'FM'. *Poems/R&M*, i, 1167–8 notes the title from Virgil, *Aeneid*, VI, 269, describing the entrance to Hades. Fair copy (*c*. 1925) in VHE Papers in Bodleian Library: c. 624. f. 10. *Sparrow*, 631, gives the date as *c*. 1924. Unpublished in VHE's lifetime.

120   *VHE's poem like Eliot:* See TSE's slighter early poem, 'In silent corridors of death', undated, unpublished in his lifetime, *Poems/R&M*, i, 275–6.

120   *VHE implored strangers:* Recalled by TSE to EH (18 Aug 1932). From a letter HWE sent his mother, dated 4 June 1926, in Houghton, it appears that TSE and VHE parted with HWE and Theresa at Milan station. This can't be verified because HWE's letter spares his mother by leaving out VHE's scene.

121   *'soaked in bromides':* Explanation to HWE in July 1926. Though a deranged VHE became the standard view of TSE's contemporaries, and the conclusion handed on to posterity, there is evidence (see note below on VHE divining her husband's mind) that the truth, implicating Eliot in VHE's terrified state of mind, is more complex. Noteworthy is the fact that TSE induced his wife's doctor to believe that he was his wife's helpless victim, her captive in a dungeon, in the face of the fact that VHE was the one who, in actuality, was in danger of being shut up for good. This could happen only if there were a medical and legal consensus that she was permanently out of her mind.

122   *'I managed . . . ':* VHE, writing from Malmaison, to Murry (6 July 1926),
       L, iii, 208.

122   *divined her husband's mind:* TSE to HWE (30 Aug 1927), *L*, iii, 674. The date of the
       following insight into TSE's wish is exactly eleven years before it came to
       pass. 'You will say: kinder to her, and far better for me, to put her away in
       a Home at once. But that is difficult in England, except when the patient is
       willing.' English doctors, he goes on, are 'scared pissless about committing
       people to asylums'. From this it can be inferred that VHE was not paranoid
       in fearing what did eventually befall her.

122   *'the kink in my brain':* TSE to HWE (2 Jan 1923), *L*, ii, 5.

122   *'emotional derangement':* TSE to Aldington (6 Nov 1921), *L*, i, 603.

122   *'a great many mistakes':* To Pound (15 Nov 1922), *L*, i, 788.

122   *'in a state of dark, dry death':* TSE to EH (7 Apr 1931), box 1, f. 4. He says this was
       about five years before the date he was writing, which makes the date *c.* 1926.
       His memory for dates was exceptionally accurate.

123   *VHE at Divonne-les-Bains:* Gordon George, pseudonym Robert Sencourt, *T. S.
       Eliot: A Memoir* (1971).

123   *third person in the marriage:* TSE to EH (4 Feb 1931) assured her that the failure
       of his marriage had nothing to do with her. The context was the question
       whether their renewed tie is 'wrong'.

123   *the blackest moment of his life: L*, ii, 592.

123–4 *the idea of perfection in the twelfth and thirteenth centuries:* TSE to Herbert Read
       from La Turbie (11 Dec 1925), *L*, ii, 797. The context is his thinking of his
       forthcoming Clark lectures in Cambridge, UK.

124   *TSE planned to write a 'Hymn to the Virgin':* TSE to Marguerite Caetani, *L*, iii, 260.

124   *'Salutation':* Eventually part II of *AW*.

125   *Olga's infatuation with EH:* The two love-letters came in Jan–Feb 1927 when EH
       was preparing to sail to Rome. EH showed TSE these letters early in 1937.

10: 'ROSE OF MEMORY'

127   *Margaret Thorp on TSE:* Untitled impressions and *pensées*. Thorp Papers, box 14.

128   *belated:* Anthony Cuda has lectured brilliantly on 'Belatedness' in TSE.

128   Marina *as TSE's favourite:* He said this to Aurelia Bolliger in 1931–2, Bolliger
       Papers, Bryn Mawr.

128   *granite islands:* Specifically Roque Island, off the coast of Maine, where TSE
       used to sail. He put this in by hand on a draft of *Marina* in the Bodleian
       Library, Oxford.

128   *'something very strong . . . ':* TSE to EH (18 Sept 1931), box 2, f. 1.

129   *'an unusual spiritual maturity' and 'beautiful':* TSE to EH, first love-letter
       (postmarked 3 Oct 1930), box 1, f. 1.

129   *'I am heartily sorry . . . ':* Ibid.

129   *TSE's link of AW with EH:* Begun with 'Salutation' in Dec 1927 and published as
       a whole in Apr 1930.

129   *'Lady of silences' and 'Rose of memory':* Lines in 'Salutation'.

130   *'multifoliate rose': Paradiso*, Canto XXX. At apex of Heaven, the empyrean, Dante
       sees an enormous rose, the petals of which are the souls of the faithful. All
       the souls Dante has met in Heaven, including Beatrice, have their home in
       this rose. Angels fly around the rose like bees, distributing peace and love.

131   *lecture on Dantean love:* Clark Lectures, Trinity College, Cambridge, 1926,
       published as *Varieties of Metaphysical Poetry*, ed. Ronald Schuchard (1993).

132   *'sign':* Lost to Gerontion who longs for a sign. The interconnections between
       TSE's poems bear out his idea that we have to read all a writer's works
       to understand any one of them (speaking of Shakespeare in essay, 'John
       Ford', in *SE*).

132   *disappointment with AW:* TSE to A. L. Rowse (14 May 1930), *L*, v, 179.

136   *'Your outcasted friend':* VHE to OM (31 Jan 1928), *L*, iv, 28.

136   *'If you hear . . . murdered':* *L*, iv, 'Biographical Commentary', xviii.

136   *EH asked if anything could improve TSE's marriage:* TSE to EH (4 Mar 1931).
       Characteristically, he takes time to consider a difficult question and then
       replies on 2 May 1931.

137   *'monastic':* Robert Sencourt (real name: Gordon George), *T. S. Eliot: A Memoir*
       (1971), 112, 120. He stayed with the Eliots in Oct 1930, the month when TSE was
       waiting for EH's verdict on a future relationship.

137   *tea with the Woolfs:* VW/*Letters*, v, 370–1. Eliot gave VW's letter to EH, who gave
       it to her friend, Ruth George, who taught English literature at Scripps
       College, California. The letter was left to Scripps College.

138   *'hornets'; TSE 'leaden and sinister':* VW/*Diary* (8 Nov 1930), iii, 331.

138   *difficult to have VHE certified:* TSE to HWE (30 Aug 1927), *L*, iii, 674. See
       Chapter 9, above.

140   *the Master of University College to TSE:* TSE to EH (10 Jan 1931), box 1.
       Background to the exchange and to TSE's choice of the Bodleian Library:
       on 16 Dec 1929, TSE had replied to an initiative on the part of the Master,
       Sir Michael Sadler, about preserving a manuscript in the Bodleian
       Library: he explained (*L*, iv, 714–15) that his early manuscripts, including
       WL, were in the John Quinn collection in NY. He offered to write out a
       fair copy of *AW*.

140   *'favourable light':* TSE to EH (12 Jan 1931), box 1.

141   *'There will be so much in existence . . . ':* TSE to EH (19 Feb 1932), box 2, f. 7

141   *'what I do not yet understand . . . '; 'selfish motive'; and misunderstood always:* TSE to EH (15
       Mar 1932), box 2, f. 8.

142   *'canker':* Ibid. This is the letter where he argues that his life and work would
       be 'misunderstood until the end of time'.

142   *'entrust [letters] to Thorp . . . ':* TSE to EH (6 July 1932), box 3, f. 4. The letters were
       her 'property'.

143   *GF an alternative to Thorp:* TSE to EH. TSE had already given the Bodleian
       a few manuscripts of poems via Sir Michael Sadler, the Master of
       University College.

143   The Aspern Papers: TSE to EH (6 Mar 1933). The class was English 26: English
       Literature from 1890 to the Present Day'. For his lecture notes see *Prose*,
       iv, 771–3.

143   *relations 'peculiar':* TSE to EH (30 Apr 1933), box 4, f. 2.

144   'I might have thrown poor words away': 'Words', Yeats, *Collected Poems*, 100–1.

II: ACTOR AND MUSE

145   *TSE's low view of theatre people:* TSE to EH (8 Dec 1930).

145   *'And so you are now . . . ':* TSE to EH (New Year's Day 1931) addressing her as 'My

dear Saint'. Linn Cary Mehta asked a perceptive question (on 4 Jan 2020): was Eliot really writing to Emily Hale?

145 *make-up would not show her beauty 'to advantage!'*: TSE to EH (5 Jan 1932), box 2, f. 6. He refers to the play again on 19 Feb 1932, pleased to hear of its success.

146 *'I should like to see you in the role of Beatrice!'*: TSE to EH (7 Sept 1931), box 2, f. 1.

146 *TSE advising strong female roles*: TSE to EH (18 May 1931), box 1, f. 5.

146 *'madonna Olivia'*: TSE to EH (13 Feb 1931), box 1, f. 2.

146 *TSE responding to Berkeley Square*: TSE to EH (4 Dec 1931), box 2, f. 5.

147 *TSE to EH, discussing her poem on a painting*: TSE to EH (31 Aug and 4 Sept 1931), box 2, f. 1.

147 *TSE would like to write every day*: TSE to EH (7 Jan 1931), box 1.

147 *'a dizzy sense of awe'*: Ibid.

147 *'Well, my paragon . . . '*: TSE to EH (27 Jan 1931), box 1.

148 *'Terminate torment . . . '*: 'Salutation', later *AW*: II.

148 *'clam-like'*: TSE to EH (27 Jan 1931), box 1.

149 *'a certain kind of corrupt vulgarity'*: TSE to EH (23 Feb 1931), box 1, f. 2.

149 *'Turtle'*: TSE to EH (31 Apr 1931). A cherished turtledove recalls the songbird Pipit. Is the bird image related to the nightingale (another endearment for EH) and the hermit thrush of the water-dripping song in *WL*? Yet to come is the bird call in *BN*: I. Might all these birds be related in some sense to EH?

149 *'Hidden under the . . . '*: *Poems/R&M*, 275. Dated 1912–13 by Stayer, 292.

149 *'O hidden under the dove's wing'*: 'Triumphal March', *Poems/TSE*, 126. TSE addressed EH as 'Dove' in letters.

151 *'I like Beethoven so much . . . '*: TSE to EH, box 1, f. 3. TSE repeats the gist of this twelve days later, on 28 March, to Stephen Spender, where he speaks of a wish to go beyond poetry as Beethoven in the late quartets wished to go beyond music. TSE repeats the idea a third time in a lecture he did not publish on 'English Poets as Letter Writers' delivered at Yale on 23 Feb 1933. *Prose*, iv, 848: 'To get beyond poetry, as Beethoven, in his later works, strove to get beyond music.'

151.* *TSE on Tchaikovsky's quartets*: TSE to EH (12 May 1931), box 1, f. 5.

151.* *TSE on the Razumovsky quartet*: See Chapter 11, below.

152 *'blast'*: TSE to EH (17 Dec 1931), box 2, f. 5.

153 *TSE's homily on humility*: TSE to EH (11 August 1931), box 2, f. 1.

153 *'I should like to send you a good kiss'*: TSE to EH (31 Aug 1931), box 2, f. 1.

153 *turned talk back to himself*: TSE to EH (7 Sept 1931), box 2, f. 1.

155 *impulse to turn the job down*: TSE to EH (28 Aug 1931), box 2, f. 1.

155 *'I don't know . . . see you'*: TSE to EH (8 Dec 1931), box 2, f. 5.

156 *'pattern' in existence*: TSE to EH (31 Dec 1931), box 2, f. 5.

156 *EH accepted the Scripps post*: TSE to EH (Feb 1932), box 2, f. 7.

156 *'You are just what I would have you be!'*: TSE to EH (16 Feb 1932).

156 *Penelope would take the best care*: TSE to EH (15 Jan 1932), box 2, f. 6.

156 *TSE worried about her*: TSE to EH (9 Feb 1932), box 2, f. 7.

156 *'O when will the creaking heart cease?'*: 'Lines to a Persian Cat', *Poems/R&M*, i, 141.

156 *'monkeyshines'*: TSE to EH (16 Feb 1932), box 2, f. 7.

156 *'violently' dependent*: TSE to EH (4 Mar 1932), box 2, f. 8.

157 *EH 'washed out'*: TSE to EH (24 Mar 1932), box 2, f. 8.

158 *TSE and the Thorps on sabbatical in London, 1931–32*: TSE to Thorps (25 Aug 1931),

Thorp Papers. The papers include Margaret Thorp's *pensées* and description of TSE and VHE, 1932, in her 'Journal'.

159   *VHE's party well-organised:* TSE to EH (15 Jan 1932), box 2, f. 6.

159   *TSE recalling* Tristan *performance with Margaret present:* TSE to EH (15 Jan 1932), box 2, f. 6.

159   *thinking 'of what we are to each other':* TSE to EH (2 Mar 1931), box 1, f. 3.

159   *TSE on EH's ears and neck:* TSE to EH (20 Jan 1931), box 1.

159   *'"Too late?"':* TSE to EH (18 Aug 1931), written by hand at the bottom of this letter.

160   *'western star':* TSE to EH (3 Feb 1931), box 1.

160   *nursing EH; 'cling':* TSE to EH (4 and 10 Feb 1931), box 1.

160   *dab eau de cologne:* While in Cambridge, Massachusetts, TSE repeats (15 Oct 1932) his nursing fantasy, box 3, f. 6.

160   *TSE freed from strain of celibacy:* TSE to EH (4 Feb 1931), box 1.

160   *'operation without anesthetic':* TSE to EH (18 Aug 1931), box 1, f. 4

161   *absent presence:* I owe this phrase to Rosie Alison (email, Jan 2020).

161   *fount; 'new verse'; 'vision':* AW: IV: 'the fountain sprang up'. 'The new years walk, restoring . . . / With new verse the ancient rhyme.' 'The unread vision in the higher dream'.

12: A QUESTION OF DIVORCE

162   *inventory of TSE's books:* A copy in the Bodleian Library, discovered by Robert Crawford, who wrote about it to EVE in 1983. *L*, vi, 274n.

163   *dreaded:* TSE to EH (23 Aug 1932), box 3, f. 5.

163   *Mirrlees on camera:* 'The Mysterious Mr Eliot' (3 Jan 1971), BBC TV.

163   *VHE 'ashy-white':* Hope Mirrlees papers, discovered by Clare Reihill. With thanks for passing this on.

164   *bag including lecture notes:* TSE told HWE the bag contained his pyjamas and toothbrush, and this got around, but Monro, who was there, denied she had been inaccurate.

165   *punishment and disgrace:* TSE to EH (19 Nov 1933), box 5, f. 2.

165   *'a void'; 'toward asceticism or sensuality':* (12 Feb 1929), *L*, iv, 432–3.

166   *'vivacious and ornamental':* Margaret Thorp reporting to EH (Jan 1934), Thorp Papers.

166–7   *TSE's sermon to EH:* EH's word repeated in his reply to her (3 May 1932), box 3, f. 2.

167   *EH laid TSE flat:* TSE to EH (13 May 1932), box 3, f. 2.

167   *Age had not diminished his passions:* Ibid.

167   *TSE's assent to tour with EH:* TSE to EH (21 June 1932), box 3, f. 3.

167   *a glimpse . . . beautiful ritual:* TSE to EH (31 May 1932), box 3, f. 2.

167   *retreat suggestion:* TSE to EH (14 June 1932), box 3, f. 3.

168   *Lady Ottoline on TSE in her journal:* (1 and 7 Apr 1934), British Library, cited *L*, vii, 131–2n.

168   *EH criticised* TSE's radio broadcasts: TSE to EH (13 May 1932), box 3, f. 2.

168   *'dear Lady Bird':* TSE to EH (28 June 1932), box 3, f. 3.

168   *EH's protests:* e.g. TSE to EH (26 July 1932), box 3, f. 4.

168   *Lady of silences:* AW: II.

168   *barbarous:* TSE to EH (21 June 1932), box 3, f. 3.

169 *Talking to her more frankly:* TSE to EH (20 Apr 1932), box 3, f. 2.

169 *inseparable from unsatisfied need:* TSE to EH (5 June 1932), box 3, f. 3.

169 *sacrifice of personal desire:* TSE to EH (13 May 1932), box 3, f. 2.

170 *natural vs unnatural debate:* TSE to EH (16 Aug 1932), box 3, f. 5.

170 *'crook':* TSE to EH (9 Sept 1932), box 3, f. 5.

170 *Prince Mirsky:* Otherwise called D. S. or Dmitry Mirsky. His full name was Dmitry Petrovich Svatopolk-Mirsky.

170 *'deep phobia of life':* 'Eliot and the End of Bourgeois Poetry'. Published originally in French as 'T. S. Eliot et la Fin de la Poesie Bourgeoise'. Enclosed to EH (20 Apr 1932), box 3, f. 2.

170 *TSE on memories of New England:* TSE to EH (24 Sept 1931), box 2, f. 2.

171 *'The Altar of the Dead':* James, *Complete Stories 1892–1898* (Library of America), 460. TSE also mentioned 'The Velvet Glove'.

171 *'The Friends of the Friends':* Original title was 'The Way It Came' (1896). Title revised 1909 for the New York Edition. The man and woman share certain traits and tastes, as well as an openness to the supernatural.

171 *'the greatest significance':* TSE repeats the attraction to these two tales to Stephen Spender, who wanted to write a book on James (9 May 1935), *L*, vii, 618: a person who gives himself completely to James, TSE says, will not ignore 'The Altar of the Dead' and 'a story which is to me of the greatest significance, *The Friends of the Friends*. I think that a thorough study of the latter would perhaps make otiose and irrelevant your questions about James's virility.'

172 *here he was an Eliot:* TSE to OM (14 Mar 1933), *L*, vi, 562.

172 *VW questioning TSE on where he was off to:* (15 Jan 1933), VW/*Letters*, v, 150–1, in reply to letter from TSE in Nov 1932.

172 *TSE on New Mexico:* TSE to F. O. Matthiessen (12 Mar 1935), *L*, vii, 552.

172 *TSE's arrival in Claremont:* Between 27 and 29 Dec. Editor John Haffenden gives both possible dates in the *Letters*.

172 *'a man of extremes':* Reported in Scripps paper, *Scripture* (12 Dec 1932). TSE, writing to GF in 1936, says that he was drawn to the 'extreme' of depravity and degradation. A Dostoevsky range. TSE told his brother of his affinity with men who were 'failures', which might in part explain his later identifications with Richard III and Charles I.

172 *TSE with eyes only for EH:* Margaret Thorp relayed this observation to EH (Jan 1933), Thorp Papers.

172 *photographs of TSE in EH's room:* Recalled by Laurabel Neville Hume. Scripps College archives.

172 *EH joked:* Recalled by Faith McAllister, Sept 1988. *IL*, 245, 578. The joke is about Boston exclusiveness and turns on a well-known saying that the Lowells speak only to the Cabots and the Cabots speak only to God.

172 *McSpad, recalling TSE and EH:* Letter to me (8 Sept 1986).

172 *EH to Margaret on TSE's visit:* (8–12 Jan 1933). Margaret Thorp (at 142 Nassau Street, Princeton) to EH, discussing what EH had told her of the feelings. TSE to EH, box 14, f. 2.

175 *outpouring to Alida, including 'the poison . . .' and 'hideous farce':* (26 Feb 1933), *L*, vi, 552–3.

175 *'I do not believe . . .':* TSE to OM (14 Mar 1933), *L*, vi, 563.

176 *'I like to . . . curse the people I am fondest of'*: Quoted by Michelle Taylor in
     New Yorker.

176 *'hatred of life'*: 'Cyril Tourneur', *SE*, 166.

176 *'the nightmare of evil'*: TSE to MT (24 June 1944). 221 letters in Houghton bMS
     Am 1691.2.

176 *'to talk thus wildly to you'*: TSE to EH (13 Jan 1939), box 9, f. 4.

176 *'abnormal state'*: TSE to EH (8 Oct 1937), box 8, f. 1. He expands on 'a kind
     of intemperate, feverish aggressiveness' and says that he would like to
     suppress all his lectures of that time because the feverishness had been out
     of proportion to his subject matter.

176 *'Two Masters'*: Substantially revised as 'The Modern Dilemma', *The Christian
     Register* (Boston), 19 Oct 1933, repr. *Prose*, iv, 810–16. on this. The conclusion
     of the lecture is quoted in *L*, vi, 582n. Jewel Spears Brooker, *Eliot's Dialectical
     Imagination*, Chapter 10, is particularly good.

177 *'the supernatural is the greatest reality'*: *Prose*, iv, 813.

177 *HWE shamed*: HWE to TSE (12 Sept 1935), *L*, vii, 754.

177 *'He is an actor'*: Edmund Wilson to Dos Passos, cited in *IL*, 253.

178 *TSE link of free-thinking Jews and Unitarians*: (10 May 1940), *L*, ix, xxviii, 518. He put
     it to J. V. Healy, who protested against antisemitism in these Page-Barbour
     lectures: 'The Jewish religion . . . shorn of its traditional practices,
     observances and Messianism . . . tends to become a mild and colourless
     form of Unitarianism.'

178 *model dress 'for Tom's return'*: Diary (4 Dec 1934), www.tseliot.com/vivien. Quoted
     in *Sparrow*, 417.

178 *'shocking' neglect*: VHE to OM (31 Mar 1933), *L*, vi, 570–1.

178 *VHE named HWE as executor*: VHE to HWE (17 Mar 1933), *L*, vi, 564–5.

179 *brutal letter*: VW/Diary (10 July 1933), iv, 167. Jack Hutchinson came to a party at
     the Woolfs. VW reports, 'J. read one of Tom's last letters [to VHE], & describes
     it as a very cold & brutal document, saying he has made no money.'

13: A POSSUMA FOR TOM POSSUM

180 *photo of TSE in NH*: Sent to EH, box 4, f. 6. In *IL*.

181 *TSE's hideaway and Sukey's pram*: Photos sent to EH.

182 *photo of VHE*: Houghton MS Am 3041 (355).

182–3 *Abigail Eliot's visit to VHE in summer 1933*: From her memoirs, *A Heart of Grateful
       Trust*, 61.

183 *TSE's night dream of EH*: TSE to EH (9 Aug 1933), box 4, f. 7.

183 *'in solitude and silence'*: TSE to EH (11 Aug 1933), box 4, f. 7.

183 *EH on TSE to Seattle friend*: Mrs Krauss, writing from Europe, to EH (16 July
     1933), in TSE to EH, box 14, f. 2. The quotations are from Mrs Krauss's letter,
     repeating what EH had said.

183 *TSE's 'Last Will & Testament'*: Enclosed to EH (28 July 1933), box 4, f. 7.

184 *a nearby rose bush*: He calls it a rose garden to his brother (8 July 33), *L*, vi, 601.

184 *'rather a nuisance'*: TSE to EH (17 Aug 1933), box 4, f 7.

184 *'tender and passionate solicitude'*: TSE to EH (c. Sept 33), box 5, f. 2.

185 *TSE on Foucauld*: TSE to EH (1 Oct 1933), box 5, f. 1.

186 *Ada Sheffield writing to EH*: Dated 26 Oct 1933. EH retained this with TSE's letters
     to her in the Princeton collection.

187   *'a great toad'*: VW/*Diary*, iv, 208.

187   *'dissimulation'*: TSE to EH (24 July 1934), box 5, f. 5.

188   *TSE on the dominating people:* TSE to EH, written after the weekend, on his return to London (30 July 1934), box 5, f. 5.

188   *'by constantly pressing myself . . .'; 'tormented', etc:* TSE to EH (2 Aug 1934), TSE's comeback to EH's challenge of 1 August, box 5, f. 6.

189   *6 August:* TSE to EH, box 5, f. 6. In this reply, TSE quotes back some of EH's words and phrases.

191   *'what I stand for':* TSE quotes this accusation and underlines it to EH (17 Aug 1934), box 5, f. 6 (a folder covering Aug–Dec 1934).

191   *'bacchanalian':* TSE to EH (19 Sept 1934), box 5, f. 6.

191   *Beethoven's Razumovsky Quartet:* The F major quartet, Op. 59, no. 1, was commissioned by Prince Andrey Razumovsky, the Russian ambassador to Vienna, in 1806 and published in 1808.

192   *'a very twisted creature':* TSE to EH (19 Oct 1934).

192   *star sapphire ring:* EH recalls in letter to TSE, 16 Oct 1949: 'the first gift of such a personal character' and 'the beautiful star sapphire you gave me long ago on my birthday in Chichester!' There was certainly an intention to celebrate her birthday there and the ring was chosen in advance, but since they went to Chichester at the end of November, they either went there twice or the birthday visit was postponed.

192   *found EH entertaining:* TSE reporting afterwards to EH (13 Dec 1934), box 5, f. 6.

193   *EH's opinion on SA:* TSE to EH (8 Oct 1935), box 5, f. 3 (misfiled in the archive). He must be recalling this from the previous year because the date of this letter, at the time she is moving to London, is before she attends a rehearsal or performance in 1935.

193   *'Secret'; 'I live in Kensington . . .':* TSE to VW (3 Nov 1934), *L*, vii, 368. TSE invited VW to take tea with the Perkinses and suggested bringing *'an American friend'* to meet her.

193   *'respectable' china:* VW/*Diary* (31 Mar 1935), iv, 294. A tea party on 30 March appears to have been VW's first visit to his rooms.

193   *play about Furies a follow-on from SA:* TSE to Hallie Flanagan (9 Feb 1934) about starting 'something new of the same kind' as Sweeney, *L*, vii, 64. Early scenarios for *FR* in HWE Collection, Houghton bMS Am1691 (box 1).

194   *possession:* (8–10 Dec 1933), *L*, vi, 740. Theresa Eliot recalled this way of thinking about VHE, *L*, vi, 741n. Cited also in Tomlin, *T. S. Eliot*, 171, heard from Theresa Eliot: TSE suggested that mental disturbance gave way to something more horrible.

194   *'the oppressive gravity of mistakes':* The Europeans.

195   *'a part of herself':* 'Sibylla's Fear of a Tête a Tête', *Sparrow*, 669.

195   *signing her own death warrant:* GF to VHE, quoting her sentence (13 Jan 1934), *L*, vii, 30.

196   *30 November:* The date was traced by Helen Gardner, *CFQ*, 35. Her friend Elsie Duncan-Jones, daughter-in-law of the Dean of Chichester, Arthur Duncan-Jones, found TSE's signature, together with those of EH and the Revd and Mrs Perkins, in the visitors' book. EH gave her address as Scripps College, California.

196   *'only a POSSUMA can pet a possum':* TSE to Pound (29 Nov 1934), *L*, vii, 390.

196 *'a smile and shake of the hand'*: With thanks to Frances Dickey for spotting the connection.

197 *'What is the future . . . '*: TSE to EH (20 May 1932), box 3, f. 2.

14: 'WE'

198 *'Riven'*: VW/*Diary* (21 Nov 1934), iv, 262.

198 *'in this country . . . liberty'*: TSE to EH (3 Jan 1935), box 6, f. 1.

198–9 *VHE refused entry to men collecting TSE's property*: TSE to EH (9 Nov 1934).

199 *'I want to put the seriousness . . . '*: Same day, *L*, vii, 342.

199 *TSE's justification to Mary Hutchinson*: (20 Sept 1933), *L*, vi, 640.

199 *'If you meet my husband . . . '*: VHE to MHW (3 Sept 1935), *L*, vii, 732.

200 *VHE advertising*: On 18 September 1934 she put in a notice that Eliot had 'abandoned' her. *The Times* did not run the item.

200 *'shut up . . . I cannot get away'*: TSE to EH (22 Mar 1935), box 6, f. 1.

200 *hunted by the Furies*. TSE conceived of a latter-day Orestes (guilty of murder) in March 1935 and again to JDH on 2 May 1935.

200 *'I take notes . . . '*: *L*, vii, 540.

200 *Morley's liking for VHE*: 'Afterwards', *Sparrow*, 494.

201 *'MY dear Tom . . . '*: (14 July 1935), *L*, vii, 693.

201 *nine lines*: These lines, following the exit of the Second Tempter, were composed at the request of EMB to liven up the second Priest, and then cut as non-dramatic. In the 1970s Gardner discovered this from a draft in the McKeldin Library, University of Maryland. *CFQ*, 82.

201 *'right way'*; *'sanctuary'*; *'presumption'*: TSE to EH (25 Mar 1935), box 6, f. 1.

202 *burdened by women*: TSE had only £500 a year from Faber and contributed more than half to VHE. *L*, vii, 458 offers details: VHE's father left an estate of £30,000, which meant that VHE had *c.* £350 a year, plus one-third income from Irish rents (between 1927 and 1933 she received *c.* £569). Together with the £260 that TSE gave her annually, she had an ample income of nearly £600 a year. Her mother had £600 a year, so VHE would have more when her mother died, as well as the trust CCE had been compelled to make over to her, going against her husband's will with a codicil in VHE's favour. This made VHE better off than TSE's single sisters. TSE to HWE (21 Feb 1935), *L*, vii, 531: 'The notion of her having a considerably larger income than Marion or Margaret does not appeal to me.'

202 *'Olympian hypocrisy'*: TSE to EH (2 Apr 1935), box 6, f. 1.

202 *EH's lunch with TSE*: *L*, vii, 592.

203 *'We'*: 'Footfalls echo in the memory / Down the passage which we did not take / Into the rose-garden.' Draft of *MC* in spring 1935, which TSE repurposed for *BN* later that year. The rose-garden was at first imaginary, a follow-on from 'Rose of memory'. On 3 Oct 1935 TSE writes to EH of his pleasure in using 'we' instead of 'you' and 'I'.

203 *outing to the Ballet*: TSE habitually uses a capital B. Faber was due to publish book on ballet ((3 May 1935), *L*, vii) and TSE commissioned 'The Year in Ballet' from Rayner Heppenstall, *C*, xv, 57–64.

203 *'The Anniversary'*: *Poems/R&M*, i, 291, 1195, ii, 602. 'Miss Emily' was afterwards eliminated, as well as her visibility in a verse TSE wrote for her later in

the year, renamed 'A Country Walk'. Of a piece with an archive curated to eliminate EH from record.

204   *occurred again to TSE to give his Lady a dog:* TSE consulted his dog-loving friend Ralph Hodgson (now in Japan and married to Aurelia Bolliger): (11 May 1935), *L*, vii, 622. TSE does not name EH but alludes to Chekhov's 'The Lady with the Dog' (1899).

204   *her head on his shoulder:* This gesture, beginning in July, is recalled in a letter to EH on 29 Aug 1935.

204   *Furtwängler:* He made his debut with this work at Covent Garden on 20 May 1935. That night EH said 'something' to TSE about Tchaikovsky, relevant to her participation in *BN*. TSE recalled it as he completed the poem (16 Jan 1936), box 6, f. 6. This 'concert' figured along with an accumulation of 'moments' in EH's company in the run-up to the poem in the course of 1935.

204   *'O dark dark dark':* TSE quotes from Milton's *Samson Agonistes* in *EC*: III. That very summer TSE's family (Uncle Christopher and Abigail Eliot) visited to East Coker. Relayed to him directly when he had them together with niece Dodo for tea in London at the end of August.

205   *'I have said this already':* The sentence is crossed out.

·205   *lunch under a hawthorn tree:* As TSE recalled in letter to EH (July 1943).

205   *'The moment in the arbour where the rain beat':* *BN*: II.

205   *'the summer star-evening':* TSE to EH (10 Jan 1936), box 6, f. 6.

205   *lecture on letter-writing:* 'English Poets as Letter Writers', *Prose*, iv, 846–9.

206   *'My nightingale!':* Undated handwritten note from Ty Glyn in Wales. TSE said the nightingales were particularly good that summer in a letter to Ralph Hodgson (11 May 1935), *L*, vii, 622: 'The Nightingales HAVE been something extra this year I heard them all around Pikes Farm this last weekend that ever was singing all night and all day I never heard so many . . . though you know my convictions a good mockingbird can beat the nightingale all holler . . . and I think the hermit thrush superior on his own habitat . . . '

206   *favourite image:* Said in Oct 1946, box 12, f. 8.

207   *'The Lost Bower':* In 1973, Helen Gardner mentioned this source for *BN*, which she had recently discovered, along with others, *Alice in Wonderland* and Kipling's story, 'They'. *CFQ*, 40–1. The crest of a hill above the garden at Elizabeth Barrett's childhood home, Hope End, near Ledbury, in the Malvern Hills, was the scene of this poem and an actual experience.

207   *'I can only tolerate roses':* Handwritten addition to letter (4 Sept 1935), box 5, f. 2.

207   *date of visit to Burnt Norton:* TSE mentions this (undated) visit in a letter to EH from London on 10 September. Frances Dickey suggests this took place amongst the many excursions at the end of July. There is no proof, but it seems likely that the visit happened close to the date when TSE mentions the place. I agree with Dickey that the moments in late July infuse the moment of 'reality' experienced or imagined at Burnt Norton. That it was 'real' for TSE, and that it involved EH, is implied when he told her afterwards that *BN* is a love-poem of a special kind. Climactic lines, 'human kind / Cannot bear very much reality' originated with Becket speaking just before his martyrdom in *MC*: Part II (*Plays*, 43; *Poems/TSE*, 176).

15: INTIMACY

209   *TSE's appearance:* VW/*Diary*, iv, 343–4.

210   'A Valedictory': Poems/R&M, i, 292, in section of Uncollected Poems.

210   *Donne, 'A Valediction':* Written before Donne left on a journey to Continental Europe. *The Metaphysical Poets,* ed. Helen Gardner (Penguin, 1957), 71–2.

210   *'I was almost one of the family':* To Edith Perkins (11 Dec 1935), *L*, vii, 855.

211   *celebration of EH in his finest letter:* TSE to EH (30 Sept 1935), box 6, f. 3.

211   *'Cape Ann' sent to EH:* After it came out in December 1935.

211   *birds familiar to TSE:* He was a keen birdwatcher. His mother gave him *Birds of the Eastern United States* for his fourteenth birthday.

211   *garden known only to themselves:* TSE to EH (2 Aug 1943), box 12, f. 3. 'I have never heard of any reader of the poem finding it; and I don't see how they can unless we tell them.' TSE wrote to EH that he imagined Burnt Norton as a secret garden. He thought that no one but themselves would know of it. In fact, a boarding school for girls occupied Burnt Norton during the war, as noted by Gillian Avery in *The Best Kind of Girl.*

212   *yew for buttonhole:* TSE to EH (3 Oct 1935), box 6, f. 4.

212   *additions to TS of* BN: In pencil in the draft TSE sent to Morley and cancelled in ink on the proof copy sent to EH on 24 Mar 1936.

212   *happiest birthday: L*, vii, 780–1.

212   *'the full radiance':* Remembered Apr 1936. TSE to EH, box 6, f. 7.

213   *buttoning neck of her dress:* TSE to EH (9 Nov 1936), box 7, f. 3.

213   *rehearsal of* MC: TSE to EH (29 Oct 1935), box 6, f. 4.

213   *'collaborating':* TSE to EH (22 Oct 1935), box 6, f. 4.

213   *fancy to play opposite EH:* TSE to EH (Dec 1935), box 6, f. 4.

213   *Lady Ottoline at Windsor:* TSE to EH (20 October 1935), box 6, f. 4.

214   *did not have 'the intimacy of writing':* TSE to EH (22 Oct 1935), box 6, f. 4.

214   *'and can never be undone':* TSE to EH (30 Oct 1935).

214   *'companion':* TSE quotes the word back to EH on 3 Oct 1935.

214   *'natural':* TSE to EH (14 Nov 1935).

215   *TSE gave EH the typescript of his lecture:* Untitled. EH eventually gave this as a gift to Harvard. Houghton bMS Am 1691 (27).

215   *'More bitter than the love of youth':* The line is scribbled in pencil on the typescript Houghton bMS Am 1691 (20a) 'Words for an old man'. Published as 'Lines for an Old Man' (28 Nov 1935). Poems/R&M, i, 855. TSE claimed that his source was a detective story by R. Austin Freeman in which a man banged his head.

216   *EH sat with him while unwell:* Recalled 11 Feb 1936. TSE to EH, box 6, f. 6.

216   *their shoulders brushed:* Recalled Apr 1940. TSE to EH, box 10, f. 5.

216   *'the most intimate' excursion:* Recalled on 10 Jan 1936. TSE to EH, box 6, f. 6.

216   *countless kisses:* TSE to EH (22 Nov 1935), box 6, f. 4.

216   *'most beautiful body':* TSE to EH (22 Dec 1935), box 6, f. 4.

217   *'Rose of memory' stanza: AW:* II.

217   *'quite out of date':* OM's Journal (17 Mar 1934), cited *L*, vii, 80n.

217   *Woolf was put out:* VW herself could have loved Eliot, she admitted to her sister, if only they hadn't been in the 'sere and yellow leaf'. VW to VB (1936), *L*, vi, 59.

218   *EH's letter on VW to Ruth George:* Scripps College archives. Quoted in full in *IL*.

220　*pre-departure emotions:* Pre-departure love-letters are in box 6, f. 4.

220　*infusing intellectual ideas with intense emotional value:* HWE to TSE (12 Sept 1935), *L*, vii, 752.

220　*VHE sent out joint Christmas cards:* TSE to HWE (2 Feb 1936), *L*, viii, 52n.

221　*'gnaw like acid':* TSE to EH (3 Oct 1935).

221　*incorrect conjecture that EH stayed the night:* This was against their principles and disproved by statement on 11 Jan 1937, box 7, f. 4 where TSE recalls that EH 'came' to his room in the morning she was due to leave.

221　*'the Courtfield rooms belong to us':* TSE to EH (2 Jan 1936), box 6, f. 6.

222　*TSE on ring EH gave him:* TSE to EH (31 Dec 1935), box 6, f. 4, recalled on 3 Jan and 10 Jan 1936, box 6, f. 6. Quoted in *New Yorker* article by Michelle Taylor, 5 Dec 2020.

222　*record of their farewell scene:* TSE's letter addressed to EH's Liverpool hotel (11 Dec 1935).

223　*knelt together:* TSE recalled to EH (16 Jan 1936), box 6, f. 6.

16: 'THE WAY DOWN'

224　*EH 'frivolous and childish':* TSE quotes her words back to her (3 Jan 1936), box 6, f. 6.

224　*'That my Lady should love me . . . ':* TSE to EH (2 Jan 1936), box 6, f. 6.

224　*'ejaculations of ecstasy' and 'naturally':* Ibid.

224　*'breathe your breath':* TSE to EH (6 Jan 1936), box 6, f. 6.

225　*'my Self':* TSE to EH (2 Jan 1936), box 6, f. 6.

225　*'the blessings of intimacy':* TSE to EH (6 Jan 1936), box 6, f. 6.

225　*'puzzled':* To JDH (c. June 1936) and again to Edith Perkins (30 July 1936), *L*, viii, 312.

226　*'new period'; 'new kind of love poem'; BN done; and 'our' poem:* TSE to EH (13 and 16 Jan 1936), box 6, f. 6.

226　*'still point': BN:* II. Eliot's affinity for ballet had to do with the inner rhythm and emotion that gather when the dancer stills himself for action, what in ballet is called preparation. Susan Jones has explained how dancers apprehend and control the 'centre' as the origin of movement, its 'focal point', which in great performers is a strongly felt 'inner point'. At that centred moment, a dancer fills up with maximal energy, before he takes off. 'At the still point', *Literature, Modernism & Dance* (OUP, 2013), 235.

226　*18 November:* Date pinpointed, TSE to EH (16 Jan 1936), box 6, f. 6.

227　*discipline of St John of the Cross:* 'The soul cannot partake of the divine union unless it divests itself of the love of created beings.' At the very nadir of the Eliots' marriage in 1926, Eliot had quoted this as an epigraph to *Sweeney Agonistes.* Eliot's friends were taken aback. On 26 Oct 1936 TSE again stood by this precept, and on this date told EH it is the same as the epigraph to *Sweeney.*

229　*TSE on Ada:* TSE to EH (19 Feb 1936), box 6, f. 6.

230　*'Light' added to end of the poem:* TSE sent a draft of *BN* earlier to Morley, possibly the one Morley took to Brace in NY. Houghton bMS Am 1691.14 (34) with revisions in Eliot's hand. At the end, after 'waste time . . . ', TSE tried to repeat the effect of 'quick now' and 'loss' in the on-off flash of words spaced on the page.

First try:

Light
Light
Light of light

Gone

Then he contracts it:

Light
       Gone.

(He crossed out three repetitions of 'Light'.)

Finally, he gives up on this verbal experiment and leaves the finale as 'waste time'.

230   *a feeling of being alone*: To Paul Elmer More (11 Jan 1937), *L*, viii, 42.

230   *a really ascetic . . . order*: To Geoffrey Curtis (14 Feb 1936), *L*, viii, 66. See also *L*, vii, 648n, about Foucauld.

230–1 *'Tom is an orthodox Churchman . . . '*: TSE to EH (10 Feb 1934 and 21 Mar 1934), *L*, vii, 80–1.

231   *'our developing union'*: Seduction through words, Hannah Sullivan suggests about the love-letters of 1935–Jan 1936 in 'The Moment of Embalming: T. S. Eliot's love letters', *TLS* (31 Jan 2020), invoking 'To his Coy Mistress'.

231   *selflessness as narrowing*: TSE to EH (Ash Wednesday, 1936).

232   *TSE intolerant and oppressive*: TSE repeats this back on 24 Mar 1936.

232   *'woolly counsels'*: TSE to McPherrin (26 Oct 1936), *L*, viii, 360.

233   *EH's invitation fell through*: TSE responded to this report on 7 May 1936.

233   *TSE disliked EH's acting role*: TSE to EH (26 May 1936).

234   *'waiting for things to happen'*: TSE to EH (30 July 1936), box 7, f. 1.

234   *EH's sense of failure*: TSE to EH (24 July 1936).

234   *Alarmed*: TSE, looking back, to McPherrin (20 Aug 1936), *L*, viii, 335.

234   *'wrung'*: TSE to EH (24 July 1936), referring to her last letter on 9 July.

234   *'we shall be together'*: TSE to EH (30 July 1936), box 7, f. 1.

234   *'lay foundations'*: TSE to EH (11 Sept 1936), box 7, f. 2.

234   *TSE to help EH make a start at Smith*: To McPherrin (20 Aug and 26 Oct 1936), *L*, viii, 335, 360.

235   *'moments' and bell-buoy*: The moment on the beach and the sound of the bell will be recalled on 4 April 1940, as Eliot looks ahead to the first summer in years that he would not be with EH. She herself, however, did return to Woods Hole that July, and Eliot will think of the bell and keep imagining her by the sea (26 July, 4 and 13 August 1940). He referred to the potential writing of a new poem on October 8, and *DS* was completed within a few months in 1941.

     DS is tied to Eliot's time with EH as much as *Burnt Norton* is. There was this private reason for the shift of the *Quartets* to America. The poem now can be read not only as the retrieval and reconfiguration of a childhood memory through poetry, but as recording the experience of the lived recurrence and reframing of that memory. The Gloucester of childhood is displaced and refracted through the bell heard again in 1936 and through the presence of the 'Lady' (*DS*: IV), who is not the dedicatee of a Gloucester church, as was thought, but the epistolary persona of EH, often addressed as 'Lady'.

236 *TSE's view that the depression would pass:* To McPherrin (26 Oct 1936), *L*, viii, 360.

236 *worried women who lie awake:* EH is present in the women who are thinking of a man they love who is out at sea – the sea emblematic of the spirit's voyage out.

236 *EH behind women's insomnia and other details in DS:* With thanks to Katerina Stergiopoulou for connecting EH with *DS*: I and II. In conversation at Princeton in Jan–Feb 2020. I'm indebted also to Frances Dickey who writes on the links between the letters and *DS* in *Time Present* (spring 2021): 'The biographical dimension of this *Quartet* . . . adds a personal depth to this otherwise philosophical poem. When we see the role that Hale plays in this poem, it is no surprise that he did not mention it to her, for this is not a love poem, but a poem of the end of love.'

236 *'when the past is all deception':* Poems/*R&M*, 194.

237 Ars Amandi *and a* Sermon on Death: TSE to GF (10 May 1936), *L*, viii, 202.

237 *'I almost smelt the grapes':* TSE to EH (17 Oct 1936), box 7, f. 2.

237 Show Boat: TSE had recalled the steamboats on the Mississippi in a letter to EH (Feb 1933), box 4, f. 1, soon after he visited St Louis on the return leg from California. In 1936 he was further delighted with a print of old St Louis, a Christmas present at the end of the year from his niece Dodo. He wrote to her (*L*, viii, 429) that he had owned a Mississippi steamship print but had not managed to retrieve it from VHE.

238 *'a whole Thibet':* FR, Part II, scene ii. Plays, 104.

17: 'BROKEN STONES'

239 *'late wife', 'took to my heels', 'shaky':* (28 July 1936), *L*, viii, 305, 311.

239 *woollens underwear:* TSE to EH (28 Dec 1939), box 10, f. 4.

240 *family photos in TSE's office:* A letter of 2 Feb 1936 says how it delighted him to have Cranch photos (ancestry through his paternal grandmother: the first American Cranch held high judicial office for fifty years, passed on by HWE). TSE framed these. Aunt Susie (Hinkley) too had sent photos. TSE placed a photo of the Revd Charles Chauncy, a President of Harvard, over his mantelpiece, flanked by the Revd Andrew Eliot. Another photo, Major Thomas Stearns, stood on bookcase. In this way, TSE surrounded himself with members of family as he thought up a drama of a renegade reunited with his family after a long period abroad.

240 *VHE's fictional portrait of TSE:* 'Fête Galante', C (July 1925). Sparrow, 570–7. 'The Paralysed Woman' was prepared for publication the following October, but then that issue was scrapped at the point when TSE joined Faber & Gwyer, with a projected change in the journal. Conceivably, TSE was so disconcerted by VHE's knowing close-up of him that he stopped promoting her career. He told her father that she was bitterly disappointed by rejections, but he did not admit that what must have been the most devastating of the two she had was his own.

241   *'grim, prim . . . female':* Quoted *L*, viii, 578n.

242   *TSE's movements in July 1937:* Dates approximate, deduced from letters of TSE to EH in box 7, f. 5.

242   *Desire as spur to spiritual development and mental and spiritual intimacy:* TSE to EH (30 Sept 1936), box 7, f. 2.

242   *ten layers of composition of* FR: *IL*, Appendix V.

242   *new draft of* FR *sent to EH in Oct 1937:* Discussed in letter from TSE to EH (24 Oct 1937), box 8, f. 1

243   *'Something should come of this':* Houghton 1691.14 (38). Part I, scene ii. TSE cut this. See also Houghton 1691.14 (39) 'TS C'. This draft of the scene is fascinating for granting more character and agency to Mary and for the latent promise in the relationship with Harry which EMB encouraged TSE to develop. The scene offers some kind of commentary on the relationship of TSE with EH as separateness hardened in view of Harry's 'push', his alleged dark deed, in the script EMB read in spring 1938. EMB's advice to TSE was to develop rather than curtail Mary: EMB to TSE (11 Mar 1938), *L*, viii, 837. His page references are to typescripts loaned by EH and passed on finally to HWE. Noted by HWE in Houghton: MS Am 1691 (11).

243   *EH had a holiday in Charleston:* TSE to EH (7 Apr 1938), box 8, f. 6.

244   *wife had contaminated Harry:* TSE to EMB (19 Mar 1938), *L*, viii, 846.

244   *women unclean; Harry de-sexed':* *L*, viii, 845. TSE acknowledged to EMB that the play does not convey the sexual disturbance he had in mind.

246   *'the future was long since settled':* FR, Part 1, scene iii. *Plays*, 87.

247   *MHW appalled:* MHW to TSE (14 July 1938), *L*, viii, 909–10.

18: VIVIENNE'S COMMITTAL

248   *doctor* 'fairly *satisfied'* with *VHE's state:* MHW to TSE (14 July 1938), *L*, viii, 909–10.

249   *early typescript of* Old Possum *inscribed for EH:* Ella Strong Denison Library, Scripps.

249   *'nor do we want actual certification . . . ':* (21 July 1938), *L*, viii, 911n.

249*   *Cyriax massage for both TSE and VHE:* Sparrow, 168.

249–50   *TSE offers a supplement for VHE in an asylum, an offer 'inseparable from certification':* TSE to G. F. Higginson (9 Aug 1938), the day he authorises certification, recalls saying this at the office consultation, *L*, viii, 927.

250   *MHW to deal with the next step:* TSE to EH (19 July 1938), box 9, f. 1.

250   *'Soft you; a word . . . ':* Othello, V, ii, 335.

251   *drowned brother and sister in 'The White Ship':* Resonating too in the attachment of the drowned brother and sister may be Poe's tale of a brother and sister who are too bound for one to outlive the other: they go down together into a tarn at the close of 'The Fall of the House of Usher'.

251   *shivering painted shadow:* Amy in *FR*, Part I, scene i.

251   *EH's critique in the back garden:* Recalled again, 29 June 1941. TSE to EH, box 11, f. 4.

251   *VHE 'better'; against forcing a critical interview:* Dr Miller to MHW (21 July 1938), *L*, viii, 911n–912n.

251   *Dr Miller speaks on behalf of VHE to TSE:* (23 July 1938), *L*, viii, 912.

252   *No one could be sure what was wrong with VHE:* Ann Pasternak Slater in *Sparrow* diagnoses the illness as Munchausen's syndrome, in which a patient invents or enacts illness in order to get love and sympathy. This would

explain a host of minor ills, from bad teeth to a wonky womb (the result, VHE claimed, of standing up too much), in the early years of the marriage. In her *Guardian* review of *Sparrow*, Kathryn Hughes concedes that VHE's drug addiction and supposed anorexia in the twenties are plausible diagnoses, but does not agree that these conditions were 'self-inflicted'.

253 *spoon:* There seems no obvious connection with the *Spoon River Anthology* by Edgar Lee Masters (1915).

254 *TSE's authority for VHE to be certified:* Elizabeth Lowry, 'Marriage Made in Hell', *Literary Review* (8 Dec 2020) comments: 'It's hard to acquit Eliot of shabby dealing at the end of the marriage', unless he was coping with PTSD. 'There can be no doubt that he was genuinely terrified of her. But his passivity . . . looks ugly: his letter to Vivien's brother, Maurice, of 1938 authorising her certification for insanity and incarceration in an asylum is a masterpiece of queasy sidestepping. When at last the deed was done, Macavity wasn't there.' This review of *Sparrow* is sensitive to all parties, TSE included, and Lowry says 'ugly' with regret.

255 *Higginson on confiscating VHE's money:* (10 August 1938), *L*, viii, 929.

256 *nurses coming for VHE; 'fairly cheerful':* MHW to TSE (14 Aug 1938), *L*, viii, 930–1.

256 *TSE's sympathy with 'all the extreme failures of life':* To GF (10 May 1936), *L*, viii, 202.

256 *TSE's letter ('babblings') to Mrs Perkins:* (24 Aug 1938), *L*, viii, 939–40.

257 *'I am glad that it was Maurice who took this step':* *L*, viii, 930n.

257 *VHE and the Lunacy Law reformers:* In 1993 Basil Saunders wrote to me about his mother's involvement with the Lunacy Law reformers in the thirties. I am grateful to Mr Saunders, who died soon after writing down this history, and also to his son.

257 *Mary Wollstonecraft's protest against incarcerating a wife:* In the Victorian age, Dickens tried to put over his wife's insanity, and managed a separation that excluded her, even from her children, though she was harmless – only inert from what was probably depression.

257 *'more docile':* TSE to Mr Higginson (17 Oct 1938), *L*, viii, 972–3.

258 *VHE's piano request and 'some little happiness':* *L*, ix, 100.

258 *TSE declined to see VHE:* *L*, ix, 100.

259 *letters from VHE to TSE via Faber & Faber:* Houghton, Benson Papers.

259 *'sensible & normal', 'extremely wretched':* *L*, ix, 534n.

259 *VHE could not be moved to safety:* TSE to MT (24 June 1944), *MME*, 46.

259 *Maurice found his sister sane:* In old age he reportedly acknowledged the 'wrong' done to her. Ann Pasternak Slater quotes this with the following meticulous note in *Sparrow*, 489: 'Cited by Michael Hastings in his Introduction to *Tom and Viv* (Penguin Books, 1985), pp. 21, 23. Cut from the author's later, new introduction (Penguin reprint, 1992) and a further reprint by Oberon Books.' During this interview Maurice was asked if he took the lead in their action. He denied it, saying, 'What Tom and I did was wrong. And Mother. I did everything Tom told me to.'

This statement is questionable because the interviewer had an anti-Eliot agenda and Maurice could have been pressured by his perennial financial need. His statement, though, would explain the haste to get committal done.

19: WAR YEARS

260   *high moral ground 'along the edge of the precipices':* TSE to EH (1 Sept 1939), box 11, f. 1.
He visited for three days.

260   *'breathless fortnight':* Recalled 24 Aug 1940. TSE to EH, box 11, f. 1. This included
a visit to ruins of Hailes Abbey, not too far from Campden (24 July 1939),
box 10, f. 1.

260   *TSE in fancy-dress as Crippen:* VW/*Letters:* To Elizabeth Bowen (29 Jan 1939), vi, 313.
VW went as Cleopatra in a mask. Her brother Adrian Stephen and his wife
Karin, both psychoanalysts, gave the party in Regents Park.

261   *'perhaps brutally':* (27 Sept 1938), *L*, viii, 959.

261   *EH's face 'screwed up':* TSE to EH (4 Sept 1939), box 11, f. 1.

262   *they will remain part of Campden and Campden part of them:* TSE to EH (13 Sept 1939),
box 10, f. 2.

262   *'gulf of years':* TSE to EH (3 July 1944), box 12, f. 5.

262   *'since 1934':* The London and Chichester autumn when they exchanged rings.

263   *'The moment of the rose . . . ':* LG: V. TSE adds to the 'moments' in letters 1935–6
and also in letter of 24 July 1939, box 10, f. 1.

263   *'our Quartets':* (5 Dec 1944), box 12, f. 5. (Faber printed the four poems together
in 1944. They had already appeared together in the U.S. in 1943.)

263   *'our next play!':* TSE to EH (11 Jan 1940), box 10, f. 5. First mentioned even earlier,
two months before *The Family Reunion* went on stage, as 'another play' with
more surface plot (27 Jan 1939), box 9, f. 4.

263   *had 'to get rid of':* TSE to EH (14 Apr 1939), box 9, f. 6.

263   *in the grip of destiny:* It is not known how much of this play TSE foresaw in 1939.

263   *EH's advice to write for New York:* TSE to EH (30 Nov 1939), box 10, f. 4.

263   *EH sent American plays:* TSE read some without specifying.

264   *'narrow' and 'intolerant':* TSE, quoting back her words, to EH (18 Sept 1938),
box 9, f. 2.

264   *EH on 'diversities of forms of worship' and 'broadmindedness':* TSE repeats her position
(7 Oct 1939), box 10, f. 3.

264   *'why is it so difficult . . . ':* TSE to EH (24 Nov 1939), box 10, f. 4.

264–5 *Sam Eliot's productions:* TSE to EH (8 Dec 1939), box 10, f. 4.

265   *chorus from* Electra*:* Towards the end of the fall semester, 1939.

265   *TSE's response to de Blasio's thesis:* (10 July 1939), *L*, ix, 198–9. Her third son, Bill de
Blasio, would later become mayor of New York mayor.

266   *TSE's advice to EH to 'push':* TSE to EH (15 Feb 1940), box 10, f. 5. On 9 Mar 1940,
TSE repeats what he has heard from EH, box 10, f. 5.

266   *jealousy 'one of the most violent emotions':* TSE to EH (9 Mar 1940), box 10, f. 5.

266   *scholarly edition of Columbo and Bolo:* TSE to Clive Bell (1941), Hayward Collection
at King's College, Cambridge. First noted by McIntyre, followed by
Michelle Taylor. At this time TSE had also sent a Columbo stanza to JDH
(24 Aug 1940, headed 'St Bartholomew's Day'), *L*, ix, 621. *Poems/R&M*, ii, 249.

266   *no longer regretted desire, etc:* (9 Nov 1939), *L*, ix, 348.

267   *'spectre of a Rose':* LG: III. In the first draft this is a 'ghost' of a rose. *CFQ*,
Appendix A, 230. TSE to JDH (5 Aug 1941): 'I was thinking of the Ballet',
L, ix, 884.

267   *'beyond desire':* First draft of *LG* (spring 1941): part III. *CFQ*, 205. Over the
following year TSE revised 'the end of desire' to read 'beyond desire'.

267 *adagio:* Defined by Alastair Macaulay, ex-dance critic of *New York Times*, in a wonderful lecture on Petipa, the French choreographer of classical ballets in late nineteenth-century Russia. St Hilda's College, Oxford, 2019.

267 *'trying':* EC: V. 'For us, there is only the trying'.

267 *'humility is endless':* EC: II.

268 *'and the sun had risen':* This follows the compound ghost at the close of part II. *CFQ*, Appendix A, 229.

268 *'stuck':* TSE to EH (20 May 1941), box 11, f. 3.

268 *TSE to EH on the death of VW:* (22 Apr 1941), *L*, ix, 794n. TSE said the same to JDH (p. 803) and Enid Faber (p. 815).

268 *'a ghost':* To JDH (21 Apr 1941), *L*, ix, 803–4.

268 *'clear the deck':* minutes of meeting (6 Oct 1941) where the President declared the speech department was 'over-staffed'. Smith College Archives.

268 *'frills':* Minutes of Feb 1942 departmental meeting. Smith College Archives.

268 *TSE and Hallie Flanagan:* Eric Bentley, *Hallie Flanagan*, 149, cited in *L*, vii, 79n: TSE and Flanagan had lunch (Sat, 3 Mar 1934) and tea next day. She recalled: 'We had the most crazy and amusing times, and we talked entirely in Sweeney-ese. Eliot thinks [her production of] Sweeney the best play he ever saw, and of course this makes me think him very discerning.'

   TSE refers to Smith's 'grandiose' offer to Flanagan in letter to EH (13 July 1942), box 12, f. 1. He may be reflecting back information from EH. This was letter number 6 (they numbered their letters in wartime, given censorship and submarines, so that they could know if a letter had gone astray).

269 *TSE's relation to Sam Eliot too remote:* TSE to EH (21 July 1942, wartime letter marked 7), box 12, f. 1. This could be true, but it is one of several excuses to EH that summer. Abigail Eliot does not convey any sense of remoteness when she records a family gathering with Sam Eliot in London (correspondence with her parents, *c.* August 1920, Abigail Eliot Papers.) On 4 Sept 1955, TSE entertained Sam Eliot and wife in London. He mentions this to EH blandly, box 13, f. 4.

269 *'brave' and socks for TSE:* TSE to EH (27 Aug 1942), letter marked 10. TSE disparaged the socks to MT, saying that they were so big that they could have gone over his boots.

269 *TSE turned the offer down:* The idea of a visit to Princeton remained in his mind as evidenced by a dubious letter about being there later that year. TSE wrote to MT (7 Dec 1942), mentioning the scarcity of eggs in wartime London and the contrasting luxury of boiling himself two eggs for breakfast every morning in Princeton. This letter indicates that he had only recently returned to London (PRS). An earlier letter (HOU) from TSE to MT, dated 15 Sept 1942, had agreed to a talk for MT's students in Nov 1942. There is no corroborating evidence of a visit to America: nothing in letters to EH and he could hardly have been in Princeton without the Thorps knowing. It looks as though the egg-letter was a blind for cancelling the November talk on the grounds of having to go abroad. In that case, this letter would not be worth mention but for the glibness of the excuse to MT, of a piece with continuing excuses to EH. Where is the line between the social excuse and deceptiveness which EH could not at length accept?

269 *'I belong to England':* TSE to EH (18 Aug 1942), wartime letter marked 9, box

12, f. 1. There is no wartime letter 8, which either went astray or else TSE miscounted. I am grateful to Katerina Stergiopoulou for alerting me to the possibility of missing facts.

270 *'I want to continue to feel . . . ':* TSE to EH (13 Oct 1942), box 8, f. 4.

270 *seven more lines to write:* TSE to EH (27 Aug 1942), wartime letter 10, box 12, f. 1.

270 *'spiritual aridity':* TSE to EH (13 July 1942), wartime letter 6, box 12, f. 1.

271 *two-faced versus multi-faceted:* Since TSE often referred to his divided self, we might consider this in terms of EH's accusation and TSE's reply about facets. Facet no. 2 is a detached, cruel if need be, writer who stood apart from facet no. 1, the ardent, loving, exceptionally loyal Eliot who now and then stood before EH in person and told her that he belonged to her and she to him, reinforcing their pact. Facet no. 2 belonged to nobody, perhaps not even himself. No. 2 was a trespasser on Emily's life and feelings who undertook no responsibility. (I am indebted to Frances Wilson for her convincing way of showing D. H. Lawrence's shifts between Self 1 and Self 2 in *Burning Man*.)

271 *'I was certainly not repudiating the past':* TSE to EH (13 Oct 1942), after a hiatus in the correspondence, looks back to what was said in the summer, most likely in late August.

271 *'very, very lonely':* TSE to EH (16 Sept 1942), letter marked 12, box 12, f. 1.

272 *'the fountain dries':* TSE to EH (1 Jan 1943), box 12, f. 2.

272 *disparagement of Burnt Norton:* TSE to Helen Gardner (2 Dec 1942). Correspondence, Bodleian Library, Oxford.

272 *TSE on his 'sombre tinge' belonging to his ancestors more than to Anglicans:* TSE to EH (24 Jan 1943), box 12, f. 2.

273 *FQ in 1943:* Published first by Harcourt in New York. The UK edition appeared a year later.

273 *'as a kind of monument to you':* TSE to EH (7 July 1943), box 12, f. 3.

273 *EH asked TSE to make selection of her letters:* Inferred from TSE's letter of 30 Aug 1943, box 12, f. 3, which harks back to EH's letter dated 13 July, which of course we don't have.

273 *not to write letters as if for publication:* TSE to EH (17 July 1943), box 12, f. 3. With thanks to Katerina Stergiopoulou for drawing attention to this letter while we were reading in Special Collections in Jan–Feb 2020.

273 *'my purposes'* TSE to EH (30 Aug 1943), box 12, f. 3.

273 *'Your letters would go . . . to the Bodleian':* TSE to EH (30 Aug 1943), box 12, f. 3. At the foot of this letter, he informs EH that JDH would be his executor only for his literary remains, which don't include letters; i.e. letters would not fall into his province.

273 *Pygmalion:* Book 10 of Ovid's *Metamorphoses*. The statue-woman harks back to 'La Figlia che Piange', which TSE claimed was inspired by a *stele* he saw in Italy.

273 *TSE's 'talent for publicity':* HWE to TSE (12 Sept 1935), L, vii, 755.

274 *sonnet CXXII:* TSE to EH (4 Oct 1943) notes this from her.

274 *TSE on the role of Hermione:* TSE to EH (19 Apr 1944).

274 *TSE wishes something may be settled:* TSE to EH (10 July 1944), box 12, f. 5. Readers of *Sense and Sensibility* will recognise a variety of John Dashwood.

275 *TSE on his volunteers:* TSE to EH (31 July 1944), box 12, f. 5.

275 *'I confess I seem to myself rather less self-centred'*: Ibid.

275 *jealous*: Ibid.

20: MISS HALE IN HER PRIME

279 *'reports from the past'*: TSE to EH (26 Feb 1945), box 12, f. 5.

282 *TSE's answer on 22 May 1945*: TSE to EH, numbered 15, box 12, f. 6.

282 *to wish for VHE's death would be sinful*: TSE to EH (28 May 1945), box 12, f. 6.

283 *'... regret ... becomes passionate'*: TSE to EH (15 July 1945), box 12, f. 6.

283 *'withdraw from life'*: TSE quotes her phrase in a letter of 9 Sept 1945. See the parallel with the unlived life in James's great tale, 'The Beast in the Jungle', in *IL*, Chapter 11.

285 *visit to EH in Vermont*: July 1946. After he returned to London, TSE sent a postcard to MT dated 15 Aug 1946. It pictures a swimming pool in a marble quarry in Dorset, Vermont. The water is exquisitely blue and clear between piled blocks of white marble.

285 *'I'll be in costume'*: Recalled by Sally Foss in phone interview (14 Jan 2020).

286 *deep freeze and now reanimated*: Phrase from Jonathan Bate on the Sonnets in *The Genius of Shakespeare*.

286 *'four very happy days'*: TSE to Thorps (5 Aug 1946). Thorp Papers.

287 *'a serious difference to our relations'*: TSE to EH (16 Oct 1946), box 12, f. 8.

287 *'My whole nature cries out ...'*: TSE quotes her words back in inverted commas on 9 Nov 1946, box 12, f. 8.

288 *flaw in the pact*: TSE to EH (2 Nov 1946), box 12, f. 8.

288 *EH flouting sacredness of communion*: Previously, TSE had ordered EH not to 'mess' with the body of Jesus Christ, warning her of Hell for such as do.

21: THE PLAY'S THE THING

289 *'normal'; 'inevitable'; 'decorum'; 'the future, for a year hence'*: TSE to EH, box 13, f. 1.

290 *Enid Faber on VHE's funeral*: Afterword in *Sparrow*.

291 *TSE in touch with EMB to discuss next play*: Mentioned in letter to EH (8 Mar 1947), box 13, f. 1. The same day, TSE tells EMB that he'd like to discuss future possibilities.

291 *'bad conscience'; 'intense dislike of sex'*: TSE to EH (3 Feb 1947), box 13, f. 1.

291 *'there are times when I desire you'*: TSE to EH (18 Aug 1931), box 2, f. 1.TSE adds at bottom by hand his answer to EH's query if their tie had developed 'too late'.

291 *'all I do'*: TSE to EH (3 Feb 1947), box 13, f. 1.

293 *'stranger'*: TSE to EH (14 Feb 1947), box 13, f. 1.

293 *'I recoiled ...'*: TSE to EH (Easter/6 Apr 1947), box 13, f. 1.

293 *'a nightmare' and 'demons'*: Ibid.

294 *'you'll find yourself another little part to play'*: draft of *CPy*, Houghton bMS Am 1691.7.

294 *'the kind of faith that issues from despair'*: *CPy*, Act II.

294 *'insane' or 'dishonest'*: TSE to EH (Easter/6 Apr 1947), box 13, f. 1.

294 *past tense, 'had'*: TSE typed 'had' and then added 'has' before 'had' in pen, as Hannah Sullivan noted, to soften the past-ness. *TLS* (31 Jan 2020).

296 *Celia cast out of the marital narrative*: Later, in the context of a fulfilling second marriage, TSE was to reject Noel Annan's imputation that in *CPy* he denied the redemptive power of sexual love. 'T. S. Eliot Replies [re *Cocktail Party*]. To the Editor of *Encounter*'. *Prose*, viii (May 1960), 418.

296   *Celia's holy destiny:* Margaret Leighton played Celia at the start of the London run and Irene Worth took over the role. At the close of the run, in Feb 1951, TSE told EH that he thought Worth was too much inside the part – living rather than acting it (14 Feb 1951, box 13, f. 4). He had the same criticism of Robert Speaight as Becket. TSE seems opposed to Method acting derived from Stanislavsky and the Moscow Art Theatre. Marlon Brando, for instance, gave a Method performance in the Elia Kazan movie of *The Streetcar Named Desire* (1951).

296   *the doctor a divine agent:* TSE to MT in PRS: Harcourt-Reilly, Alex and Julia are 'immortals' and don't change. The other four characters 'develop'.

297   *'chaotic noise':* Draft of Act I Scene ii: Houghton bMS Am 1691.7 (67).

297   *'Transhumanised':* Julia's word in *CPy,* Act II.

298   *visit to be different from last time in Vermont:* TSE to EH (1 Mar 1947), box 13, f. 1.

298   *'ruins' of post-war London:* Ibid.

298   *'numbed':* TSE to EH (19 May 1947), box 13, f. 1.

298   *'agony':* TSE to EH (2 July 1947), box 13, f. 1.

298   *TSE's notes for Address at EH's school:* Typescript, Houghton bMS Am 1691 (folder 46), 3 June 1947. 'On Poetry: An Address by T. S. Eliot on the Occasion of the Twenty-Fifth Anniversary of Concord Academy, Concord, Massachusetts, June 3, 1947'. *Prose,* vii, 11–18.

299   *'framed in the doorway':* TSE to EH (25 June 1947), box 13, f. 1.

299   *not 'unified'; 'something most valuable':* TSE to EH (30 Nov 1947), box 13, f. 1.

299   *'my only love':* TSE to EH (2 July 1947), box 13, f. 1.

300   *his sagging belly:* He joked too about the dental plate that replaced his upper teeth in October. It left him afraid of leaning over railings and munching in a corner, in case the plate dropped into his soup.

300   *the ghosts of those Richard had wronged: Richard III:* V, iii.

301   *EH's 'theatrical art':* TSE to EH (14 Aug 1947), box 13, f. 1.

301   *EH on TSE to Lorraine Havens:* Lorraine Havens visited me after *Eliot's New Life,* with its portrait of EH, was published in 1988. She brought this letter.

302   *'too obscurely emotional to understand':* NWEH.

302   *TSE sent EH a list of poems read on the BBC:* TSE to EH (8 Feb 1948), box 13, f. 2.

303   *EH's rented rooms in Concord:* TSE to EH (17 Dec 1947), box 13, f. 1.

303   *EH gave reading of A. A. Milne play:* On the afternoon of Tuesday 8 June 1948; this was the first of the Summer Literary Readings.

304   *'One can hardly refuse':* TSE to EH (7 Sept 1947), box 13, f. 1. On that occasion TSE was going to Aix and giving a lecture there.

304   *Gomorrah:* To MT, written on board the SS *America* of the US Lines (autumn 1948), Houghton. *MME,* 83.

305   *King George VI to TSE:* TSE recounting the King's words to MT (5 May 1949). PRS. Quoted in *MME.*

305   *TSE's fear of fame and EH's advice:* TSE to EH (4 Feb 1948).

305   *TSE at the Royal Horticultural Society on behalf of Aunt Edith:* TSE's letter to Mrs Perkins, headed 'Presentation of Lantern Slides by T. S. Eliot' (3 Mar 1948), and the report in the *Evesham Journal* (13 Mar 1948), are in Houghton bMS Am 1691 (folder 48). Letter to Edith Perkins in *Prose,* vii, 103–5.

307   *'very poignant memories' of Petersham:* TSE to EH (16 March 1948), box 13, f. 2.

307   *TSE on EH's fantasy:* Ibid.

308   *'Since the future is not to give me . . .'*: EH to TSE (25 May 1948). Written
        from Concord.

308   *TSE did not 'relish' Millay and Amy Lowell*: TSE to EH (1 May 1949), box 13, f. 2.

309   *invitation to Princeton Institute of Advanced Studies*: Letter from Frank Aydelotte,
        Director of IAS (29 Sept 1947).

309   *TSE's view of Margaret Thorp*: TSE to EH (15 Aug 1948), box 13, f. 2.

309   *EH drove north through Maine*: TSE to EH (8 Aug 1949). Amongst strangers during
        a summer holiday at The Flying Jib on Grand Manan Island in August–
        September 1948, she longs again for Eliot to be there with her. 'I had so
        hoped we might come together here, that I cannot quite accustom myself
        to the change.' (24 Aug 1948).

309   *My spirit I confess . . .*: EH to TSE (13 June 1949).

310   *embarrassed and guilty*: TSE uses these terms in an explanatory letter about his
        past to MT in 1950. See Chapter 13, above.

310   *TSE thought Henzie unsuitable for CPy parts*: TSE to EH (15 May 1949), box 13, f. 3.

310   *'Do you not like to write any more?'*: TSE to EH (12 June 1949), ibid.

310   *EH read scene of Celia's rejection*: Originally this scene was in Act II, and at a late
        stage it was transferred nearer to the beginning of the play Act I, scene ii.

310–11   *'smear the victims . . . ants'*: Lines crossed out in pencil on Edinburgh typescript.

311   *EH's protest over CPy*: EH to TSE (8 Aug 1949).

311   *Celia's immolation*: Helen Gardner (whose brilliant book, *The Art of T. S. Eliot*, came
        out that same year) reviewed the play in *Time and Tide* (25 Mar 1950). She too
        deplores the cruelty to Celia's flesh: 'The wonderful truth and beauty of [Celia's]
        self-exposure deserve a better fate than the sensational fantasy of her death.'

312   *EH's loss of the ring*: EH to TSE (16 Oct 1949). From Abbot Academy.

312   *EH on the 'personal' allusions in CPy*: To TSE (16 Oct 1949). From Abbot Academy.
        A previous blind for EH happened when TSE wrote *FR* and told EH that in
        this play he was creating a small part for her or the eminent English actor
        Edith Evans. He does not say which part this was, but it turns out that he
        was thinking of Evans for the part of Harry's commanding and blinkered
        mother Amy. The role eventually went to Helen Haye, but the situation
        of Mary and that of EH was almost identical, and I imagine that TSE was
        covering up EH as source for the rejected Mary.

312   *'There is universal distaste'*: Houghton bMS 1691 (80). Sherek expanded on the
        'jolly little ants' in his letter after the Edinburgh opening (Sept 1949),
        Houghton bMS Am 1691 (65). EMB too deplores the ants: (26 Feb 1950),
        Houghton bMS Am 1691 (81).

313   *TSE toned down the martyrdom*: TSE to EH, box 13, f. 3.

313   *TSE's self-defence against charge of antisemitism*: To Sherek (Sept 1949), filed with
        CPy material. Houghton bMS Am 1691.

313   *'Oh, it's YOU again, Julia.'* MT reports this in her diary entry for 24 Nov 1949,
        drawn on for PRS. Cited by Humphrey Carpenter in his superb talk for the
        English Association, 1988, and published in their journal, *English*, in 1989.

22: ENTER A GUARDIAN

315   *MT's invitation to TSE*: MT's suggested 13 Oct 1935 as the date for his reading,
        and she renewed the invitation in July 1935. TSE wrote formally to MT as
        'Madam' to confirm the arrangement on 18 July 1935. *L*, vii, 696.

315–16   *TSE's dramatisation from the Bible:* Nehemiah, IV–VI.

316   *gun in the Prophet's holster: The Rock*: V.

316   *Tenebrae service:* 'That great, dark, magnificent service' is described in PRS early Apr 1953. Described again on Maundy Thursday, 7 Apr 1955. This was TSE's favourite Anglican service and it became customary for MT to join him.

316   *TSE as Nehemiah:* (Oct 1955), PRS.

317   *Nehemiah in Puritan New England:* For the model of Nehemiah in Puritan biography and sermon, and for the Puritan idea of history, see Sacvan Bercovitch, *The Puritan Origins of the American Self,* Chapter 2: 'The Vision of History', 63–70.

317   *'Fare forward':* TSE draws on Whitman.

317   *'distraught refugee face':* (1 May 1949), PRS.

317   *one of us: V W/Diary,* iv, 324.

317   *London a 'tough nut':* (10 Aug 1920), *L,* i, 490.

319   *MT on TSE's reading in 1940:* (11 Oct 1940), PRS.

319   *first lunch:* Date uncertain. MT is unreliable about early dates in her friendship with TSE. Under 1941 in PRS.

320   *'alien':* 'Virginia Woolf' in *Horizon,* iii (May 1941). *Prose,* vi, 313–16.

320   *TSE's lost galosh:* (22 Oct 1949), PRS.

321   *'Say gal':* (7 Apr 1955), *MME,* 201.

321   *TSE's warnings to MT:* (15 Sept 1942), PRS.

322   *TSE prayed for MT daily:* TSE to MT (May 1955), a conversation when he was leaving for America. PRS.

323   *'so much of her is me!'* (18 August 1949), *MME,* 101.

323   *'a painful light . . .:* Ibid., 118.

324   *MT's letters must be preserved:* TSE to MT (autumn 1944). Houghton.

324   *jeep to take in the Rhineland Offensive: MME,* 58–9. Letter dated 5 Mar 1945.

324   *MT crossed German border: I'll Walk,* 91.

324   *MT's impressions like WL:* Ibid., 94.

325   *'In the year that King Uzziah died . . . ':* TSE to MT (16 Nov 1944). Houghton. Quoted in *MME.*

325   *'Man of Action':* TSE to MT (30 Oct 1944), quoted in PRS and *MME.*

325   *fifty thousand:* The number who passed through the Albert by April 1945.

325   *'scum list' and sacking:* Wonderfully vivid letter to me, *c.* 1989.

326   *MT to survey educational needs:* (1947), *MME,* 72.

326   *Martha May Eliot:* Ibid., 80–1, 283–4, cites Harvard's School of Public Health: 'Child health pioneer Martha May Eliot: A woman ahead of her time'.

326   *'working relationship':* (1949), *MME,* 87.

327   *'Tom gave me many indications':* Ibid.

327   *'(Before leaving I wrote to Tom . . .)': MME,* 94, and TSE's reply, 94–6.

328   *'Why should we both be lonely?'* Ibid., 115.

329   *'I have never told anyone else':* Ibid., 117.

329   *'I don't suppose the lady will ever understand':* Ibid.

329   *Donald Hall's reminiscence of TSE:* I first heard this in 1999, repeated, always vividly, from time to time at Bennington College Summer Writing Program. TSE was interviewed by Donald Hall for the *Paris Review* (1959), the best interview he ever did. Hall, *Remembering Poets: Reminiscences and Opinions* (NY: Harper & Row, 1978). Quoted in *MME,* 133.

330   *'to save my nerves':* MT to TSE (29 Nov 1951), PRS.

331   *'Women always get me . . . wrong'; 'neurotic':* (21 Mar 1956), *MME*, 222.

332   *'you sound like a spirit released':* (27 Nov 1951), PRS.

332   *'I just rang up . . . ':* (29 Dec 1953), *MME*, 173.

332   *'a relief . . . what we really mean':* (4 Aug 1953), *MME*, 163.

332   *TSE on his confessions:* PRS: talk of confession happened more than once. See 27 Nov 1951 and early April – Holy Week – 1953.

333   Wee Dolly Sayers: To MT (11 Mar 1944), Houghton. *Poems/R&M*, ii, 197.

333   *'usual representation of Central European ghettos':* TSE to MT. Letters in Houghton.

333   *'intolerance':* (Oct 1955). PRS.

334   *TSE on Jewish girl in the Tandy household:* TSE to EH (11 Jan 1940), box 10, f. 5.

334   *EMB's 'very Jewish looking' sons:* TSE to EH (7 Feb 1942), box 11, f. 6; repeated 15 Jan 1945, box 12, f. 6. In the mid-forties, TSE also disparaged Robert Helpmann (playing Hamlet) as a Jew.

335   *'jilted':* MT, Diary (9 Aug 1953), PRS, quoted *MME*, 164.

336   *encounter with the Huxleys: MME*, 205.

23: THE POSTERITY PLAN

338   *Fame did not worry him:* TSE to EH (8 Dec 1930), box 1, f. 1.

338   *tiger eye:* The poem tells of 'The tiger in the tiger-pit . . . ', *New English Weekly* (28 Nov 1935), ten days after Vivienne accosted the poet at Dorland Hall). Typescript/manuscript Houghton bMS Am 1691 (20a). Osbert Sitwell noticed TSE's 'yellow' eyes at a reading in 1917. Note also, 'Came Christ the tiger' in 'Gerontion'.

339   *'the wild eye':* VW/*Diary* (22 Nov 1934), iv, 262. She described also his looking at her with the jewelled eyes of a toad.

339   *'humility is endless':* EC: II.

339   *'the unattended / Moment':* DS: V.

339   *'spectre':* TSE to EH (4 Sept 1935), box 5, f. 2.

340   *EH suggested they write once a month:* EH wrote from 9 Lexington Road, Concord, to TSE (17 Dec 1947). She hoped if he wrote less often, his letters might have more substance. Her post-pact letters are held by the Eliot estate.

341   *loneliness would always be with her:* EH to TSE (13 June 1949).

341   *honorary degree from Aix-en-Provence:* Spring 1948.

341   *exhausting:* EH's word, from TSE's 'very detailed' letter of 2 May about his French trip (25 May 1948), from Concord.

342   *'public symbol':* EH quotes TSE's phrase. EH was writing hastily before a midweek journey to Andover on 21 April 1948.

342   *'outburst':* TSE to EH (15 Nov 1953), box 13, f. 5.

342   *disparaged* Pygmalion: TSE to EH (14 Nov 1954), box 13, f. 5.

342   *supposed fortune from writings:* TSE to EH (15 Nov 1953), box 13, f. 5.

342   *income tax of £25,000 after CPy ended its run:* TSE to EH (8 July 1951), box 13, f. 4. At the end of 1952, he told MT that he had a demand for £17,000 income tax after *CPy* had made about £35,000, of which he got about £4,000 (cited in *MME*). It seems that TSE inflated the amount he stated to EH.

343   *1955 visit to US, saw EH once:* TSE to EH (27 June 1955), box 13, f. 5.

343   *promise that Princeton would keep letters safe:* Thorp Papers, box 5, f. 3. EH's further correspondence with the Thorps about her TSE letters is mainly in this

collection, though there are some letters to Margaret Thorp in box 14 in the Eliot–Hale collection.

343   *drafted first act of ES:* TSE to EH (13 Dec 1955), box 13, f. 5.

343   *'rest cure' earlier in TSE's mind:* TSE to EH (8 May and 27 June 1955), box 13, f. 5.

343   *'a peach of a girl':* (18 Jan 1956), PRS, quoted in *MME*, 219.

343   *drafted second act of ES:* TSE to EH (9 Jan 1956), box 13, f. 6.

344   *'It's Never Too Late to Say I Love You':* Song by Keith Varnum, sung by Brenda Lee. One line is 'I love you too much to part'. Maisie's lines pick up a line Eliot had given to his earlier dramatisation of EH as Mary, waiting around for Harry in a draft of Part 1, scene ii of *The Family Reunion*: 'Something should come of this conversation. / It is not too late ... ' He had cut the line in the process of playing down Mary's role.

345   *Minnesota lecture:* 'The Frontiers of Criticism', repr. *Prose*, viii, 121–38.

345   *TSE read Cat poems in Abbot Hall:* Sara Fitzgerald's commentary, with Frances Dickey, in their online edition of *NWEH*.

345   *TSE said no to EH's question if he had preference for a particular depository:* EH to WT (26 July 1956), Thorp Papers, box 5, f. 3. She says here that she had checked with TSE in the spring.

346   *EH's report of Margaret's cremation:* TSE to EH (2 July 1956), box 13, f. 6.

346   *EH came to decision about letters:* EH to WT (26 July 1956), Thorp Papers, box 5, f. 3.

346   *15 Aug 1956 letter from EH to TSE:* EH's letter does not survive. Its date is referred to by TSE. The content can be inferred from his reply.

348–9 *friction over TSE's writing of a Cotswold poem:* TSE to EH (2 Mar 1941), *L*, ix, 542n. 'I wondered at your implying that I had never written a poem about the Cotswolds, because if "Burnt Norton" is not about the Cotswolds, what is it about? In the way of local setting, that is. Perhaps you forgot Burnt Norton, or perhaps you consider it geographically out of the area – but certainly not out of it emotionally.'

350   *'progressively clearer idea' of the letters' 'richness':* TSE to EH (11 Dec 1956), box 13, f. 6.

350   *EH asked TSE to shorten the embargo:* TSE did not tear up this particular letter of 23 Nov 1956. He retained its details in order to be precise in rebutting details the following month.

350   *TSE's emotional appeal to EH:* (27 Nov 1956), quoted in *Poems/R&M*, i, 514n.

350   *vultures:* TSE had previously mentioned being prey to a vulture. TSE to EH (13 June 1952), box 13, f. 4.

351   *'novice':* EH to TSE (23 Dec 1956). Eliot Estate.

351   *She would now ask Dix:* Ibid. In fact, Dix had done so already. On 19 Nov 1956 he had given formal thanks on behalf of the library and set out an interim memo to EH where he notes her agreement. Thorp Papers, box 5, f. 3.

352   *'tempest':* EH recalling events to Mr Dix (15 July 1957), Thorp Papers.

352   *'how very little I understand [TSE]':* (3 Dec 1956), *MME*, 243.

352   *EH's 'jellyfish existence':* To Margaret Thorp (11 Jan 1957), Thorp Papers.

352   *curating his archive:* Rosie Alison, film director, in conversation June 2019.

352   *'O hidden':* 'Difficulties of a Statesman', *Poems/TSE*, 128.

24: THE DISCIPLE'S STORY

353   *'distinctly':* John Haffenden in conversation with EVE, recalled in 'Valerie Eliot: Editing the Letters', *L*, v, xxxiv.

354   *EVE 'had to get to Tom'*: Interview, *Observer* (20 Feb 1972).

354   *EVE and Dylan Thomas*: EVE to Eleanor Hinkley (20 Aug and 26 Oct 1957),
       Houghton bMS Am 2244.

356   *comfortable in her own skin*: With thanks to Clare Reihill.

356   *EVE's arms swung*: Observed by Gwen Watkins, writer and widow of Vernon
       Watkins, a Faber poet. In conversation.

356   *'tiresome'; 'creeps'*: Quoted in *MME*, 249.

356   *secretaries interchangeable*: TSE to MT (Oct 1949), PRS. Miss Fletcher had been in
       post for just over a month and TSE was easy about the odd mistake.

357   *TSE's reaction to EVE with Dr Ghosh*: TSE to MT (28 Oct 1950), from
       Chicago, Houghton.

357   *depression and Miss Fletcher's home visits*: TSE to MT (6 Feb 1955), Houghton.

357   *JDH on a Lady with the Lamp*: John Malcolm Brinnan, *Sextet: T. S. Eliot & Truman
       Capote & others* (London: Andre Deutsch, 1981), 274.

358   *EVE determined to marry TSE or no one*: TSE to Eleanor Hinkley (25 Oct
       1958), Houghton.

358   *Higginson as best man*: Peter Ackroyd, *T. S. Eliot* (London: Hamish Hamilton,
       1984), 319.

359   *marital poems*: *Poems/R&M*, i, 316–19. Discussed in 'T. S. Eliot and the sexual
       wasteland', *New Statesman* (15 Nov 2015).

359   *'Valerie's Own Book'*: Eliot estate.

361   *booklet on George Herbert*: (London: Longmans), repr. *Prose*, viii, 498–528.dc

361   *'The Blameless Sister of Publicola'*: *Poems/R&M*, ii, 290.

361   *Valeria*: *Coriolanus*, V: iii. Coriolanus declares her to be 'chaste as the icicle /
       That's curdied by the frost, from purest snow'.

362   *'burst into Bolovian song'*: On 1957 wedding announcement, cited *Poems/
       R&M*, ii, 249.

362   *copied Bolo verses into 'Valerie's Own Book'*: *Poems/R&M*, ii, 249.

362   *when EVE went out*: EVE to Eleanor Hinkley (25 Aug 1963), Houghton.

363   *unexploded mine*: Comment by Isobel Dixon.

364   *'out of his mind'*: Quoted in *MME*, 260.

364   *TSE opening heart to EVE's dedication*: Erica Wagner, *MME*, 248.

364   *'conversion'*: Comment by Isobel Dixon.

364   *'a tall girl'*: TSE to EH on the appeal of her 'height (tall girl)', together with
       her spiritual loveliness (12–13 Dec 1935), box 6, f. 4. He wrote this letter to her
       ship on the eve of her departure for Boston, after their farewell embraces.

365   *MT on 'strong sexual impulses'*: PRS, quoted in *MME*, 251.

365   *'a great "runner-away"'*: Ibid.

365   *'Perhaps you and I mean . . . different things by friendship'*: Quoted *MME*, 255.

365–6 *letters between TSE and MT in 1957*: *MME*, 255–8.

367   *MT as dangerous*: Thanks to Isobel Dixon for pointing this out.

367   *witnessed streak of sadism*: *MME*, 203.

367   *refuge*: On 31 Dec 1956, TSE thanked Collin for offer 'to give me refuge'
       before the wedding, and on 4 Jan 1957 EVE wrote to confirm the stay.
       Correspondence between TSE and EVE with the Brookses is at Washington
       University's Special Collections, St Louis.

367   *'puzzled'*: To Anne Ridler, poet and TSE's one-time secretary (3 Feb 1957),
       Modern Archives Centre, King's College, Cambridge. Cited *MME*, 247.

367 *'my jilting'*: MME, 259.

367 *'so great a sadness'*: Postscript, PRS.

368 *'Have John and I known . . . the real man?'*: MME, 260.

368 *MT's rougher diary of conversations with TSE:* That diary no longer exists, according to Humphrey Carpenter.

25: CURATING THE PAST

369 *Chapter title:* With thanks to Rosie Alison, in discussion, June 2019.

371 *imaginary stand-in, Monica:* Helen Gardner was candid with TSE in preferring the figures from the past to what she judged the less convincing figure of Monica. Bodleian Library: MS.Eng.Lett.d.294, including photocopies of Gardner's replies to TSE.

371 *'real' love:* When EH was due to sail for Boston in Dec 1935, the poet's message was that their love was becoming more real. Box 6, f. 4.

371 *'Dedication' to 'My Wife':* Poems/R&M, i.219.

371 *repurposes:* This word comes from Frances Dickey. Another phrase is from Katerina Stergiopoulou: 'reorienting towards Valerie Eliot'. Thanks to both.

371 *'I believe . . .':* TSE to EH (13 Jan 1936), box 6, f. 6. This was after EH's return to Boston.

371 *TSE revised the record:* He said to Eleanor Hinkley (25 Aug 1963) that he had never before had the experience of mutual love. Houghton.

372 *the question of 'mitigating circumstances':* EH to Margaret Thorp (16 Jan [1957]), Thorp Papers.

372 *four days after:* EH writes 'Ack Jan 14' on the top of TSE's letter dated 29 Dec, addressing her as 'Dearest Emily'.

372 *'very fine letter'; 'very much pleased':* TSE to EH (10 Feb 1957), box 13, f. 6.

372 *TSE hoped EH might come to England:* Ibid.

372 *EH writing first draft of NWEH:* To Margaret Thorp (Feb 1957), Thorp Papers.

373 *'a crazy idea?':* Ibid.

373 *'Your critical writing':* EH to TSE (10 March 1957), from Andover.

375 *EH's 'strange behaviour':* TSE to Eleanor Hinkley: Houghton bMS Am 2244 (52–54), f. 32.

376 *third letter on EH to Eleanor:* Houghton bMS Am 2244 (55-58), f. 33.

376 *'an endurance test':* EH to Marjon Ornstein (1968), her one-time colleague at Abbot. Thanks to M. Ornstein for sharing this letter in 2020, also her beautifully phrased impression of EH on the phone, as well as her photo of EH.

377 *'strictly private':* TSE to EH (15 Feb 1938), box 8, f. 4.

377 *TSE's letter to posterity:* Prose, viii, 595–600. This is the revised version of 1963.

378 *wipes the slate clean:* Rosie Alison, in conversation in Princeton (12–13 Jan 2020).

378 *a woman who professes no inconvenient needs:* Thanks to Isobel Dixon.

379 *The Solid Gold Cadillac:* Information in email (14 Apr 2019) from Sara Fitzgerald (working on her novel, *The Poet's Girl*) in conversation with Abbot pupils who went to Smith. The young Judy Holliday played the role on screen.

379 *'revulsion against the whole story':* EH to WT (18 Aug 1963), Thorp Papers.

381 *burning EH's letters:* We may wonder how letters that filled thirteen boxes

(the fourteenth box contains related extras) at Princeton could have been
stuffed into one metal box. John Haffenden, co-editor with Valerie Eliot
of *The Letters of T. S. Eliot*, suggests in his tribute to EVE, *Letters*, v, xxi, that
TSE's letters from Vivienne were burnt at the same time. Peter du Sautoy
spoke of one container. If another container was given to him, he would
have mentioned it. According to Jewel Spears Brooker (Zoom lecture, 24
Sept 2021), by March 1963 TSE already had it in mind to destroy the contents
of two containers. On leaving for Bermuda, he asked du Sautoy to do so
if he and EVE lost their lives in a plane crash. Brooker noted that TSE and
EVE dined in Bedford Square with du Sautoy and his wife to celebrate
TSE's birthday on 26 Sept, and she suggests that this could have been when
the plan to burn the letters went ahead. John Haffenden, editor of TSE's
Letters, reports this (email on 30 June 2022) as too large a gathering for private
discussion. He thinks it likely that EH's letters could have been burned
before this date. This makes her reminder to TSE (on 12 Sept 1963, about her
side of their correspondence) irrelevant to his action.

381   *no coal-burning stove in Eliot's flat:* Thanks to Jewel Spears Brooker for this fact.

382   *I have the greatest dislike:* TSE to EH. Printed [n.d.] in John Haffenden's tribute
to EVE, *Letters*, v (2014), xx–xxi. Haffenden calls it 'an unusually ill-tempered
letter, begotten by shock'.

382   *'something has changed his mind . . . ':* EH to WT, Thorp Papers.

382   *I have* almost *a suspicion . . . ':* EH to WT (5 Jan 1964), Thorp Papers.

383   *'miles' of tape:* To WT (17 Feb 1965). I wondered if her taped readings from TSE's
letters could have survived, and Princeton kindly made it possible to hear
an old and fragile tape amongst the Thorp Papers but, sadly, there was
nothing by EH.

383   *' from my own feeling for shielding . . . ':* To Margaret Thorp (8 Feb 1965),
Thorp Papers.

383   *'miscarriage':* EH to WT, from Concord (17 Jan 1965), Thorp Papers.

383   *revised* NWEH: On 1–3 Mar 1965. Revised copy dated 19 April 1965.

384   *EH told herself that TSE burnt her letters to protect her:* EH to WT (27 Nov 1965),
Thorp Papers.

384   *'in the background':* EMB to EH (11 Nov 1966).

384   *aerogramme and card:* EH to EVE, Eliot estate.

386   *passion for the stage:* EH to WT (7 Mar 1967), Thorp Papers.

387   *would not have missed . . .:* EVE to me (1975).

388   *'On medical advice . . . ':* EVE to Spender (8 Oct 1974), cited by John Haffenden in
L, v: 'Valerie Eliot: Editing the Letters', xix–xxxvii.

388   *EVE stood by TSE claim: L*, viii, 932–3.

388   *'I live in terror':* (1 Mar 1969). On 4 Nov 1968 she had examined *WL* manuscript
in New York and undertaken to edit it.

388   *the great god Pan:* 'A Musical Instrument', quoted by EVE in letter to
Eleanor Hinkley (11 May 1965), Houghton bMS Am 2244 (99–100).

389   *'pet':* EVE to Eleanor Hinkley (Oct? 1958), Houghton.

389   *'utterly unreal . . . ':* (11 May 1965), Houghton bMS Am 2244 (99–100).

389–90   *EVE's achievements:* She purchased works of art and manuscripts that would
have left the country without her intervention. She set up the T. S. Eliot
Memorial Lectures at the University of Kent and the T. S. Eliot Poetry

Prize. She gave £2.5 million to the London Library and donated £1 million to Newnham College, Cambridge to fund a fellowship in English. She gave £50,000 to the V&A towards the £3.8 million purchase of Becket's Casket. On her death, her net estate was £13,736,705, which went into Old Possum's Practical Trust, a sum that includes the £6.5 million from the sale of her art collection at Christie's.

391   *letters 'bypass his directive':* Haffenden, op. cit.

EPILOGUE

395   *women came closer to him than any man:* It could be argued that his brother was close to him, and this would be true from Henry Ware Eliot's point of view, but though Henry understood his brother in a very intelligent way, I think the poet did not concede this understanding and tended to see his brother first as something of a resource and later as a failure in contrast with himself.

395   *chummed up to an Anglican wit:* Carpenter on MT and TSE.

395   *pattern of closeness and withdrawal:* Thanks to Isobel Dixon for her comment on the flawed, often cruel patterning of creative closeness and retreat.

396   *'I get flashes':* TSE to EH (31 Dec 1931), box 2, f. 5. Jewel Spears Brooker rightly draws attention to this in 'Eliot in Ecstasy' (2021).

396   *'Occasionally, very rarely':* TSE to EH (9 Aug 1933), box 4, f. 7.

397   *'our own past is covered . . . action':* DS: II.

397   *'pastimes':* DS: V.

397   *pattern in the carpet:* 'Pattern' is one of TSE's iconic words. Henry James's tale 'The Figure in the Carpet' is about the pattern to be discerned in the oeuvre of a great writer, who died without disclosing this hidden clue, which only the rare reader can find and which changes that reader's life. 'It's my life,' says Gwendolyn, a reader in the know.

397   *'dark, dark, dark':* EC: III.

397   *'To be redeemed from fire by fire':* LG: IV.

397   *'reality':* BN: I.

397   *'waste sad time':* BN: V.

397   *'Quick now . . . ':* BN: V.

397   *the sequence which culminates in faith:* 'The "Pensées" of Pascal' (1931), SE, 360.

SOURCES

Primary sources

Manuscript sources

Benson, Linda Melton, Eliot's secretary in the 1940s, preceding Valerie Fletcher. Houghton Library, Harvard bMS Am 2706

Bolliger, Aurelia. The Ralph Hodgson and Aurelia Bolliger Hodgson papers, Bryn Mawr College, Pennsylvania. Special Collections BMC – M49. See 'Notebooks concerning T. S. Eliot: biography notes with accounts of Eliot's and Vivienne Eliot's home life and some of Vivienne Eliot's dresses', box 25, f. 6–7. This includes fascinating detail on 'Boyhood of T. S. Eliot' in a ring-bound notebook. See also Bolliger's correspondence with Valerie Eliot (nine letters, 1978–82), box 5, f. 9

Eliot, Abigail. Papers, including Travel Diary 1919–20 and letters 1921. Schlesinger Library, Radcliffe College, Cambridge MA. MC 327, boxes 1–2

Eliot Family Collection. Houghton Library bMS Am 2560

Eliot, Henry Ware. 15 letters to his mother, Charlotte Champe

(Stearns) Eliot (1924–9). Houghton Library bMS Am
1691.10-1691.12

Eliot, Martha May. Papers. Schlesinger Library, Radcliffe
    College, MC 229

Eliot, T. S. Two letters advising Emily Hale in her work (Sept–Oct
    1930). Emily Hale Collection, Special Collections, Firestone
    Library, Princeton University C1294, box 1, f. 2

———. 1,131 letters to Emily Hale (1930–56). 14 boxes, sealed from
    December 1956 until October 2019 (fifty years from Hale's
    death). Special Collections, Firestone Library, Princeton
    University C0686

———. To Willard and Margaret Thorp. Willard Thorp Papers,
    Special Collections, Princeton University C0292, box 4, f. 4

———. T. S. Eliot Papers at Harvard. Houghton Library
    bMS Am 1691

———. Typescripts of *The Family Reunion* and correspondence to
    do with the many revisions of the play. Houghton Library.
    Typescript drafts of the play, called drafts A, B and C, have
    been catalogued as MS Am 1691.14 (37,38 and 39), but are not
    to be found at that location. These are in boxes 1 and 2 of
    assorted material collected by Henry Ware Eliot. For Hale's
    'TS B' with her marginal suggestions see bMS Am 1691(2), i.e.
    box 2 of Henry Ware Eliot's collection

———. Two drafts of *The Family Reunion* (1938). Inscribed to John
    Davy Hayward, King's College Archive Centre, Cambridge
    (KCAC). The layers of composition behind this play are
    listed in chronological order in an Appendix to *The Imperfect
    Life of T S Eliot*.

———. Hale's aunt, Mrs Perkins, donated her garden slides to the
    Royal Horticultural Society, 80 Vincent Square, London,
    and Eliot stood in for her at an event on 2 March 1948. For his
    letter to Mrs Perkins, headed 'Presentation of Lantern Slides
    by T. S. Eliot', on 3 March and a report in the *Evesham Journal* (13
    March 1948) see Houghton Library bMS Am 1691 (f. 48)

———. Letter in folder RHS/P3/4. Education: lecturers/lectures. 'Presentation of lantern slides by T. S. Eliot'. Royal Horticultural Society Library

———. 221 letters to Mary Trevelyan (1940–56). Houghton Library bMS Am 1691.2. The letters are interleaved with her notes. Extracts from these letters are in her memoir, 'The Pope of Russell Square'. See Trevelyan, below

———. Typescript 'Notes for a talk to the Ecumenical Club' (1955), sent to Mary Trevelyan and included in 'The Pope of Russell Square'

———. 67 letters to the Hinkleys. Houghton Library MS Am 2244

———. 27 letters (1947–64), including joint letters with Valerie Eliot, to classmate (Harvard class of 1910) Leon Magaw Little. Houghton Library MS Am 1691.4 and MS Am 1691.13 (5-6), (10-13)

———. Letters to John Hayward, KCAC. Also photocopies of letters from Hayward to T. S. Eliot, L/13/1-3

———. Letters to E Martin Browne and dramatic compositions with notes by Browne. Houghton Library bMS Am 1691.7. See f. 16. Edinburgh script of *The Cocktail Party* is in f. 69 with producer Sherek's comments

———. Pencil draft of *Marina*. Bodleian Library, Oxford Ms Don.c.23(1)

———. Dame Helen Gardner correspondence. Bodleian Library MS.Lett.d.294. (See *New Summary Catalogue*, i, p. 369, no. 41721.) Letters from Eliot to Gardner, with Xerox copies of her replies and her accounts of contexts, 1942–64. 88 leaves

———. Drafts of *The Cocktail Party*. Houghton Library bMS Am 1691.7. See, in particular, Houghton Library bMS Am 1691.7 (67) for first draft of Act I, scene ii, written close to events

———. Book of *The Cocktail Party* in the Eliots' flat has corrections

———. Typescript draft of *Burnt Norton* sent to Frank Morley (the same sent to Hale) with significant additional ending. Houghton Library bMS Am 1691.14 (34)

———. Arrangements and payment for stay at the Institute for Advanced Studies, Princeton (1948) put together as a file by librarian, Marcia Tucker https://albert.ias.edu/handle/20.500.12111/2915

———. Personal clippings 1936–47. Houghton Library HWE Collection, series IV: MS Am 2560 (426), (429) and (432); and series VI (378 on *The Cocktail Party*)

Eliot, Theresa Garrett. Letters in HWE Collection, series I: correspondence. Box 2. MS Am 2560 (43)

Eliot, Valerie Fletcher. Letters to Eleanor Hinkley. Houghton Library MS Am 2244

——— and Eliot. Letters to Collin and Lillian Brooks. Special Collections, Washington University in St Louis

Hale, Emily. Substantial collections at Smith College, Northampton MA and Scripps College, Claremont CA, as well as at Princeton

———. Correspondence with Margaret and Willard Thorp about her letters from T. S. Eliot. Thorp Papers, Princeton C0292, box 5, f. 3

———. *Narrative Written by Emily Hale* (1957/ 1965) a brief memoir introducing Eliot's letters to her. Special Collections, Princeton C0686, box 14. Digital scans of her handwritten and typed versions are in the finding aid for the Emily Hale letters written to T. S. Eliot

———. Letter to Eliot (26 Apr 1945). Eliot–Hale Letters, Special Collections, Princeton C0686

———. 26 letters to Eliot, 1947–61. Eliot Estate

———. Copy of last letter to Eliot (1963). Princeton

———. 'They flash upon the inward eye': typescript memories of Chipping Campden. Hale Papers, Smith College Archives. Extract published in *Campden Historical Society: Notes & Queries*, v, no. 4 (spring 2007). See *The Letters of T. S. Eliot*, viii, 273

———. Letters to Willard Thorp. Hale Collection, Princeton C1294

———. Correspondence with the Thorps, Thorp Papers,
    Princeton C0292, box 4, f. 4

———. Correspondence with the Thorps (1955–67) about
    depositing her collection of Eliot letters at Princeton.
    Thorp Papers, Princeton C0292, box 5, f. 3

———. Letter (16 Oct 1968) from 9 Church Green, Concord, to
    Marjon Ornstein who had been a young colleague at Abbot
    Academy. She also provided the lovely photograph Hale, on
    leaving Abbot, gave Ornstein as a memento

———. Correspondence with J. J. Hayes (1929–30), writer on Irish
    theatre and reviewer for the *Boston Globe* and *New York Times*.
    Hale Collection, Princeton C1294, box 1, f. 3

———. Correspondence with Cecil E. Armstrong, writer on
    theatre. Hale Collection, Princeton C1294, box 1, f. 1

——— (signing herself 'Tubby'). Letters to Louise Andrews Kent
    in Kent Family Papers, Vermont Historical Society. In 2001
    Professor Rosamond Kent Sprague, daughter of Louise
    Kent, wrote to me about her mother's fifty-year friendship
    with Emily Hale. Leahy Library, Vermont History Center,
    Louise Andrews Kent Collection Doc K-26, K-27, K-28, K-29

Hayward, John Davy. Letters to Frank Morley. KCAC JDH/26/72

Hutchinson, Mary. 'T. S. Eliot', short, unpublished biographical
    sketch. Harry Ransom Center, Austin, Texas

McPherrin, Jeanette ('Jeanie'), pupil and friend of Hale. Letters to
    Eliot. Scripps College. Some printed in *The Letters of T S Eliot*

Monro, Alida. Henry Ware Eliot to Alida Monro (10 July 1935).
    British Library Add MS 83366

Morrell, Lady Ottoline. Letters (on Vivienne and Eliot) to Bertrand
    Russell. Papers in Harry Ransom Center, Austin, Texas

———. Journal. Goodman Papers, British Library Add MS
    88886/04/034

Russell, Bertrand. Letters to Lady Ottoline Morrell on Vivienne
    Eliot and her husband. McMaster University Library,
    Hamilton, Ontario

Smith College Archives, Neilson Library. Minutes of meetings
of the Department of Speech (1936–42). With gratitude to
curator Nanci Young for finding this during lockdown

Thorp, Margaret Louise Farrand. Papers (1917–60). Thorp Papers,
Princeton C0292. These include writings, correspondence,
journals, notebooks and photographs. Her journal
contains notes on meeting Eliot in the early thirties

Thorp, Willard. Papers (1923–81). Princeton, C0292. These include
correspondence, writings, class lecture notes, journals,
diaries and photographs

Trevelyan, Mary. 'The Pope of Russell Square', a memoir of
her friendship, correspondence and conversations with
Eliot. Bodleian Library. For substantial and well-chosen
extracts see below, Mary Trevelyan and Erica Wagner, *Mary
and Mr Eliot*

Sound and audio

Live recording of Eliot's December 1950 reading at the 92nd Street
Y in New York, including informal remarks: https://
soundcloud.com/92y/t-s-eliot-reads-from-his-work-
december-4th-1950-at-92nd-street-y/s-BX8Vo

Foss, Sally, daughter of Hale's schoolfriend Mary Foss.
Wonderfully vivid and articulate recorded interview with
Princeton representative in January 2020, when she was
ninety-six. She spent time with Emily Hale and Eliot in
Dorset and Brattleboro, Vermont, in summer 1946

Digital

www.tseliot.com. Includes 'Poetry' by Hannah Sullivan, 'Prose'
by Ronald Schuchard and 'Life' by Lyndall Gordon;

photographs; and Ann Pasternak Slater's digital edition of
Vivienne Eliot's diaries and ledgers

Dickey, Frances. Reports from the Emily Hale Archive. https://
tseliotsociety.wildapricot.org/news. Illuminating blog with
chronological summaries of Eliot's letters to Emily Hale
during the thirties

Princeton University Library's Spring Event, 2021: 'T. S. Eliot &
Emily Hale Letters: Re-examined'. https://mediacentral.
princeton.edu/media/T.S.+Eliot+%26+Emily+Hale+Letters
A+Re-examined/1_7vtzmy35

Television

BBC documentary (1943) of TSE reading one of his poems, owned
by William Macquitty, Pinewood Studios, who found it in
September 1957 and gave it to Eliot

On 16 Oct 1955 Eliot told Emily Hale (box 13, f. 4) that he had to
do a five-minute television interview for the opening of a
McKnight Kauffer exhibition. It went out five days later

The Mysterious Mr Eliot, BBC (1 Jan 1971). See especially the vivid
memories that Hope Mirrlees had of Vivienne. 'Eliot's Life',
The Listener, 85 (14 Jan 1971), 50

Arena documentary, BBC2 (2009)

Return to T. S. Eliotland by A. N. Wilson, BBC4 (8 Oct 2018). Includes
Dana Hawkes's tour of the Eliot house at Eastern Point near
Gloucester MA

3 Compayne Gardens, a film about the West Hampstead house belonging
to Vivienne Eliot's parents, where she and Eliot stayed in July
1915 after their marriage. Narrated by Edward Petherbridge

Eliot's Search for Happiness by Adrian Munsey, Sky Arts (15 Dec 2019)

Into The Waste Land, Arena, BBC2 (2022), to celebrate the centenary
of *The Waste Land* produced by Rosie Alison and directed by
Susanna White, with their superb commentary

Film footage

Eliot in Canterbury to see a performance of *Murder in the Cathedral*
on 22 June 1935, a week after its opening. E. Martin Browne
as Fourth Tempter and Speaight as Becket, as well as the
Women of Canterbury, the killers and the Four Knights.
Three minutes. Filmed by Stanley Bligh in the Cathedral's
Chapter House. From Screen Archive South East and
available through the BFI. On website of the *T. S. Eliot Society
Newsletter* (10 Jan 2021)

Rare footage of T. S. Eliot at the opening of the Sheffield
University Library, 1959. Available at Sheffield University
Digital Special Collections

Valerie Eliot filmed a smiling Eliot emerging from their flat in the
sixties. First public showing by Nancy Fulford, the Estate's
researcher, at the Eliot Summer School in July 2019

Printed primary sources

———, *La Vita Nuova* [*The New Life*], trans. Mark Musa (Oxford:
World's Classics, 1992)

Berger, Patty Wolcott, 'T. S. Eliot: An Auspicious Event in the
Life of the Academy', a report on TSE's visit to Concord
Academy on 3 June 1947 with photographs of Miss Hale's
special girls

Bhagavad-Gita, trans. Lionel D. Barnett (London: J. M. Dent, 1905).
Temple Classics edition. Houghton, with name 'TS Eliot'
and 'Cambridge 1912' on flyleaf and marginal lines

Brooker, Jewel Spears (ed.), *T. S. Eliot: The Contemporary Reviews*
(Cambridge: CUP, 2004). Eliot told Hale he particularly liked
the review of *East Coker* by J. J. Sweeney in the *Southern Review*
(spring 1941). Also Helen Gardner's inspired review of the
first three *Quartets*, 'The Recent Poetry of T. S. Eliot', *New*

Writing and Day-light (August 1942). John Lehmann passed it on to the poet, who told Gardner it gave him 'great pleasure'.

Carpenter, Humphrey, 'Poor Tom: Mary Trevelyan's View of T. S. Eliot', *English: Journal of the English Association*, 38:160 (1 March 1989), 37–52

Chapman, Frank M., *Handbook of Birds of Eastern North America* (New York: Appleton, 1897). Given to TSE, a keen birdwatcher, by his mother when he turned fourteen. Relevant to his pet name for Emily is the mockingbird, p. 377, described as 'our national song-bird' whose song thrills the listener: 'on moonlit nights many birds sing throughout the night'

Dante Alighieri *The Divine Comedy*. Eliot read the Temple Classics edition in three volumes with Italian text and English translation, ed. Israel Gollancz (London: J. M. Dent, 1909). Copy without his name in Houghton Library, Harvard. Also *Dante's Inferno, Purgatorio* and *Paradiso*, Italian text with English translation and commentary by John D. Sinclair (New York: OUP, 1939 and 1946, repr. 1970)

Dostoevsky, Fyodor, 'The Plan of *The Life of a Great Sinner*', trans. S. S. Koteliansky and Virginia Woolf, first published by Eliot (along with *The Waste Land*) in the first issue of the *Criterion* (Oct 1922), then immediately after in 1922 by the Hogarth Press. Repr. in *Translations from the Russian* by Koteliansky and Woolf, ed. Stuart N. Clarke (Virginia Woolf Society of Great Britain, 2006)

Eliot, Abigail Adams, *A Heart of Grateful Trust: Memoirs of Abigail Adams Eliot*, transcribed and ed. Marjorie Gott Manning (n.d.)

Eliot, Charlotte Champe Stearns, poems printed in Unitarian magazines. Boxes of Eliot Family Papers, Houghton Library, Harvard University

———, *Easter Songs* (Boston: James West, 1899). Geneva Series of small white booklets. Praised by the *Journal of Education*

as an 'inspiration to higher thinking and nobler
living'. Her contribution was three poems: 'At Easter-
Tide'; 'Ring Easter Bells!'; 'Be Glad and Gay'. Copy in
Houghton Library

Eliot, T. S., lecture notes for undergraduate Harvard course in
Feb–May 1933 in the *Complete Prose*, iv

———, blurbs for Faber publications. See Toby Faber, below

———, Eliot's final edition of *Collected Poems 1909–1962* (London:
Faber; New York: Harcourt, 1963)

———, *Poems Written in Early Youth* (New York: Farrar, Straus and
Giroux, 1967)

———, *The Varieties of Metaphysical Poetry*, ed. Ronald Schuchard
(London: Faber, 1993). The Clark Lectures at Cambridge,
delivered in 1926

———, *Inventions of the March Hare*, ed. Christopher Ricks (London:
Faber, 1996)

———, *The Letters of T. S. Eliot*, i–ii, ed. Valerie Eliot and Hugh
Haughton (London: Faber; New Haven: Yale University
Press, 2009)

———, *The Letters of T. S. Eliot*, iii–, ed. Valerie Eliot and John
Haffenden (London: Faber; New Haven: Yale 2012–). Yale's
publication ceased after volume vi

———, reply (n.d., probably unsent) to Hale's last letter, where she
asks what he intends to do with her thousand or so letters
to him from 1930–47. He has destroyed them, he tells her.
Printed in John Haffenden's tribute to Valerie Eliot, *Letters*, v
(2014), xx–xxi. Haffenden calls it 'an unusually ill-tempered
letter, begotten by shock'

———, *The Poems of T. S. Eliot: The Annotated Text*, i–ii, ed. Christopher
Ricks and Jim McCue (London: Faber; New York: Farrar,
Straus and Giroux, 2015)

———, unpublished lecture in *Agenda* (2017)

———, statement on the opening of the Emily Hale letters at
Princeton University. Houghton Library MS Am 1691.5 (19).

This is the poet's letter to posterity, publicised according to plan on 2 Jan 2020. Printed in *Prose*, viii, 595–600

———, *The Complete Prose of T. S. Eliot: The Critical Edition*, i–viii, ed. Ronald Schuchard et al. (Baltimore: Johns Hopkins University Press, 2021). Online at the Project Muse website, 2014–18, https://about.muse.jhu.edu/muse/eliot-prose

———, *The Waste Land: A Facsimile and Transcript of the Original Drafts*, ed. Valerie Eliot (London: Faber; New York: Harcourt, 1971; repr. in colour by Faber, 2022)

Eliot, Valerie, interview, *Observer* (20 Feb 1972)

———, 'The Poet's Wife and Letters', interview, *The Times* (17 Sept 1988)

———, 'The Two Mrs Eliots', interview by Blake Morrison, *Independent on Sunday* (24 April 1994), repr. in Morrison, *Too True* (London: Granta, 1998)

Eliot, Vivienne Haigh-Wood, published (1924–5) and unpublished fiction and poems, edited with biography and commentary by Ann Pasternak Slater in *The Fall of a Sparrow: Vivien Eliot's Life and Writings* (London: Faber, 2020), along with digital editions of her diaries and ledgers at www.tseliot.com

———, numerous letters in *The Letters of T. S. Eliot*

Faber, Toby, *Faber & Faber: The Untold Story* (London: Faber, 2019) draws upon the words of Faber's editors, staff and authors. Includes Eliot's blurbs

Haffenden, John, biographical summaries introducing each volume of his edition of Eliot's *Letters* and a permanent treasure of deeply researched notes lay down the basis of a biography, as his co-editor Valerie Eliot initiated and anticipated

———, 'Vivien Eliot and *The Waste Land*: The Forgotten Fragments', *PN Review* 175, 33:5 (May–June 2007), 18–23

———, 'Valerie Eliot: Editing the Letters', *L*, v, xix–xxxvii, a tribute to Valerie Eliot's lifelong labour in collecting TSE's correspondence, a piece which brings her vividly to life. See other use of 'TSE' and 'EH'

————, '"Literary Dowsing": Valerie Eliot Edits *The Waste Land*', *The T. S. Eliot Studies Annual*, 2 (2018), 133—50

Hale, Emily, letter (1947) to Lorraine Havens about Eliot's decision not to marry her. Privately owned; printed in Lyndall Gordon, *Eliot's New Life* (New York: Farrar, Straus and Giroux, 1988) and in *The Imperfect Life of T. S. Eliot* (1999; repr. London: Virago, 2012)

————, extract from 'They Flash upon the Inward Eye', *Campden & District Historical and Archaeological Society: Notes & Queries*, 5:4 (spring 2007), 47—8. Original typescript (with manuscript annotations) in Smith College Archives

Hinkley, Eleanor, in *Plays of 47 Workshop* (New York: Brentano, 1920)

Huxley, Julian, *Memories* (London: Allen & Unwin, 1970). Huxley advised TSE on Dr Vittoz in Lausanne

Mansfield, Katherine, *The Collected Letters of Katherine Mansfield, Volume 5: 1922*, ed. Vincent O'Sullivan and Margaret Scott (Oxford: OUP, 2008)

McCue, Jim, 'Vivien Eliot in the Words of TSE', *Review of English Studies*, 68:283 (Feb 2017), 123—64

Mirsky, D. S., 'T. S. Eliot et la fin de la poésie bourgeoise', *Échanges*, 5 (1931), 44—58. TSE enclosed an English translation in a letter to EH, calling this brilliant

Morrell, Lady Ottoline, *Ottoline: The Early Memoirs of Lady Ottoline Morrell*, ed. Robert Gathorne-Hardy (London: Faber & Faber, 1963)

————, *Ottoline at Garsington: Memoirs of Lady Ottoline Morrell, 1915—1918*, ed. Robert Gathorne-Hardy (London: Faber & Faber, 1974)

Morris, *Leslie A., Gore Vidal Curator of Modern Books and Manuscripts, Houghton Library*, 'The Love of a Ghost for a Ghost: T. S. Eliot on his Letters to Emily Hale', Houghton Library Blog, Harvard University, blogs.harvard.edu/houghton/the-love-of-a-ghost-for-a-ghost-t-s-eliot-on-his-letters-to-emily-hale/

Newman, John Henry, *Parochial and Plain Sermons* (n.p.: CrossReach
     Publications, 2018). TSE read his sermons in Aug 1933

Pritchard, Jane, *Diaghilev and the Golden Age of the Ballets Russes*
     (London: V&A, 2010)

Stravinsky, Igor, 'Memories of T. S. Eliot', *Esquire* 64.2 (1965), 92–3.
     Eliot's intense response to *Tristan und Isolde*

Taylor, A. E., *The Faith of a Moralist* (1931; repr. Andesite Press, 2017).
     Eliot said to Hale in August 1933 that he was 'in agreement,
     admirable'

Trevelyan, Mary, obituary, *The Times* (12 Jan 1983)

———, 'The Unpublished Letters and Diary of Mary Trevelyan',
     Appendix 1 in Barry Spurr, *Anglo-Catholic in Religion: T. S. Eliot
     and Christianity* (Cambridge: Lutterworth Press, 2010), 250–2

——— and Erica Wagner, *Mary and Mr Eliot: A Sort of Love Story*
     (London: Faber; New York: Farrar, Straus and Giroux, 2022).
     Draws substantially on Trevelyan's memoir of Eliot

Tucker, Cynthia Grant, *No Silent Witness: The Eliot Parsonage Women
     and Their Unitarian World* (New York: OUP: 2010; revised edn
     Bloomington: iUniverse, 2015)

Vittoz, Roger, *Treatment of Neurasthenia*, 1921 edition read by TSE,
     translation of *Traitement des psychonévroses par la rééducation du
     côntrole cérébrale* (1911)

Woolf, Leonard, *Letters of Leonard Woolf*, ed. Frederic Spotts (London:
     Weidenfeld & Nicolson, 1990)

Woolf, Virginia, *The Diary of Virginia Woolf*, i–v, ed. Anne Olivier Bell
     (Harmondsworth: Penguin, 1979–85)

———, *The Letters of Virginia Woolf*, i–vi, ed. Nigel Nicolson and
     Joanne Trautmann (London: Hogarth Press, 1975–82)

Prime literary sources for Eliot

King James Bible
St Augustine, *Confessions*

Bhagavad Gita
Dante: *The Divine Comedy, The New Life*
Dickens: *Bleak House, Oliver Twist, Our Mutual Friend*
Dostoevsky: *Crime and Punishment, Notes from the Underground,* 'The Plan
       of *The Life of a Great Sinner*'
Hawthorne, *The House of the Seven Gables*
James, 'The Altar of the Dead', 'The Beast in the Jungle', *The*
       Europeans, 'The Friends of the Friends', *The Portrait of a Lady,*
       The Sense of the Past, Washington Square
Poe: 'The Fall of the House of Usher', 'Ligeia'
Shakespeare: *Hamlet, Othello, Pericles, Richard III*
Twain: *Huckleberry Finn*
Virgil, *The Aeneid*

Ballets Russes

Le Spectre de la Rose. Created by Michel Fokine with Vaslav Nijinsky
       and Tamara Karsavina
Petrouschka. Created by Fokine, with music by Stravinsky,
       and Nijinsky as the puppet clown. Source for 'The
       Hollow Men'

Music

Beethoven: *A Minor Quartet, Corialan Overture, Razumovsky Quartet,* 7th
       Symphony (2nd movement)
Stravinsky, *Petrouschka, Le Sacre du printemps*
Tchaikovsky, String quartets
Wagner, *Tristan und Isolde*

Secondary sources

Exchanges: Newsletter of the T. S. Eliot Society of the United Kingdom
The Journal of the T. S. Eliot Society (UK)
The T. S. Eliot Studies Annual (Liverpool University Press)
Time Present: The Newsletter of the International T. S. Eliot Society

Alexander, Michael, *Medievalism: The Middle Ages in Modern England* (New Haven: Yale University Press, 2018). Chapter on 'Modernist Medievalism' includes Eliot and Pound

Bentley, Joanne, *Hallie Flanagan: A Life in the American Theater* (New York: Knopf, 1988)

Bradshaw, David, '"Those Extraordinary Parakeets": Clive Bell and Mary Hutchinson', *Charleston Magazine*, in two parts: 16 (1997), 5–12; 17 (1998), 5–11

Brooker, Jewel Spears, 'Dialectical Collaboration: Editing *The Waste Land*', in *The Cambridge Companion to* The Waste Land, ed. Gabrielle McIntire (New York: CUP, 2015), especially pp. 106–7, expounding the opposite tugs between Vivienne Eliot's and Ezra Pound's views

——, 'Eliot's Exilic Triptych', lecture, Eliot Summer School (2017)

——, *Eliot's Dialectical Imagination* (Baltimore: Johns Hopkins University Press, 2019)

——, 'Eliot's Ghost Story: Reflections on his Letters to Emily Hale', *Time Present*, 101 (summer 2020)

——, 'Good and Evil in Eliot's Letters to Emily Hale', *The Glass*, 33 (autumn 2020), 19–25

——, 'Eliot in Ecstasy: Feeling, Reason, Mysticism', talk at MLA (2021)

——, 'Eliot Reading Eliot: Pipit, the Hyacinth Girl, and the Silent Lady', *The T. S. Eliot Studies Annual*, 4, (2022), 25–42

Bush, Ronald, *T. S. Eliot: A Study in Character and Style* (Oxford: OUP, 1984)

—— (ed.), *T. S. Eliot: The Modernist in History* (New York: CUP, 1991)

————, '"As if you were hearing it from Mr. Fletcher or Mr. Tourneur in 1633": T. S. Eliot's 1933 Harvard Lecture Notes for "English 26 (Introduction to Contemporary Literature)"', *ANQ* 11:3 (summer 1998), 11–20

————, 'Intensity by Association: T. S. Eliot's Passionate Allusions', *Modernism/modernity*, 20:4 (November 2013), 709–27

Buttram, Christine, 'T. S. Eliot and the Human Body: The Corporeal Concerns of his Life, Prose and Poetry', PhD thesis (1995)

Carroll, Steven, *The Lost Life* (Sydney: HarperCollins, 2010). Fiction

————, *A New England Affair* (Sydney: HarperCollins, 2018). Fiction

————, *Goodnight, Vivienne, Goodnight* (Sydney: HarperCollins, 2022). Fiction

Carver, Beci, 'Eliot's Humble Tennis', lecture, Eliot Summer School (July 2022). On a portrait that challenges the viewer to detect Eliot's hidden faces

Cheyette, Bryan, 'Eliot and "Race": Jews, Irish, and Blacks', in *A Companion to T. S. Eliot*, ed. David E. Chinitz (Chichester: Wiley-Blackwell, 2014), 335–49

Chisholm, Anne, *Nancy Cunard* (New York: Random House, 1979; Penguin, 1981)

Chinitz, David E., 'T. S. Eliot's Blue Verses and their Sources in Folk Tradition', *Journal of Modern Literature*, 23:2 (winter 1999–2000), 329–33

————, *T. S. Eliot and the Cultural Divide* (Chicago: University of Chicago Press, 2003), on Eliot's taste in popular culture

———— (ed.), *A Companion to T. S. Eliot* (Chichester: Wiley-Blackwell, 2014)

————, lecture on 'Over-Annotation', Eliot Summer School (2018 and 2019)

Christ, Carol, 'Gender, Voice, and Figuration in Eliot's Early Poetry', in *T. S. Eliot: The Modernist in History*, ed. Ronald Bush (New York: CUP, 1991), 23–40

Christiansen, Karen, 'Dear Mrs Eliot …', *Guardian* (29 Jan 2005)

Cooke, Rachel, '*The Fall of a Sparrow* by Ann Pasternak Slater review – T. S. Eliot's troubled first wife', *Observer* (29 November 2020)

Cooley, Martha, *The Archivist* (New York: Little, Brown, 1998). Fiction about the Emily Hale Bequest

——, 'My Novel Centered on the Eliot–Hale Letters. Now, We Can Read Them', Lithub.com (14 Jan 2020)

Crawford, Robert, *Young Eliot: From St Louis to* The Waste Land (London: Jonathan Cape, 2015; repr. 2022)

——, 'A Cousin of Colonel Heneage', *London Review of Books*, 41:8 (18 April 2019). Review of *Letters*, viii

——, *Eliot After* The Waste Land (New York: Farrar, Straus and Giroux, 2022)

Cuda, Anthony, *The Passions of Modernism: Eliot, Yeats, Woolf, and Mann* (Columbia: University of South Carolina Press, 2010)

——, 'The Poet and the Pressure Chamber: Eliot's Life', in *A Companion to T. S. Eliot*, ed. David E. Chinitz (Chichester: Wiley-Blackwell, 2014), 3–14

——, 'The Waste Land's Afterlife' in *The Cambridge Companion to* The Waste Land, ed. Gabrielle McIntire (New York: CUP, 2015), 194–210

——, 'A Precise Way of Thinking and Feeling: Eliot and Verse Drama', in *The Edinburgh Companion to T. S. Eliot and the Arts*, ed. Frances Dickey and John D. Morgenstern (Edinburgh: EUP, 2016), 116–30

——, 'Reasons not to be late: Eliot, Narrative and Belatedness', lecture, Eliot Summer School (July 2018)

——, 'Back, Late, from the Hyacinth Garden', *The T. S. Eliot Studies Annual*, 4 (2022), 57–72

de Courcy, Anne, *Five Affairs and A Friendship: The Turbulent Life of Nancy Cunard* (London: Weidenfeld & Nicolson; NY: St Martin's Press, 2022)

de Villiers, Rick, 'Banishing the Backward Devils: Eliot's Quatrain Poems and "Gerontion"', in *The New Cambridge*

Companion to T. S. Eliot, ed. Jason Harding (Cambridge: CUP, 2016), 55–70

——, *Eliot and Becket's Low Modernism: Humility and Humiliation* (Edinburgh: EUP, 2021)

Dickey, Frances, *The Modern Portrait Poem: From Dante Gabriel Rossetti to Ezra Pound* (Charlottesville: University of Virginia Press, 2010)

——, 'Eliot and St Louis', lecture, Eliot Summer School (2018). This is one of her fine series on Eliot's sensory experiences in turn-of-the-century St Louis

——, '*Hydraulic*: The Company and Its Archive', *Time Present*, 99 (fall 2019)

——, 'Eliot's Personal Theory of Poetry', *Time Present*, 100 (spring 2020)

——, 'May the Record Speak: The Correspondence of T. S. Eliot and Emily Hale', *Twentieth-Century Literature*, 66:4 (Dec 2020), 431–62

——, 'Eliot's Emilia: From Poetry to Life', Annual Burnt Norton Lecture, Eliot Summer School (2022)

—— and Bradford Barnhardt, '"My Madness Singing": The Specter of Syphilis in *Prufrock and Other Observations*', *The T. S. Eliot Studies Annual*, 2 (2018), 3–24

—— and John D. Morgenstern (eds), *The Edinburgh Companion to T. S. Eliot and the Arts* (Edinburgh: EUP, 2016)

Duncan-Jones, Elsie, 'Ash Wednesday', in Balachandra Rajan (ed.), *T. S. Eliot: A Study of His Writings by Several Hands* (London: Dennis Dobson, 1947)

Duplessis, Rachel Blau, 'Gender', in *T. S. Eliot in Context*, ed. Jason Harding (Cambridge: CUP, 2011), 295–304

Fitzgerald, Sara, *The Poet's Girl: A Novel of Emily Hale and T. S. Eliot* (n.p.: Thought Catalog Books, 2020)

——, 'Searching for Emily Hale', *Time Present*, 100 (spring 2020)

——, 'Reconsidering Emily Hale', *Journal of the T. S. Eliot Society (UK)* (2020), 45–58

————, 'The Love of her Life: Emily Hale's Theatrical Career', *The T. S. Eliot Studies Annual*, 4 (2022), 61–96

————, '"Because You Are You": Emily Hale's Letters', *Journal of the T. S. Eliot Society (UK)* (2022)

Ford, Mark, *This Dialogue of One: Essays on Poets* (London: Eyewear, 2014)

————, 'Eliot's London', lecture, Eliot Summer School (2018)

————, 'Beginning and Ending: Little Gidding', Annual Little Gidding Lecture, Eliot Summer School (2022)

Gardner, Helen, *The Art of T. S. Eliot* (London: Cresset Press, 1949), taking off from her 1942 essay on the *Quartets*

————, *The Composition of* Four Quartets (London: Faber, 1979)

Geary, Matthew, *T. S. Eliot and the Mother* (New York: Routledge, 2021)

Gish, Nancy K., *Time in the Poetry of T. S. Eliot* (London: Macmillan, 1981)

————, '"A Divided Man"', *Time Present*, 103 (spring 2021)

———— and Cassandra Laity (eds), *Gender, Desire, and Sexuality in T. S. Eliot* (Cambridge: CUP, 2004), including Gish, 'Discarnate desire: T. S. Eliot and the poetics of dissociation', 107–129

Gold, Matthew K., 'The Expert Hand and the Obedient Heart: Dr Vittoz, T. S. Eliot, and the Therapeutic Possibilities of *The Waste Land*', *Journal of Modern Literature*, 23:3/4 (summer 2000), 519–33

Goldstein, Bill, *The World Broke in Two* (New York and London: Bloomsbury, 2018)

Gordon, Lois, *Nancy Cunard: Heiress, Muse, Political Idealist* (New York: Columbia University Press, 2007)

Haffenden, John, biographical introductions to his edition of *The Letters of T. S. Eliot*, together with his informed and invaluable notes

Hann, Jennie, '"*The Aspern Papers* in Reverse": The Hale Letters as Dramatic Monologue', *Time Present*, 103 (spring 2021)

Harding, Jason, *The Criterion: Cultural Politics and Periodical Networks in Inter-War Britain* (Oxford: OUP, 2002)

———— (ed.), *T. S. Eliot in Context* (Cambridge: CUP, 2011)

——, *The New Cambridge Companion to T. S. Eliot* (Cambridge: CUP, 2016)

Hargrove, Nancy Duvall, *T. S. Eliot's Parisian Year* (Gainsville: University Press of Florida, 2009)

——, 'The Remarkable Relationship of T. S. Eliot and Mary Hutchinson', *Yeats Eliot Review*, 28:3–4 (fall–winter 2011), 3–14

Harries, Richard, *Haunted by Christ: Modern Writers and the Struggle for Faith* (London: SPCK, 2018)

——, draft of book on *Four Quartets*

Helmore, Edward, 'T. S. Eliot's hidden love letters reveal intense, heartbreaking affair', *Guardian* (2 Jan 2020)

Hollis, Matthew, The Waste Land: *A Biography of the Poem* (London: Faber; New York: Norton, 2022)

Hughes, Kathryn, '*The Fall of a Sparrow* review – Vivien Eliot, T. S. Eliot and "utter hell"', *Guardian* (8 Dec 2020)

Jones, Susan, '"At the still point": T. S. Eliot, Dance, and a Transatlantic Poetics', in *Literature, Modernism, & Dance* (Oxford: OUP, 2013), especially 234–9

——, 'Eliot and Dance', in *The Edinburgh Companion to T. S. Eliot and the Arts*, ed. Frances Dickey and John D. Morgenstern (Edinburgh: EUP, 2016), 225–43

Keegan, Paul, 'Emily of Fire & Violence', *London Review of Books*, 40:20 (22 Oct 2020), 7–16

Kennedy, Sarah, '"Let These Words Answer": *Ash Wednesday* and the Ariel Poems', in *The New Cambridge Companion to T. S. Eliot*, ed. Jason Harding (Cambridge: CUP, 2016), 89–102

——, Sarah, *T. S. Eliot and the Dynamic Imagination* (Cambridge: CUP, 2019)

——, 'Eliot's Glance', lecture, Eliot Summer School (2022)

Lowry, Elizabeth, 'Marriage Made in Hell', *Literary Review* (Dec 2020). Review of *The Fall of a Sparrow*

Marx, William, *Naissance de la critique moderne: la littérature selon Eliot et Valéry* (Arras: Artois Presses Université, 2002)

——, 'Paris', in *T. S. Eliot in Context*, ed. Jason Harding (Cambridge: CUP, 2011), 25–32

——, 'T. S. Eliot, Notes sur le cours de Bergson au Collège de France (1910–1911)', in *Annales bergsoniennes, IX: Bergson et les écrivains*, ed. Arnaud François, Clément Girardi and Camille Riquier (Paris: Presses universitaires de France, 2020)

McDonald, Gail, 'Through schoolhouse windows: women, the academy, and T. S. Eliot', in *Gender, Desire, and Sexuality in T. S. Eliot*, ed. Cassandra Laity and Nancy K. Gish (Cambridge: CUP, 2004), 175–9

——, 'Eliot and the New Critics', in *A Companion to T. S. Eliot*, ed. David E. Chinitz (Chichester: Wiley-Blackwell, 2014), 411–22

——, 'Gender and Sexuality', in *The New Cambridge Companion to T. S. Eliot*, ed. Jason Harding (Cambridge: CUP, 2016), 162–74

McIntire, Gabrielle, 'An Unexpected Beginning: Sex, Race, and History in T. S. Eliot's Columbo and Bolo Poems', *Modernism/modernity*, 9:2 (2002), 283–301

——, *Modernism, Memory, and Desire: T. S. Eliot and Virginia Woolf* (Cambridge: CUP, 2008, repr. 2011)

—— (ed.), *The Cambridge Companion to* The Waste Land (New York: CUP, 2015)

——, 'Love's Errors and Effacements: T. S. Eliot and Emily Hale', *Time Present*, 101 (summer 2020)

Mizruchi, Susan, *A Very Short Introduction to Henry James* (New York: OUP, 2021)

Monk, Ray, *Bertrand Russell: Spirit of Solitude, 1872–1921* (London: Free Press, 1996)

Patmore, Brigit, *My Friends When Young* (London: Heinemann, 1968)

Pearson, Graham, 'Mrs Edith Carroll Perkins and Chipping Campden Gardens', *Signpost: The Journal of the Chipping Campden History Society*, 8 (spring 2018), 11–14

Perry, Seamus, 'Eliot's Liberalism', lecture for the Eliot Society at Merton College, Oxford (15 Nov 2021)

——, 'Eliot at Margate', lecture, Eliot Summer School (July 2022)

——, 'What Did They Expect?', *The T. S. Eliot Studies Annual*, 4 (2022), 121–30

Peters, Julian, comic-book illustrations for 'The Love Song of J. Alfred Prufrock', available at julianpeterscomics.com

Piette, Adam, 'Eliot's Breakdown and Dr Vittoz', *English Language Notes*, 33 (September 1995), 35–9. With thanks to Valerie Fehlbaum for sending a copy

Pondrom, Cyrena, 'Conflict and Concealment: Eliot's Approach to Women and Gender', in *A Companion to T. S. Eliot*, ed. David E. Chinitz (Chichester: Wiley-Blackwell, 2014), 323–34

Pritchard, William H., 'The Prose Eliot', *The Hudson Review*, 68:1 (spring 2015), 125–32

Query, Patrick, '"The pleasures of higher vices": Sexuality in Eliot's Work', in *A Companion to T. S. Eliot*, ed. David E. Chinitz (Chichester: Wiley-Blackwell, 2014), 350–62

——, 'T. S. Eliot and Radical Hope, 1939', lecture, Eliot Summer School (2022)

Quigley, Megan, 'Eliot's Fictional Afterlives', Zoom talk (18 June 2020)

——, 'Mature Poets Steal: Eliot's Fictions', lecture, Eliot Summer School (July 2022)

Ramazani, Jahan, *A Transnational Poetics* (Chicago: University of Chicago Press, 2009)

——, *Poetry and Its Others: News, Prayer, Song, and the Dialogue of Genres* (Chicago: University of Chicago Press, 2013)

——, *Poetry in a Global Age* (Chicago: University of Chicago Press, 2021)

——, 'Burying the Dead: *The Waste Land*, Ecocritique, and World Elegy', *The T. S. Eliot Studies Annual*, 4 (2022), 7–24

Redford, Bruce, 'Figures in the Carpet: *A Choice of Kipling's Verse* and Occult Autobiography', *Time Present*, 103 (spring 2021). Good on TSE and *The Aspern Papers*

Ricks, Christopher, *T. S. Eliot and Prejudice* (London: Faber, 1994)

Roe, Sue, *Virginia Woolf and Friends: T. S. Eliot and Katherine Mansfield* (n.p.: Virginia Woolf Society of Great Britain, 2011)

Schuchard, Ronald, *Eliot's Dark Angel: Intersections of Life and Art* (Oxford: OUP, 1999)

———, 'Burbank with a Baedeker, Bleistein with a Cigar: American Intellectuals, Anti-Semitism, and the Idea of Culture', *Modernism/modernity*, 10:1 (January 2003), 1–26

———, 'Goodnight Mrs Tom', *Royal Society of Literature Review* (2013)

———, 'Eliot in the Wartime Classroom 1916–1919', lecture, Institute of English Studies, Senate House, London (16 May 2017)

———, on TSE as Critic for www.tseliot.com

Seymour, Miranda, *Ottoline Morrell: Life on a Grand Scale* (1992; London: Faber, 1998 repr.)

Seymour-Jones, Carole, *Painted Shadow: A Life of Vivienne Eliot* (London: Constable; NY: Doubleday, 2001)

Shell, Alison, 'P. D. James: "Lighten Our Darkness"', in *Anglican Women Novelists: From Charlotte Brontë to P. D. James*, ed. Judith Maltby and Alison Shell (London: t&tclark/Bloomsbury, 2019)

Sherry, Vincent, '"Where are the eagles and the trumpets?": Imperial Decline and Eliot's Development', in *A Companion to T. S. Eliot*, ed. David E. Chinitz (Chichester: Wiley-Blackwell, 2014), 91–104

Sigg, Eric, 'New England', in *T. S. Eliot in Context*, ed. Jason Harding (Cambridge: CUP, 2011), 17–24

Slater, Ann Pasternak, *The Fall of a Sparrow: Vivien Eliot's Life and Writings* (London: Faber, 2020)

———, 'Vivien Eliot's Life: Difficulties, Deceptions, Discoveries, Disillusion – and her Real Literary Gifts', lecture, Eliot Summer School (2022)

Smith, Carol H., 'Eliot's "Divine" Comedies: *The Cocktail Party, The Confidential Clerk*, and *The Elder Statesman*', in *A Companion to T. S. Eliot*, ed. David E. Chinitz (Chichester: Wiley-Blackwell, 2014), 251–62

Spark, Muriel, review of *The Confidential Clerk* in the *Church Times*, which Eliot approved, in *The Golden Fleece: Essays by Muriel Spark*, ed. Penelope Jardine (Manchester: Carcanet, 2014)

Spurr, Barry, *Anglo-Catholic in Religion: T. S. Eliot and Christianity* (Cambridge: Lutterworth Press, 2010)

Stayer, Jayme, 'The Short and Surprisingly Private Life of King Bolo: Eliot's Bawdy Poems and Their Audiences', *The T. S. Eliot Studies Annual*, 1 (2017), 3–30

——, *Becoming T. S. Eliot: The Rhetoric of Voice and Audience in Inventions of the March Hare* (Baltimore: Johns Hopkins University Press, 2021)

——, 'Snuggling Up to the Abyss', *The T. S. Eliot Studies Annual*, 4 (2022), 145–60

Stergiopoulou, Katerina, '"For Whom the Bell Tolls": Reading the *Quartets* after the Letters to Emily Hale', *Time Present*, 100 (spring 2020)

——, Roundtable discussion of Eliot–Hale letters at T. S. Eliot Society conference (Oct 2020)

Sullivan, Hannah, 'Classics', in *T. S. Eliot in Context*, ed. Jason Harding (Cambridge: CUP, 2011), 169–79

——, chapter on Eliot's accretive composition of *The Waste Land* in *The Work of Revision* (Cambridge MA: Harvard University Press, 2013)

——, 'The Moment of Embalming: T. S. Eliot's love letters – a report from the archive', *TLS* (31 Jan 2020)

——, 'Poetry', www.tseliot.com

Taylor, Michelle, 'The Secret History of T. S. Eliot's Muse', *New Yorker* (5 Dec 2020)

——, '(In)discreet Modernism: 'T. S. Eliot's Coterie Poetics', *College Literature*, 47:1 (winter 2020), 34–64

Toda, Kit Komiko, lecture at the International Eliot Society Conference, Rapallo (2016)

Varry, Cécile, 'Opening up the Archive: T. S. Eliot's Letters to Emily Hale', *The Modernist Review* (31 Dec 2019)

————, 'T. S. Eliot and the Anxious Body', online lecture (2 Sept 2020) in University of Durham series

————, 'Looking for Relief in Eliot's French Poems', *The T. S. Eliot Studies Annual*, 4 (2022), 279–92

Virkar, Aakanksha J., '"Heart of Light": Emily Hale and The Birth of Tragedy in *The Waste Land*', *The T. S. Eliot Studies Annual*, 4 (2022), 43–56

Whittier-Ferguson, John, 'After such knowledge', *Time Present*, 100 (spring 2020)

————, '"I would meet you upon this honestly": The Repudiation of Mary in *The Family Reunion*', *The T. S. Eliot Studies Annual*, 4 (2022), 215–28

ACKNOWLEDGEMENTS

This book is dedicated to three Eliot readers, firstly my mother, Rhoda Stella Press, who taught the Bible to women's groups and to children in her native Cape Town. She was attentive to the moral perceptions in children and amongst them was 'the philosopher'. He was a thumb-sucker, and now and then would remove his thumb from his mouth to offer a deep thought. Her spiritual journey was akin to Eliot's in her need for solitude, facing life as a set of tests and alert to what she called her failings. As a Jew she did mark Eliot's antisemitism but had too keen an awareness of human fallibility to allow this and other flaws in his make-up to undermine her recognition of his greatness.

A. Walton Litz, born in Arkansas, was a Modernist at Princeton. He detected the Jamesian element in Eliot: the American on trial in Europe, a mind evolving beyond human limitations with a haunted susceptibility to the unseen, the ghosts who accompany a journey to somewhere else.

The pre-eminent Eliot scholar Helen Gardner was born in London and a scholarship took her to St Hilda's College, Oxford, in the late twenties. This was a time when Eliot was on students' lips. She would greet a friend on the High with a line about Sweeney testing a razor on his leg and expect an amusing return from the same poem. Her own experience of the flawed soul on a journey pervaded her empathy for Eliot and her understanding that he was an explorer not an expounder.

Among admirable Eliot readers and scholars of my generation are Ronald Bush, one of Walt's students, and Ronald Schuchard, who set up the International Eliot Summer School. Both write exceptionally well.

When the Eliot–Hale archive opened in January 2020, there were about six readers and our responses to the letters animated exchanges between half past eight and nine each morning, as we waited for the doors to open. Most readers came for a short time and tended to concentrate on a particular period: it might be 1935, when Eliot's relationship with Emily Hale was at its height, or 1947, when Eliot decided not to marry her. Two of us were reading through the whole collection, every day and every hour that the archive was open before lockdown. The other reader was Frances Dickey, who was putting out an informative blog for the Eliot Society. She was resolved to convey the contents of unpublished (unquotable) letters to the many who could not come to the archive, and she did this accurately, discerningly, via the poet's published (quotable) work. Dickey's reports of what Eliot said to Hale are even in tone and self-effacing, yet they reveal facets of Eliot that were unknown or not fully known. This present book took shape in the course of our talks both in Firestone Library and after hours, including emails mulling over issues by night.

I want to thank others in the archives, Katerina Stergiopoulou, Jennie Hann, Hyonbin Choi, Sara Fitzgerald, Jewel Spears Brooker and John Whittier-Fergusson, for impressions they shared. Katerina's insights into the links between Eliot's experience with Emily Hale on the New England shore in September 1936, followed by reminiscent letters to her, and his American quartet, written in 1941, were especially telling.

Jewel's low-voiced question, as we sat side by side at one of the long tables, 'why didn't she [Hale] walk away', resonated throughout the writing of this book. Michelle Taylor, a student from Harvard, was at the far end of that table; a long, stimulating talk actually took place later at my home in Oxford. Another student of Eliot, Cécile Varry, from the University of Paris, doing new and exciting work on the body, also came for talks over cups of tea in the garden during lockdown.

The International Eliot Summer School, run now by Anthony Cuda from North Carolina, provides a forum for new ideas (like Tony's lively work on 'belatedness'), and over the years I've enjoyed discussions with him, Jahan Ramazani, Megan Quigley and many others cited in the Notes and Sources.

Valerie Fehlbaum, a past pupil who became Professor of English at the University of Geneva, wrote on 15 November 2018: 'I "escaped" to Lausanne today to see if I could find Ave des Tilleuls.' Here was the house where Eliot went for treatment with Dr Vittoz; then, the following month, Valerie arranged for her Geneva friend Monika Turner to accompany me to Lausanne and for Lise Jequier, who lives there, to guide us around the Eliot sites.

In the course of writing I have been touched by the interest of friends, past pupils and members of family. These include Freddie Baveystock, Philip Clark, Finuala Dowling, Philip Getz, Lauren Goldman, Susan Jones, Pamela Norris, Linn Cary Mehta, Sage Mehta, Marie Philip, Hilary Reynolds, Jennifer Roth and Miranda Seymour. Special thanks to Susan Mizruchi of Boston University and to Paula Deitz for supporting an application to Princeton for a visiting fellowship in the Library. As editor of *The Hudson Review*, Paula Deitz published an early excerpt from this book, 'Eliot Among the Women', in volume LXXIII/4, the winter issue of 2021.

I would like to acknowledge a fellowship granted by the Friends of the Princeton library, which provided for travel and accommodation. Since 2017 it has been a pleasure to correspond with warmly helpful AnnaLee Pauls in Special Collections, and I appreciate the kindness too of the Head of Special Collections, Don Skemer, followed by the Deputy Head, Daniel J. Linke, the University Archivist. Mr Linke's letter about rights to quote Emily Hale was a model of probity and diligence. That letter and my American agent Georges Borchardt's belief in the importance of retrieving the voice of Eliot's 'Lady of silences' proved invaluable. Georges's comments, to include more on John Hayward, were as always apt. Cora Markowitz in the Borchardt agency is similarly prompt and professional.

I am fortunate too in my UK agent, Isobel Dixon, and especially with this particular book. As a poet herself, she understands Eliot, and as the daughter of an Anglican minister, can follow the religious path Eliot took. At the same time she saw the problems that women had to confront. Her abundant comments on reading the manuscript at the point of delivery were wonderfully empathic.

One difficulty in writing this during lockdown came when needs arose for material in American archives. I have benefited from the alacrity of curators, Nanci Young at Smith College and Allison Mills and Marianne Hansen at Bryn Mawr, who took the trouble to find and send manuscript material. In 2001, Professor Rosamond Kent Sprague, a daughter of Louise Andrews Kent, wrote to me about her mother's fifty-year friendship with Emily Hale. Marjorie Strong of the Vermont Historical Society sent me a batch of their letters from Leahy Library. Jennifer Fauxsmith at the Schlesinger Library of the History of Women at Radcliffe College located the papers of Eliot's distinguished Boston cousins Martha May Eliot and Abigail Eliot.

Though Karen Kukil has now retired from Smith, I have not forgotten her numerous acts of generosity, amongst them sending items from Smith's Emily Hale Collection back in the eighties; also Judy Sahak, who was at that time curator at Scripps College, who went beyond the call of duty in sending items I hadn't known were available and putting me in touch with Hale's pupils. It was lovely to see Judy again at the Princeton archive.

Leslie A. Morris is the curator of the Eliot family collection at the Houghton Library, Harvard. It was thoughtful of her to send me Eliot's letter to posterity and at the end of February 2020 we discussed its image of Hale. She spared the time for a long, congenial talk over morning coffee. While in Boston, I stayed a night at the Eliot House at Eastern Point, cared for by Dana Hawkes.

Sally Foss and Marjon Ornstein, who both recall Emily Hale with Eliot, shared vivid memories on the phone.

Thanks to the Eliot Estate for permission to quote from Eliot's unpublished as well as published works, and thanks also to Nancy Fulford, Archivist for the Estate, and to Becky Taylor in Faber & Faber's Rights department for her courtesy. Acknowledgement is due to Faber & Faber Ltd as Eliot's publishers.

Going far back to 1973–5, Helen Gardner shared her discoveries about Emily Hale, Eliot's visits to her in Campden, and an invaluable batch of letters that Eliot as a young man had written to Conrad Aiken. What Dame Helen said has been unforgettable, including her class on the *Quartets* in Trinity term 1974 and her last lectures on Eliot in the following year, just before she retired. In the later seventies, I was glad for permission from Maurice Haigh-Wood to quote from his sister's letters. In the eighties, Humphrey Carpenter kindly let me read and drawn on the memoir by his aunt Mary Trevelyan, and filled me in about her character.

This book is soaked Eliot's published letters, edited by John Haffenden with superb notes, on the basis of groundwork by Valerie Eliot. My final draft had the benefit of his corrections and queries. He shared my sadness over what came to light in Eliot's letters to Hale, and was rightly honest about the limitations of any present record of Mrs Eliot.

At intervals, beginning in Princeton in January 2020 and continuing through the last two years, have been illuminating discussions with two film-makers, Rosie Alison and Susanna White. Their thoughts and phrases entered into what I was writing. The talk was like an Oxford tutorial. It was as though our minds moved together with ease.

Lastly are those for whom words fail. I cannot do justice to what is owing to the Chair of Virago, Lennie Goodings. She read and edited the drafts at least four times all the way through, and certain chapters even more often. Her work has been transforming, driven by a sure sense of what a book has to be. Once again, Zoe Gullen has copy-edited with meticulous care and good judgement, and again too I am thankful to Susan de Soissons for undertaking publicity and to Linda Silverman, the picture researcher at Little, Brown UK. At Norton, I thank Alane Mason, who acquired the book and then passed it to John Glusman, whose major suggestions, to do with Eliot's conversion and posterity plan, made a great difference.

Anna Gordon has stood ready to read every chapter and given unstinting support. Her deep feeling for Eliot was borne out by a first-class mark for her Cambridge dissertation on the poet's language. Olivia Gordon, an editor at the Department of Education (as well as her two published memoirs), brought a quick, discerning eye to a late draft, working in tandem with my editor. From the outset Siamon Gordon discussed and read every draft, bearing out my conviction that though he chose science, he could have excelled as well on the arts side. There are no words adequate to my gratitude for his collaboration in this book.

INDEX